23.95

YOUTH JUSTICE:
THEORY AND PRACTICE

Cavendish
Publishing

364.36094

YOU

HE   STL

YOUTH JUSTICE: THEORY AND PRACTICE

Edited by

Jane Pickford, LLB (Hons), LLM, Cert Ed, Dip Social Work
Senior Lecturer in Law, University of East London

Cavendish
Publishing
Limited

London • Sydney

First published in Great Britain 2000 by Cavendish Publishing Limited,
The Glass House, Wharton Street, London WC1X 9PX, United Kingdom
Telephone: +44 (0)20 7278 8000   Facsimile: +44 (0)20 7278 8080
Email: info@cavendishpublishing.com
Website: www.cavendishpublishing.com

British Library Cataloguing in Publication Data
Youth justice: theory and practice
1 Teenagers – Legal status, laws, etc – England
2 Teenagers – Legal status, laws, etc – Wales
3 Juvenile justice, Administration of – England   4   Juvenile justice,
Administration of – Wales
5 Juvenile delinquency – England   6 Juvenile delinquency – Wales
364.3'6'0942

ISBN 1 85941 534 2

Printed and bound in Great Britain

In memory of Doris May Nelson

FOREWORD

Young people – young males – breaking the law have been at the centre of the criminal justice 'theatre' for a long time now. Housebreaking, street crime, drugs and, above all, car crime, have provided the motifs for an image of youth out of control. This image is one that successive governments have periodically fostered not only for the sake of law and order policies but as a symptom of social (family / community) disintegration.

The last few years have seen the enactment of two major pieces of legislation, the Crime and Disorder Act 1998 and the Youth Justice and Criminal Evidence Act 1999, which signal significant institutional reordering. In some ways, these represent trends of earlier years, for example, the emphasis on multi-agency policing and, going back even earlier, the emphasis on prevention and early intervention. The indicators of the 'at risk' child will seem to many reminiscent of predictive multi-factorialism. On the other hand, the invocation of community is wistfully invoked in the sanction of the curfew. Not a popular option for magistrates, it nonetheless has a symbolic resonance: withholding the 'citizenship' of the public place.

Do current measures, in fact, represent a 'new' approach or are they just a reworking of the same problematics – notably of welfare and justice – that have structured thinking about youth crime since the late 19th century? What broader frameworks may be brought to bear to understand Britain's 'youth policy' (or lack of it)? What framing, equally, is appropriate to analyse the imaging of the young person and their relation to the delictual?

These are some of the questions that are explored in this extremely interesting collection of essays.

This book is, in fact, quite unusual. For, while many may claim to offer a 'wide ranging' conspectus, or to draw together practitioners and theorists in a space where their writings may 'speak' to each other, here for once is the fulfilment of such promises. The contributors do come from a range of backgrounds (legal, social work, police) and also a variety of theoretical locations: cultural studies, criminology, legal theory, international law. Each essay offers a new twist, a different angle, the possibility of seeing things otherwise. What emerges is a refreshing and informative set of essays that keep 'turning the kaleidoscope' on the questions in hand.

Professor Beverley Brown
London
July 2000

CONTRIBUTORS

THE EDITOR

Jane Pickford is Senior Lecturer in Law at the University of East London, where she lectures in youth justice, criminal law and criminology. She has postgraduate qualifications in both law and education, and is a qualified social worker. She has had extensive experience of youth justice practice and worked as a court officer for the London Borough of Haringey, She has facilitated the training of youth magistrates.

FOREWORD

Professor Beverley Brown has published in the fields of feminist criminology and legal theory and is co-author of *Sex Crimes on Trial* (1993, Edinburgh UP). She was Professor in the Law Department at the University of East London from 1996–99.

THE CONTRIBUTORS (IN ORDER OF APPEARANCE)

Dr Wayne Morrison is Director of the University of London External Programme in Law and Senior Lecturer in Law at Queen Mary and Westfield College. He has written extensively in the area of legal theory and criminology and his 1995 book, *Theoretical Criminology: From Modernity to Postmodernism* 1995 (Cavendish Publishing), is regarded as a major contribution to criminological discourse at the end of the last century.

Dr Mark Fenwick is Lecturer in Law at the University of Kyushu, Japan. Having graduated in law from Queen Mary and Westfield College, he went on to complete a Masters of Philosophy and a Doctorate at the Institute of Criminology, University of Cambridge, and was postgraduate research fellow at the University of East London. He has written various articles in the field of criminology, and his research interests also cover legal theory and new technology and the Law.

Keith Hayward is Lecturer in Law at the University of East London. He was educated at Brunel University and at the Institute of Criminology, University of Cambridge. He is currently completing a Doctorate entitled 'Crime, Consumerism and the Urban Experience'. His research interests include criminological theory, architecture and popular culture.

Elizabeth Stokes is a Lecturer in Law at the University of East London. She is a graduate of Oxford University and completed a Masters in Philosophy at the Institute of Criminology, University of Cambridge. She teaches criminal law, criminal justice and criminology and has contributed to the development of undergraduate and postgraduate courses in this area. She has previously published papers on the censure of hunt saboteurs and their media representation. Her current research interests include processes of criminalisation and the interrelationship between criminological theory and the formation of criminal justice policy.

Stuart Vernon is Principal Lecturer in Law at the University of East London, where he teaches students of law, social work, criminology and criminal justice, and legal studies. He teaches a number of courses on youth justice and sat as a magistrate in Hounslow, West London. He is a member of the Social Work Law Research Group and as such is the joint author of a number of reports for the Central Council for Education and Training in Social Work and articles on social work law. He is the author of three editions of *Social Work and the Law* (Butterworths) and a joint author of *Disability and the Law* (1996, Jessica Kingsley).

Deirdre Fottrell is Lecturer in International Law and Human Rights at the Institute of Commonwealth Studies, University of London. She is a graduate of University College Galway, and a postgraduate of the London School of Economics. Her recent publications include *Minority and Group Rights in the New Millennium* (edited with Bill Bowring) (1999, Kluwer) and 'Children's rights', in Hegarty, A and Leonard, S (eds), *Human Rights: An Agenda for the 21st Century* (1999, Cavendish Publishing).

Issy Harvey is a research associate at the Institute of Education where she is currently developing a research project, 'Getting Creative', which aims to explore young people's creative uses of digital media beyond the school gates. She has two first degrees, in psychology and photography, and is a Master of Social Work, as well as being a qualified social worker. She has 16 years' experience of working as a youth justice social worker, working for both the Junction Project (an innovative community-based scheme offering full time programmes of group work and education to serious and/or persistent young offenders) and for the London Borough of Haringey. Issy has also worked in the voluntary as well as the statutory sector across the full range of youth work, education, group work, youth justice and counselling services.

Susannah Hancock trained and worked as a probation officer in London before moving into development work in the areas of substance misuse, community safety and crime. She worked as Development Officer for Lewisham's Youth Offending Team, which is acting as a government pilot site and Youth Justice Board pathway site. She is now Operational Manager at Southwark's Youth Offending Team.

Bill Whyte lectures in social work at the University of Edinburgh and is Programme Director of Advanced Social Work Studies in Criminal Justice at the University of Edinburgh and Stirling. He has written many articles about the Scottish Youth Justice System.

Malcolm Bentley is a youth magistrate. Malcolm graduated from Reading University with a degree in economics and worked for the Inland Revenue, investigating corporate fraud/evasion cases until he retired in the 1990s. He is currently undertaking a Masters of Philosophy at the University of East London.

Matt Long is a lecturer at Bramshill Police College. After graduating, Matt undertook postgraduate research at both Manchester and Cambridge University. He is currently completing a Doctorate on the topic of the rise of managerialism with the police.

Phil Cohen is Professor of Applied Cultural Studies at the University of East London, where he currently directs the Centre for New Ethnicities Research. He has researched and published widely on changing patterns of education, popular culture, youth, race and identity in contemporary Britain. His most recent books are *Rethinking the Youth Question – Education, Labour and Cultural Studies* (Duke 1999) and *New Ethnicities, Old Racisms* (1999, Zed).

Dr Patrick Ainley is a Reader in Learning Policy, University of Greenwich School of Post-Compulsory Education and Training. Recent publications include: *Learning Policy, Towards the Certified Society* (1999, Macmillan) and *Apprenticeship: Towards a New Paradigm of Learning* (edited with Helen Rainbird) (1999, Kogan Page). Past publications include *The Business of Learning: Staff and Student Experiences of Further Education in the 1990s* (with Bill Bailey) (1997, Cassell); *Degrees of Difference, Higher Education in the 1990s* (1994, Lawrence & Wishart); *Class and Skill, Changing Divisions of Knowledge and Labour* (1993, Cassell); *Training for the Future: The Rise and Fall of the Manpower Services Commission* (with Mark Corney) (1990, Cassell); *From School to YTS* (1988, OU Press).

Caroline Hunt is an inspector for the United Nations. She is a barrister who worked in a London law centre in the 1980s and, in the late 1980s and early 1990s, worked as Director of an alternative to custody scheme in Delaware. Caroline worked as a researcher for the Dutch Ministry of Justice for two years. After completing a MPA at Harvard University, Caroline went on to work for the United Nations High Commissioner for Refugees on various humanitarian projects.

CONTENTS

TABLE OF CASES

TABLE OF STATUTES

INTRODUCTION

A NEW YOUTH JUSTICE FOR A NEW CENTURY?

Jane Pickford

INTRODUCTION

> The youth justice system in England and Wales is in disarray. It simply does not work. It can scarcely be called a system at all because it lacks coherent objectives. It satisfies neither those whose principal concern is crime control nor those whose principal priority is the welfare of the young offender.[1]

This collection is published at an interesting juncture. Jack Straw, the current Home Secretary, would have us believe that there is a revolution taking place within the practice of youth justice in this country. Over the next few years, the implementation of two ground breaking pieces of legislation (the Crime and Disorder Act 1998 and the Youth Justice and Criminal Evidence Act 1999) will certainly completely redesign the juvenile justice landscape, producing the most radical change in the way we treat young offenders since the inception of the Children Act 1908, which set up a separate system for the treatment and punishment of young law breakers.

In relation to youth justice theory, however, do the legislative changes represent any real transformation in the philosophies that dominated the youth crime debate over the 20th century and provide us with a new approach for the new millennium? Or do they really amount to no more than a reworking and mixing of the old justice versus welfare dichotomy, which seems to have confused and fragmented youth justice policy for so long? Is this current approach merely tough on youth crime, or can it also be described as tough on the causes of youth crime? These are the questions this introduction and the following chapters will seek to answer.

Throughout this introductory chapter, we will examine whether this seemingly substantial shift in youth justice practice indicates a concomitant shift in the dominant ideologies of youth justice. In the Labour Party's Consultation Paper, *Tackling Youth Crime, Reforming Youth Justice* (1996), the Home Secretary alleged that it did, stating that the proposed reforms would provide a 'radical overhaul of the youth justice system' which would indeed amount to a 'fundamentally different approach to youth crime'. He commented that the root of the problem with the youth justice system was a fundamental confusion over philosophy:

---

1   Home Office 1997c.

> At the heart of the crisis in youth justice is confusion and conflict between welfare and punishment. Too many people involved with the system are unclear whether the purpose is to punish and to signify society's disapproval of offending or whether the welfare of the young offender is paramount.[2]

The solution seemed clear. A re-focus of philosophy was needed:

> This confusion cannot continue. A new balance has to be struck between the sometimes conflicting interests of welfare and punishment.

This would involve:

> ... resolving some of the confusion between the relationship of welfare and punishment in dealing with young offenders.[3]

This introductory chapter examines whether the promise to vanquish the theoretical tensions and contradictions has been fulfilled by the new reforms and, indeed, whether it is possible to resolve them.

THE LEGISLATION

The Crime and Disorder Act 1998 and the Youth Justice and Criminal Evidence Act 1999 are being implemented in stages over the next few years. Pilot schemes and pathway projects are currently acting as testing grounds for the complete implementation of these statutes. Additionally, the Human Rights Act 1998, which gives children, young people and adults further access to the freedoms and rights enshrined in the European Convention on Human Rights and Fundamental Freedoms, is likely to be implemented by October 2000. This Act represents the most significant statement of human rights in this country since the Bill of Rights in 1689. It is possible that, under this legislation, legal challenges could be mounted to the way that we, as a country, treat children and young people who come before our justice system, as it will be unlawful for any public body to act in a manner which is incompatible with the spirit of the Convention rights (s 6 of the Human Rights Act 1998). Furthermore, a requirement will be placed upon all courts to interpret any legislation which appears incompatible with Convention rights in a way which accords with rights given under s 3 of the Human Rights Act 1998. (We will return to this topic later in this introduction in order to examine possible challenges to our new youth justice system which could be anticipated under the Human Rights Act 1998.)

---

2 Labour Party 1996:9.
3 Labour Party 1996:9–18.

THE HISTORY OF COMPETING PRINCIPLES AND CONFUSED PRACTICE

Prior to 1908, there existed no separate system for dealing with young offenders. The Children Act 1908 created the juvenile court, although these were presided over by the same magistrates who sat in the adult courts. Since then, the history of the politics of youth justice over the last century has been, at best, chequered, and can be characterised as a seemingly interminable philosophical feud between the welfare and justice (or punishment) approaches. The question has been whether the young offender needs treatment or deserves punishment, care or control (alternatively known as the debate concerning issues of deprivation or depravity). In Chapter 1, Wayne Morrison argues that the justice versus welfare dichotomy is problematic on two fronts. First, it represents a polemical oversimplification of the youth justice discourse and, secondly, it reflects a possible inability on the part of theoreticians to adequately represent the actual practice of youth justice in abstract terms.

Justice versus welfare

What do we mean by the justice and welfare approaches? A justice model would arguably contain the following features:

(1) *due process* – adherence to a fixed procedure to ensure that all accused persons are treated in the same manner;

(2) *legalism* – an emphasis on 'formal justice': legal procedure and legal representation to ensure that all young people who come before the courts are treated equally and fairly. The presence of lawyers is important in order to provide an articulate voice for the defendant and to advise on and explain legal matters;

(3) *adversarial procedure* – a traditional focus on legal battles between the defence and prosecution lawyers in an effort to find the truth;

(4) *formalism* – a sombre procedure in a courtroom is adhered to, which purportedly reflects and reinforces the serious nature of matters being raised. In Crown Courts, lawyers wear gowns and judges preside and direct proceedings;

(5) *proportionality* – to ensure fairness and consistency, the defendant should be sentenced in proportion to the seriousness of the offence;

(6) *responsibility* – any person aged 10 or above in this country is presumed capable of forming the level of culpability (*mens rea*) required for the crime and should, therefore, be made to face up to the effects and full consequences of their behaviour;

(7) *act orientation* – throughout, the emphasis is on the crime, on the action performed, rather than the person who performed it. Appropriate disposals will be decided upon which have regard to the act rather than the actor.

On the other hand, a welfare model would probably display the following features:

(1) *adaptable procedure* – there is no fixed procedure. Procedure is adaptable to the case/issues being discussed. The hearing is conducted by a tribunal rather than a court;

(2) *various professionals may be present* – lawyers will generally not be required. Other professionals may take part in the hearing (for example, social workers, teachers, youth workers and health workers) in order to discuss solutions to the alleged problem behaviour;

(3) *inquisitorial procedure* – a non-confrontational approach to fact finding will be preferred without conflictual confrontations. Each party will be encouraged to verbalise their account/views;

(4) *informality* – the hearing will take place in an informal atmosphere and any representative will not be robed. There may, for example, be a round table discussion of the alleged offending event and possible solutions. All parties, including the young person and parent(s), are encouraged to speak;

(5) *tailor made disposal* – primarily to fit the needs of the offender rather than to reflect the seriousness of the offence. Emphasis is placed upon what kind of intervention is needed to help the young person desist from negative behaviour patterns. Sentences should be aimed at the need to reform and reflect the idea that young people can move away from criminal behaviour;

(6) *reasons for offending* – are investigated in order to provide suitable intervention. The young person's capability/capacity to form the required level of culpability is considered along with a number of concerns related to the young person's welfare and upbringing. Potential solutions are suggested;

(7) *person orientation* – throughout the proceedings, the emphasis is upon the actor rather than the act.

The dual role of juvenile justice

The establishment of the juvenile court in 1908 indicated a certain understanding that the reasons why children and young people commit crime and the needs of children and young people who come before the courts may not be the same as adults (or at least points to a recognition of this perspective). However, it can be seen that some confusion arose at this inception stage between the quite different approaches required for those children who are in need of care and those who had committed criminal offences and were before the court to be tried and sentenced, since the Act gave the juvenile court jurisdiction over both criminal and care issues. The unfortunate coupling of these dual roles (care and control) had the practical effect of making the same judicial body responsible for dealing with both the so called depraved and deprived. This led to a tension which persisted, at least up until 1989, when the Children Act of that year separated these two quite distinct functions, largely transferring care issues away from the (then soon to become) youth court, and placing them in the hands of social service departments. However, the unease created by this joint role has probably stretched beyond the removal of the sentence of a criminal care order from the youth court in 1989, and the youth justice system in England and Wales has undoubtedly become infused with tensions between juridical and welfare approaches towards young law breakers.

A recognition of the differences between adults and young people, in terms of responsibility and blameworthiness, was embodied in the 1908 Act. Its creation of a distinct system of youth justice gave birth to a latent and, perhaps, concomitant acknowledgment of a process of distinguishing between different types of young people who came before the youth justice system – between those who deserved punishment and those who needed help to overcome their difficulties. The tacit appreciation of this difference is, arguably, a tenuous but early manifestation of the bifurcated approach[4] to dealing with different kinds of young people who came before the youth courts that developed over the course of the 20th century.

Essentially, the introduction of a distinct system for dealing with young offenders represented a 'modification' of adult justice – a 'compromise' which resulted in the cross-fertilisation of principles of adult responsibility with notions of welfarism and protectionism. As noted earlier, a justice approach, based upon classicist ideas of culpability and responsibility, would involve a strict legal due process system, which sentenced using notions of proportionality and seriousness, and provided a sanction which was befitting to the offence rather than the offender. A welfare based approach would involve a less formal and adaptable procedure which would contextualise the offending behaviour, allowing for mitigation (and a recognition of the possibility of limited responsibility part of neo-classicism). Such an approach would enable non-legal experts to enter the decision making process and produce a disposal which would fit the offender rather than the offence. The Children Act 1908 effectively opened up the possibility of these two styles being blended (or possibly muddled) in the context of dealing with young offenders.

---

4   See below, p xxxiv.

This early discovery of the potential for conflict between the polemic welfare versus justice dichotomy was to produce various further compromise solutions over the course of the century. After outlining the major pieces of legislation which shaped the youth justice landscape since the Children Act 1908, we will return to this issue of forms of compromise and analyse the various guises these have taken. Moreover, we will examine recent legislation and consider whether the reforms will result in a radical change, or merely result in a further form of compromise.

The prevention principle

It could additionally be suggested that a third principle of youth justice emerged in embryonic form at that stage. This is the prevention principle which has, arguably, always been a nascent feature of welfarism. This principle emerges more obviously in the Children and Young Persons Act 1969 and, in a distinctly overt form, in preventative measures introduced by the Crime and Disorder Act 1998 such as curfew and child safety orders. Although purportedly welfare based, it will be argued later that preventionism produces net widening effects, drawing more young people, who may not yet have committed any criminal offences, into the ambit of the criminal justice system and is, therefore, essentially a latent form of social control.

The Maloney Committee

The next significant piece of legislation after the Children Act 1908 was the Children and Young Persons Act 1933. This Act provides a further example of the conflict between the opposing approaches of justice and welfare. The Act was passed as a result of the Report of the Maloney Committee in 1927, which contained a blend of classicist and positivist explanations of criminality in children and young people. It may be useful here to briefly outline the classicist and positivist approaches to crime so that these terms, which may be referred to later, are understood.

(a) The classicist approach

The pre-criminology philosophy of the classical school of thought (which arguably supports the justice approach to youth justice) viewed offending behaviour as, basically, a matter of choice. It asserted that all people are free but, in its utilitarian version, that they are by nature self-seeking – they will seek out pleasure and seek to avoid pain – and so everyone is capable of committing a crime if they think that it will benefit them and that those benefits will outweigh the costs. However, there exists a consensus in society regarding the need to protect personal welfare and property whereby, to prevent anti-social behaviour, all persons freely enter into the social contract. The social contract involves individuals abandoning some of their freedoms in return for protection from the State. Crime is thus essentially irrational and punishment must be used in order to deter people from violating the rights of others and to demonstrate the irrationality of law breaking behaviour. The State has been given the right to punish via the social contract and punishment must be prompt, certain and public in order to act as a deterrent. Punishment must be proportionate to the interests violated (that is, the harm done) not for reformation or retribution. Laws and legal procedures should adhere to a strict process so that everyone is treated equally. All people are responsible for their actions. Under neo-classicist revisionism, the lack of criminal capacity of young children was acknowledged and mitigation was allowed, but only as an explanation and not as an excuse for criminal behaviour.

(b) The positivist approach

The positivist school of thought can be viewed as a critique of the legal system, viewing it as an inept means of dealing with crime as a social problem because of its focus on the morality of acts rather than on the dangerousness or reformability of the offender. The focus for positivism is upon the criminal him or herself and, whilst it distinguishes 'mere' law breakers from 'true' criminals, one of the main features of the positivist school of scientific criminology is its focus upon determinism. Using this approach, the 'true' offender is destined to become a criminal due to (a) biological or genetic factors; (b) psychological or individualistic factors; or (c) social factors. In essence, the belief is that the offender simply cannot help him or herself – certain genetic, psychological or environmental factors have influenced his or her behaviour and their existence means that he or she is almost pre-programmed to become a criminal. With this in mind, one of the great contradictions of the positivist approach to crime is its focus on reformation and rehabilitation. Taylor, Walton and Young 1973 refer to this as the 'therapeutic paradox' – if the criminal is totally determined, how is reform possible? While this has sometimes been seen confusing, the argument has been advanced that what is necessary is an alteration in the determining factors.

A positivistic system of justice requires a broad range of possible sentences/treatments so that professional discretion can be used to choose the disposal most likely to produce reformation. The Crime and Disorder Act 1998 and the Youth Justice and Criminal Evidence Act 1999 have, arguably, created a vast range of possible disposals for young people who come before the penal system. This, coupled with a focus on preventionism, indicates a possible move towards a positivist approach within the youth justice system.

The Maloney Committee in 1927 adopted both classicist and positivist explanations of youth criminality (although they are in stark contrast to each other) in regarding law breaking as a deliberate act of defiance which had to be dealt with by formal court procedures and sanctions, whilst recognising, at the same time, that delinquent behaviour may be caused by psychological or environmental factors beyond the young person's control. Morris and Giller 1987 contend that the report thus presented:

> ... dual images of the delinquent [which] were placed not side by side but in sequence. In the first instance ..., the offence was used as a conscious act of wickedness. Once the act was proved or admitted, however, it was viewed as a product of personal or external forces [p 71].

The Children and Young Persons Act 1933

This allowed a sequencing strategy to develop, which attempted to compromise between the conflicting principles of justice and welfare. It subjected the young person to justice procedures in relation to trial and conviction and then to welfare principles in relation to disposal via mitigation and made available a wide range of welfare orientated disposals in the juvenile court. The Children and Young Persons Act 1933 was instrumental in establishing what became known by professionals as 'the welfare principle', which is still of paramount importance for the court when dealing with young offenders. Under s 44 of the Act, a court must:

> ... have regard to the welfare of the child or young person and shall in a proper case take steps for removing him from undesirable surroundings or for securing that proper provision is made for his education or training.

This, in turn, raised the question of the segregation of offending and non-offending children in need: linked by deprivation and hence welfarism, should such children be dealt with through common procedures and institutions?

The Children Act 1948

The immediate answer was 'no' as can be seen in the report of the Care of Children Committee in 1946, which accepted that it was undesirable for approved schools to provide identical services and regimes for non-offenders and offenders in the same institution. However, the report also precipitated the formation of the local government Children's Authorities, a social service department which was established by the Children Act 1948 as a service provider for deprived children and children subject to criminal court orders.

This common tension between ideas of treatment and punishment continued and had repercussions throughout the history of the juvenile justice system in the second half of the century.

The Children and Young Persons (Amendment) Act 1952

The Children and Young Persons (Amendment) Act 1952 allowed courts to remand young offenders to local authority accommodation and created an approved school licence release whereby those released from approved schools were to be supervised within the community by local child care officers. This Act, in effect, created two provisions whereby the systems of control (the criminal justice system) and of care (the welfare system) became intertwined when dealing with young people who became subject to such orders.

The Ingleby Report

In 1960, the Ingleby Report produced a more liberal understanding of youth criminality than had been seen previously, perhaps reflecting a recognition of the influence of criminological debates of the time that focused upon social and environmental, rather than individualistic causes of crime and an acknowledgment of labelling theory, which had flagged up the negative results of stigmatising young people who took part in anti-social behaviour, not only the effects on their life chances but also the likelihood of re-offending. The report recommended a reduction in the criminal jurisdiction of the juvenile court, via the diversion of non-serious offenders away from the formal criminal justice system, and a focus upon welfare provision for those who came before it. This warming towards welfarist models, coupled with professional doubts about the effectiveness of punishment for young offenders amongst social work personnel, continued throughout the 1960s and was reflected in the policy debates concerning youth criminality over that period.

The Children and Young Persons Act 1969

An appreciation of deprivation and social inequality as causal factors in juvenile delinquency by the reformers, together with a recognition of the stigmatising effects of early criminalisation, was also clearly visible in a radical White Paper published in 1965. It proposed that young offenders should be completely removed from the court system and dealt with exclusively by social service departments. This radicalism of the mid-1960s met with vociferous opposition mainly from lawyers within the Conservative Party and led to a justice orientated backlash. The result was an uneasy compromise in the form of the Children and Young Persons Act 1969, introduced by the then Labour Government. The introduction of the 1969 Act was clearly a legislative manifestation of the tensions between the two distinct approaches of justice and welfare. Some of the more welfare orientated provisions of that Act, such as the raising of the age of criminal responsibility to 14 and the proposal to allow local authorities to deal with most juvenile delinquents by means of supervision and care arrangements, never came into force due to the incoming Conservative Government's refusal to implement them. However, as will be explained in Chapters 8 and 9, in the same period in Scotland there was little opposition to a welfare model of youth justice as proposed by the Kilbrandon Report, and a treatment approach was implemented north of the border at the same time as a justice backlash was occurring in England and Wales.

One particular provision which was implemented by the 1969 Act clearly illustrates the introduction of a double-edged measure in another attempted compromise which purported to fuse the two approaches of treatment and punishment. The Act granted the criminal court the power to pass a criminal sanction on a young person which effectively amounted to a welfare provision: this was the criminal care order. In that sentence, the 'deprived' and the 'depraved' became as one: the welfare measure became a criminal sanction. Issues of deprivation and depravation were not only jointly acknowledged, but became merged as both the problem of juvenile delinquency and its solution. (This problematic theoretical fusing was recognised some time later and the criminal care order became discredited and was infrequently used from the late 1970s onwards, until it was finally abolished by the Children Act 1989.)

The battlefield of the debates surrounding the passing and implementation of the 1969 Act resulted in a youth justice landscape which, in the 1970s, produced:

> ... a widening of the net of control as elements of the new system brought into being by the 1969 Act were absorbed into a larger system which retained its traditional commitment to imprisonment.[5]

In effect, the 1969 Act created greater powers of discretion for social workers and did nothing to stem a rising tide of custodial disposals. Social workers were able to expand their client group – a kind of professional entrepreneurialism – which resulted in many non-serious delinquents being drawn into the social control net of the youth justice system under the guise of preventionism, a nascent concomitant of welfarism which, as noted earlier, has been (albeit latently) evident as a feature of youth justice since 1908.

---

5   McLaughlin and Muncie 1996:267.

Conservative youth justice – the bifurcation approach

The Conservative Party's victory in the 1979 general election saw the start of the Thatcher era and a move towards individualism and consumerism. (In Chapter 2, Keith Hayward and Mark Fenwick examine the links between the growth of consumerism and youth criminality, analysing crime as a commodity of post-modern life.) The 'rule of law' and 'law and order' rhetoric, which dominated the Conservatives' election campaign, was implemented by the 'short, sharp shock' and the Criminal Justice Act 1982, which transformed borstals into youth training centres that aimed to give young offenders an experience more akin to an adult prison. Nevertheless, behind the rhetoric, the re-orientation of the duality of approach towards young law breakers which had developed was to take on a new guise. A policy of bifurcation was pursued by successive Conservative governments. The policy, which represents a further form of compromise implemented to resolve the inevitable conflict between principles of justice and welfare, arguably continued until the post-Bulger panic in the early 1990s. This practice involved 'getting tough' on those deemed to be serious and persistent young offenders, whilst endeavouring to divert first time and non-serious juvenile offenders away from the more stigmatising effects of the criminal justice system, thus indicating a recognition of the effects of criminalisation as a possible causative factor of further criminal behaviour. Indeed, a general trend away from incarceration can even be seen as early as the 1982 Act, which created the specific activities order as a high tariff community disposal, that was later to become a direct alternative to custody under the Criminal Justice Act 1988. (In Chapter 12, Caroline Hunt looks at the use of intensive alternatives to custody projects as a disposal for more persistent young offenders, focusing on a case study of such a scheme in Delaware, USA.) As McLaughlin and Muncie 1986 state in relation to bifurcation strategies:

> Some categories of offenders are represented as more serious and menacing while others, who had previously been regarded as a threat, are represented as relatively unproblematic. The activity of a small number of offenders is 'dramatised' while that of others is 'normalised'. Bifurcated penalties increased the penalties imposed upon the dramatised group while reducing those imposed upon the normalised group [p 265].

Bifurcation policy provides a convenient justification for the continued use of both justice and welfare measures within the same youth justice system and, thus, the continuation of what is and was, in effect, a schizophrenic practice of youth justice. This is because the policy of bifurcation permits a welfare based approach towards the normalised, non-threatening group, and yet allows for the full rigours of the justice model to bear down upon those young people whose activities are amplified and who are defined as problematic.

The 1980s and early 1990s represented a further attempt to mix principles of justice and welfare within the practice of youth justice via the progressive development of the bifurcation strategy, with each measure being separately aimed at what were defined as quite distinct offender populations. Various Home Office circulars over this period officially encouraged the use of cautions for young offenders and, in many areas, resulted in the practice of multiple cautioning of some young people. The diversionary tactic of cautioning at this time arguably allowed flexibility for professionals in dealing with young offenders who were regarded by them as non-serious and likely to 'grow out' of their delinquency. This discretion has largely been lost by the creation of the more rigid final warning system in the Crime and Disorder Act 1998. The new final warning system amounts to a diversionary tactic which, nevertheless, adheres to an anti-discretionary due process model and has all the features of the formalism of a justice approach.

Additionally, the Conservative governments of the 1980s provided local authorities with funds to set up intermediate treatment centres and programmes for young offenders. These centres concentrated on creating positive learning environments for juveniles, with a focus on education and training as a means of breaking the cycle of offending (unfortunately, funding for these was reduced in the late 1980s). Similarly, the Children Act 1989 placed a duty upon local authorities to establish diversionary schemes, attendance at which could be ordered as part of a court sentence. The Act also required social service departments to provide alternatives to secure accommodation remands for young people awaiting trial.

The Criminal Justice Act 1991

Then, in 1991, the Criminal Justice Act represented an unusual fusing of various approaches. Whilst it was arguably imbued with classicist notions of proportionality, in youth justice terms it also appears to move towards ideas of welfarism in relation to non-serious offenders, elements of which can be viewed as part of the further development of the bifurcation strategy witnessed over the 1980s. In fact, it could be argued that the Act represented an acceptance of the effectiveness of diversionary practices for certain young delinquents. Although it can be accepted that, in terms of sentencing policy generally (that is, of adults and juveniles), the Act can be regarded as a move towards justice ideas of proportionality in sentencing,[6] welfare orientated provisions for young offenders are in evidence in a number of measures introduced by the Act. These include:

(1) an expansion of the upper age limit in the youth court to include 17 year olds;

(2) a reduction of the maximum custodial sentence in a Young Offender Institution to 12 months (excluding very serious offences which are covered by section 53 of the Children and Young Persons Act 1933);

---

6   See Gibson 1993, Chapter 3.

(3) a raising of the minimum age that a young person can be sentenced to a custodial punishment to 15;

(4) the expansion of community sentences for 16 and 17 year olds; and

(5) the creation of new remand arrangements (including remand fostering) for 15 and 16 year olds.

Ironically, perhaps, certain more general provisions of the Criminal Justice Act 1991 regarding proportionality of sentencing were not well received by the more conservative magistrates who seemed to believe in a type of 'welfarism' in the sense of individualised disposals. These magistrates felt that their discretionary powers to sentence the offender (rather than the offence) had been severely curtailed. (In Chapter 4, Stuart Vernon speculates on how magistrates might respond to the discretion they may gain as a result of the Crime and Disorder Act 1998 and the Youth Justice and Criminal Evidence Act 1999.) As a result of such criticisms, the Criminal Justice Act 1993 removed the classicist tariff based restriction placed on those sentencing in both the adult and youth courts (which were imposed in 1991), and allowed for the full offending history of the defendant to be taken into account when deciding an appropriate disposal. Also, offences committed on bail were to be regarded as an aggravating factor and the controversial unit fine system was abolished.

The Bulger effect – the Criminal Justice and Public Order Act 1994

The 1993 Act can be viewed as the beginning of a march towards more justice orientated policies within the criminal justice system generally. However, this march was to become a sprint after the killing of James Bulger and the populist crisis in morality debate which ensued. This was largely fuelled by the media highlighting cases of persistent young offenders who, it was argued, were simply 'getting away with it' due to the youth justice system's inability to deal adequately with those children and young people who engage in anti-social behaviour. The Bulger case eventually led to the abolition of the presumption of innocence for 10–13 year olds in the Crime and Disorder Act 1998 (see Chapter 3, where Elizabeth Stokes analyses the possible effects of the abolition of the doctrine of *doli incapax*). Children were no longer to be regarded as innocent; they were potential murderers. Notions of childhood innocence were replaced by demonising images of young people who display troublesome or lawless behaviour. Something had to be done – and it was.

The Criminal Justice and Public Order Act 1994 represented a politically motivated, knee-jerk lurch towards a justice orientated punitive response to child and young offenders. The use of police detention and secure remands was introduced for those as young as 12 years old; secure training centres were to be established as a custodial sentence for persistent offenders aged 12 and over; the maximum Young Offender Institution sentence was increased to two years; and s 53 procedures became operational from the age of 10. This statute was followed up by a Home Office Circular, which officially restricted the use of more than one caution for young offenders.

A HISTORY OF COMPROMISE STRATEGIES

From our summary of the major pieces of legislation that have shaped the modern youth justice system, it can be seen that there have been various attempts to produce solutions to the unavoidable conflict which is created when seeking to create a system which combines the polemical theoretical approaches of justice and welfare. As we have seen, these solutions have taken the form of a variety of compromise strategies whereby elements of justice and welfare have been distributed over the system in a bid to resolve this inevitable tension. These attempts can be summarised as follows:

(1) *bifurcation strategy* – distinguishing between different types of children and young people who come before the justice system. This involves differentiating those who need help from those who deserve punishment; serious offenders from non-serious offenders; and persistent offenders from those whose behaviour can be 'nipped in the bud';

(2) *sequencing strategy* – creating different types of procedures/processes which utilise divergent approaches; for example, a justice approach in relation to trial and conviction; a welfare approach in relation to mitigation and sentencing; pre-trial/court diversionary schemes, and so on;

(3) *institutional strategy* – developing practices whereby different institutions/organisations will deal with different types of young offenders; for example, informal tribunal-style hearings such as the new Youth Offender Panels as opposed to the courts; social services as opposed to the formal youth justice system, etc;

(4) *'double-edged' strategy* – the introduction of measures which have both a welfare and justice function; for example, the criminal care order introduced by the Children and Young Persons Act 1969 (now abolished);

(5) *career criminal strategy* – a young offender may experience a more welfare oriented approach at the start of their offending career, for example, by the use of cautions/reprimands and final warnings or other diversionary measures; if he or she continues to offend, more justice orientated procedures and sanctions will be implemented.

All the above forms of compromise amount to techniques or splitting strategies which attempt to distribute potentially incompatible elements across the system in different ways.

Does the new legislation indicate a radical overhaul of the youth justice system? Are they in fact new or are they a re-worked version of some of these compromise strategies we have witnessed over the last century?

A NEW YOUTH JUSTICE?

Is a new landscape being created in terms of our approach towards juvenile offenders, or are we about to witness significant changes in the practice of youth justice which have not been fully thought through at the level of theory? Will significant practical change to a system succeed without an arguably necessary concomitant change to the theoretical foundations of that system? It appears that the dominating conflictual discourses may continue to create discord in the 'new' youth justice of the 21st century. Is yet another compromise strategy being developed to plug the inevitable conceptual holes which will undoubtedly develop in a system which houses two separate and incompatible approaches? Is it time not only to overhaul youth justice practice, but also to overhaul youth justice theory? This may require not merely a repair or reconditioning job, but, perhaps, a scrapping of the dominating divergent discourses in order for any attempted radicalism at the level of practice to have any chance of success.

As Paul Boateng, Minister of State for the Home Office, said in his address to a conference on the new legislation hosted by NACRO and the Juvenile and Family Courts Society in July 1999, 'It is quite intolerable that one in three young men have a criminal record. We must change this'.[7]

A further question which needs to be asked is whether the radical proposals contained in these new pieces of legislation really address the problem of criminalisation of young people, particularly of young men from low status socio-economic backgrounds. Will they succeed in removing what Boateng called 'the mark of Cain' from them, a mark which is often counterproductive, affects their life chances and, arguably, pushes them even further into a career of dysfunctional law breaking behaviour? (See Chapter 1, where Wayne Morrison examines the possibilities of reintegrative shaming for young offenders which focuses on social inclusion, rather than exclusionary practices of justice.)

The quasi-hysteria about the 'problem' of youth crime at the time of the 1997 General Election appears to make little sense when we analyse the statistical data. According to criminal statistics published by HMSO the number of young offenders aged 10–17 who had been found guilty or cautioned for an indictable offence fell by 30% between 1987 and 1997. Furthermore, according to NACRO:

---

7   Boateng 1999.

... since 1987, the number of male juvenile offenders has fallen by 33% and female young offenders by 17%. The decline in the number of known young offenders over the 10 years is only partly accounted for by the decline in juvenile population. Between 1987 and 1997, the number of juveniles in the population fell by 2%.[8]

However, the number of young people receiving custodial sentences rose over that period. Whereas the number of young offenders who were detained under sentence fell by approximately 50% between 1980 and 1993, this figure rose by almost 56% in the four years up to and including 1997. The reasons for this increase can only partly be explained by the seriousness of the offences being committed, and is, arguably, linked with two other facts: first, the development of a definition of the so called 'persistent offender' over this period and the 'get tough' policies in relation to those so categorised; and, secondly, the media hyping of 'youth out of control' type stories (remember 'Boomerang Boy', 'Ratboy', 'Spider Boy' and 'Blip Boy'? ((1999) *The Guardian*, 25 March)) following the murder of James Bulger and the consequential media driven moral panic about anti-social behaviour amongst young people which ensued on a grand scale.

Prior to their election in 1997, the Labour Party, desiring to be seen to be 'getting tough' on crime due to the increased politicisation of the youth crime issue, put forward its proposals for the reform of the youth justice system in their Consultation Paper, *Tackling Youth Crime* (1996), in an attempt to dislodge the Conservative Party from their traditional image as the party most concerned about law and order.

Tackling Youth Crime focused upon the need to remove the confusion over justice and welfare approaches that had perplexed youth justice policy for most of the 20th century. Whilst acknowledging that each approach was, in essence, theoretically quite different from the other, it promised to establish a new balance between these conflicting interests within the practice of youth justice. Indeed, the Home Secretary, Jack Straw, in his first speech to the Police Federation following the general election in May 1997, specifically referred to the problems within the youth justice system which, he indicated, were directly related to the marrying of these two disparate philosophies:

> ... many young offenders have suffered erratic parenting – indulgent one minute, overly harsh the next. The last thing the criminal justice system should do is mimic the faults of a bad parent, but it often does.

The Crime and Disorder Act 1998

Following a second Consultation Paper in 1997, entitled *No More Excuses – A New Approach to Tackling Youth Crime in England and Wales*, the Crime and Disorder Act was passed in 1998. This Act proposes a 'root and branch'

8   NACRO 1999.

overhaul of the youth justice system and will be implemented over a number of years, following the establishment of, and feedback from, pilot schemes and pathway sites which will test the ground of the new reforms. Due to this extended period of implementation, it remains to be seen whether the Act can successfully fuse the justice and welfare approaches into the new youth justice system, or whether it is merely another attempt to reach a compromise in the conflict between these, perhaps, mutually exclusive principles.

Section 37 of the Act emphasises the primary aim of prevention and states that:

> It shall be the principal aim of the youth justice system to prevent offending by children and young persons ...

It also places a duty on all personnel working within the youth justice arena to have regard to this paramount aim whilst carrying out their duties. In a Home Office paper published in September 1998, Jack Straw referred to this primary focus of preventing offending and recidivist behaviour:

> The Government wants to see the youth justice system make a real difference to the lives of the children and young people with whom it deals by preventing those children and young people from offending. Too many young people begin offending at a very young age. Too many continue offending in their adult lives. Young people who offend and re-offend damage their own lives. They cause disruption, harm and distress to others. Preventing offenders is in the best interests of all concerned and should be a priority for all those working within the youth justice system.[9]

In order to deliver that principal aim, the Home Office Juvenile Offenders Unit set out six key objectives for the reformed youth justice system:

(a) tackling delays – by halving how long it takes for young offenders to be processed from arrest to sentence from an average of 142 days in 1996 to a target of 71 days by the time of the next election;

(b) confronting the young offender with the consequences of their offending and encouraging responsibility for their actions;

(c) intervention into 'risk factors', including family, social, personal and health factors (see Chapter 6, where Issy Harvey discusses the need for Youth Offending Teams (YOTs) to develop serious initiatives in relation to drug use amongst young people and the links between drug use and criminality);

(d) introduction of a new range of penalties to enable sentencers to punish in proportion to the seriousness and persistence of offending;

(e) encouragement of reparation;

(f) reinforcement of parental responsibilities.

---

9   Home Office 1998 (Preface).

The Act sets out six key themes that will supposedly assist in achieving the above six objectives. It is useful to briefly outline what each of these six themes consists of in terms of the new measures being introduced. General comments about these themes will follow.

(a) Partnership and multi-agency working

Sections 6 and 7 of the Crime and Disorder Act encourage the development of local partnerships to provide a local framework and strategy for identifying crime and disorder problems within a particular locality and to provide a response. (In Chapter 10, Matt Long asserts that the task of tackling youth crime can only succeed if there is a truly local approach to youth delinquency, where local agencies work in partnership to tackle crime issues particular to their area.)

Section 39 of the Act required local authorities to establish multi-agency YOTs by April 2000, bringing together professionals from social services, police, health, education and probation. The team must produce an annual youth justice plan for tackling crime within their area of responsibility. (In Chapter 7, Susannah Hancock analyses how the new legislation is being implemented in the London Borough of Lewisham, whose YOT is both a government pilot site and a pathway site for the Youth Justice Board.)

(b) Tackling offending behaviour and providing early intervention

The key theme of tackling offending through early intervention is addressed by the following measures:

- child safety orders (s 11), which are placed on a child under the age of 10 to prevent him or her from growing into criminal behaviour;
- local child curfews (s 14), aimed at preventing anti-social behaviour in local areas by children under the age of 10;
- final warnings (s 65), replacing the cautioning system and providing for a significant punishment if anti-social behaviour is continued;
- action plan order (s 69), which combines elements of reparation, punishment and rehabilitation to help prevent re-offending and include parental involvement.

(c) Focus on reparation

Section 67 establishes the reparation order, which is designed to make the young person face up to the consequences of their offending behaviour. The courts can require a young person to make reparation to the actual victim of their crime or to the local community generally.

(d) Focus on parenting

Section 8 of the Act reinforces parental responsibility by setting up the parenting order. This is aimed at 'helping' parents through support and guidance to control the anti-social behaviour of their children. Such an order may place specific responsibilities on a parent, for example, to impose a curfew on their child.

(e) More effective custodial sentences

Section 73 establishes a new detention and training order, implemented from April 2000. This purports to be a constructive and flexible custodial sentence that will have a clear focus on preventing re-offending behaviour. This is a new custodial sentence for young offenders that can be used by Youth and Crown Courts in respect of all young offenders under the age of 18 who have been convicted of an offence which, if committed by an adult, would be an imprisonable offence. If the child is aged 10 or 11, a further order will be required by the Home Secretary to allow such a sentence to be passed.

(f) A national framework

Section 41 sets up the framework for the operation of the national Youth Justice Board. This is to encourage and monitor nationwide consistency in the implementation of the system of youth justice, to draw up standards for service delivery and to help disseminate good practice.

The notion of responsibility

In addition to the primary aim of the Act – that of the prevention of (re-)offending – it is clear that traditional classicist notions of responsibility also form a thread which runs throughout the Act. The culpability for delinquent behaviour appears to be jointly placed upon the shoulders of the young person and at the door of his or her parent or guardian. Under the legislation, both can be 'punished' for the same act, amounting, in effect, to a dispersal of responsibility. When the Government pledged £35 million in September 1999 to facilitate the establishment of projects aimed at preventing offending by children and young people, Lord Warner, chair of the Youth Justice Board, said:

We will no longer accept excuses for criminal behaviour from young offenders or their parents. Young offenders need to take personal responsibility for their actions and parents need to face up to their failure to act.[10]

The creation of a parenting order, in addition to the existing powers to fine and bind over parents, represents a further move to hold parents responsible for the sins of their offspring and provides the Government with a way of punishing parents by means of a criminal sanction for their presumed failure to provide welfare (that is, to properly care for/bring up their child). In March 2000, a mother in France was jailed for a month for failing in her parental duties in relation to the delinquent activities of her sons.[11] The judge invoked a rarely used Article of the French criminal code (Art 227) which permits a court to imprison a parent for up to two years if they 'without legitimate reason shirk the obligations of parenthood'. It remains to be seen how much further we, in this country, will move down the pathway of parental punishment. It will also be interesting to see how far we will continue to usurp and supplant the parental rights of those we consider to be bad parents by the use of anti-social behaviour orders, curfew orders, remands into local authority accommodation, care orders and custodial measures. It may also be useful to monitor the types of parents who become subject to parenting orders and other intrusive orders in terms of their socio-economic backgrounds and whether it is predominately single parents or co-parents who are targeted for such interventions.

The theme of responsibility is also evidenced by the creation of a reparation order (s 67, see above), which encourages a young person to contemplate the actual effects of their behaviour in terms of the injury and suffering caused to victims and the increased use of punitive measures for persistent young offenders. In November 1999, Prime Minister Tony Blair announced that young people who do not comply with court orders will be deprived of their welfare benefits.

Expanding professional discretion

The Act also promotes a more proactive management of the youth crime problem. YOT officers will be drawn from a broad range of professionals associated with the care of young people and will be required to adopt multi-agency strategies for tackling the youth crime problem in their local area. The focus upon preventative work and the involvement of parents will inevitably result in YOT officers dealing with a broader range of service providers and service users and, therefore, the net widening effect of the Act will arguably be a natural consequence of these initiatives.

---

10   (1999) *The Guardian*, 30 September.
11   See (2000) *The Sunday Times*, 12 March.

The boundaries of traditional youth justice social work have been breached by these reforms, with YOT officers being effectively given more power to decide how to deal with young people who have been made subject to one of the new court orders. Discretion always raises problems of accountability and of possible dangers of over-enthusiasm in the name of welfare of the young person, leading to a greater amount of State intervention than may have ensued had he or she been made subject to sanctions given under a justice orientated framework. Practitioners within the new YOTs should guard against using unnecessary, excessive, or disproportionate interventions in the lives of young people and their families. If the new legislation is creating a new framework for discretionary intervention, then the net widening effect of the Children and Young Persons Act 1969 could be repeated. Civil liberties, including personal and family rights and autonomy, should be respected by professionals who are being encouraged by the Government to take a more proactive approach. If caution is not exercised, it is possible that this new proactivity will result in even greater State intervention in, and control of, the lives of marginalised communities lacking social or economic power and who are most at danger of being labelled as 'problem families'.

Contract culture and the Youth Justice and Criminal Evidence Act 1999

The Youth Justice and Criminal Evidence Act 1999 gives effect to further reforms proposed in the 1997 White Paper, *No More Excuses*. It creates a new sentence of a referral order for young people convicted for the first time. The young person will be referred to a Youth Offenders Panel (YOP) drawn from the local community (established by YOTs) for a period of between three and 12 months. A 'contract' will be drawn up with the young offender and his or her parents, specifying the details of the order which will be tailor made to suit the needs of each young person.

There has been a rise in the contract culture within social work practice generally over the last decade and it is worth commenting on its growing use and significance within the context of the youth justice arena. A contract represents a democratic freedom (albeit in economic terms) and, therefore, the presence of two principles in modern legal philosophy: (a) an equality in terms of status and bargaining power in relation to contractual terms; and (b) a focus upon individual rights and responsibilities regarding the performance of the contract. In terms of social work interaction, these two principles are somewhat diluted.

Regarding the first principle, there is no real equality of bargaining power; social work contracts are often presented to the young person or parent simply to sign after the contents have been briefly explained. The young person or their parent will certainly not be under the impression that the contents of the contract are negotiable and, indeed, apart from a few minor details, effectively, they are not. It is a 'take it or leave it' situation; if the young person 'chooses' to leave it, then he or she is taken back to court for non-co-operation.

In relation to the second principle – the creation of individual rights and responsibilities – the contract acts as a further means of reinforcing classicist notions of individual responsibility for actions; the responsibility to comply is imposed upon the young person, so that non-compliance with the terms of the contract is clearly seen as being caused by individual non-co-operation. The notion of personal responsibility and culpability for anti-social behaviour, which is emphasised in the new legislation, provides a reworking of the ideas of responsibility as expressed in the justice model, but here it is incorporated into a purportedly welfare based measure. The idea of responsibility is additionally reinforced by the use of contracts with young people on court orders. Furthermore, what are their 'rights' under this contract? Presumably, they include the 'right' to access social work services to enable compliance with the court order. The young person (quite reasonably) may not view this as a 'right' at all, but as a form of coercive social control.

Regarding this growing contract culture within youth justice and social work practice, the discourse of citizenship in relation to the Welfare State has, according to Donzelot (1979), generated a distinction between those who can attain full independence as freely contracting individuals through economic activity and those who are unable to achieve such status and for whom special provision must be made. So, the Welfare State notion of citizenship has always manifested a split between contract and tutelage, so that those who receive any State entitlements or services are inevitably in a compromised position. As Yeatman argues in relation to such tutored citizens:

> The administration was and is designed to impress upon them their client status, their lack of contractual freedom of choice.[12]

The referral order is designed to address offending behaviour in an attempt to prevent further offending. The order should include reparation and can involve community work, curfews, mediation, contact with the victim or participation in specified activities or education programmes, and is structured a further part of Jack Straw's commitment to the 'three Rs':

> I want the youth justice system to promote the 'three Rs' of restorative justice: restoration and apology to the victim; reintegration into the law abiding community; and responsibility on the part of offenders and parents.[13]

---

12 Yeatman 1994:85.

13 (1998) *The Times*, 24 February.

If the young person does not co-operate with the requirements of the order, he or she will be referred back to court for the imposition of another sentence.

Young offenders who appear for the first time in the youth court will be automatically referred to a YOP, unless the crime is serious enough to merit a custodial sentence, or the court passes an absolute discharge. The Home Office Juvenile Offenders Unit asserts that, 'making referral orders the norm for first time offenders ensures an opportunity for most young people to make their first court appearance their last'.[14]

Scottish similarities

These new YOPs resemble the system adopted in 1971 in Scotland to deal with young offenders (see Malcolm Bentley and Bill Whyte, Chapters 8 and 9). The similarities with the Children's Hearings north of the border are clear: parents are to play a crucial role in attending and being asked to help prevent anti-social behaviour; other significant adults, such as social workers or teachers, may also be required to be present; victims will be able to attend YOP meetings and explain to the young offender the effects of their criminal behaviour and suggest appropriate reparation; the meetings will be conducted informally, possibly without the presence of a legal representative; and the young person will be encouraged to participate fully in the proceedings. Indeed, Jack Straw made no secret of the fact that he has looked north of the border for evidence of good practice to include as part of his reform proposals:

> We have sought to identify the aspects of the Scottish system which could fruitfully be incorporated into the different legal framework in England and Wales to improve the efficiency and effectiveness of the system south of the border.[15]

The media at the time was very much aware that Jack Straw was trying to learn some lessons about youth justice from Scotland:

> The Home Secretary has tailored part of his overhaul of the youth justice system in England and Wales by borrowing elements from the Scottish Children's Panel System.[16]

The YOPs in England and Wales will be required to undertake a full examination of the causal factors which have contributed towards the offending behaviour of the young person, with the emphasis on providing a suitable, individualised programme to help tackle this behaviour, encourage responsibility and prevent further offending. So, in relation to first time offenders, we are adopting a system which has been practised for all but the most serious young offenders in Scotland for some 30 years.

---

14 Home Office 1999.
15 Labour Party 1996.
16 (1998) *The Times*, 24 January.

The referral order is being piloted for 18 months in specific areas from April 2000 (the date by which all YOTs became operative). The order is expected to be available to the courts by 2002–03. The referral order clearly represents a welfare based approach for first time offenders; its nature and characteristics arguably fit squarely into the welfare model. The focus upon informality, lack of due process, the absence of lawyers and its inquisitorial approach towards causative factors, and so on, all point to a method of dealing with non-persistent young offenders in a purely treatment orientated manner. This approach is further evidenced by the fact that the Rehabilitation of Offenders Act 1976 has been amended in relation to the referral order, so that the rehabilitation period runs only until the end of the order and is considered spent at that point, removing the so called 'mark of Cain' from these young people.[17] This move for first time offenders contrasts very starkly with the increased punitive measures introduced for offenders regarded as serious or persistent in the Crime and Disorder Act 1998, and indicates the continuation of the development of a bifurcated youth justice system for dealing with juvenile law breakers in England and Wales.

A REVOLUTION IN YOUTH JUSTICE OR POLITICAL PRAGMATISM?

So, do the reforms presented in the Crime and Disorder Act 1998 and the Youth Justice and Criminal Evidence Act 1999 mark a radical change in the way we practise youth justice in this country? Do they really represent a fresh philosophical direction and an inspirational departure from the traditional theoretical tensions which have dominated youth justice over the last century? Is it really out with the old and in with the new, or do the changes, in fact, represent a dazzling, well stage managed reworking of the familiar conflicts which have dogged the way we have dealt with young delinquents for too long?

The Government believes that its reforms to the youth justice system are pivotal to their crusade to remedy the crime and disorder problem. They are spending a lot of money to ensure that the reforms have some chance of success. As well as the general cost of setting up new YOTs and YOPs throughout England and Wales, Jack Straw pledged £35 million to pay for the establishment of locally based programmes to help challenge youth offending, in addition to the £11 million pledged to the eight pathway project areas.

---

17 In Scotland, although the rehabilitation period similarly runs until the end of the supervision order, as the period of the order is indeterminate, the fact of the order must be disclosed in any job applications until it is terminated. This could stretch well into the young person's late teens and, as such, is arguably contrary to the whole ethos of the Scottish youth justice system (Rehabilitation of Offenders Act 1976, s 3, as amended by the Children (Scotland) Act 1995, Sched 4).

Tough on crime ...?

During the general election campaign of 1997, Jack Straw was keen to appear to be as 'tough on crime' as the then Conservative Home Secretary, Michael Howard. The Labour Party knew that they were not traditionally the party of law and order but, by 1997, we had become a society obsessed with law and order, fearing victimisation and uneasy about anti-social behaviour amongst young people. This was an Achilles heel election issue. The image of the Labour Party as soft on young offenders had to be turned around, and it was. In the run up to the election, with every punitive measure Michael Howard proposed for reforming the criminal justice system, Jack Straw followed close on his heels, either agreeing with proposed measures (for example, the 'three strikes and you're out' rule for burglars) or proposing hard line policies himself, so that it seemed, by the time of the general election, that not even a hair's breadth of space could be seen between the 'toughness' of Conservative and Labour policies in relation to the crime 'problem'.

However, many Labour supporters believed that:

> ... once in power, Straw was supposed to throw off the cloak, take out the false fangs and reveal a decent, reforming, though solid and sensible Home Secretary beneath (he said that Roy Jenkins was his model). But no one told him that the election is over.[18]

It seems likely that Jack Straw will carry though the promises that he made during the political frenzy which characterised the crime and disorder debate in the run up to the general election. If elected for a second term, it is probable that this reforming spirit may well continue.

The legislative changes are, therefore, aimed at middle England and it is hoped that they will satisfy the many Conservative voters who decided to defect to Labour in 1997. The reforms are aimed at keeping them happy and encouraging them to trust Labour enough on this key issue to vote for them again.

Tough on the causes of crime ...?

The Crime and Disorder Act 1998 and the Youth Justice and Criminal Evidence Act 1999 have been trumpeted as the most far reaching shake-up of the youth justice system since the setting up of the juvenile court in 1908. They have certainly been depicted as clearly representing research based, sensible and impartial proposals. The creation of new orders aimed at preventing offending behaviour prior to the commission of any real offences – such as the curfew order, the child safety order and the anti-social behaviour order – has obvious dangers in relation to the labelling of certain powerless groups within

---

18   Toynbee 1999.

our society. Will curfews be imposed in Hampstead or Knightsbridge? Probably not. It is easy to predict the kinds of children who will find their freedom of movement restricted because they live in a particular area which is classified as troublesome, due to the activities of a handful of children in that area. (It may be that curfew orders will fall foul of the Human Rights Act 1998 when it comes into force in October 2000, as Art 8 of the European Convention on Human Rights stipulates that a public body should not interfere with private family life unless it is for the prevention of crime.)

Moreover, the net widening effect of this and other initiatives is similarly clear. The virtual scrapping of the conventional use of absolute and conditional discharges for young offenders, due mainly to the introduction of the referral order, will result in such offenders effectively being 'up-tariffed' – finding themselves subject to a higher level of supervision under the referral order and, therefore, being subject to a greater involvement within the criminal justice process than would have previously been the case, when an absolute or conditional discharge may have been considered a satisfactory means of disposal by magistrates.

Additionally, the abolition of the cautioning system and its replacement with a reprimand, followed by a final warning if necessary, will result in a considerable number of non-serious delinquents (who were previously able to receive a series of cautions before being subject to more serious criminalisation strategies at court) being pushed into the formal court system earlier, with arguably damaging effects upon their life chances which will, perhaps, make them more likely to develop into career criminals.

Prison works ...?

The increase in the number of young people confined in custodial or secure establishments has continued to rise since 1997 and, with the introduction of the detention and training order and the power to remand young people in such establishments upon their first appearance at court, this increase will probably continue. Indeed, Jack Straw has made it clear that he agrees with Michael Howard's view that 'prison works', as evidenced by the rise in the general prison population from 60,000 when the Conservatives left office to 64,000 and rising by the end of the last century. The crisis of numbers is highlighted by the proposed use of tagging of young offenders as a means of coping with an expected increase of juveniles held in youth jails and other youth detention facilities.

The continued rise in the use of incarceration to deal with young offenders is particularly worrying in the light of reports of brutality, for example, the use of wrist and neck locks to control offenders aged 12–14 in Medway

Training Centre in Kent[19] and the comments of the Chief Inspector of Prisons Sir David Ramsbottom. He noted, in a report on Feltham Young Offenders Institution published in March 1999, that the inspection was 'without a doubt the most disturbing' he had ever made.[20] Many young prisoners were found to be locked up for 22 hours a day in cells that were dirty, dilapidated and cold, often sleeping on thin mattresses that were damaged, without the provision of blankets. Most had no opportunities for outside exercise and there had been little progress on the 187 recommendations the Inspector had made about the institution some three years earlier. Further concerns relating to young offender Institutions were raised in November 1999, when the Prison Service was accused of dragging its feet over calls for an investigation into Portland youth jail in Dorset, where 10 former inmates had accused officers of systematic brutality, including physical and emotional abuse. In March 2000, the Chief Inspector of Prisons stated that Portland was an unsuitable place for young people and, in effect, recommended closure.

NEW RIGHTS VERSUS NEW YOUTH JUSTICE: POSSIBLE CHALLENGES UNDER THE HUMAN RIGHTS ACT 1998

The Human Rights Act 1998 will come into force in October 2000. This Act, in effect, incorporates the European Convention on Human Rights into domestic law so that all current and planned legislation must be implemented in a manner consistent with the rights and freedoms set out in the Convention. Additionally, the Act also includes the adoption into domestic law of the UN Convention and linked protocols including (very significantly from a youth justice standpoint) the Beijing Rules (the UN Standard Minimum Rules for the Administration of Juvenile Justice 1985). How will the inclusion of these international provisions effect the practice of youth justice in this country? Could legal challenges be mounted under the Human Rights Act 1998 to the way young people are treated who are deemed to be anti-social or who are suspected of or convicted for a criminal offence? What influence could such challenges, if successful, have upon the Labour Government's crusade to transform the practice and, purportedly, the philosophy of youth justice in England and Wales? (See Chapter 5, where Deirdre Fottrell examines the growth of international legal standards in relation to juvenile justice practices.)

---

19 See (1999) *The Times*, 15 January.
20 (1999) *The Guardian*, 26 March.

The impact of *Thompson and Venables*

The implications of the incorporation of the European Convention on Human Rights via the Human Rights Act 1998 have, arguably, already been felt in the ruling of the European Court of Human Rights in the Bulger case in December 1999, where the court ruled that:[21] (a) the process in the Crown Court was unfair in that it was unsuitable for the two defendants, Thompson and Venables (aged 11 at the time), because it was intimidating and incomprehensible for them; (b) sentencing should be left to judges to decide and recommendations should not be overruled by politicians (the boys were originally sentenced to eight years by the trial judge, which was raised to 10 years by the Lord Chief Justice Lord Bingham, and then to 15 years by Michael Howard, the then Home Secretary); and (c) that decisions about release should not be decided by the Home Secretary, but by an independent judicial body such as the Parole Board.

As a result of the ruling in this case, in March 2000, Jack Straw handed over the decision on how long Thompson and Venables will remain in custody to the Lord Chief Justice. In future, the sentencing of juveniles convicted of the gravest crimes will be set by the Lord Chief Justice on a recommendation from the trial judge. Further, under the Criminal Justice and Court Services Bill 2000, in addition to provisions relating to release dates, it is planned that new limits will be placed on the reporting of trials involving juveniles and attendance in court by the press and public.

By October 2000, young offenders will not have to go to Strasbourg to obtain such rights. The implications beyond the change already implemented by the Home Secretary and planned in new legislation seems clear – children should not be subject to adult court procedures. Changes may have to be made to the system of trial for children and young suspects in the Crown Court, especially those at the youngest end of criminal responsibility (that is, 10–13 year olds).

A further challenge could possibly be taken in relation to the provisions in the Crime and Disorder Act 1998 regarding anti-social behaviour orders and curfew orders. A magistrate can order an anti-social behaviour order in respect of any person over the age of 10. Although this order is civil in nature, its breach can involve criminal sanctions. Such orders can be made for up to two years and its potential for constituting an intrusion into individual and family privacy seems clear. Furthermore (as noted earlier), the curfew which can be imposed on a group of children under the age of 10 for an extendable period of 90 days, appears similarly intrusive. As with the anti-social behaviour order, no criminal behaviour need be proved before a curfew is

---

21 *R v Secretary of State for the Home Department ex p Venables and Thompson* [1996] AC 1, p 40C–D.

imposed. Article 8 of the European Convention on Human Rights states that every person has the right to respect for his or her individual, private and family life, unless an intrusion is necessary for (amongst other things) the prevention of crime. It may be difficult to justify severe restrictions on the liberty of a child who has not committed any criminal act. Article 8 may also cover situations where a young person has been remanded in local authority accommodation and, due to a shortage of specialised places (especially of secure accommodation), he or she is placed some considerable distance from his or her family, possibly for a number of months whilst awaiting trial.

Article 6 of the Convention covers the right to a fair trial. Possible issues arising under this provision are threefold. First, it has been noted earlier that criminal sanctions can be applied for breaches of civil orders under the Crime and Disorder Act 1998 (for example, anti-social behaviour and curfew orders). For a civil order to be made, the standard of proof is on the balance of probabilities; a much lower standard than the criminal law requirement of proof beyond reasonable doubt. Furthermore, parental bindovers are deemed to be civil in nature and criminal sanctions can accrue for breach. Additionally, the referral order established by the Youth Justice and Criminal Evidence Act 1999, enables a court to refer a young person to a YOP, a body which is outside of the 'official' criminal justice system, where the accused may not have a right to legal representation yet the body is authorised to pass criminal sanctions. Arguably, as such provisions and procedures are either, in reality, criminal in nature or have criminal consequences, they legitimately fall into the ambit for scrutiny by Arts 6 and 8 of the Convention (particularly as no rights of appeal are set out in either the Crime and Disorder act 1998 or the Youth Justice and Criminal Evidence Act 1999).

Secondly, s 35 of the Crime and Disorder Act 1998 permits an adverse inference to be drawn from a defendant's silence at interview or trial stage: this provision now applies from the age of 10. Article 6, in its assertion of the presumption of innocence and the right to a fair procedure, arguably sits uneasily with s 35 in relation to young suspects. Also, it can perhaps be implied that Art 6 requires that an appropriate adult be present when the young person is cautioned, so that they can be properly instructed as to the full implications of their silence.

The third possible challenge in relation to Art 6 of the Convention concerns reprimands and final warnings under s 65 of the Crime and Disorder Act 1998. Issues about proportionality in relation to such sanctions – coupled with the continued debate about the possibility that young people, in their eagerness to rid themselves of any further involvement with the criminal justice process, may confess to things they might not be found guilty of in a court of law, may be open to question in relation to fairness of procedure. Additionally, as any failure to co-operate with the requirements of these disposals may result in the breach being cited in court and possibly to a harsher sentence being given in any future court appearances, a challenge of the system which has replaced the old cautioning system seems a likely source of legal challenge.

Article 3 of the European Convention covers the prohibition of torture which includes degrading treatment or punishment. Linked to this, the Beijing Rules state that, when a young person is sentenced, it should amount to a 'fair reaction' – in other words, it should adhere to the principle of proportionality. It could possibly be argued that the Crime and Disorder Act 1998 impliedly sanctions the use of deterrent sentences in order to dissuade others from certain behaviour and that such sentences may, therefore, fall foul of the Human Rights Act 1998.

Lastly, if a young person is refused bail, the consequence of this may be that their relationship with their parents is severely affected. In an adversarial process where there may have been only a short time to respond to an application to refuse bail, the parent may not be involved at all in the decision making process. Certain decisions to refuse bail may possibly breach Art 8 (noted above) and Art 5 of the Convention, which covers the right to security and liberty.

So, it appears that there is the potential for a number of challenges to our youth justice system when the Human Rights Act 1998 comes into effect in October 2000. The Government, the Youth Justice Board and YOTs should perhaps prepare themselves for such challenges.

CONCLUSION

It could be argued that a bifurcated approach to youth justice, started by the Conservative Government in 1979, is continuing to develop under Labour. Custody and justice orientated measures for serious and persistent young offenders are being implemented, alongside measures designed to help prevent young people getting into a life of crime, aimed at early intervention and diversion away from the more damaging effects of contact with the criminal justice system. Such preventative measures may inevitably draw more service users into the scope of the youth justice industry.

The old mix of services designed to deal with the depraved and the deprived, administered under the youth justice system, seems set to continue in the form of the multi-disciplinary YOTs. These teams will bring together personnel from various career disciplines, including both service providers from the social work and education professions, trained in responding to the needs of children and young people from a welfare perspective, and also professionals such as the police and probation officers, who are clearly drawn from vocations within the criminal justice system and, therefore, represent occupations which have a tendency to categorise any anti-social behaviour as troublesome and as requiring a more punitive approach.

The fusing of divergent professions and professionals alongside the amalgamation of philosophical approaches of treatment and punishment under the same new youth justice system is interesting, but might prove to be confusing, as inherent conflicts may inevitably begin to manifest themselves.

The fundamental shake-up in juvenile justice practice which is presently taking place across the country is evident. By April 2000, new YOTs were set up and the business of youth justice is undoubtedly being transformed. One hundred and fifty YOTs are now in operation with some 2,500 staff drawn from police, probation, health, education and social work backgrounds. Lord Warner, Chair of the Youth Justice Board, in March 2000, commented on their proliferation:

> The Youth Justice Board has been acting like a football coach, helping teams to establish themselves and prepare for their first season. Across the country, these teams have been training together, developing shared information systems, pooling budgets and starting new programmes for preventing offending.

The Youth Justice Board has funded 450 local programmes, covering reparation, mentoring, parenting, bail support and training, and will spend £55 million over the next three years.

Competing principles

Will the reforms work? Will they produce a reduction in juvenile offending? As noted earlier, surely any 'root and branch' reform involves a fundamental reconsideration of philosophy (indeed, it is arguable that the unseen part of the system, the roots of it, are its theoretical foundations). We have witnessed several forms of uneasy compromise between competing principles over the 20th century; examples of which are the multifarious strategies adopted by various governments in an attempt to resolve the conflict between conflictual ideologies. They have developed unstable splitting strategies in an effort to distribute the divergent elements across the system of youth justice using an assortment of techniques (see above, p xxxiv). No attempt has yet been successful in resolving integral clashes. Are we simply observing a further move to mix or construct a compromise between justice and welfare measures in a 'new' youth justice system?

However, previous endeavours resulted in a partitioning or distribution of welfare and justice elements across the system of youth justice; what Jack Straw now appears to be doing is attempting to fuse these two approaches together. It is questionable whether this is possible; certainly, at the level of theory, it seems impossible and youth justice history, manifested in the creation of a number of splitting strategies used to venture a compromise, implies that, at the level of practice, any amalgamating techniques will be fraught with inherent difficulties. Indeed, distribution had been attempted exactly because mixing had proved impossible.

The reforms attempt to couple and expand each approach. As noted earlier, we are witnessing a full speed expansion of welfarism by the introduction of new orders, such as parenting and referral orders, as well as an expansion of punitive measures, such as the secure training order and an increase in the use of custodial measures. In addition to this, principles of preventionism are being pursued as a paramount aim of the youth justice system (s 37 of the Crime and Disorder Act 1998). Whilst it is perhaps easy for the Government to allege that many preventative measures can be viewed as welfarist in a broad sense – in that the focus is on preventing the young person entering the youth justice system or becoming a career criminal – the effects of preventionism may lead to an expansion of social control measures (including the use of criminal sanctions) being applied to non-offending children, young people and their families (for example, anti-social behaviour orders, curfew orders, parenting orders and recent measures to control truancy). It could be claimed that we are seeing an attempt to vindicate State intervention in the lives of children and their families at the extreme end of preventionism – the predictual end. This may represent the thin end of the wedge of social control measures – measures purportedly justified by the presumption of the goal of preventionism.

The rise of positivism

The principle of preventionism arguably allows for an extension of the diversionary model, perhaps even into the realms of (unjustifiable) State intrusion and, therefore, possible breaches of rights of privacy, the rule of law and the Human Rights Act 1998.

Furthermore, it could be asserted that the sheer number of possible disposals now available within the youth justice arena amount to a positivist's dream. The range of sentences from which to choose is now so vast that a disposal can be tailor made to fit the actor rather than the act. Classicist notions of proportionality which were particularly evident in the 1980s and 1990s have now been sacrificed in favour of preventative intervention (often in the guise of welfarism) and custom-made measures of treatment.

If we are indeed moving towards a positivist approach regarding youth justice, then this theoretical direction should at least be tacitly acknowledged by the Government, who appear to persist in trying to reformulate and provide us with ever 'new' versions of the old justice versus welfare dichotomy.

Long term strategy

Do the Crime and Disorder Act 1998 and the Youth Justice and Criminal Evidence Act 1999 merely represent short term measures to 'get tough' on youth crime. Will we witness the promised longer term strategy of getting tough on the causes of youth crime coming to fruition over the next few years, should the Labour Government be re-elected? The answer to the latter question is far more complex and cannot be provided by the creation of another couple of statutes. It involves a fundamental strategy to improve education, reduce truancy and exclusion,[22] provide training and employment opportunities and reduce poverty amongst children and young people.

Do the new laws really indicate a change in philosophical direction, away from the old battles between the, arguably, mutually exclusive paradigms of justice and welfare? Can the old justice versus welfare feud now be redefined, in the light of the Government's policies, as a 'tough on youth crime' versus a 'tough on the causes of youth crime' debate? Or, is it possible, as the Home Secretary claims, to marry the two philosophies within our new youth justice system? Are we witnessing the development of a justice approach for serious young offenders and of a more treatment orientated approach for non-serious offenders – a twin approach administered under the same schizophrenic youth justice system? Is not their coupling a liaison of strange bedfellows with divergent philosophies which may inevitably cause conflict? When the pilot schemes are completed and a revolutionised youth justice system emerges from the chrysalis of the old system, will we in fact witness the successful fusing of two quite different philosophical approaches? Indeed, in the Labour Party Consultation Paper, *Tackling Youth Crime, Reforming Youth Justice* (1996), Jack Straw acknowledged that these two divergent approaches could not be merged at a theoretical level, when he described them as, in essence, 'conflicting interests'. However, by creating a new and integrated system, he appears to believe that they can be fused on a practical level. This optimism remains to be tested.

A REVIEW OF THE PAPERS IN THIS COLLECTION

This book contains a series of chapters that analyse the proposed changes within the youth justice system and which seek to predict the likelihood of successful and fruitful implementation of the Crime and Disorder Act 1998 and the Youth Justice and Criminal Evidence Act 1999. Contributors from a variety of professional backgrounds, academics and practitioners, put forward

---

22 The Audit Commission 1996 specifically cites these as factors which may predispose young people to offending behaviour.

their views and raise important questions in relation to the theoretical and practical implications of the new legislation. The book brings together both academics and those who practice in the field of youth justice to give their verdict on how this major shake-up of the system will affect the practice of youth justice, and to consider whether the legislation represents a significant theoretical shift in the philosophy behind the special treatment of children and young offenders within our criminal justice system.

In Chapter 1, Wayne Morrison provides a reflexive analysis of the ideologies, or master narratives, that have dominated youth justice over the last century, and also asks what kind of 'justice' is being practised within the youth justice arena at the turn of the century. He analyses whether the current reforms to the youth justice field represent a move towards a system that can cope with the 'problem' that youth criminality will pose in a consumerist, desire driven late or post-modern, society.

Morrison alleges that the welfare versus justice dichotomy, which has traditionally dominated youth justice discourse, represents not only a polemic over-simplification of the possibilities of youth justice practice, but probably also reflects an essentially modernist inability amongst practitioners and theoreticians to describe appropriately what was actually happening in the practice of youth justice or the experiences of those young people who came into contact with police and court systems. He asserts that criminological investigations over the period of modernity were principally dominated by positivistic enquiry and, therefore, definitions of youth 'delinquency' were interpreted via this dominant discourse as, in essence, negative and socially dysfunctional; thus, the rigours of social control processes to 'civilise' the wayward youngster were required.

The growing trend in the US and UK to transmit notions of adult responsibility for actions is analysed here, alongside the 'recriminalisation' of delinquency, as evidenced by various provisions in recent legislation – more especially, the abolition of the presumption of *doli incapax* and the move towards restorative justice as a means of confronting personal responsibility. The latter requires the discourse of youth justice to be reconstituted and, as emotion may enter what was essentially a legalistic, stark due process model, a new language to describe youth justice is required.

To this end, Braithwaite's reintegrative shaming techniques are examined. These have historically worked within a *communitarian* or republican setting. The implementation of restorative justice models will, in Morrison's view, require a major transformation of orientation for Western individualist societies. A reconstitutive youth justice system is required for a late modern society which consists of subjects dominated by desires generated by the global market and the seductions of consumerism. This new system will require a reflexive and interdisciplinary mixing of diverse epistemologies. As the modernist criminological discourse has proved inadequate in constructing ideas about delinquency and justice, it will have little to offer the process of reconstruction of notions of youth 'justice' for this new century.

In Chapter 2, Mark Fenwick and Keith Hayward examine how the 'new cultural criminology' can assist in structuring a new theory of youth crime. This combines the phenomenology of transgression with a sociological analysis of post-modern culture (where criminal behaviour is analysed as a method of 'resolving certain psychic conflicts' linked to living a late modern life).

Katz's seminal work, *The Seductions of Crime* (1988), is a starting point for their investigations. This reconstitutive post-modern analysis of criminological discourse, with its focus upon the thrilling or seductive nature of social transgression, will, they argue, assist them in developing a theory of youth crime which is fitting for the turn of the century.

Fenwick and Hayward then go on to examine the work of authors who have built upon Katz's basic argument in their analysis of the 'socio-cultural context' of transgression, arguing that these authors identify a flaw in Katz's analysis: '… namely, its failure to examine what it is about contemporary social life that makes the pursuit of excitement via transgression so seductive.'

They contend that the increased pressure of consumerism and its inherent emphasis on individualism causes conflicts for some young people, the pressure of which can be relieved by resorting to criminal activities. They assert that, in a post-modern society, crime has developed into a commodity, to be consumed – a 'lifestyle choice' – a way of living in the midst of mundaneness. This consumption consists of the 'rush of excitement', coupled with a feeling of being in control.

In Chapter 3, Elizabeth Stokes examines the implications of the abolition of the presumption of *doli incapax* by the Crime and Disorder Act 1998. Since the implementation of this provision, the presumption of criminal incapacity which applied to children aged 10–14 has passed into history.

Stokes notes that critics have denounced this abolition as yet another attempt to undermine the important distinction between childhood and adult criminal responsibility. Whilst supporting the arguments behind such concerns, she suggests that the abolition will make little practical difference to the criminalisation of young people at the turn of the century. The significance of the presumption was, she argues, primarily symbolic.

The development of the presumption and its use within the practice of youth justice prior to its demise is examined and it is asserted that the previous legal position merely facilitated the perpetuation of a 'fiction' of protection that was obscured by legal forms. Stokes's chapter concludes that we should not, perhaps, be mourning the death of a doctrine, but seizing the reconstructive moment which its removal presents. By abolishing the presumption of *doli incapax*, the arbitrary and strict age of criminal responsibility in England and Wales will become more apparent and, therefore, more difficult to justify on any principled basis.

In Chapter 4, Stuart Vernon examines the significant theoretical discourses that have dominated youth justice practice over the last century. The tension between theoretical approaches, it is alleged, has hindered the construction of a successful way of dealing with young offenders. Vernon examines contemporary legislation and asks whether the new statutes represent a re-focus or re-orientation of youth justice theory.

Vernon analyses the conventional role of youth magistrates and the nature of the youth panel, investigating how the magistrates – the 'old beaks' – will adapt to the major changes being produced by implementation of the new laws. With such a fundamental shake-up, both in theory and application, he asks whether the justices of the peace will be easily taught the 'new tricks' of being a youth magistrate in the reformed youth justice system of the 21st century.

In Chapter 5, Deirdre Fottrell asserts that over the past decade we have witnessed a revolution in international legal standards relating to juvenile justice. A range of 'hard' and 'soft' legal rules and guidelines have been formulated in order to establish minimum standards of protection to which all juvenile offenders are entitled and which States must guarantee in the domestic arena. It is notable that the United Nations Convention on the Rights of the Child advances the legal position of the young offender and so brings youth justice issues into the human rights arena.

She asks why our youth justice system has been heavily criticised by international human rights bodies for its failure to meet these standards. A series of court judgments where our policies have been condemned is noted. If the Government is to meet its treaty obligations, it must update its relevant laws and practices, she writes.

Fottrell's chapter reviews the international law on youth justice and examines, in particular, how our own domestic practices may be altered as a consequence of international pressure from human rights organisations. In doing this, she highlights the European Court's decision in the Bulger case.

In Chapter 6, Issy Harvey provides an insight into the issue of drugs and youth crime, alleging that the current Government has identified drug use as a 'social problem' and a major cause of crime. For the first time, agencies with responsibility for young people are being urged to develop strategies that respond to the growing number of young people using drugs. New multidisciplinary teams and partnerships are, she says, being expected to co-ordinate their service responses to this end.

Harvey's chapter critically examines the social and historical contexts which gave rise to social policies and legislation that seek to control drug use. She also addresses the theories of criminology and psychology that arose to explain drug use amongst young people. Theories of deviance assume that drug use is a marginal activity, but recent figures suggest that recreational use is now a mainstream youth activity. In Harvey's analysis, there is a conflict between the public discourses prompted by health agencies and the criminal justice system; YOTs will have a foot in both these camps. It is recognised that young offenders have often experienced multiple social difficulties and are, therefore, at risk of developing problematic drug use. In examining these issues, she urges youth justice professionals to adopt a welfare stance towards these young people and to develop holistic, child centred responses for those in need of support.

Susannah Hancock (Chapter 7) provides us with a highly contemporary, practical insight into how the legislation is being implemented at a 'grassroots' level in a YOT which has been selected as a pilot project and a pathway site for testing the new laws.

The changes and challenges faced by practitioners of youth within the new multidisciplinary YOTs justice are outlined. Having been faced with a series of legislative and practice changes in the 1990s, such practitioners now find themselves once again having to come to terms with a fundamental re-orientation of both theoretical focus and practical implementation. However, she calls this a 'brave new world of youth justice' and seems optimistic for the future. Hancock examines the joys and problems of the fusing of professionals from disparate vocational backgrounds in the new YOTs, using the metaphor of a fruit cake to describe the merging and gelling of quite different professional ingredients into one whole. She believes that the recent changes, while serious interventions, do seem to be 'evidence based', and she notes the value of YOTs developing models of working based on tried and tested research.

Hancock examines the new orders being introduced and helpfully sets out what these will mean in practice for workers within YOTs. She poses a few questions in relation to possible problem areas, noting issues of concern for YOT officers to be aware of. Hancock describes new YOT professionals as 'pioneers' in the formation of a reformed youth justice system.

In Chapter 8, Bill Whyte examines the Scottish youth justice system in the context of international human rights. He notes that many countries have reviewed their youth justice systems in recent years and that some have brought their practices within the framework recommended in the United Nations Convention on the Rights of the Child. Whyte asserts that the greater emphasis on legal rights, individual responsibility, due process and 'just deserts' seem to have been associated with a retreat from welfare and the use of non-criminal and extra-judicial processes. Recognising the special status and rights of youth on the one hand and dealing with their behaviour in politically acceptable ways on the other remains a tension.

Whyte outlines Scotland's dual track system, where most young people under the age of 16 are dealt with by non-criminal and extra-judicial processes, while those young people aged 16–18 are dealt with by the criminal justice system. This chapter examines the principles and practices of Scotland's Children's Hearing System in the context of the United Nations Convention, as well as taking into account research relating to the system's operation and effective intervention.

Malcolm Bentley (Chapter 9) continues the theme of examining good practice north of the border, where a completely different youth justice system, focusing upon decriminalisation and diversion, emerged early in the 1970s. He asks whether England and Wales can learn anything about the practice of youth justice by looking to Scotland.

Bentley examines the Scottish system from the point of view of an English magistrate, tracing the divergent histories which led to the development of distinct processes of dealing with children and young people who break the law. He posits that an average English justice of the peace would, perhaps, be initially shocked by the Scottish practice of non-prosecution of all but a minority of serious young offenders and by the very limited powers of punishment of the Children's Hearing System which deals with all other young law breakers.

The chapter provides an in-depth examination of the Scottish youth justice system and, at each stage, presents a comparative analysis with the system used in England and Wales, tracing the historical, cultural and contemporary development of each. Each system is examined in terms of the dominating ideologies of justice and welfare, and the question of whether the Scottish hearing is really a truly welfare orientated system is posed. Bentley analyses the effectiveness of each and concludes that the measures of effectiveness may be as divergent as the practices of each jurisdiction; assessing re-offending rates alone as a measure of effectiveness may, therefore, be inadequate. Nevertheless, he presents an outline of the advantages and disadvantages of each approach and finishes by summarising what an English magistrate might learn from taking a glimpse at life over the border. He concludes that the changes in Scotland introduced in the early 1970s were so far reaching that the 'Scots had the advantage of starting with a clean sheet' – the old system was, in effect, wiped out, and a brand new system was established. In England and Wales, however, the 'radical' reforms, though extensive, do not abolish the old system and, therefore, amount to merely (albeit, substantial) changes within the existing system. No blank sheet has been provided on which to write a totally new form of youth justice for England and Wales.

Matt Long's Chapter 10 explores the changes to the policing of youth crime in the light of recent legislation.

Long explores evidence which seems to demonstrate that the police have been far more willing to work towards multi-agency approaches than in the past. He then considers precisely how these types of arrangements are being consolidated by the Crime and Disorder Act 1998, with the further development of 'joined-up' services and an emphasis on the police as part of a multi-agency, holistic approach to tackling youth crime.

The 'partnership' approach to youth crime is theorised and Long explores how this ideology, in order to be sustainable, has to rediscover and then invoke the idea of 'community' as a necessary concomitant of the move away from crime control and prevention towards a notion of 'community safety'. He refers to the changing nature of social control and raises questions about the extent to which 'communities' are genuinely empowered to make decisions about how youth crime is policed. He concludes by suggesting that genuine advances in social justice and democracy can only be made in this area if there is a truly local approach to the problem of youth crime. He notes that potential conflicts may arise when endeavouring to remedy the crime problem in trying to balance the demise of the Keynesian dream of full employment against the Labour Party's communitarian ideals of stakeholding and social inclusion.

Phil Cohen and Pat Ainley, in Chapter 11, examine the history of academic enquiry into the two fields of youth studies and cultural studies in the UK and analyse the relationship between these two seemingly divergent discourses. Each field has its own peculiar history that has shaped these social scientific enquiries within the context of modernity. They assert that, in a late or post-modern society, the issue of youth is ripe for interdisciplinary investigation and that the 'youth question' potentially stands at the 'cutting edge' of the breakdown of traditional academic boundaries. Being an enquiry that spreads its tentacles into many conventional disciplines, it can act as a tool in the dismantling of the artificially constructed territories of modernist dialogue.

The youth question has an important dual role to play in academic enquiry, in that it assists a reflexive investigation of both the problems of modernity and of identity in the context of late or post-modern society. Furthermore, the youth justice issue assists a directive focus of policy debates around the contradictions of experience under post-colonialism.

However, in order to facilitate this interdisciplinary investigation, youth studies must rid itself of its tendency to focus mainly upon empiricism, and cultural studies must avoid its propensity to fully immerse itself in theoretical questions. Cohen and Ainley argue that lessons must be learned by both fields for a more realistic and useful interdisciplinary approach to be constructed, that is, an approach that transgresses the entrenched practices that have previously hindered academic pursuit in each area.

Finally, in Chapter 12, Caroline Hunt provides an analysis of the successes and failures of an alternative to custody experiment run in the State of Delaware, USA, for two years in the 1990s. Hunt, the Director of this project, the Delaware Juvenile Advocacy Project, presents a candid account of the problems and pleasures of running such a scheme.

The resistance the project faced is highlighted, which, she argues, was due to entrenched ideas amongst criminal justice personnel and politicians about the appropriateness of justice or punishment models for the treatment of young law breakers and notions that alternatives, such as those offered by the project, were, in essence, soft options which should be discouraged.

The project was an experiment initiated by the National Centre on Institutions and Alternatives, in partnership with Delaware State. It provided a high supervision alternative to incarceration, including intensive social work assistance, advocacy provision and individually designed programmes which focused on education, training and constructive use of leisure time.

The main aims of the project were de-institutionalisation and a focus on breaking negative behaviour cycles. The experiment was notable for its policy acknowledgment and practical application of international human rights standards on the treatment of young offenders. Hunt documents the history of the project, from the initial idea to its formation, its policies and procedures, successes and failures (in terms of recidivism and other measures), and systemic problems and hindrances. References are made to case study examples and comparative projects to illustrate issues raised within this chapter. She concludes by summarising lessons learned from the experiment and implications for future practice in both the USA and UK.

In this collection, academics and practitioners within the youth justice system, including social workers, YOT members, magistrates, social work trainers, police trainers, drug project workers and United Nations officers aim to provide a broadly based analysis of the recent and pending legislative changes, examining reforms from a variety of professional viewpoints. The wide ranging focus of the book should provide a wealth of information for academics, students, practitioners and researchers in the complex and fast changing field of youth justice.

CHAPTER 1

VISUALISING THE JUSTICE OF THE YOUTH JUSTICE SYSTEM: PERSPECTIVES AT THE CENTURY'S END

Dr Wayne Morrison

Crime and intolerance occur when citizenship is thwarted; their causes lie in injustice, yet their effect is, inevitably, further injustice and violation of citizenship. The solution is to be found not in the resurrection of past stabilities, based on a nostalgia and a world that will never return, but on a new citizenship, a reflexive modernity which will tackle the problems of justice and community, of reward and individualism, which dwell at the heart of liberal democracy.[1]

It is not unique to state that we require a reflexive grasp of penal and social practices. But Jock Young's recent work, *The Exclusive Society*, is distinguished by the intensity with which such a plea focuses on the difficulty of grasping the nature of justice in our contemporary world. We inhabit a globalised social order in which the hopes and assumptions that have underpinned social activism for the last 200 years – the period many scholars have come to call modernity – lie open to deconstructive analysis and sceptical doubting. Each image of social advancement and economic prosperity – and there are many in the 'advanced Western world' – can be contrasted with images of social despotism and despair. The losers in the 'justice' of world capitalism are not merely those whose political élites do not play the game according to the correct market rules (of leading disciplined selves operating with rational calculation). We need only turn to the tragedies of the Balkans, Rwanda or Sierra Leone for confirmation of this. If the US is taken as the exemplar of the 'free' world, then it appears that the price of liberty is increasingly a new gulag of imprisonment, with penality the most obvious (although prison is rendered professionally discreet) example of the social divisions of late modernity.

Attempting a reflexive grasp on the practices of 'justice' is problematic. We need to locate our perspectives, but there are many possible stories to tell and many sites to describe. Our topic is the youth justice system, an interrelation of various people, discourses, institutions, contexts and outcomes: what is its 'justice'? Deciding on this justice is a decision regarding the acceptability of the balance and nature of those interrelations. How is the question of justice decided, and what kind of decision making process is it? In *The Politics*, Aristotle argued that agreeing upon a 'rule of justice' was fundamental for a polity to live in a harmonious whole, but it was also the most difficult decision

---

1   Young 1999:199.

making process to set up. To act justly is to treat different people equally, according to settled criteria of judgment. But the criterion of equality, the measure of justice, was an essentially political judgment and, in politics, everyone starts from the position of relating to others from 'oneself'. In judging 'others', one has already, implicitly, judged oneself, and Aristotle warns that the majority of people are bad judges of themselves. Yet, if one cannot obtain objectivity from oneself, how is common agreement, arising from intersubjectivity, possible? One needs to create an 'objectivity' of judgment – a mechanism of seeing. Therefore, ascertaining justice always requires a prior agreement upon some science of recognising, some epistemology, and agreeing upon justice is only possible within the settled canons of that 'way of seeing things'.

Thus, while the search for justice is a product of human desire (why bother if we do not want justice or do not want to act justly?), it requires (social) knowledge. Yet, we are doomed never to have total knowledge. Only the gods could possess such a thing. Justice is always a human creation – a social relation. Administering justice reflects the (im)possibility of a true knowledge of humankind, situations and things. Deciding justly is dependent upon the techniques of telling the truth, but the issue of telling the truth may be historically contingent – a factor dependent upon processes of inclusivity and exclusivity, and of decisions over relevance and rhetoric.

In other words, deciding whether the system is just is always a process undertaken in changing circumstances of time and space, time and space understood both through 'personal experience' and the mediation of discourses. A reflexive concern with justice requires us to ask three things: (a) what characteristics of time and space are we concerned with?; (b) what are the characteristics of relevant discourses?; and (c) who are the personnel involved? However, such an exercise in typologising is immediately compromised, for identifying who, what and where changes in time. Moreover, the processes of discursive argumentation are neither so successful nor so finite that they reduce competing perspectives to a nullity. Instead, a perspective appeals to an audience, links with sets of assumptions and already implicit judgments lodged in common dispositions and concepts, in the common sense of different groupings. Who are the people concerned with youth justice? We have three main sets: (a) the personnel who staff the system; (b) the audiences, that is, the public, academic commentators and public officials; and (c) the targets, that is, the selves of the youth who are the grist of the system.

Who are these targets: the selves of the youth? We know these selves through personal experience, the discourses of journalistic endeavour and scholarly reflection. The literature of youth justice requires a prior literature of delinquency, and this literature must achieve a resonance with its audiences. Thus, the literature of delinquency is replete with anecdotes and case studies (for example, Aichhorn 1925; Burt 1925; Goddard 1927; Bowlby 1946; and

Belson 1975), with attempts to identify typical adolescents (for example, Griffin 1985) and to locate the subject's self, in relation to wider social structures and flows (for example, Hall's 1905 work was entitled *Adolescence, Its Psychology and Its Relations to Physiology, Anthropology, Sociology, Sex, Crime, Religion and Education*). The production of this literature occurs in specific social and cultural settings. The American 'sub-cultural' studies (for example, Cloward and Ohlin 1961; Cohen 1955) give a different picture from the British (for example, Davis's 1990 work was aptly entitled *Youth and the Condition of Britain*). The kinds of selves illuminated by modernist social science range from the idea of a self-interested individual – whose behaviour is to be shaped into conduct suitable for civil society, whose passions are to be guided to protect society from the destructive effects of anarchic behaviour (the Hobbesian tradition) – to the benign sheet, the potentially virtuous self who needs to be both protected from the impositions of a corrupt social order and subjected to processes which lift, elevate, perfect, purify and realise an implicitly social humanity (the Rousseauian tradition). Classic scholars on delinquency (for example, Hirschi, who formulated his 'control' theory in 1969) draw upon both traditions, implying that it was society's duty to get the twin strategies of socialisation and control right, or else the unsociable sociability of the human condition would become rampant.

For their part, 'most people involved with the "youth justice system" like to feel that they are doing something worthwhile' and want to feel that they are acting justly. However, this basic desire does not lead to agreement regarding what exactly worthwhile activity is. Indeed, one of the major institutional faultlines that runs through 'youth justice', and this seems to hold across the Western world, is between those who see it as an arena of activity that should be imbued with the caring and welfare ethos of the social services, and those who see the legalistic ethos of individualism, rights, responsibilities and punishment as more appropriate. But few of those who belong to the legalistic camp believe that pain ought to be imposed on children and young people for pain's sake. Instead, such pain is 'punishment' and is sanctioned because 'justice' requires it.

This distinction between welfare and punishment is the most common orientating dichotomy running throughout literature on youth justice. Two dominating modes of objectivity are contrasted, but accepting this as the crucial operating distinction in youth justice is an oversimplification. Moreover, the traditional dichotomy reflects a misplaced confidence in the discourses produced by those operating in the arena to adequately describe what is really going on. The discourses of welfare and legalism/punishment might offer the participants comforting sets of glasses to orientate themselves and create a confidence in their acting justly, but we may well need to step back somewhat and adopt more external views. Whether, however, such external views can be reduced to certain master views which easily locate the social role of youth justice is another matter. Where does one begin?

THE DEPENDANT NATURE OF
THE YOUTH JUSTICE SYSTEM

The first point is that even to talk of a 'youth justice system' is to give an idea of self-containment and closure which is misleading. It would be more correct to call it an institutional sub-system of the overall social system.

The second point is that the juvenile/youth justice system is the product of modernity. The term 'modernity' does not simply denote the 'modern' or 'contemporary Western societies', but reflects the idea that there are features to 'modern' social life that are essentially unique and radically different from the ways in which human life had previously existed. 'Modernity' designates both cultural features – in that it witnesses a vigorous war waged by philosophy and sociology against tradition – and socially constructive features. Specifically, modernity denotes the creation of societies which understand themselves to be artefacts, products of humankind's social and cultural energies, and not of any 'natural law' or 'God's design'. In modernity, criminal justice systems replace, in significant aspects at least, the network of social control in which traditional values are inscribed, and we come to trust and accept modern systems to the extent that they achieve their 'rationally defined' purpose(s) to act justly. The justice of such systems is a question of the development of rational discourse(s) which structure our perceptions of role and performance. These discourses enable us to agree, for example, that the practice of the juvenile/youth justice system is such that the offender/child/delinquent is being fairly treated according to the relevant criteria of judgment. Conversely, other discourses tend to upset or critically undermine such acceptances. What have been the dominant discourses, or as some call it, the master-narratives, of juvenile/youth justice?

THE MASTER-NARRATIVES OF JUVENILE/YOUTH JUSTICE

First, what is the raw material to be understood? At the beginning of the 19th century, children and young persons received no special treatment by the penal authorities.[2] Indeed, as Ariès (1962) has suggested, childhood and adolescence were not recognised as specific stages of individual development requiring specialised and intensive surveillance or intervention. During the course of the century, various attempts were made to create a separate system

---

2   For a general view of the position of the child in 19th century England, see Walvin 1982; and Gillis 1975, Chapter 3. More generally, see, also, Thane 1981.

and various specific juvenile 'schools' or reformatories were set up.[3] Around the turn of the 20th century, special 'informal' courts, enjoying wide discretion (either juvenile courts or child welfare boards), were constituted and widespread agreement was reached that special provisions ought to be enacted for young people in trouble with the law. This criminal jurisdiction became complemented by a civil jurisdiction system under which children in 'moral danger', or latterly 'in need of care and protection', were taken into care or sent to special schools. The 'system' expanded but, in time, was criticised for unreasonably incarcerating thousands of young people, either in the guise of protecting them and acting in their best interests, or responding to offences committed by juveniles in a way that was far harsher than an adult would receive. Arguments were either raised for 'children's rights' or for the need to 'divert' young people from the system.

The system has always been a site of social rituals, tensions, conflicting perspectives, various interacting bodies and competing goals which amalgamate the claims of diverse sets of interest groups and discursive practices. The practices have varied over locality and changed over time. On the one hand, some have been, and are, legal practices which are usually a formalised, specialised activity and are the object of manuals and legal codes. On the other hand, others have been made up of the activities of social science professionals and volunteer participants, of decision making processes laden with operational discretion, common sense opinions and the opinions of those with supposedly specific expertise.

To reiterate, the usual way to depict these tensions and competing interests has been to demarcate the competing ideologies of 'legalism/justice/punishment' and 'welfare'. To act justly under the welfare orientation demands that we diagnose the underlying problems of the young person, and either treat those problems in some therapeutic fashion, by removing the person from his or her harmful environment, or provide intensive supervision. Legalistic justice represents the traditional demand for appropriate punishment when an offence has been committed, but also requires procedural fairness and the protection of the innocent against unfair decisions. These two orientations have never been freestanding, but are deeply embedded in the grand narrative of modernity's progressive overcoming of the past and its creation of just societies.

---

3   Ariès argues that the steam engine and the adolescent were joint creations of the industrial revolution. At first, 'lower class children were mixed with adults ... They immediately went straight into the great community of men, sharing in the work and play of their companions, old and young alike'. In the 19th century, 'traditional apprenticeship was replaced by the school, an instrument of strict discipline, protected by the law courts and the police courts ... The school shut a childhood which had hitherto been free within an increasingly severe disciplinary system ...' (1962:412–13).

THE NARRATIVES OF SOCIAL PROGRESS

The battles between proponents of welfare and legalism have largely been understood within a dominant narrative organised around the motif of social progress. Thus, the development of a juvenile justice system is portrayed as part of the process whereby the child was recognised as a separate personality, needing to be saved from the harshness of the adult system; increasing attention was also paid to preventing children from becoming criminals. Until recently, this dominant narrative gave a formal history of the development of justice systems in modernity in terms of the progressive march of humanitarian impulses, rationalisation and the victory of 'scientific knowledge' over superstition, tradition and ignorance.[4] The meta-narrative of social progress held central roles for commitment to knowledge, the idea of the progressive advancement of knowledge and the expectation of a future which would be better than the past.[5] It depicted juvenile justice, largely, as originating with a critique of the (philosophically) universal claims of liberal criminal justice, a critique which had the practical outcome of differentiating juveniles from adults in the name of humane treatment and social justice. To a large extent, this history of juvenile justice parallels the distinction in many criminological works between the approaches of classical (neo-legal) and positivist (social scientific) criminology, holding that positivism had its greatest success in the creation and legitimation of a separate system for juveniles. These two approaches contain separate sets of assumptions on human nature, offending and policy recommendations on responses to juvenile deviancy and offending. Adults 'ought' to be treated as legal subjects, but, as the child did not possess sufficient rationality and autonomy to fit the idea of the modern legal subject, to treat him or her as if what he or she did was clearly socially unjust. In some versions, it was not that punishment was ruled completely inappropriate, it was rather that punishment needed to be done under a special mandate and in the light of specific narratives of legitimation. In the pure classical approach, the socialisation scheme was one

---

4   Most pre-1960s texts share this. The massive American text by Barnes and Teeters, *New Horizons in Criminology*, simply asserted that criminal justice programmes were the logical and orderly result of evolutionary practices. As with advances in scientific knowledge, criminal justice developed through trial and error and what did not work was discarded over time. Thus, the then present system was better than the past and would improve in the future (1951:342–43).

5   Thus, Turgot could depict the new man of the enlightenment in 1750 as 'possessor of the treasure-house of signs ... he can assure himself of the possession of all his acquired ideas, communicate them to other men, and transmit them to his successors as a heritage which is always being augmented. A continual combination of this progress with the passions, and with the events they have caused, constitutes the history of the human race, in which no man is more than one part of an immense whole, which has, like him, its infancy and its advancement' (1973:63). In Hans Blumenberg's huge study of the legitimacy of the modern age, 'the idea of progress ... is the continuous self-justification of the present, by means of the future that it gives itself, before the past, with which it compares itself' (1983:32).

in which an individual member of society is opposed to the civilised social whole and he or she must learn to enter society on its terms. Thus, the child was to learn the rules of the social bond and to be punished when, as a youth, he or she did not obey its requirements. The development of a separate juvenile justice system acknowledged the weakness of this model and deemed that it needed to cater for the reality of the child/juvenile as not being responsible for the conditions of his or her own socialisation. Hence, the State needed to supervise the socialisation (to stand in relation to the juvenile as *parens patriae* – the ultimate guardian) and, in time, take over where the young person was out of the control of the parents or where measures needed to be taken in 'the best interests of the child'.

In this dominant narrative, the history of the system, and the disputes over justice, can be observed by reference to government reports and the interjections of concerned individual reformers.[6] The confidence and coherence of this type of narrative starts to be undercut in the 1960s and, in time, a series of revisionist histories came to be written.

REVISIONIST NARRATIVES

The first stage of revisionism was to provide narratives, cast in terms of social-political conflicts and the ideological demands of a class structured economic order, which provided the context for the approaches to the socialisation of youth and the responses to offending. In broad outline, it is possible to see that classicism was a doctrine necessarily linked to the development of 'rule of law States' over feudal society, of the rights of the bourgeoisie over aristocratic privileges, and of the creation of a more free social space for the abstract 'market' to function, as opposed to the settled hierarchies and status interactions of late feudal society. Positivism can likewise be seen as responsive to a different set of demands, linked first to the demand to spread political influence into the growing middle class and, secondly, to the difficulties that the newer social control agencies were facing. But revisionist social historians expressly saw these control measures in terms of a class struggle and the containment of the lower classes. The tenants of positivism allowed new forms of legitimation to complement the all too obviously class biased nature of the criminal justice system. But positivist criminological writings largely assumed a benign State, acting progressively in the search for a humane justice. The organisation of society became a 'social question', with ideas on the enlarged role and functions for the State and the idea of conscious planning and organisation of the society. For the Scottish neo-Marxist revisionist Garland (1985), penalty needed a new form of legitimation and

---

6   An outstanding example of this mode of writing is Radzinowicz and Hood 1986.

found it in the critique of classicism and the setting up of a 'mission for criminology', that of identifying the criminal and the conditions under which he or she was produced. The variability of crime was turned into practicable objects, namely juvenile delinquency, and adult criminality, which could be the subject of a positivist study and the object of practical policy. As a social problem, criminality could possibly be reformed, extinguished or prevented; for the young person, a new object of analysis, the delinquent, was identified and a whole body of institutions set up and texts formulated with protecting society and saving the youth as their mission.[7] The concept of the delinquent divided the working classes against each other and allowed intensive surveillance and policing apparatuses to be accepted in the name of welfare and the prevention of delinquency.

A seminal influence was provided by Michel Foucault, whose startling work *Discipline and Punish* (1977), began by contrasting a horrific public execution, carried out in the name of the King in 1757, to the detailed timetable of a juvenile reformatory some 80 years later. Commentators relativised the positivist claims to be guided by the progress in knowledge and looked with Nietzschean speckled eyes to see plays of power and ideology everywhere. If the new knowledges of the 'human sciences' could not be trusted to provide a non-ideological standard, then the desire for reflexivity demanded one simple question: whose justice was it? But it became increasingly difficult to see any particular group determining the conditions of justice. Tony Platt's rather neo-Marxist 1969 reading, which saw the 'Child Saving Movement' as a middle class, Anglo-Saxon, Protestant campaign for control over the practices of the working class Catholic immigrant families, creating a professionally dependent client group for middle class decision makers,[8] gave way to wider images which saw juvenile justice as a discretionary site of disciplinisation involved in the wider creation of 'normalcy'. Foucault linked the institutions of 'punishment' into sets of

---

7   For revisionist, social control or class aware accounts of discovering the delinquent and child saving in the 19th century, see Platt 1978; Humphries 1981; Pearson 1983; Clarke 1975; Donajgrodzki 1975, particularly the 'Introduction' and Chapter 2; Fox 1952; Gillis 1975, particularly Chapter 3); Hagan and Leon 1977; Strang Dahl 1995:83; Weinberger 1993. More generally, see Weiner 1990. For current attempts to see juvenile justice mainly through this perspective, see 'Juvenile justice, history and policy' (1991) 37(2) Crime and Delinquency (Special Issue).

8   For Platt, while the individuals responsible for the child saving movement were genuinely concerned with the need to step in and aid in the socialisation of those at risk, they were in the grip of a subtle class conflict and an eagerness to control the poor of the developing cities and keep minorities within their assigned social and geographic spaces. According to Platt, 'The child savers viewed themselves as altruists and humanitarians dedicated to rescuing those who were less fortunately placed in the social order. Their concern for "purity", "salvation", "innocence", "corruption", and "protection" reflected a resolute belief in the righteousness of their mission' (1969:3). Behind the 'justice' of these moral entrepreneurs, Platt reads the development of juvenile justice legislation in the US as responsive to the successful labelling of immigrant Catholic families as primitive in their socialisation methods, a labelling process which was reinforced by racism and class discrimination.

processes which not only aimed to control disturbed and ill adjusted individuals, but transformed our potential understanding of techniques of resistance to new patterns of 'civilisation' into a pathology of deviancy by constituting the notion of delinquency. For Foucault, contrary to the individualist ethos of the discourses of reforming delinquency, modernity required delinquents as targets for disciplinary practices.[9] Thus, we came to expect many children to be in danger of becoming 'disturbed adolescents' and accepted a whole gambit of appropriate mechanisms to interrogate and supervise them.[10]

If Foucault's vision appeared to many as unduly pessimistic, most commentators came to appreciate juvenile justice in terms of the social control mechanisms of modern societies. A crucial relationship was posited between the family, education and delinquency. For the new ideal – the stable (middle class) family – educational practices reinforced the primary, successful socialisation of the family unit. The nuclear family was to be the cornerstone of Western modernity. Delinquency was not only an individual feature, but demonstrative of failing families. In Donzelot's analysis, for example, the juvenile court's real target was those working class families who failed to adopt modern child rearing practices.[11] How were the failings to be remedied? Fashions change and, at one time, the social sciences and the administrative network encouraged an interest in control within closed institutions and in the imposition of discipline and behavioural regulations. In time, however, de-institutionalisation and de-carceration became fashionable concepts (for example, Scull 1977). Presently, we see a strong interest in creating and maintaining multi-agency networks of control in the city and in enhancing the capacity for self-control and purposive interaction for the subject. At the turn of the century, what went for juvenile justice was

---

9 Foucault thus traces the power plays in the texts of the 'ideal' institutions he studied to wider practices. Thus, his discussion of the children's prison at Mettray, France, in 1840, was that it stands as a model for the emergence of disciplinary techniques which become the taken for granted normal underpinning for a whole range of welfare practices. Foucault writes that: 'The chiefs and their deputies at Mettray had to be not exactly judges, or teachers, or foremen, or non-commissioned officers, or "parents", but something of all these things in a quite specific mode of intervention. They were in a sense technicians of behaviour: engineers of conduct, orthopaedists of individuality. Their task was to produce bodies that were both docile and capable ... The modelling of the body produces a knowledge of the individual, the apprenticeship of the techniques induces modes of behaviour, and the acquisition of skills is inextricably linked with the establishment of power relations; strong skilled agricultural workers are produced; in this very work, provided it is technically supervised, submissive subjects are produced and a dependable body of knowledge built up about them' (1977:294–95).

10 For Springhall 1986, the difficult or disturbed adolescent is as much a product of societal expectations as any individual features.

11 See Donzelot 1979. Thus, the juvenile court was a space 'where the mode of appearance before the court implies the placing of the child and his family in a setting of notables, social technicians and magistrates: an image of encirclement through the establishment of a direct communication between social imperatives and family behaviour, ratifying a relationship of force prejudicial to the family' (1979:3).

concerned with creating and enforcing a consistent and methodical way of behaving from the youth it had to deal with, a fashioning of these youth into good members of the working class. Now, with the demise of the working class and the more fluid forms of social structure that a late (or post-)modern penalty has to contend with, we have juvenile/youth justice systems becoming more diffuse and de-institutionalised in their forms of social control.[12]

Other commentators depict juvenile justice as a set of institutions of last resort which aim to teach young people the moral values of the society or to remedy defective socialisation. The orientating criteria of justice would in this case view the processes as assisting in the preparation for citizenship of society's most difficult youth.[13] In these narratives, juvenile justice picks up on the failure of the primary institutions of socialisation (the family, the school) and deals with double victimisers (youth who may be victimised by their parents and environment and who go on to victimise others).

MODERNITY AS AN ORGANISING CONCEPT

Recognition of changing social and cultural contexts enables some intermixing of the foregoing narratives concerning the social process of modernity, each of which highlight certain aspects while downgrading others. Thus, the concept of modernity comes to be used in a search for a wide enough set of assumptions that may provide orientation, whilst not falling into the trap of either a narrow, *a priori* perspectivism, or mindless eclecticism. Social order in modernity continually poses problems of integration. Each of the earlier narratives touches particular aspects of a complex, multidetermined process. Juvenile justice, as part of the control process of modern societies, reinforces (or, as the labelling perspective feared, often goes against) socialisation processes. But we must always ask, 'what are the conditions of socialisation?'; 'into what exactly are the youth being socialised?'; and 'what is the form of correct socialisation?'. The question of the justice involved in this relationship is less often asked.

REFLEXIVE LATE MODERNITY

What of the present? For most commentators, contemporary social theory no longer addresses the issue of the construction of states of social justice under

---

12 Meyer 1977, in his French analysis, draws upon the explicit portrayal in French civil law of the (middle class) family as the basis of civilised sociality. For a British work in a similar vein, see Harris and Webb 1987. See, also, Cohen 1985.

13 Eg, Bailey 1987.

an implicit paradigm of 'building modernity', but must face a situation where we are the products of modernity, but are no longer in it. Both the terminology and the identification of the problems varies; for some we are now in late modernity, for others post-modernity.[14] In general, the meta-narratives of social progress and social justice appear less believable. The problem of social justice, that is, how we judge the nature of the relationship of the one to the other, and the nature of the context, intensifies. Each unit in the equation(s) becomes more difficult to grasp in a coherent fashion. To take the simple example of self-consciousness or 'identity'. For the late modern person, the question of personal identity is not defined by one's position in the order of things, some embedment in localised tradition and custom which ultimately seems to reflect some 'natural' participation of self and cosmos, but by an insulated individualism mediated by concepts such as authenticity, choice and the 'rationality' of ends-means relations. How can we conceptually grasp the 'subject' of justice systems? The adult criminal justice system deals with this issue by conceptually creating a 'legal subject', identified in the discourse of the criminal law and insulated from the claims of the social sciences (for example, the criminal law judges 'criminal intent' and *not* social motivation),[15] but the subject of the juvenile justice system has been a multiple and overburdened subject at the intersection of numerous disciplinary discourses, discourses which respond to the destruction of the settled life of tradition and custom and need to relocate the newly constituted subject in a modernist network. We can refer to this process as one of disembedment and re-embedment.

In these processes we can separate out three periods or stages,[16] namely:

(1) From the 17th century until the mid-19th century, the critical deconstruction of traditional synthesis in the philosophical construction of liberal modernity, a process which occurred at the same time as the social processes of industrialisation, urbanisation and imperialism. For all the discourse of philosophical freedom, the reality of life for the masses was one of unbending poverty and drudgery.

---

14 Radical changes have occurred over the last 30 years. To describe these changes, social theorists have coined various labels including the Media Society, the Society of the Spectacle, the Consumer Society, the Bureaucratic Society of Controlled Consumption, the Post-Industrial Society and lately, and most fashionably, the description of post-modernism. Certain key writers are responsible for this term, among them Jean-Francois Lyotard who, in a well known book, *The Post-modern Condition*, 1984, coined the term 'post-modern' to reflect changes in the level of science and technology. In particular, Lyotard notes the development of computers, mass communication and the increasing emphasis upon language in social and cultural studies. Others have referred to the post-capitalist age and announced that we no longer need labour for successful production: machines, in particular computers, have largely made (or are in the process of making) mass labour redundant. Thus, we appear headed for a world without the need for vast sections of its population.

15 See Norrie 1993.

16 Influenced by Wagner 1994.

(2) From the mid-19th century until the 1950s, the sociological reconstruction of liberal modernity into an organised social structure; in the West, becoming Fordist (the factory and the strength of manufacturing and industrial production). A social order focused on production and exchange and reasonably settled social expectations emerged as a result.

(3) The recent development of a more complex structure focused on consumption rather than production as well as creating a plurality of social identities; on the issue of rights we see the movement from liberal or abstract and formal legal rights, to demands for substantive or social rights. In terms of personal desire, we witness the multiplication and universalisation of personal wants and the constant demand for gratification. In these late modern (post-modern) conditions the pressures on the individual intensify and the individual unit needs increasing amounts of social and intellectual skills as well as 'self-control'. Those without such skills or self-control run the risk of becoming a new 'underclass', 'learning not to labour' (Stafford 1982).

Modernity involved destruction and construction, liberty and freedom. The process occurs at both the level of the social structure and the individual; neither can be treated in isolation. In the meta-narratives of social progress, modernity was a process that freed humans from traditional identities, turning them into civilised selves able to function in a 'civilised social order'. Such a civilised social order depended upon the functionality of the roles required by economic and industrial formations, as well as political and philosophical aspirations. As political subjection gave way to political citizenship, the selves of the previously excluded, namely, the property-less, the working class, had to be re-constructed in order to fit the functionality of the places on offer. The modern individual must be continually constructed and reconstructed so that they may take their places in the social order – civilisation requires disciplinisation. This idea of the civilised human being, a man possessed of a civilised mind-body complex, can be distinguished from the positivist, naturalised forms or the disciplined self which Foucault feared the bureaucratic society demanded. Norbert Elias (1978; 1982), for example, tends to give a picture of functional dependency whereby the emerging modern personality is developed, not as a consequence of some imposed pattern, but as a consequence of the increasing differentiation of social patterns and functions. The growing need for self-control is part of the self-steering mechanism of individuals involving reflexivity (or self-scrutiny) and foresight.

In Elias's narrative, modern democracy is dependent upon the existence of certain kinds of subjects who do not require continual external policing. The external constraint of village supervision, and then the urban police, was transformed into an internal constraint upon the conduct of the self, the formation of subjects who were prepared to take responsibility for their actions and for whom the ethic of discipline was part of their mental fabric.

There is a subtle dialectic in play: participation in the differentiated roles opening up with modernity results in experiences and forms of self-scrutiny which create the fully modern person, but only the fully modern person is deemed fit to participate in these roles. This 'modern' person comes to know him or herself through processes of self-scrutiny using the lens of the human sciences.

However, the positivist sciences of criminology lacked reflexivity and were not engaged in promoting social participation or inclusivity under any active criteria of justice. They were, rather, legitimating differentiation and placement. There was little intellectual opposition.[17] There were few, if any, attempts to read the behaviour of youth as a positive expression of their resistance to the 'civilising' processes, or as reflections of a class position which required an appreciative or empathic understanding. Rather, they were read as caused by the reduction or disintegration of social control.[18]

The qualities sought to be instilled in working class youth were not that of independency or free thought: these were instead kept back for the middle classes. The routine of the reformatories was one of unrelenting monotony and discipline. At no time were the subjects of this discipline asked for their views or expected to contribute actively to this process. They were simply the object of pressures brought and imposed upon them to conform, entities to be shaped into a desired product. Attempts at resistance stood little chance of success.[19] Above all, it was preparation for one's place in the industrial network that was required.[20] The youth could not hope to go beyond his or her allotted position.[21]

In the formal narratives, this was termed rehabilitation or dealing with the child in his or her own best interests. But the child was not allowed (at least ideally) to develop other than as 'normal'. The transformative process involved processes of repression of 'otherness' and of disorder. Were they

---

17 Even Marx's collaborator Engels saw criminality not only among the deprived working class, but also in the 'surplus population' of casual workers, those whom Marx called 'the lowest sediment' and others called 'the residuum' (1958). While Engels saw their problem in terms of their culture which had developed as a response to their social and physical location, others claimed constitutional defects.

18 See, eg, Stedman-Jones 1977.

19 See the oral memories quoted in Humphries 1981.

20 Willis's ethnographic study, *Learning to Labour*, 1977, is a reading on the continual presence of a 'caged resentment' among youth who do not openly confront the control mechanisms.

21 As the following quotation from Alexander Paterson, one of the 'greats' of penal reform, makes clear, the attitude persisted into this century: '... by the end of his training ... he will be able to keep any sort of job, however laborious and monotonous it may be ... Many were born to be hewers of wood and drawers of water ... For them, labouring work, arduous and continuous, is the best preparation for the life that ensues ... It is the duty of every Borstal officer to preach the gospel of work, not because it is easy or healthy or interesting, but because it is the condition of an honest life' (*The Principles [of Borstal]*, 1932, quoted in Fox 1952:373).

successful? The accounts which tell us that a new social order was produced have a certain validity. To a very real extent, order was imposed on the wildness of the city and the lower classes were transformed. A social structure of organised modernity was created, at least in large part, which was mirrored in the hegemony of structural functionalism in sociology from the 1930s until the 1960s. But the dream of a thoroughly organised modernity – full of modern 'rational' agents – has today been undercut. Late or post-modernity has arrived.

A settled social order organised around the idea of almost full male employment in Fordist systems of production, with female support in the family, has given way to high levels of male unemployment existing inside a mass consumer society inhabiting a globalised economy and a rapidly changing communication network.[22] Consumption power, rather than location in the structure of production, can be the dominant structural ascriber of identity/class.[23] Towards the end of the Thatcher/Regan 'social revolution', commentators such as Bauman (1987), could offer a picture of the present as the failure of the projects aimed at constructing a thoroughly rationalised society. Bauman argued that the ruling intellectual and political élites had turned away from any grand ideas of constructing socially just societies, or establishing faith in bureaucracy (although, paradoxically, bureaucracy keeps expanding), to the market. It appears as though a new dialectic of social control had been created. On the one hand, Bauman suggested, we have those who are tuned into the market who become seduced by its items and messages; a group of people who are now effectively and efficiently integrated through a new cluster of mechanisms of public relations, advertising, growing needs, institutional and individual bargaining. Opposed to these are the new poor, who are not really consumers since their consumption does not matter. They will provide both the grist for the mill of youth justice and the imagery for new fears regarding the future.

Thatcher and Regan may have lost political power, but no one suggests that the market has receded. Taylor (1999) defines contemporary Europe as 'market-Europe', a consequence of the social transformations of the late 20th century which have ushered in a 'post-Fordist market society'. The solidity of modernist ideas of social structure and functional positioning is replaced by the fluidity ushered in by post-Fordism, globalism, individualist market conceptions of worth, with the concomitant effects of personal dislocation. A 'fear of falling' resonates with a growing 'fear of the other' and leads to popular cries to place barriers in defence 'against others' in the interest of local and national peoples. Taylor's text, largely written from the locality of the

---

22 For accounts of the changing position of youth in late modern Britain, see Riddell 1989; Roberts 1995; Williamson 1993 and 1997; Pilcher and Wagg 1996; Osgerby 1998; MacDonald 1997; Jenks 1996; Furlong and Cartmel 1997.

23 On culture, see Brake 1990; McRobbie 1994; Thornton 1995.

North of England, is suffused with the notion of crisis; a crisis of increasing alienation and cynicism at a personal level for large numbers of people, and crises of masculinity, family, notions of parenting and the explosion of penalty. Daily life becomes a task of managing risk and arranging insurance. In Fordist modernity, 'only a proportion of any one new cohort of youthful social actors can escape the "destinies" which these situated processes of social production inscribe for them in adult life' (Taylor 1999, p 12), but late modernity dislocates such destinies while the post-modernist culture of contingency is full of messages to take control of one's life and 'do what you want to do' (Morrison 1995).

WHAT IS THE LATE MODERN STANDARD OF JUSTICE?

Attending to the conditions of late modernity, two readings of trends present themselves. Both, at least rhetorically, recognise that everyone is entangled intimately in the fate of everyone else. Thus, rage among the dispossessed and rejected can terrorise anyone and everyone even if it is unable to realise positive ends itself. But one reading leaves this at the level of rhetoric and clings to a modernist paradigm of 'mastering' the situation and 'ordering from above'. Governmental power is asked to penetrate more and more thoroughly into life, partly in response to the threat of resentment, revenge and unpredictable violence engendered by historical patterns of past repression, inequality, confinement and exclusion. Power penetrates, but without a grand design – the utopia of the just, well ordered social order being lost – enabling a social order which is 'ordered' by power while being fragile and susceptible to 'crisis' and deterioration.[24] A dialectic of instability and the application of power(s) both from above and within results in an endless circle of rhetorical justification, penalty, exclusion, silencing and displacing of 'otherness'.[25] Social order becomes a dialectic of techniques of communication and 'geographies of exclusion'.[26] The desire for justice must ultimately recognise the limits of what can be done, and thereby is rendered of little bite.

The second reading has its source in the optimistic 'natural law' of the enlightenment, namely, that of attunement to an intrinsic set of conditions and purposes inherent in human life. But in this rendition, the drive to master, assimilate, level and mobilise power around the criteria of the one, the normal, to discipline in the name of civilising, is relaxed and 'nature' is seen as

---

24 Thus, the images of problematic youth being read as part of an 'angry brigade' responding to 'anarchy'. See Vague 1997.

25 The notion of 'displacing', as with ethnic cleansing, replacing the ideology of conquering and assimilation.

26 To borrow the title of the text of Sibley 1995.

a foundation of difference. The rights of human difference are granted priority over the tradition of mastery and fashioning normality. In this reading, justice lies in criteria of recognition. Such a perspective on justice discards any foundation of the security of the subject's prior self-knowledge. For the pursuit of justice becomes inherently reflexive: through mutual recognition of 'other(s)' one recognises oneself as different but worthy. This project lies at the heart of the post-modernist clamour of 'deconstruction' and promotion of 'difference'. But it is a criterion of justice which is constantly in danger of irrelevance and of being lost in the continuing discourse of 'normalising individuality', restrictive community and State hegemony. It is a problematic understanding which seems compromised, both for its inability to establish itself in the current settings of political debate, and in its (at least) initial inability to specify exactly its implications for particular practices of law, welfare, gender, race, the ethics of responsibility and international relations. Its appeal lies less in any demonstrable ability to institute itself in political conduct, than in the fact that current (at least to 'critical' lenses) strategies of established politics foster a politics of discipline and destructiveness.[27]

And what of the criminological discourse of the self? Few would have confidence in the body of criminological discourse to capture the aetiology of youth offending. If the drive of the enlightenment was fixed first on the primacy of self-knowledge, it presupposed an (at least possible) correspondence between inner life and the public resources of discourse – that the hidden could be made knowable in the technologies of articulation; that the deeply personal could be represented for public consumption; and that strategies of dependency, repeatability and prediction could be developed. Under this model, intrasubjective agreement could be facilitated by obeying the grammar of representation. The discourse(s) of delinquency were meant to capture the being of the young offender within a certain logic of articulation, to establish the webs of social position, to display the pushes and pulls of interaction and to demonstrate the bonds and the strains. Perhaps the delinquent was different, but this difference was understood through the discourses of delinquency and thus rendered capable of change, of returning

---

27 Its links with the critical demonstration of material inequality are also underdeveloped. For 'critical' writers, a demonstration of the continuing and increasing inequality in the conditions of late modernity, as in Taylor 1999 and Young 1999, results in claims of grotesque unmeritocracy and appears to refashion 'distributive justice'. Young writes: 'We must construct a new contract of citizenship which emphasises diversity rather than absolute values, and which sees such diversity not as a catalogue of fixed features but as a plethora of cultures, ever changing, ever developing, transforming themselves and each other' (1999:198). But the fundamental problem of political liberalism remains. It appears impossible to agree a standard of intrasubjective ranking outside of a structure where the power to judge has been given up to some mechanism (the sovereign, the market). It remains the case that, outside of some 'social' reason to include the 'other' (such as a Benthamite fear of social revolution), recognition of the other as different can simply imply a politics of practical ignoring (negative tolerance) in which the other is partitioned off to personal despair and alienation so long as they do not turn to a coherent social revolution.

the relation of the delinquent and the social order to one of (imaginary?) homogeneity. Differentiation presupposed the idea of assimilation. Ideally, then, the reformed, rehabilitated self is re-embodied in the social order as an integrated unity.

But the post-modern spirit cannot believe in the integrity of any stable criminological or pseudo-criminological disciplinary language. The thesis of professionally correct ontological recognition, of the one epistemology which reveals the essence of the delinquent as masterable, reformable and, thus, assimilable, is no longer acceptable either by the audience of the public (which finds more resonance with other popularist discourses on crime)[28] nor with the subjects (who object to being captured) whose desire is usually not represented nor do they recognise the strategies of denial and techniques of neutralisation offered. One does not have to be a follower of the Nietzschean-Foucault axis of thought, the wider suspicion is that the disciplinary web of discourse and 'therapy' reduces unique and particular experiences and struggles to a common vocabulary, inserting the imperatives of a particular social form into the interior of the individual, whilst leaving that which motivates and individuates the self to come from more creative dimensions of language that do not find ample expression in those theories which seek to bring the inner life of the self into neat co-ordination.[29] The late modern self is an active desiring subject; but few criminological texts pay any attention to what the discourse of cultural studies has latterly become aware of, namely, that the simulation of desire is the crucial arena for the understanding of motivation. As many of the texts of moral theory made clear (for example, MacIntyre 1985; and, in criminology, Wilson 1991; 1993), the late modern subject is an especially 'selfish' unit. In these texts, the classic image of the self-possessed person of character has been replaced by a self understood through the self-calculating rationale of neo-economic discourse, as a manifestation of individualist psychology, or as a bearer of materialistic possessiveness. Modernity freed the personality from the 'natural order', setting in train the processes of self-assertion and aggressive desire. In the narratives of social progress, this aggressive desire was to be civilised through the institution of rationalised social procedures and the inscription of desire and motivation in the discourses of the human sciences,[30] human sciences which have latterly proved incapable of rendering the self knowable, except as a function of this or that perspective. But, if the discourse(s) of delinquency cannot provide a stable and coherent epistemology within which we may consider ourselves acting justly, what is the fate of youth justice without a settled overreaching

---

28 As Taylor 1999 notes, the sections in bookshops devoted to popularist accounts of 'real' crime contain far more texts than the sections containing scholarly accounts.

29 Thus, the appeal of the writings of Katz 1988 and the continuing resonance of the work of Matza 1964, 1969, which are rather existential readings of delinquency.

30 Hobbes 1651 was the earliest writer to capture this precisely.

coherence? Is it to become responsive to sets of popularist, political strategies? And, if so, how could that be reflexively defended? Perhaps it cannot. Thus, legalism, with its self-reproducing epistemology, becomes even more attractive, but with its legitimation being reinforced by appeals to popularism, or simply by doing what the rules demand.

The weakness of this appeal can be seen in two contrasting strands of youth justice: (a) the arguments for removing separate systems for 'juveniles' in various jurisdictions (particularly in the US) and; (b) the rise of the rhetoric of 'restorative justice'.

ESCAPING THE CONCEPTUAL MORASS OF 'DELINQUENCY' THROUGH RECRIMINALISATION: DOES DOING ADULT CRIME REQUIRE ADULT TIME?

In both Britain and the US, the concept of delinquency is being undercut by processes which break down the difference between youth and adult justice.[31] In the US, debate over the future of the juvenile court and the right to send youth from that court to adult courts to be dealt with as adults ('waiver procedures') has been heavily influenced by public concern with the problem of school violence, particularly youth gun violence.[32] The widespread media perception that juveniles are only younger criminals who need to be held accountable and receive just punishment for their offending – linked to the catch-cry 'adult crime – adult time' – has resulted in statutory exclusions which automatically disqualify an increasing number of youth from juvenile courts.[33]

Some American commentators warned in the late 1980s that 'treating juveniles as adults when they are 16 or 17 years old may seem appealing as a "get tough" measure. However, there is no creditable evidence that such policies are effective crime control measures' (Schwartz 1989, p 71). 'Critical' British commentators refer to a 'blacklash' against critical analysis of youth justice and 'child centred policies and practices' (Scraton 1991, p 185). The move to recriminalise delinquency occurs at the same time as international recommendations and conventions (Council of Europe Recommendations; United Nations Convention on the Rights of the Child 1989) have stressed the

---

31 See Singer 1996, whose text is simply entitled *Recriminalising Delinquency*.

32 In the UK, the media debate was influenced by the Bulger case (*R v Secretary of State for the Home Department ex p Venables and Thompson* [1997] 1 All ER 327; [1997] 3 All ER 97, HL). (See James and Jenks 1996; Young 1996; Davis and Bourhill 1991.)

33 Eg, statutory waivers which, at the end of 1998, existed in 37 States and concurrent jurisdiction statutes which allow prosecutors to file specified cases in either the adult or juvenile court (10 States plus the District of Columbia). On the other hand, 22 States have provision for reverse waiver, allowing criminal court judges to transfer cases from the criminal court to the juvenile court.

need to protect childhood and minimise the use of custody for youth. The UK has proceeded with the introduction of secure training centres and reducing the scope of the *doli incapax* principle (see Scraton 1991; Stokes, Chapter 3 in this book).

THE RISE OF RESTORATIVE JUSTICE: CHANGING LENSES FOR VIEWING YOUTH JUSTICE?

At perhaps the other extreme to the neo-criminalisation of youth justice lies the demand to reconstitute the discourse of youth justice in terms of 'restorative' or 'relational' justice. At its most basic, the claim is simple: 'we need a new language' (Zehr 1990, p 200). Welfare discourse encourages passivity while legalistic discourse appears simple: 'Do not commit offences because they are against the law. Those who do wrong deserve to get hurt' (Zehr 1990, p 198).

Moreover, language stimulates emotion: the enlightenment discourse whereby crime demands State sponsored and administered punishment results in the emotionality of popularist law and order. The modernist due process model is consciously designed to treat offenders as strangers (for example, the composition of the jury changed in the UK from people who knew the accused to representatives of the society who did not know the accused), and helps to enhance a public fear of crime by strangers, yet crime (including violent crime) by non-strangers is more likely.

The restorative justice movement unites a diverse band of hitherto 'fringe' individuals – who draw upon religious ideas (in particular, Quaker and Mennonite traditions) and the more recent criminological traditions of peace making, mediation, the victims movement and abolitionism – who write and speak at international conferences with the confidence of entering into a new crusade. Their appeals find resonance with some public officials who become interested in the 'traditional' or experimental justice systems of other cultures (for example, British interest in the Maori 'justice' of New Zealand). But, if the restorative justice movement explicitly orientates itself with a global grasp, quickly exchanging ideas and experiences from certain key schemes (with good use of late modernity's central innovation, the internet),[34] many of its proponents' claims for effectiveness lie in the recognition of justice as a locally focused entity. This localisation reflects the desire for a different from of

---

34 Eg, Braithwaite has since 1996 put certain papers on the net at a website called *realjustice.org*.

democratic participation in criminal justice employing mediators or facilitators from the local community (police officers, social workers, volunteers).[35] The procedure places emphasis on personal dialogic relations and concrete subjects (such as victim and offender),[36] while battles over the positions of such schemes (should they be integrated into the criminal justice process and thus 'overseen' by a court and so on, or should they take place at a pre-trial stage where they are included as part of social services) are also questions of ownership (criminal justice is usually in the hands of central government) and of the potential for involvement in a process which may have diverse benefits.[37] A key concept is the idea of mutual recognition by

---

35 Several policies and programmes have been introduced in Australia which are designed to take account of the 'sociology of apology and the psychology of forgiveness'. Reform in the area of juvenile justice in New South Wales began in 1994, when a pilot scheme was introduced following the Government's White Paper entitled *Juvenile Justice*. Under the auspices of the office of Community Justice Centres, the Community Youth Conferencing Scheme was implemented in six rural and metropolitan regions throughout the course of 1995, the first being in Wagga Wagga, Australia. Conferences are conducted by two facilitators and the parties involved are the juvenile offender, the victim (if they so choose), and family supporters belonging to each side. Specifically excluded are legal representatives and the conference proceeds on the basis that the offender is guilty. The purpose of the conference is to bring together the offender and victim, so that the offender can see and hear the effects of their crime on the victim. The aim is not to exact punishment, but to bring about reconciliation through the offender making some form of restitution to the victim. The conference follows four stages. Initially, the offender is given the opportunity to explain what happened and how they felt at the time of the crime. The victim (if present) is then invited to respond and state how they were personally affected. During the third stage, the aim is to have the two parties discuss how they feel now, given the developments of the conference. This may include talking about the (possibly) changed perceptions of both people towards each other and the crime itself. In the final stage of the conference, the participants decide what can be done now to rectify the harm. Here, the role of the conveners is to ensure that the restitution is 'fair and appropriate' and able to be implemented. South Australia became the first State in Australia to legislate a family group conference model based on the one in New Zealand, so that, now, all but the most serious cases are diverted to this approach from the Youth Court. Victoria's first Victim-Offender Reconciliation Programme is different from the others in that it involves adults and is not an alternative to legal proceedings but merely a pre-sentencing option. Moreover, it is limited to cases where offenders plead guilty to property offences and some crimes involving violence (not domestic violence or rape).

36 The claim is that restorative justice means a criminal justice system which is more victim centered, thereby providing a number of positive opportunities for both the victim and offender which are not available in the traditional system. Eg, victims have the chance to express any pent-up feelings of anger, frustration, fear or anxiety and can (psychologically) benefit from receiving an apology. With the offenders, rather than playing a passive role of simply accepting punishment, they can play an active role in trying to put things right by taking responsibility for their actions, apologising to the victim and making atonement. Combined, the victim and offender are directly involved in the resolution, which allows them the opportunity to regularise their relationship.

37 Representative quotes from Zehr: 'Faces should take the place of stereotypes ... Part of the tragedy of modern society is our tendency to turn over problems to experts ... In doing that, we lose the power and ability to solve our own problems. Even worse, we give up opportunities to learn and grow from these situations' (1990:204).

offender and victim – of each as real personalities.[38] Thus, offenders are encouraged to take responsibility and, in undertaking the restorative process, they can 'bring emotional closure to the offence' and, particularly in the hands of a skilled mediator, can experience an 'empowering' outcome (Zehr 1990). The distance that professional discourses – legitimating strategies of State power – have created between troubles and real people must be broken. The State's 'theft of conflict' (Christie 1977) has to be overcome.

Such appeals are never straightforward, both 'conservative' and 'liberal' camps can voice the urgent need to have greater concern for the victims of crime; 'victims', however, are not similar; their emotionality cannot be captured in some pre-packaged assumption.[39] But now we hear claims that 'restorative' justice has been used in a number of countries for more than 20 years with over 800 programmes now reinterpreted to fit into the rhetoric of a paradigm shift. For juveniles/youth, the discourse may be strongest in New Zealand (where it underlies the revolution of the 1989 Children, Young Persons and their Families Act),[40] Australia and South Africa, but it has vocal proponents in the US, Canada, England and Germany. Among the most popular types of programmes held out as 'restorative' are victim-offender reconciliation programmes; victim-offender mediation; court diversion programmes; community justice conferencing; peer mediation; and victim impact and empathy panels.

What unites these diverse projects? Harry Mika and Howard Zehr (1996) postulate 10 rules, referred to as commandments, that must be adhered to in 'restorative justice'. These are:

(1) Focus on the harms of crime rather than on the rules that have been broken.

(2) Be equally concerned about victims and offenders, involving both in the process of justice.

---

38 District Court Judge McElrea of Auckland, New Zealand and an influential figure in the acceptance of the Children, Young Persons and their Families Act 1989, quotes Taylor's definition of personality: 'To accept responsibility for one's feelings, actions and beliefs is to exercise one's personality. To fail to accept such responsibility is to refuse to be a person' (quoted in McElrea 1994:13).

39 Eg, Jung 1995, distinguishes three groups and three sets of demands in the victims movement. These are: (a) those asking for restitution and/or restoration; (b) those asking for more participation and protection during the process; and (c) those asking for protection and/or increased criminalisation.

40 The Children, Young Persons and their Families Act 1989 marked a significant shift in the administration of juvenile justice in New Zealand. Restorative justice, reintegration and communitarianism are all features of the practical application of the Act and Family Group Conferences (FGC) are the central mechanism, not only for decision making in a reintegrative way, but also as a diversionary technique from the formal criminal justice processes (see Morris and Maxwell 1993). The objectives of the Act, and their application, are concerned with accountability, responsibility, 'just deserts', de-institutionalisation and community based sentencing options.

(3) Work towards the restoration of victims, empowering them and responding to their needs as they see them.

(4) Support offenders while encouraging them to understand, accept and carry out their obligations.

(5) Recognise that, while obligations may be difficult for offenders, they should not be intended as pain.

(6) Provide opportunities for dialogue, direct or indirect, between victim and offender as appropriate.

(7) Find meaningful ways to involve the community and to respond to the community bases of crime.

(8) Encourage collaboration and reintegration rather than coercion and isolation.

(9) Be mindful of the unintended consequences of your actions and programmes.

(10) Show respect to all parties – victims, offenders, justice colleagues.

Reading the literature, one is presented with promises of a new role for youth justice, where it actively contributes to the rebuilding of communities and uplifts individuals through their participation. The strongest legislative support for 'restorative' youth justice lies in New Zealand and in Australia where 'restorative' justice is the buzz word for dealing with young offenders of non-violent crime.[41] As the New South Wales Youth Justice Conferencing Handbook 1998 puts it:

> The young offender's actions cause hurt, loss or damage to other members in that community. At a youth justice conference, the young offender and the community meet together to heal the hurt and help the young person take steps towards a responsible future.

Ideally, the process is not to rely upon any external discourses to recognise the offender. Instead, the young person is to be 'recognised' as a multifaceted personality and, in direct opposition to the perceived alienation of juvenile court or welfare tribunal hearings, they are now given the chance to explain or say sorry for what they have done and agree an outcome. Moreover, court appearances are seen as fostering rebellion against authoritative figures, with detention periods likely to harden him or her, rather than soften their resolve to challenge authority.

---

41 The programmes have various titles but, in essence, the concept is the same. In New South Wales, the scheme is known as Youth Justice Conferencing, while in the country's capital, Canberra, the approach is referred to as Diversionary Conferencing. The Juvenile Justice Department of New South Wales has teamed up with the Attorney General's Department, the New South Wales Police Service and the Director of Public Prosecutions, to launch the New South Wales Youth Justice Conferencing initiative. The scheme was formed after the sanctioning of the Young Offenders Act 1997 and has been lauded as a radical new approach to youth offending.

Likewise, Canberra's Diversionary Conferencing strategy is premised upon claims to 'strengthen the moral bonds between the offender and the community'. Rhetorically, the dichotomy between 'justice' and community is overcome with a practical criminology of reintegrative shaming,[42] drawing upon the work of one of the strongest advocates, the Australian John Braithwaite, whose theory of reintegrative shaming is specifically connected with a political philosophy of 'republicanism'.

RESTORATIVE JUSTICE AND REPUBLICAN JUSTICE: THE THESIS OF JOHN BRAITHWAITE

Braithwaite develops a theory of 'reintegrative shaming' as a general integrative framework linking control, labelling, sub-cultural, opportunity and learning theories. Control theories identify the role of initial bonding; labelling theory focuses on the impact of stigmatisation and opportunity theories explain the role of criminal sub-cultures. Braithwaite purports to draw upon comparative research and claims that those societies which most effectively shame criminal conduct are the ones that have the lowest crime rates. Such societies have a high degree of social cohesiveness and moral consensus operating and function more as a 'communitarian' than an 'individualist' society. An example of a communitarian society would be Japan.[43] Communitarianism, denoting interdependency at a societal level,

---

42 See Sherman and Strange 1997; for South Australia, see Sarre 1994.

43 According to Braithwaite 1989, 'Japan's low and declining crime rate can be read as support for the notion of high interdependency ... highly developed communitarianism ... fostering a shaming of offenders which is reintegrative'. Thus, when an individual is shamed, the shame is often borne collectively by the group to which that individual belongs, eg, the school, family or the company. Reintegrative shaming is thus claimed as a feature of Japanese society, the family being the key social unit which assumes responsibility for reintegrating the offender: '... family life teaches us that shaming and punishment are possible while maintaining bonds of respect', writes Braithwaite. In sharp contrast to the West, Japan's legal system relies heavily on positive reinforcement, with an emphasis on loving acceptance in exchange for genuine repentance, with apology having a central role to play in the wake of legal proceedings and restoration ceremonies performed to signify reconciliation between the warring parties. The failures of Western systems are not philosophical, but lie in the neglect of human intersubjectivity: 'In theory [they] administer just, proportionate corrections that deter. In practice, [they] fail to correct or deter, just as often making things worse as better'. Outweighing prison's ability to reduce crime is, he argues, its pervasive stigmatising effects, which not only affirm criminal identities, but lead to those similarly outcast being attracted to and becoming members of criminal sub-cultures and 'who treat prison as an educational institution for learning new skills for the illegitimate labour market'. Braithwaite's use of Japan is one-sided. Nowhere does he discuss the issues of individuation or conformity. Bizarrely, he relates an incident in a Japanese prisoner of war camp in which the vast majority of the Western prisoners perished and in which the existence of shame within inmate culture operated. Nowhere does he discuss the thesis made popular by Ruth Benedict in 1946, that it was Japan's culture of 'shame', in contrast to the Western one of 'blame', which allowed the conformity of Japanese personnel and their obedience of criminal orders.

involves relationships of trust and loyalty, along with interdependency at a more individual level, which is reflected in a person's relationship to home, work and school. Communitarianism is claimed to lie at the heart of societies where shaming is most powerful and successful. 'All social processes of expressing disapproval which have the intention or effect of invoking remorse in the person being shamed and/or condemnation by others who become aware of the shaming.' Thus, informal sanctions have a much stronger effect on deviance than formal legal sanctions because a loss of respect in the eyes of people important to us weighs more heavily on the conscience than the actions or opinions of criminal justice officials. How are we to read the nature of youth crime, most of which can be described as low to medium level 'predatory crime'? Braithwaite reads predatory crime as a symptom of underlying social disintegration which is primarily due to a lack of integration of individuals into society, in particular, those societies which are unable to integratively shame deviant individuals back into a moral consensus. Reintegrative shaming is 'conceived as labelling that reduces crime' (1989, p 20); it aims to 'restore harmony based on a feeling that justice has been done' (1996, p 4). Thus:

> ... the solution ... is to advocate vigorous moralising about guilt, wrongdoing and responsibility which is informed by the theory of reintegrative shaming, in which the harm-doer is confronted with community resentment and ultimately invited to come to terms with it. The climate of moralising must be such as to put the accused in a position where he must either attempt to persuade the community that he is innocent, to persuade them that his deviance is harmless diversity which should be tolerated, or express remorse and seek to compensate for the harm he has done. It should be a society where retreat into a world of exclusion is difficult for either the accused or his accusers to accept. Reintegrative shaming implies opposition to both a *laissez faire* approach which renounces community responsibility for caring for weaker citizens ... and opposition to therapeutic professionalism which uses inclusionary slogans to justify widening the net of coerced State control over deviants. Community moralising is the antithesis of both professional technocracy and *laissez faire* [1989, p 156].

The question is, how can individualised reintegrative shaming ceremonies be a feasible option in complex, highly populated and mobile urban settings? Braithwaite argues that such variables can actually increase, rather than limit, the feasibility and potential of shaming. Changing the focus of justice systems away from the process of blaming and isolating offenders will reinstate and re-energise a role for proximate 'others':

> ... shaming will be most powerful within proximate groups (particularly families) where the conditions of communitarianism are maximally satisfied, where interdependency is so strong that family members care deeply about approval and disapproval [1993, p 11].

But will this mean such a radical shift in orientation for 'justice' in Western, individualist, neo-liberal societies that it has no hope of joining with the current organisational and philosophical modes? For Braithwaite, the answer is clearly 'no'; while the mainstream arguments in criminal justice resound to popularist arguments for punishment and 'just deserts', Braithwaite not only attempts to argue for the historical importance of shaming,[44] but argues that reintegrative shaming fits with a (reinterpreted) tradition of liberal political philosophy, namely, republicanism (Pettit and Braithwaite 1993). The linking concept is that of personal dominion, a neo-liberalist account of liberty, by reference to which the justice system is to be organised in such a way in order to promote the maximisation of dominion.

Dominion is a freedom derived socially; crimes are acts which diminish this freedom to enjoy life as people choose. Crimes deny personal dominion in three ways:

(a) when a criminal act involves the domination and subjugation of the victim to the will of the offender, it deliberately disregards, or is oblivious to, the personal dominion of the victim;

(b) in some types of crime, an individual's dominion may be completely destroyed or greatly diminished, for example, rape will destroy a woman's dominion, while theft of a person's property will reduce it; and

(c) each criminal act occasions communal harm, often creating fear and apprehension among those not immediately victimised, thereby endangering the dominion enjoyed in society generally.

If crime represents a denial of and damage to dominion, then the goal of the criminal justice system is to promote dominion by putting the harm right. Accordingly, the task of the courts in sentencing offenders is to try to rectify the damage caused by their crimes, making it possible for the dominion status of the victim to be restored.

Rectification has three stages: (a) recognition; (b) recompense; and (c) reassurance. The first involves an apology by the offender for their crime, which not only represents a recognition of the victim's personal liberty, but also facilitates the return of their former dominion. It is hoped that some sort of reconciliation between offender and victim would also occur. Recompense as acknowledgment of the harm done to the individual's personal dominion is the next stage and would involve some form of restitution and/or compensation. Finally, the promotion of community reassurance can be accomplished by the courts seeming to take all crimes seriously and dealing

---

44 Braithwaite's historical analysis highlights the growing 'triumph of shame' (1993:9) during the Victorian and Edwardian eras, which was replaced by the 'just deserts' or retributive policy shift later in the 20th century. This neo-classical revival which dominates current political practice in law and order policy focuses on stigmatisation and exclusion, rather than reintegrative practices.

with them accordingly. Whether, in practice, rectification in this form can be achieved is an open question.

WHAT PRACTICAL INTERVENTION MEASURES AND STRATEGIES FOLLOW?

Braithwaite argues that the republican response to crime seeks minimalist intervention on the part of the State to the offender (the principle of parsimony), favouring instead a reintegrative approach which considers the needs of the victim, community and offender. There are two key directives: first, we need to reinstate a role for mediating disputes rather than demanding punishment; and, secondly, we may be able to break the often counterproductive cycle of offending-punishment-further offending through understanding the mechanisms of shame. Shame operates on two levels to effect social control. First, it acts as a specific deterrent against criminal behaviour because of a threatened loss of social approval; and, secondly, deeper cultural changes take place whereby shaming and repentance build self-sanctioning consciences which internally deter criminal behaviour. Even without any external shaming attached 'the real power of ... shaming is at the level of prevention, conscience building' (Braithwaite 1992). Stigmatising shaming, where the offender is labelled an evil person and is cast out permanently, is the kind of shaming that is humiliating and disrespectful. In contrast, reintegrative shaming seeks to shame the evil deed while still maintaining a relationship with the offender based on respect. Thus, the shaming is finite and the offender is then given the opportunity to re-enter society by way of recognising that what they did was wrong, apologising for it and demonstrating repentance.

Braithwaite appears to offer a holistic criminological theory which explicitly links the explanatory thrust of criminology with crime prevention. It provides a well grounded political theory which is commensurate with the liberal underpinnings of Western democracies, respecting the rights of victims and offenders and restating the importance of the family and local community figures. Moreover, the restorative justice approach, based on conferencing, addresses the emotionality of the victim-offender experience in a cost effective manner which humanises the otherwise distant and alienating formal process of justice. While critics may see a man looking through rose tinted glasses,[45] Braithwaite positions the movement for restorative justice in such a way that it can join forces with the traditional main players, by arguing that criminal justice must use a combination of informal and formal processes of social control, particularly in the areas of juvenile justice, business practices and domestic violence. Formal institutional shaming should be utilised after community shaming; not just youth justice systems, but all criminal justice systems should aid in a process of developing and promoting individual conscience and the building of a 'public' conscience. Abusive situations, such as domestic violence, need public scrutiny and community disapproval. For many officials in criminal justice/social services, accepting the potential of 'restorative/relational' justice offers a new image of participating in justice, a new feeling of doing good,[46] while government officials may welcome it so

---

45 Criticisms of Braithwaite's theory are: (a) it does not really look at the causes of crime. Rather, it examines a number of variables at the level of both society (communitarianism) and the individual (interdependency) which are linked with crime, eg, age, gender, parental attachment, urbanisation, moral beliefs, social class and criminal friends. Thus, while providing a description of the characteristics of the 'typical' offender, there is no discussion of how an interaction between them and the given environment leads to offending; (b) it works on the premise that a state of moral consensus exists within society. Yet, nowhere does he define the nature of the moral or whether the consensus is meant to reflect what people say or what they do; (c) it depends on the actual existence of a community into which people can be integrated, but in reality, this does not exist, it is only an abstraction; (d) it focuses on interdependency, on the idea that we need each other. Yet, if an offender is already marginalised from society and/or dislocated from their family, then there is no point in 'reintegrating' them. It is just not possible to shame people into wanting to belong to broader society – identification must primarily exist; (e) while, at the conceptual level, a sharp distinction can be drawn between stigmatisation and reintegrative shaming, it is not so clear cut in practice. This is especially relevant when one considers the range and number of people involved in a family group conference and the prominent role of the police in several such programmes operating around Australia; (f) how can the concept of shaming's success be measured? Braithwaite's ideal is for shaming to lead to changes within the individual which will reduce the chance of re-offending. However, how can one know whether the offender is merely complying with what the group wants (which is not internalised) or is displaying true repentance and conformity (which is internalised)? All involve processes of informal social control, but only the latter can 'build consciences which internally deter criminal behaviour'; and finally (g) Braithwaite's theory of reintegrative shaming is used with certain crimes (predatory) and offenders (juvenile) in mind. This begs the question of how successful it would be if applied to, eg, white collar offences like embezzlement and fraud. Braithwaite's critics say that he expects the shaming process to function in all other societal institutions as it does in the family. However, the reality behind his assertion of the 'supremacy of conscience over rational calculation' in the corporate world is that self-interest is of paramount importance. Therefore, any shaming of corporate executives is effective because its 'appeal to self-interest bolsters its moralising content'.

46 Restorative justice conferencing has also been formally trialed in Wagga Wagga using the Braithwaitean model (Braithwaite and Mugford 1994). The leading police official, Sergeant O'Conner, has become famous for advocating that the police can change their focus and be at the centre of a restorative justice revolution that can tackle any type of crime, perpetrated by any age group.

long as the programmes run within existing resources and can be rationally assessed to be effective.[47] For the critics, this may amount to a sellout;[48] with the real possibilities for creating a new, late modern justice which is understanding of the costs of modernity lost in the need to legitimate the new in terms of cost and effectiveness, rather than in returning 'justice' to communal discourses and ways of viewing.

---

47 The most richly funded research project in Australian criminological history is the Reintegrative Shaming Experiments (RISE) for Restorative Community Policing being conducted by the Research School of Social Sciences, Australian National University, Canberra and headed by John Braithwaite. The study is based on a randomly controlled trial involving 900 drink driving offences, 300 juvenile property offences and 100 violent offences. Half of each group is randomly assigned to a conference and the remainder to court in the usual way. The aim is to compare conferences with court processing according to a number of key criteria. Adopting Braithwaite's principles, Canberra police have diverted confessed offenders from court to an alternative approach called Diversionary Conferencing. The framework and procedure of the conference is very similar to that already outlined, with the focus being on the crime as opposed to the criminal. According to observers, initial results show that conferences are superior to court in soliciting expressions of remorse from offenders and in evoking forgiveness from victims in response to their offender's apology and contrition. From the perspective of the victims, results show that conferences provide greater satisfaction in several ways. Eg, almost all victims feel that they are owed an apology and, the more personal the victimisation, the stronger victims feel about having a greater role to play in the justice process; conferences meet both these needs. Moreover, conferences appear to make victims feel safer than court. As one commented: 'You realise they aren't the monsters you'd made them out to be ... I don't have to feel conscious of people walking past and thinking, are they the ones? Are they the enemy?' As for the offenders, the results so far indicate that they are more deterred from repeat offending after having gone through diversionary conferencing than through the court system. One reason can be found in a new theory of crime prevention called 'procedural justice' which argues that, the more offenders believe they have been treated fairly, the greater the likelihood that they will obey the law in the future.

48 Blagg considers that there are significant limitations in the process, particularly for Aboriginal offenders. This is because the justice system, including the conferencing processes, remains 'mono-culturalist' (1997:482). In Australia (unlike in New Zealand), the police are the 'gatekeepers', thus increasing their powers and enhancing their role, although for Aboriginal people the police have virtually been agents of oppression. By contrast, Braithwaite argues that this makes the police more accountable: 'I have seen conferences where mothers criticise the police for excessive force or victimisation of their child in a way they would never be allowed to do in court ... [which] makes the police more accountable, not less ...' (1997:503–04). Blagg considers the Australian versions of restorative justice in the juvenile sector to be a 'reconfiguration' (1997:483) of existing structures rather than constituting the overhaul of police powers and introduction of specialised facilitators seen in New Zealand. In other words, Blagg argues that 'the process of cultural regeneration in New Zealand, as exemplified by the conferencing system, are engaged not simply with the retrieval of lost practices but the removal of alien ones' (1997:486). Because of the entrenched dispossession of Aboriginal people through the doctrine of *terra nullius* (empty land) and the enforced assimilation of Aboriginal people, Blagg suggests that any appeal to shared 'communitarian' traditions are redundant in Australia. He also questions the relevance of 'shaming' for Aboriginal communities. Braithwaite, however, counter-argues that 'no community can defend itself against threats to its survival if it cannot mobilise social disapproval in a way that bites ... the procedural minimalism of conferences creates the possibility for participants to use procedures that are culturally meaningful to them' (1997:504). Nonetheless, Braithwaite concedes that a fully de-colonised justice system in Australia is unlikely to be achieved.

IN PLACE OF A CONCLUSION

There is no simple way of judging the adequacy of contemporary social institutions. Each perspective that can be brought to bear finds itself challenged and alternatives proposed. Youth justice is no exception. Undoubtedly, few would accept any claim that the field should be the unquestioned preserve of 'experts', but negotiating the demands of popularist reactions needs new strategies for claiming justice. The ability of criminal law discourse to present its own image of acting justly (that is, following the correct procedure) is likely to retain its strength, but arguments to reinstate the community as the locus for decision making and the key legitimating factor for youth justice will be difficult to sustain, not least for the acknowledgment of the relentless dissolving power of the market.[49]

The late modern world seems dominated by the market and the ethics and technologies of communication. The market is not an abstract economic mechanism but is social and cultural. It not only actively disempowers 'community' but activates the late modern 'individual' as a created locus of desire. Attempting to reconstitute epistemologies for 'justice' in a globalised world market will require a thorough intermixing of our interdisciplinary and reflexive understandings of the way in which we are individuated and motivated.

Criminological understandings have traditionally been weak on their analysis of the social order in which justice systems operate. Rephrasing mainstream criminology, crime and deviance has been assumed to stem from the 'emancipation' of desire from established forms of order. Identifying the nature of social order in late or post-modernity is even more complicated. The writings of cultural studies now stress that social order is inherently symbolic.

The modern individual is empowered by the freeing of desire from the patterned forms of imitation which bind subjectivity to an order of nature as represented by central sovereign will and either/or diverse forms of organic ritual and ceremony. Under market conditions, such rituals have been replaced by the manifold techniques of communication, stimulation and simulation of desire; the desire to possess, the desire to become and the desire to be and do what you want to be and do. The late modern individual is to be 'free' and happiness lies in the self-recognition that one is free. But free to do what? and how is the recognition achieved that gives satisfaction? Late modern forms of alienation arise when desire loses its bearings under the impression that it is free to transcend social formations, free to position itself outside the symbolic order of society, while in fact it remains bound by a

---

49 Thus, for critical writers on restorative justice, the discourse of 'community' in the rhetoric of community justice is neo-populist and the culture of neo-populism distances forms of popular justice from the State while disempowering the community.

series of social codes and social controls; when the urge to be recognised as free runs up against the reality of the 'exclusive society'.

An optimistic theory of youth justice which acknowledges that which is truly modern – the transformative potential of desire – while grasping the deeply human – the need for recognition – seems to have little choice but to build upon the ideals of communication and recognition of difference which find some expression in restorative or relational justice. A pessimistic account refuses to let go of questions of power and domination, that is, questions about who and what establishes the models of desire and the ability to achieve desired ends. In that reading, those who seek a new form of youth justice – one which responds to the inarticulate expression of the need to be recognised by young 'offenders' – may find that late modern life has few resources to sustain such a communicating, reflexive citizenship.

CHAPTER 2

YOUTH CRIME, EXCITEMENT CONSUMER CULTURE: THE RECONS OF AETIOLOGY IN CONTEMPO THEORETICAL CRIMINOLO

Dr Mark Fenwick and Keith Hayward

That every order tends to criminalise resistance to itself and outlaw its assumed or genuine enemies is evident to the point of triviality. What is less obvious, yet seems to emerge from our brief survey of the forms which the pursuit of purity has taken in modern and post-modern times, is that the object of particularly zealous and intense outlawing are the radical consequences of the order's own constitutive principles [Bauman 1997:15].

Since its emergence in the mid-19th century, criminology has sought to establish a 'scientific' account of the causes of crime. From the early research of Lombroso, Garofalo and Ferri, through to more recent work on the possible genetic basis of anti-social behaviour, the aetiological question has provided one of the central concerns of the criminological enterprise. Unsurprisingly, many of the substantive findings of this tradition have been rejected, and yet the question 'why do certain individuals feel compelled to transgress social norms?' continues to inspire criminologists across all theoretical persuasions and strands of the discipline.

In point of fact, recent years have seen something of a revival of interest in the aetiological question. It is one of the central contentions of this chapter that some of the most thought provoking work in this area can be found in contemporary theoretical criminology. Utilising an eclectic mix of intellectual influences, both from within and beyond conventional criminological territories, a body of writing has emerged which explicitly sets out to develop a 'post-modern' theory of crime.[1] One might say that a phenomenology of transgression has been fused with a sociological analysis of post-modern culture in what O'Malley and Mugford 1994, refer to as an 'historically contextualised phenomenology'. Criminal behaviour is reinterpreted as a technique for resolving certain psychic conflicts, and these conflicts are regarded as indelibly linked to various features of contemporary life. Whilst it is undoubtedly the case that many of these themes can be found elsewhere in the criminological tradition (most obviously in the writings of David Matza and Robert Merton), we do feel that contemporary theoretical criminology offers something new, not least because of its engagement with debates on the transition into post-modernity. It is not surprising, therefore, that this work has been grouped under the moniker, 'cultural criminology'.[2]

---

1   See Henry and Milovanovic 1996; O'Malley and Mugford 1994; Morrison 1995; Salecl 1993; Presdee 1994; Van Hoorebeeck 1997.

2   See Ferrell and Sanders 1995; Redhead 1995.

In this chapter, we propose to examine how the various insights of this new cultural criminology might be utilised for developing a theory of youth crime. The chapter will begin with a discussion of what we regard as one of the pivotal texts in the post-modern reconstruction of aetiology, namely, Jack Katz's *The Seductions of Crime*, 1988. Katz's emphasis on the seductive quality of transgression represents a refreshing alternative and, arguably, has a particular resonance for anyone attempting to construct a theory of youth crime. As many commentators have observed, the thrill of transgression is central to a whole range of criminal activities popularly associated with youth. In the second part of the chapter, we will go on to examine the work of a number of authors who have attempted to develop Katz's argument by examining the broader socio-cultural context within which this pursuit of excitement takes place. In doing so, we will address what many commentators identify as the central weakness of Katz's work, namely, its failure to examine what it is about contemporary social life that makes the pursuit of excitement via transgression so seductive. Developing some of the themes of the new cultural criminology, we will suggest that the rise of consumer culture and concomitant forms of subjectivity place an extreme burden on young people, a burden that is, in many cases, resolved through crime. We will suggest that, in the context of post-modernity, crime has become commodified and that it is consumed like any other 'lifestyle choice'. What is being 'consumed' is twofold: not only the rush of excitement associated with criminal acts, but also a sense of control. Transgression is seductive, not only because of the excitement it brings, but also because it offers a way of taking control of one's destiny; in effect, of 'living' in the face of the routine of everyday life.

THE SEDUCTIONS OF CRIME

One of the central lacunae in the criminological tradition has been the failure to provide a satisfactory account of the phenomenology of the criminal act. Most obviously, criminology has failed to consider the emotional dimension of offending. Wayne Morrison has suggested that the 'existential' tradition can help fill this gap:

> Existentialism seeks out the meaning of things as they are in their full empirical actuality – thus, in understanding the human personality the emotions should be analysed, not ignored as 'accidental' or inconsequential, therefore, such emotions as fear and dread, boredom and passion are at the core of activity not peripheral; the results of this centrality are not always to our liking.[3]

Criminology, as a discipline, has translated the lived reality of crime into the banal platitudes of rational discourse. In contrast to this banality, there is the

---

3   1995:352–53.

existential tradition associated with figures such as ͏
and Bataille. This approach suggests that any understa͏
must begin with the passions, with the violent feelings
both in offenders and victims. Something of the spiɪ
approach can be found in the work of Katz. Given the
work to this chapter and to the new cultural criminolog͏
explore his work in some detail.

The central contention of Katz's theory of crime is that there are 'moral
and sensual attractions in doing evil' (to quote the book's sub-title), and that a
fully comprehensive account of 'anti-social behaviour' has to begin with this
fact. Yet, as Katz is keen to point out, this fact has been deliberately
overlooked by the criminological tradition. Criminal behaviour, Katz
suggests, has historically been reduced to one of three interpretations: first, as
an illegal, but rational, quest for the goals that all of us strive for; secondly, as
a more or less automatic response to certain 'background' traits or
characteristics, such as age, gender, race or class; or, thirdly, as the irrational
product of a physical or psychological pathology (Katz 1988, p 3). Katz finds
all of these accounts problematic, observing that none of them focuses on
what he calls, the 'experiential facts of crime'. Katz's central thesis is that
criminal behaviour cannot possibly be understood unless one examines how it
is experienced by the actors involved. He addresses this very issue by asking a
question that most criminologists either ignore or take for granted, namely,
'what is an individual doing when they engage in criminal behaviour?'.
Criminologists have tended to assume that they know the answer to this
question. By engaging in crime, individuals seek to acquire money or hurt
someone. Too often we impose our own interpretation on what the criminal is
doing without bothering to find out what the individual involved thinks or
feels. Criminology has failed to take up 'the challenge of explaining the
quality of the deviant experience' (p 3). Without an 'interpretative, emotional'
understanding of the criminal experience, our grasp of the phenomenon is
superficial and/or imperialistic. Katz argues that the various mechanisms
which move actors between 'background factors and subsequent acts' have
been a kind of 'black box', assumed to have some motivational force, but left
essentially unexamined (p 5). Katz proposes to open and examine the contents
of this 'black box'.

If we grasp the subjective aspect of the experience, Katz argues, we find
that crime has a deeply sensual, magical and creative appeal that is lacking in
most conventionally law abiding acts. Transgression is seductive: the 'central
problem' for the criminologist, therefore, is 'to understand the emergence of
distinctive sensual dynamics' of crime (p 4). Doing evil, he suggests, is
motivated by a quest for 'moral self-transcendence' in the face of boredom,
humiliation or even the chaos of everyday life (p 10). Deviance has an
authenticity and an attractiveness that uplifts, excites and purifies. To

ceptualise crime as another form of rational activity, or as the result of some innate or social pathology, is to totally miss the point. Deviance is presented as the existential pursuit of passion and excitement, a desperate attempt to escape the humdrum realities of 'regular' life.

Katz goes on to argue that the criminological tradition has always sought a general theory of crime, a project which necessarily assumes that all crimes are, in certain fundamental respects, the same. Criminology textbooks, for example, often present a range of theoretical frameworks, creating the impression that each framework can be applied equally well to all types of crime. Katz challenges this claim by emphasising that different types of crime may have their own distinctive thrills, all of them thrilling to its participants, but in different ways and for different reasons. To understand crime, one must look as closely as possible, at the distinctive 'foreground', that is, at the action itself and the actors' lived experience of it. To simply bundle all criminal activity together is to miss the distinctiveness of different types of criminality.

Katz offers a number of case studies of different types of crime. These range from the 'sneaky thrills' of shoplifting through to cold-blooded, 'senseless' murder. Let us take Katz's discussion of robbery as an initial example of his approach. Katz begins by suggesting that a cost-benefit analysis – at least one that sees benefits in purely financial terms – cannot account for robbery. In fact, the very features which deter most of us from robbing are intensively attractive to those who engage in it. Its sensual attraction is not the money gained, but the chaos, the excitement, the danger and the thrill of the act. Katz also suggests that the thrill of being pursued and even caught and publicly subdued is part of the allure. Robbers want to be thought of as 'real' or 'hard men' who court danger. 'In virtually all robberies', Katz writes, 'the offender discovers, fantasises, or manufactures an angle of moral superiority over the intended victim' (p 169). In an act of robbery, the stick-up man 'has succeeded in making a fool of his victim' (p 174).

The fact that robberies are so rarely planned (most of them are 'spur of the moment' affairs) might seem irrational to most of us. Surely this spontaneity increases the danger of being caught?[4] And yet, for the committed robber, this thrill of impulsive hedonism is part of the appeal. The robber wants to be 'open to whatever might seduce him' and be 'prepared for anything' (pp 204, 219). The chaos that robbery generates in the lives of those who live with it – victims, law enforcement officials and offenders – is embraced rather than shunned: it is the robber's own creation. The robber's survival in such a world is proof of the strength of his or her will. It demonstrates that he or she has managed to 'transcend the control of the system' (p 231). Crime is – to use Robert Lyng's instructive concept – a form of 'edgework' – in which the

---

4   There is an extensive amount of empirical work which supports this claim: see Harin and Martin 1984; Kappardis 1989; and Wright and Rossi 1985.

individual struggles to maintain control over a situation that verges on complete chaos.[5]

Murder, too, has its appeals, although these are very different from robbery. According to Katz, murder is best conceived as a 'delirious extirpation' of impotence. Common to all acts of 'righteous slaughter' – which it is suggested encompass most (although not all) criminal homicides – is a sense of rage born of humiliation. Killers are unable to 'ignore a fundamental challenge' not to life and limb, but to selfhood, a sense of dignity, self-respect and self-worth (p 19). 'From the killer's perspective, the victim ... teases, dares, defies, or pursues the killer' (p 20). The killer sees himself (Katz tends to focus his discussion on men) as defending his self-image. His identity has been challenged – perhaps by an insult, an argument, an infidelity or a lost fight. This 'eternally humiliating situation' becomes transformed into a blinding rage. There is a passionate desire to wipe away this stigmatising stain through the transcendent act of righteous slaughter (pp 18–19). Rather than random and chaotic, rage is 'coherent, disciplined action, cunning in its moral structure' (p 30). A necessary ingredient of righteous slaughter is that the actor 'does not kill until and unless he can fashion violence to convey the situational meaning of defending his rights' (p 31). Emotion is inscribed in both the form and content of vengeance.

It is worth emphasising that the importance which Katz places on emotion, in what is, after all, an aetiological theory of criminality, is genuinely innovative. Whilst other accounts have focused on 'experience' of crime, none have focused upon emotion as central to their explanatory framework. Emotions are correctly identified as a generative force which simultaneously compels and seduces individuals into committing illegal acts. Of central importance is excitement; the adrenaline rush associated with the limit experience. Katz offers a powerful analytic framework which re-injects passion into the age-old question of the causes of crime:

> We have entered the sort of world Peter Greenaway presents in *The Cook, The Thief, His Wife and Her Lover*, a world of violence, chaos, power and control, a world of multiple realities, of fantasies, of over-determinations, but criminology texts do not talk about this. Why? Because they offer *logos* – reasoned speech – and so criminology cannot talk about the existentialism of crime. It destroys crime, packages it up for symbolic consumption – it washes the blood from crime and renders it into materialism, into innovation, into a loss of self-control – and renders itself at a distance from the very subject it is meant to know. Thus, we risk increasing crime, for our passions may not be constrained – sterilised – we may need words and forms of analysis which understand the reality of passionate action.[6]

---

5   Lyng 1990.
6   See Morrison 1995:379.

Such themes are echoed in a range of other work: Renata Salecl's (1993) account of serial killers; Stuart Henry and Dragan Milovanovic's (1996) baroque 'constitutive criminology'; and Wayne Morrison's (1995) own reading of the criminological tradition, to give but three examples.[7]

Significantly, Katz's work on the thrill of transgression has also been utilised by a number of commentators in an attempt to understand contemporary youth crime. Chris Stanley (1996), for example, describes how excitement is central to a range of deviant practices associated with youth culture. In the case of the computer hacker, for example, he describes how the excitement involves 'the demonstration of power in breaking into a system, the excitement of entering a system which is apparently impregnable and running the risk of discovery' (p 165). For the joyrider, there is not only the excitement of risk-taking through driving fast, but also the thrill of being chased by the police.[8] Likewise, 'the rave exists so that individuals can partake in a collective process of excitement generated by the unique atmosphere (music, location, drugs, shared symbols)' (p 165).

This argument can easily be extended to understand a range of other activities typically associated with youth crime. Gang membership, for example, has much to do with youth expression and exerting control in neighbourhoods where, more often than not, traditional avenues for youthful stimulation and endeavour have long since been eroded. Indeed, if one reviews the literature concerning street gangs from early ethnographic studies (see Cohen 1955; Thrasher 1927; and Yablonsky 1962), through to more contemporary work (see Hagedorn 1988; and Vigil 1988), one is struck by the number of times gang members, when interviewed, describe the gang lifestyle as being exciting and a way of relieving the boredom and escaping the banal practicalities of everyday life. Similarly, graffiti 'artists' and members of 'tag crews', in both the US and in Europe, often talk at length, not only about the thrill and emotional charge experienced when breaking into buildings and compounds and defacing private property, but also about how their work serves as a means of self-expression and a way in which they can make themselves heard (see Ferrell 1995; and Lasley 1995). Furthermore, the phenomenon of vandalism, more generally, seems also to correspond with Katz's thesis. Arguably, if no material gain is likely to be forthcoming from this practice, then it must surely centre around either the excitement of perpetrating an illegal act or the exhilaration of wanton destruction.

---

7   It is worth noting that this argument challenges one of the central assumptions of much contemporary criminology, namely, the belief that most crime is routinised and, in some way, banal. This is undoubtedly the case if one adopts the perspective of the police or other criminal justice agencies, however, it is not necessarily true for those participating in criminal activity, for whom the most innocuous transgression may well represent an exhilarating form of experience.

8   The very term 'joyriding' indicates the level of emotion and excitement involved in this practice.

A similar argument might be put forward in relation to drug use which is probably the most prevalent of all youthful criminal transgressions. There can be little doubt that the drug sub-culture is inextricably linked with emotion: from the social circumstances in which the majority of teenage drug use takes place (for example, bars, clubs, raves and so on); to the anticipation involved in the 'scoring' process; continuing with the heightened sensations experienced prior to and during ingestion of the drug; and, finally, the roller-coaster of emotions one feels following the resolution of the process and the psychopharmacological high.

Finally, football hooliganism seems to be the quintessential illustration of the Katzian position. Rarely, if ever, is football hooliganism (or, for that matter, disruptive behaviour and violence connected with other sports) concerned with utilitarian gain. On the contrary, ticket prices and travel expenses ensure that following a football team home and away is a costly business. Instead, this phenomenon can clearly be seen as stemming from the emotional charge – or 'buzz' – that is engendered from the combination of the football and the related violence.[9] For example, consider this passage from Colin Ward's book *Steaming In*, a first hand account of football hooliganism in England in the 1970s and 1980s:

> There are certain events and experiences that make everyday, mundane existence seem tolerable and worthwhile. For thousands of football fans, myself included, it was the terraces. It became our life, for some the sole reason for existence ... Words can never fully express the emotions we experienced or recreate the heady atmosphere ... Most people are guilty of escapism and a desire to be famous. The terraces gave every participant a chance to be somebody.[10]

Moreover, in the 1990s, football hooliganism tended to become pre-arranged in a bid to counteract ever-more sophisticated police surveillance both in and around football grounds. These pre-arranged 'offs', served to prolong the emotional high by removing spontaneity from football violence and thus heightening and extending the anticipation and organisation periods.

Such examples serve to illustrate the point that youth crime is best understood in expressive rather than utilitarian terms. Individuals are seduced by the existential possibilities offered by criminal acts – by the pleasure of transgression – and not necessarily by, or only by, the immediate

---

9   With the exception of some excellent ethnographic work (see Giulianotti 1989; Armstrong and Harris 1991; and Armstrong 1993), research into football hooliganism typically tends to ignore the excitement or emotion that is a major factor in football violence. Instead, the vast majority of research in this area over the last 25 years has attempted to explain away football hooliganism as a straightforward phenomenon born out of one, or a combination, of factors, such as working class frustration, the class struggle or extreme right wing politics (see Taylor 1982; Robins 1984; and Williams 1986). This kind of analysis tends to overlook the fact that football hooliganism is very often an end in itself.

10   1989:5.

material or practical benefits. A key advantage of this approach is that it helps us to understand why it is that youth criminality is not solely the preserve of those groups who are economically and socially disadvantaged. These groups may well be over-represented in the criminal justice system, but this might have more to do with the social construction of criminality than higher rates of criminal participation. Youth crimes such as drug taking, 'twocking',[11] peer-group fighting and vandalism have an expressive element which is inextricably related to excitement and the exertion of control. As a consequence, they transcend social circumstances or economic inequality. Such crimes are about the thrill of transgressing rules and the pursuit of limits. This is a point that Mike Presdee has expressed well:

> It would seem that what we experience, or need to experience, in a world based on mind and rationality is the coming closer to the realms of desire and excitement, which we must deny ourselves in a civilised rather than savage society. This is what Katz has described as 'the delight of being deviant'. It is a transient, ephemeral yet sublime experience that, like all seductions, needs to be played with and experienced again and again.[12]

And yet, in spite of its originality, there is one important limitation with the kind of analytical framework that Katz proposes. With its emphasis on personal experience, such research has an inherent tendency to neglect the broader structural contexts within which all individual experience takes place (for another version of this argument, see O'Malley and Mugford 1994 and Van Hoorebeeck 1997, p 512). This is by no means a necessary consequence of focusing on the subjective and inter-subjective dimensions of social life, but it is a tendency which haunts phenomenological accounts, not least because of their methodological approach. Existential criminology is firmly located within the 'appreciative' tradition of the sociology of deviance inspired by the writings of David Matza (most famously in *Delinquency and Drift* (1964) and *Becoming Deviant* (1969)). One of the distinctive features of this tradition is that it takes seriously the first person accounts of the participants in deviant acts (for a classic example of this type of work, see Becker 1963). However, in privileging these narratives above all other sources of evidence, such work tends to neglect broader sociological concerns in favour of the participants' experiences. This is undoubtedly true of Katz's work which makes no attempt to place the subjective experience of crime in a broader sociological context. Surely the kinds of emotions he describes – humiliation, boredom, helplessness and anger – have to be read against the backdrop of contemporary social life? Broad structural trends play an essential role in generating the social conditions, within which the kinds of emotions Katz emphasises proliferate. They also give these emotions their peculiar character. A sensitivity to macro-level structures is, therefore, essential to the kind of

---

11 'Twocking' refers to the practice of taking cars without their owners' prior consent.
12 1994:182.

project which Katz advocates. His failure to locate the seductions of crime in their wider context is arguably a significant oversight, one that leaves his work open to the charge of ahistoricism and of reverting to the kind of general theory of crime from which, in other respects, he is so keen to distance himself.

This is not to take anything away from Katz's argument, but merely to highlight one possible way that it could be developed, namely, by locating the pursuit of excitement in history. This is of particular value for a discussion of youth crime. Such an approach, whilst recognising the centrality of excitement, would seek to identify what it is about the experience of young people today which makes the pursuit of excitement so seductive: *why are so many young people seduced by the existential possibilities of rule breaking?* Significantly, this line of argument is central to the new cultural criminology. A number of other authors have tried to integrate Katz's arguments into a more sociologically sensitive framework, through an analysis of various aspects of post-modern culture: (see Henry and Milovanovic 1996, Chapter 7; Morrison 1995, Chapter 13; O'Malley and Mugford 1994; Presdee 1994). In what follows, we shall focus upon one aspect of contemporary culture, namely, consumerism, and explore some of the various ways in which it interacts with youth crime – understood in Katzian terms as a seductive form of existential choice.

CONSUMER CULTURE AND THE SOCIAL PRODUCTION OF CRIME

If one wishes to understand post-modern culture and, more particularly, the experience of young people within post-modernity, it is important to understand the role of consumerism (for a general overview of this literature, see Featherstone 1991; Lury 1996; and Slater 1997). The vast majority of young people in the West live in a world in which their everyday existence is, to a greater or lesser degree, dominated by the all-pervasive triumvirate of advertising, the stylisation of social life and mass consumption. As Philip Sampson has commented, 'once established, such a culture of consumption is quite undiscriminating and everything becomes a consumer item, including meaning, truth and knowledge' (quoted in Lyon 1996, p 61). In this vein, the new cultural criminology has placed particular emphasis on the way that, within the context of post-modernity, crime becomes a particular type of consumer choice. Transgression becomes a leisure activity alongside shopping, going to the cinema and organised sports.[13] In this section, we will draw upon this work to propose a series of suggestions as to how the pursuit

---

13 Presdee 1994:182.

of excitement through transgression is cultivated by various features of consumerism.

First, however, it is worth pausing to reflect on the idea of consumer culture. In characterising contemporary society as a consumer culture, we are not referring to particular patterns of needs and objects – a particular consumption culture – but to a *culture of consumption*. To talk this way is to regard the dominant values of society as deriving from the activity of consumption. It is to highlight the way that the values of consumption have spilled over into other domains of social life. What we are suggesting, therefore, is that, in certain important respects, consumerism cultivates tendencies which find expression in criminal behaviour and that this is particularly acute in the case of young people. To return to the Bauman quote at the beginning of the chapter, youth crime is thus a 'radical consequence of the order's own constitutive principles'. This is not to say that consumer culture is bad in any simplistic sense. On the contrary, we regard consumer society as both rich and invigorating. However, we do intend to highlight some of the hidden and unintended consequences of a form of life that is increasingly significant not just in the West, but throughout the world.

Post-modern desire: 'sensation-gatherers' and the pursuit of 'the new'

In most cultures throughout human history, insatiable desire has been regarded as a symptom of moral pathology. A unique feature of consumer culture, however, is that insatiable desire – the constant demand for more – is not only normal but essential for socio-economic order. The 'very essence' of modern consumption is that it is 'an activity which involves an apparently endless pursuit of want':

> The modern consumer is characterised by an insatiability which arises out of a basic inexhaustibility of wants themselves, which forever arise, phoenix-like from the ashes of their predecessors. Hence, no sooner is one satisfied than another is waiting in line clamouring to be satisfied, when this one is attended to, a third appears, then subsequently a fourth, and so on, apparently without end. The process is ceaseless and unbroken; rarely can an inhabitant of modern society, no matter how privileged or wealthy, declare that there is nothing that they want. That this should be so is a matter of wonder.[14]

The insatiability of desire is not some unintended or unwanted 'side-effect' of consumerism, but is instead absolutely essential to its survival. If our desires were satiated we would stop consuming and, if this were to happen on a mass scale, the current order would cease to function altogether. Mike Presdee has recognised the importance of such a situation:

---

14   Campbell 1989:37.

Consumption becomes the cultural activity, which by its nature has a short shelf-life and needs to be continually reproduced. We cannot consume only one day in twenty, we must consume, we must desire commodities, all the time. New excitements and desires become an essential part of everyday life. Excitement under these conditions becomes a commodity to be bought, sold and consumed like all other objects.[15]

One of the central tasks consumer culture sets itself, therefore, is the production of subjects who are constantly on the look out for new commodities and alternative experiences – what Colin Campbell 1989 refers to as 'neophiliacs' or lovers of novelty. Consumerism is a culture of experimentation and, perhaps paradoxically, given the material benefits it brings, a culture of terminal dissatisfaction. A world where the pursuit of the new (and the ideology of 'personal growth') is valued above a more cautious satisfaction with what one has or is.

Zygmunt Bauman coins the phrase, 'sensation-gatherers' (1997, p 146), to characterise this peculiarly post-modern form of subjectivity. Focusing on the deregulation and privatisation of desire within contemporary culture, he describes how the 'soldier-producer' of industrial capitalism has been supplanted by a different type of subject who constantly craves new experience. Although Bauman does not make any generational distinction, the kinds of qualities he identifies with 'sensation-gatherers' are exactly those qualities associated with young people, namely, impulse, dissatisfaction, narcissism, spontaneity. It is in young people that this desire for 'the new' is most acutely developed, and such an argument is arguably invaluable in constructing an account of youth crime. After all, it seems clear that the kinds of activities mentioned in the previous section – joyriding, football hooliganism, drug use and gang membership – are attractive precisely because they offer novel, unconventional and, of course, illegal, forms of excitement. They represent a break with the banalities of everyday life and mark an entry into a new world of possibilities and pleasures. The seductiveness of crime may thus derive, in large part, from the new kinds of sensations which it offers. In a culture which encourages this strange combination of perpetual dissatisfaction and a longing for 'the new', it is hardly surprising that so many young people are seduced by the existential possibilities offered by criminal activities, as these contrast so sharply with the routine of their everyday lives.

Of course, unlike many other activities, crime is often – although not necessarily – harmful to others. The pursuit of excitement may well be selfish, in so far as it causes damage to property or person. If nothing else, this distinguishes it from many other (though clearly not all) types of social action. However, there is another feature of contemporary forms of desire which can

---

15   1994:181.

help us understand why individuals tend to become separated from prevailing normative values. In addition to being insatiable, consumer culture also cultivates a desire for immediate, rather than delayed gratification. Again, this represents an historical shift of some importance. Consider Baudrillard's account of Victorian concepts of ownership:

> Objects once acquired were owned in the full sense, for they were a material expression of work done. It is still not very long since buying a dinner table and chairs, or a car, represented the end-point of a sustained exercise in thrift. People worked dreaming of what they might later acquire; life was lived in accordance with the puritan notion of effort and its reward – an object finally won represented repayment for the past and security for the future.[16]

Today a new 'morality' exists where consumption has precedence over accumulation, 'where forward flight, forced investment, speeded-up consumption and the absurdity of saving provide the motors of our whole present system of buying first and paying off later'.[17]

The significance of this change lies not least in its implications for our experience of time. Whereas, in the past, personal identity was forged through a 'temporal unification of the past and the future with the present before me', the privileging of the present associated with consumerism cultivates 'an inability to unify the past, present and future of our own biographical experience of psychic life' (Jameson 1991, Chapter 1). Experience is reduced to 'a series of pure and unrelated presents', a series of 'nows'. Consequently, the experience of the present becomes overwhelmingly vivid and intense:

> The image, the appearance, the spectacle can all be experienced with an intensity (joy or terror) made possible by their appreciation as pure and unrelated presents in time. So what does it matter 'if the world thereby momentarily loses its depth and threatens to become a glossy skin, a stereoscopic illusion, a rush of filmic images without density' (Jameson 1991). The immediacy of events, the sensationalism of the spectacle (political, scientific, military, as well as those of entertainment), become the stuff of which consciousness is forged.[18]

Such a breakdown in temporality coupled with the concomitant search for instantaneous experience has real consequences, not least in terms of attitudes towards social norms. Morrison makes this point particularly clearly:

> The time horizon has been shortened; instant, rather than delayed gratification has resulted in the pursuit of short term goals at the expense of building up long term projects. This short term time horizon is said to result in a willingness to disregard the normative structures which are supportive of longer term methodologies and projects.[19]

---

16 Baudrillard 1996:158–59.
17 Baudrillard 1996:163.
18 Harvey 1989:54.
19 Morrison 1995:309–10.

Bauman refers to something similar when he observes that the 'arousing of new desires' has replaced 'normative regulation'.[20] Not only are young people constantly on the look out for new and ever more thrilling experiences, but they inhabit a world where normative systems cease to matter, or at least they are momentarily repressed in the moment of transgression. With its particular emphasis on the 'new' and the 'now', consumer culture separates young people from the consequences of their actions and makes them more likely to engage in a pursuit of excitement which may well be reckless and damaging to others.

Popular culture, identity and the consumption of crime

In the latter decades of the 20th century, the West has evolved a new type of society in which consumer choice is now the primary mode of expression, identification and social differentiation (Bauman 1992). One of the major precipitators of this continued rise of consumer culture has been the way in which goods and services have been advertised, marketed and packaged to such an extent that 'exchange-value' has triumphed over 'use-value'. More accurately, there has been an 'obliteration' of the original use-value of commodities in favour of a secondary or *ersatz* use-value, connected instead with cultural or stylistic factors. One result of this process is that products become stylised and take on a newer and more abstract social symbolism. (See Douglas and Isherwood 1980; Leiss *et al* 1986; and Hebdige 1988.) The fact that use-value has been obliterated by advertising and the corrosive influence of the mass media has profound implications in terms of our relationship to material goods. Baudrillard (1981; 1983), for example, argues that as a consequence of the obliteration of use-value, we now inhabit a world of 'sign-value signification'. Consumption is reinterpreted, not in terms of the satisfaction of material needs, but as involving the manipulation of signs. Putting the same point more simplistically, within the context of consumer culture, image is indeed everything.

In a consumer culture, individuals construct their identities through the commodities they consume and display. To paraphrase Helga Dittmar, society has reached a point where 'being' is now defined by 'having':

> In Western materialistic societies ... an individual's identity is influenced by the symbolic meaning of his or her own material possessions and the way in which he or she relates to those possessions ... Moreover, material possessions provide people with information about other peoples' identities.[21]

Again, this marks something of a break with what has gone before. Previously, a Cartesian view of identity held sway, at least in the West.

---

20   Bauman 1997:146.
21   Dittmar, quoted in Lury 1996:8.

Identity was conceived as unique, autonomous and uninfluenced by other people or socio-cultural surroundings. This view has been replaced by a more dislocated and fractured conception of identity as life 'project' – a never to be completed process of perpetual construction and reconstruction (see Campbell 1989, Featherstone 1991). Contemporary forms of identity are thus articulated through consumption. We construct and display a self-identity chosen from the shop window of our pluralised culture. Identity is constituted through the manipulation of signs. It is no longer a case of 'I think, therefore, I am', but rather, 'I shop, therefore, I am'.

Nowhere is this obsession with image more pronounced than in youth culture. Young people, probably more than any other demographic group in society, are seduced by the combined artifice of advertisers and marketers into constructing their identities through the processes of consumption. The youth market for consumer goods and services has grown phenomenally during the second half of the 20th century as young people have been inexorably drawn into the all-pervading culture of consumerism (for a discussion of this trend see Lury 1996, Chapter 7). Indeed, with the pressure that is being placed on young people by contemporary society to grow up ever more quickly, in the not too distant future terms such as 'youth culture' might actually become redundant, as individuals emerge from 'childhood' at 12 or 14 and proceed straight into an adult world of materialism and rampant consumerism.

What is important in this context, however, is the way that, in recent years, corporate capitalism has increasingly come to rely on images of crime as a means of selling products in the youth market. Certainly, crime has always sold. The compelling and salacious nature of certain criminal acts ensures a ready audience for crime and it has remained a dominant theme in popular culture throughout the 20th century. What has changed, however, is both the force and range of this message. Crime has been seized upon; it is being packaged and marketed to young people as a romantic, exciting, cool and fashionable cultural symbol. It is in this cultural context that transgression becomes a desirable consumer choice. Within consumer culture, crime is aesthetisised, and thus our experience of crime is primarily aesthetic. That is to say, our collective experience of crime is given to us via the mass media.

It is worth pausing to reflect on this 're-branding' of crime within contemporary culture. One obvious example of this process is the way in which 'gangster' rap combines images of criminality with street gang iconography and designer chic to create a product that is immediately seductive to youth audiences. For instance, in recent years it has become very difficult to tell whether gangster rap imagery and styling is shaping street gang culture in the US or vice versa. Since the 1980s, many cultural symbols of rap music, such as branded sports apparel and designer clothing, have increasingly been used by street gangs as a means of 'flagging' gang affiliations. Add to this the fact that several major rap artists like Tupac

Shakur and the Notorious BIG have been murdered in a long running feud between East and West Coast rap artists and it becomes immediately apparent that, at least in the field of gangster rap, art and real life are becoming ever more intertwined.[22]

Stylised images of crime abound in many other areas of the mass media, sending mixed messages to a young audience who often take their lead from popular and consumer culture. In film, violent crime and drug dealing are glamourised by slick production values and carefully selected soundtracks. The central characters in films such as *Pulp Fiction*, *New Jack City*, *Reservoir Dogs*, *True Romance* and *Natural Born Killers* are then lionised as cool popular culture icons. Likewise, on television, crime is also being packaged as entertainment. Shows like *America's Most Wanted*, *Justice Files*, *Cops*, *Top Cops* and *America's Dumbest Criminals* in the US (many of which are shown on the increasingly important cable and satellite stations in the UK) – and *Police, Camera, Action*, *Crimewatch UK*, *Crimewatch Files* and *Crime Report* in the UK are little more than a mixture of dramatic case re-enactments and real life crime footage, cobbled together to provide audiences with a vicarious televisual cheap thrill.

Crime is also beginning to feature in the world of video gaming. Violent imagery has always played a major part in this pastime, most notably in role-playing and 'shoot 'em up" video games. However, in recent years, game developers have begun to produce games that use criminal activities as their central theme. Two notorious examples are *Carmaggedon* and *Grand Theft Auto*, both of which had their release dates put back while the content of the games was reviewed by censors. *Carmaggedon* encourages reckless and aggressive driving, while in *Grand Theft Auto* players traverse urban landscapes by hopping from one stolen car to another, gaining extra points by eluding the police. These games provide their predominantly young audience with vicarious excitement from activities that are at best questionable.

If one of the key characteristics of the culture of consumerism is indeed the fact that individuals, and especially youths, are increasingly using signs and symbols to construct identity and, if as far as consumer culture is concerned, crime is both exciting and cool, then perhaps it should not come as any real surprise that young people are being seduced by the attractiveness of these visions of excess. The seductiveness of crime – and of excessive living more generally – is a dominant theme within popular culture. Although we are not suggesting that there is any simple causal link between images of violence and crime in consumer culture and contemporary youth crime, it does seem that the distinction between representations of criminality and the pursuit of

---

22 Incorporating images of crime in music is not solely confined to rap. From the controversial Body Count album, *Cop Killer*, and the skate-punk group MDC (Millions of Dead Cops) to the sophisticated urban hip hop of the Fun Lovin Criminals, crime has become a major theme in youth orientated commercial music.

excitement, especially in the area of youth culture, are becoming extremely blurred. Returning to our question, 'why are young people seduced by the existential possibilities offered by transgression?', perhaps we need to examine more closely the way that cultural forms are tied in to the production of youth identity and, further, how images of crime are inscribed in this process (see Young 1996 for a more developed version of this line of argument).

'Edgework', control and the routinisation of everyday life

Thus far, we have suggested that various features of contemporary culture encourage a desire to pursue excitement through transgression, and that this is particularly acute amongst young people. We have considered how the pursuit of new forms of experience are fundamental to the reproduction of consumer culture and we have outlined how the marketing of 'excessive' living has arguably made it an attractive 'consumer choice' for young people struggling to construct an identity for themselves. We want to end our discussion with some observations about the relationship between self-control, consumerism and youth crime. Significantly, the question of self-control is a recurring theme in literature relating to both consumerism and the new cultural criminology. Whilst commentators on consumer culture have highlighted how the practice of consumption can be characterised as a 'controlled decontrol' or a 'calculating hedonism' (Featherstone 1991; Lury 1996), contemporary theoretical criminology has emphasised how transgression and the pursuit of excitement represents an attempt to assert control – to take control of one's fate in the face of the banality, boredom and routine of everyday life (see Henry and Milovanovic 1996; Morrison 1995; O'Malley and Mugford 1994). Both discourses identify the complex interaction between excitement and control as being central to post-modernity. In this section, we will examine this convergence and outline some of its implications for an account of contemporary youth crime.

Many commentators have observed that consumer culture encourages a very different type of relationship to pleasure to that which was predominant in industrial capitalism (see Lury 1996). As was noted earlier, we no longer live in the age of the Protestant work ethic, but rather of hedonistic consumption (Campbell 1994). The pursuit of pleasure is now not only permitted, but is something which is demanded of us all. Mike Featherstone (1991) characterises the dominant relationship towards pleasure as being one of 'calculating hedonism', a hedonism in which the individual strategically moves in and out of control, enjoying the thrill of the controlled suspension of constraints. Featherstone suggests that this calculated capacity to involve and then detach oneself from objects and people is an important aspect of consumer culture. The idea of 'calculated decontrol' should not be equated with losing control, but to the capacity of the post-modern subject to strategically decontrol the emotions – to be open to an extended range of sensations and to enjoy shifting between the pleasures of attachment and of detached distance.

It is interesting to note the extent to which Featherstone's discussion converges with that of the new cultural criminology. One of the central themes of this literature is the claim that transgression involves just such a slippage between control and chaos. As we saw in our discussion of Katz, crime can be usefully conceptualised as a particular form of 'edgework' involving as it does, a strategic decontrol, in which the individual places him or herself in a potentially catastrophic situation. Lyng suggests that the central feature of edgework is that it involves:

> A common and clearly observable threat to one's physical or mental well being and one's sense of ordered existence ... The archetypal edgework experience is one in which the individual's failure to meet the challenge at hand will result in death or a debilitating injury.[23]

Many criminal activities involve just such risk-taking. And yet, this decision to place oneself in danger is itself an assertion of control. It is, to use Featherstone's language, a strategic choice. Individuals do not place themselves in a purely chaotic situation; rather, they utilise various techniques which allow them to experience both the thrill of transgression and a sense of control – of surviving at the 'edge'. The seductiveness of crime is not only linked to the inherent excitement of the acts involved, but also to the more general feelings of self-realisation and self-expression to which they also give rise. As Lyng puts it: 'the predominant sensation for the individual is one of being pushed through everyday life by unidentifiable forces that rob one of true individual choice' (1994, p 870). It is worth noting that this is a very different conception of control to that normally found in criminological theory: (see Gottfredson and Hirschi 1990 for the classic contemporary statement of this position). Rather than being symptomatic of a lack of self-control, the new cultural criminology suggests that much crime and, importantly, much youth crime, represents an attempt to exercise control and to take responsibility for one's own destiny.

The new cultural criminology is keen to historicise this phenomenon and asks, 'why is edgework so seductive now?', or, more specifically, 'why are certain types of youth crime increasingly prevalent?' What is interesting is the shared emphasis on the question of control. Firstly, Henry and Milovanovic (1996, Chapter 7), focus on the question of diminishing control in post-modernity. They discuss the work of sociological commentators who have characterised the process of modernisation in terms of increased regulation. They utilise three approaches, namely, Weber in relation to the 'iron cage' of

---

23   1994:857.

bureaucracy, Foucault's account of disciplinary forms of social control and Deleuze and Guattari's account of the territoralisation of desire to suggest that, over time, capitalism gives rise to a loss of freedom and control. In this context, edgework represents an attempt on the part of individuals to assert themselves in the face of the rigidity of everyday life. Contemporary culture thus encourages 'edgework', that is to say, within post-modernity 'edgework' becomes 'an object of desire' as 'danger and excess stir latent and repressed emotions that ultimately hold out the promise of reassuring identity, and the experience of self-actualisation, realisation or determination'.[24] This echoes our own argument of the previous section; indeed, Henry and Milovanovic highlight the fact that the seductions of edgework have become intimately linked to the mass media:

> The 'spoken subject' is constituted by way of discursive subject positions that provide the promise of overcoming schisms, gaps-in-being, alienation, disempowerment, etc. 'Things go better with a Coke' as well as with an oozie [sic]. Here the gun is its image. The gun is the instrument of power rather than an instrument to purvey death. But the one begets the other in the tension of the edge.[25]

O'Malley and Mugford 1994 offer a similar account, albeit one that, like our own, emphasises consumerism. They suggest that alienation, commodification and the prevalence of 'clock time' create a situation in which transgression takes on a peculiar appeal:

> As commodification proceeds apace, the world becomes dominated by style, by appearance, by simulacra. In such a world, the self becomes swallowed in consumerism, but that consumerism is ultimately rather hollow and unsatisfying. The pursuit of selfhood may involve seeking liberation through consumption by indulging in more extreme forms of experience, but in so doing one risks more conformity to the consumerist imperative ... Within modern cultures there is a steady and increasing pressure towards emotionally exciting activities, including leisure activities, as a source of transcendence and authenticity with which to offset the suffocation of an over-controlled, alienated existence within the mundane reality of modern life.[26]

Finally, in a thought-provoking re-working of Merton's 'strain' theory, Wayne Morrison (1995, Chapter 13) emphasises the tension that arises within consumer culture as a result of the widening gap between desire and the impossibility of its fulfilment:

> Modernity gives us a series of expectations as to self-realisation and personal growth – we are to become other than what we have been through the choosing of identities, employment roles and seizing opportunities – but actual human beings have not fully escaped being defined by their location in

---

24 1996:157.
25 1996:157.
26 1994:206.

situations of ennoblement and restraint. Human beings will be disappointed, they wish to take control of their selves, they wish to realise their (future) self-potential, but are located in demeaning and restraining circumstances – a crisis of action develops.[27]

Like the other authors mentioned above, Morrison conceptualises transgressive forms of edgework as an assertion of control in the face of this kind of strain.

Each of these accounts leaves us with an opposition between two modes of being. On the one hand, there is the routinised alienation and boredom of everyday life – a world in which individuals find themselves over-controlled and yet without control. On the other hand, there are those activities which offer the possibility of excitement *and* control. Lyng's account focuses on extreme sports, whilst the new cultural criminology focuses on transgression. Although ostensibly dangerous, these activities offer a mode of being in which individuals take control through a calculated act of de-control. The seductiveness of crime is not only linked to the inherent excitement of the acts involved, but also to more general feelings of self-realisation and self-expression to which they give rise. It might be an unpalatable thought, but it is through such activities that individuals come alive. It is our contention that this kind of opposition can provide a useful framework for an understanding of youth crime.

CONCLUSION

In this chapter, we have suggested that an explanatory account of youth crime needs to address the question of why contemporary culture makes the consumption of transgression so seductive. We outlined a series of possible answers to this question. First, we drew upon the work of Jack Katz, to suggest that part of the answer is linked to the sheer thrill of transgression. It offers a mode of experience unavailable in 'regular' life. Whilst there is much of value in Katz's approach, we criticised his failure to locate the pursuit of excitement in a historical context.

Instead, we asked, 'what is it about *contemporary* culture which makes transgressive forms of excitement seductive to young people?'. In the second part of the chapter, we attempted a preliminary answer to this question, by examining how youth crime is linked to various features of consumer culture. We argued that consumerism cultivates certain tendencies which find expression in criminal behaviour and outlined some of the elements involved in this process, namely, the insatiability of desire and the pursuit of the new; short termism and the desire for immediate gratification; the marketing of

---

27   1995:301.

crime within youth culture; and the construction of youth identities through crime.

We ended with some suggestions as to how certain kinds of illegal 'edgework', rather than being symptomatic of a lack of self-control, are best understood as a strategic attempt to exercise and take control in the face of the routinisation of everyday life. Unfortunately, this recognition of the centrality of culture in the social production of crime mitigates against any obvious solution. If Bauman is correct in suggesting that 'the object of particularly zealous and intense outlawing are the radical consequences of the order's own constitutive principles', then the possibility of any significant change is clearly limited. Perhaps our only hope at this time is to think of new ways of channelling the pursuit of excitement by young people into less harmful forms of edgework.

CHAPTER 3

ABOLISHING THE PRESUMPTION OF *DOLI INCAPAX*: REFLECTIONS ON THE DEATH OF A DOCTRINE[1]

Elizabeth Stokes

THE AGE OF CRIMINAL RESPONSIBILITY AND THE PRINCIPLE OF PROTECTION

In England and Wales, young persons may be subject to criminal liability and prosecution from the age of 10.[2] All children under this age are considered to be *doli incapax* (incapable of committing a crime) and are therefore protected from State punishment, although they may be subject to a civil action as a result of their harmful conduct. A local authority has the power, under s 31 of the Children Act 1989, to institute care proceedings if a child's behaviour provides evidence that the child 'is suffering or is likely to suffer significant harm which is attributable to the care given to the child not being what it is reasonable to expect a parent to give, or the child is beyond parental control'. These proceedings are by no means automatic and are premised on a welfare based concern for the protection of the child.

After reaching the age of 10, however, there is nothing within the substantive criminal law which distinguishes the responsibility of young people from that of adults. This is not to overlook the different provisions applicable to young suspects, defendants and offenders within the youth justice system, which are intended to account for their vulnerability and lack of age. It is simply to observe that, in the attribution of guilt, 10 year olds and adults are subject to the same legal principles and can be the subject of a criminal conviction.

This is a recent development as, before the Crime and Disorder Act 1998, there existed a transitional period, between the ages of 10 and 14, where a rebuttable presumption of *doli incapax* applied. According to this legal doctrine, children did not suddenly become fully responsible on their 10th birthday, but would only be held criminally accountable for their actions if, in addition to committing the *actus reus* and *mens rea* of a criminal offence, the

---

1 This paper was first presented at the British Criminology Conference 1999. I would like to thank Beverley Brown, Hilary Lim and Steve Gilmore for their helpful comments on previous drafts.

2 Children and Young Persons Act 1933, s 50, as amended by the Children and Young Persons Act 1963, s 16, which raised the age from eight.

prosecution could also prove beyond reasonable doubt that, when doing the act, the child knew that what they were doing was 'seriously wrong'.[3]

The abolition of this presumption by s 34 of the 1998 Act has resulted in criticism from academics who are concerned with youth justice and feel that the Government are undermining an important distinction between childhood and adult criminal responsibility (see Bandalli 1998; Cavadino 1997; Fionda 1998; Rutherford 1998). The basis for such criticism rests upon the acceptance of a 'principle of protection' which is supposed to underlie the allocation of criminal responsibility to young people:

> 'No civilised society regards children as accountable for their actions to the same extent as adults' ... The wisdom of protecting young children against the full rigour of the criminal law is beyond argument. The difficulty lies in determining when and under what circumstances that protection should be removed.[4]

This statement has been cited with approval by the House of Lords and extra-judicially by the Lord Chief Justice, Lord Bingham.[5] The principle of protection is also recognised by the United Nations Convention on the Rights of the Child. Article 40(3) provides that:

> States Parties shall seek to promote the establishment of laws, procedures authorities and institutions specifically applicable to children alleged as, accused of, or recognised as having infringed the penal law, and, in particular:
>
> (a) the establishment of a minimum age below which children shall be presumed not to have the capacity to infringe the penal law;
>
> (b) whenever appropriate and desirable, measures for dealing with such children without resorting to judicial proceedings, providing that human rights and legal safeguards are fully respected.[6]

It is not proposed within the context of this chapter to examine this 'principle of protection' in any detail. Arguably, it is a rather nebulous concept which fails to provide sufficiently clear guidance for policy formation. Should children be protected from criminal liability or from punishment? And how is punishment to be defined within this context? It is enough for present purposes to acknowledge that this is the basis on which much academic criticism of s 34 of the Crime and Disorder Act 1998 rests. For example, Bandalli maintains that the policy of abolition was based on 'a fundamental

---

3   This was confirmed in *C (A Minor) v DPP* [1996] 1 AC 1, HL.

4   Harpur J in *R v Whitty* (1993) 66 A Crim R 462, Supreme Court of Victoria, Australia, quoting Howard 1982:343.

5   *C (A Minor) v DPP* [1996] 1 AC 1, p 40C–D; *R v Secretary of State for the Home Department ex p Venables and Thompson* [1997] 3 All ER 97, p 145E–F; Lord Bingham of Cornhill 1997.

6   See, also, Art 3. The UK ratified the UN Convention on the Rights of the Child in 1991. The UN Committee on the Rights of the Child has since suggested that 'serious consideration be given to raising the age of criminal responsibility throughout the areas of the UK', CRC/C/15 Add 34C.

misunderstanding of the presumption of *doli incapax* and of the complexity of the issues it presents' (1998, p 115) and she rejects the Government's contention that children do not need protection from the consequences of criminal liability. The debate is essentially viewed as one solely concerning the proper scope of the principle of protection.

This chapter, however, suggests that such a narrow focus is misconceived and that further reflection on the origins and operation of this legal presumption puts into question its status as a protective mechanism. By examining the principle of *doli incapax* within the criminal law, it is possible to argue that the previous legal position perpetuated a fiction of protection which was obscured by legal forms. Its abolition will, therefore, make little practical difference to the current criminalisation of young people. Instead, its significance is primarily symbolic of this trend. Finally, it is not within the scope of this chapter to consider how the question of allocating criminal responsibility should be resolved. Possible reforms and comparative solutions are adequately covered elsewhere.[7]

The presumption of *doli incapax*: an historical perspective

The rebuttable presumption of *doli incapax* had existed at common law since the 14th century. In 1796, *Blackstone's Commentaries* documented this long line of authority, which recognised that 'the capacity for doing ill, or contracting guilt, is not so much measured by years and days, as by the strength of the delinquent's understanding and judgment'.[8]

It is unclear, however, why such a legal doctrine originated at this point in history. Conventional wisdom suggests that it had a protective function, shielding the young from harsh adult justice.[9] But this fails to account for the fact that the doctrine developed 'long before modern conceptions of childhood took hold' (Allen 1996, p 30). According to the work of the French historian Philippe Ariès, at the end of the medieval period, children were perceived quite differently, and the idea of childhood as a separate stage of development, which should be cherished and protected, simply did not exist:

> Children were mixed with adults as soon as they were considered capable of doing without their mothers or nannies, not long after a tardy weaning (in other words at about the age of 7).[10]

---

7   See Allen 1996; Bandalli 1998; Cavadino 1996; Dunkel 1991; Lloyd Morris and Mahendra 1996; Sagel-Grande 1991.

8   4 Bl Com, 22nd edn, pp 23–24, cited in *C v DPP* [1995] 2 All ER 43, p 47H.

9   This is a point on which both opponents and supporters of the recent abolition agree.

10 Ariès 1973:395, quoted in Newburn 1997:615. For further reference on the construction of childhood, see Jenks 1996; Pinchbeck and Hewitt 1969.

Children who reached the age of seven (which was, in medieval times, the age of rationality), entered the adult world of labour and were considered of equal status. This is largely because of the limited life expectancy in the 14th century, when it is estimated that over half of the population were under the age of 20 (Newburn 1997).

Whilst we can be fairly certain that the presumption of *doli incapax* originated at the end of the medieval period, its precise relation to the issue of criminal responsibility is unclear. As Baker explains:

> It was settled in medieval times that a child under 12 could not be convicted of a felony if he was too young to bear criminal responsibility. Although there was an upper limit of 12, it is far from clear whether there was a lower limit before Hale, in the 17th century, adopted the civilian limit of 7.[11]

It would seem likely, therefore, that the presumption of *doli incapax* applied below the age of 12. Why should this have been the case?

One benefit of the doctrine (which is recognised by critics of its abolition today), is its focus on individual capacity and the development of understanding, rather than the arbitrary measure of chronological age. As Ariès suggests, children were only separated from adult life whilst they were physically dependant on their elders and it was the process of 'weaning' rather than age *per se* which was seen to be important. It may be that the law developed to account more accurately for this transitional stage. It would seem, however, that the focus of the test was practical and not premised on the idea of protection: 'Could he count up to 12 pence? If his father was a weaver, could he measure a yard of cloth?'[12] It was the child's ability to work, rather than the possession of an adult understanding, which determined responsibility.

It is probable that Ariès's thesis on the absence of a concept of childhood in medieval times is somewhat overstated as subsequent writers on the construction of childhood have criticised both his methodology and conclusions.[13] It is clear that the dependent infant lacked capacity during this period and Bracton observed in the 13th century, that such children were believed to possess an 'innocence of purpose'.[14] These qualifications, however, do not undermine the force of Ariès's contention that childhood is historically, and culturally, contingent. If children, at the time of the doctrine's inception, were viewed differently from today, this must inform any interpretation of the *doli incapax* presumption. It is perhaps unlikely that the 'principle of protection' was of major influence. It would have been a rather

---

11 Baker 1990:597.
12 Walker 1983:23. Walker uses this practical test to explain the high age of responsibility when compared to later standards.
13 Eg, Pollock 1983, Chapters 1–2; James and Prout 1990.
14 Walker 1983:23.

enlightened development in medieval law, extending the notional period of childhood well beyond the age of rationality to the age of 12.

There is another plausible explanation. Andrew Nichol QC has argued that 'the definition of what constituted a child (and so the boundary of who was affected by the principle) only acquired crispness after births became recorded as a matter of course'.[15] It may be suggested that the presumption conveniently avoided the difficulty of having to determine the age of suspects with any certainty in medieval England. Historians of childhood have noted an indifference to the idea of age enduring until reforms required its documentation (largely for the purposes of taxation) (see Ariès 1973, p 14; Pinchbeck and Hewitt 1969, p 7).

> Parish Registers of birth were introduced in 1538, but long after that date, registration was never kept with any exactitude. Not in fact till 1836, after the Registration of Births Act – and even then by no means in every case – was it possible in this country to ascertain a person's age with any precision.[16]

This problem was particularly acute among transient populations in developing urban areas. Pinchbeck and Hewitt note that it presented some difficulties in lawsuits, although they refer mainly to property cases and the decisions of feudal wards (which had to appoint special committees to call for detailed evidence on the question of age when necessary). With the doctrine of *doli incapax* in operation, any uncertainty about age would present no obstacle to a criminal action.

Whatever the reason for its introduction, it seems doubtful that the doctrine originated from a concern to protect the vulnerable from punishment as previously suggested. As one member of the House of Commons Standing Committee on the Crime and Disorder Bill observed:

> It would have surprised those who instituted the doctrine of *doli incapax* in the mid-14th century that they should be blamed for an alleged 'excuse culture' in the youth justice system of the late 20th century.[17]

It is, of course, possible that the doctrine changed its function in later centuries as the question of age acquired greater significance and the idea of childhood as distinct from adulthood evolved. Laws LJ in the Divisional Court judgment of *C v DPP* claims that the presumption of *doli incapax* 'took root in an earlier era, when the criminal law was altogether more draconian'. He refers to the 18th century and concludes that it is 'little wonder that, at a time when criminal guilt led to such ferocious retribution, the law developed a means by which mercy was exceptionally extended to child defendants'.[18]

---

15 Nichol 1995:5. The author was counsel for the defendant in the case of *C (A Minor) v DPP* [1996] 1 AC 1, HL.

16 Pinchbeck and Hewitt 1969:7.

17 Clappison MP (C, Hertesmere), HC Standing Committee B 12/5/98.

18 *Per* Laws LJ in *C (A Minor) v DPP* [1994] 3 All ER 190, p 198F–G.

There is no evidence, however, to support the view that the presumption of *doli incapax* acted as a protective mechanism at this time. Radzinowicz and Hood argue that proof of capacity in the 18th century 'was frequently forthcoming, even for the vast numbers of crimes carrying the death penalty' (1986, p 133).[19] Although Knell maintains that few condemned children were actually executed (1965, p 198), it was not the legal presumption, but the application of discretion, either before prosecution or after conviction, which allowed for mercy. Indeed, as Douglas Hay's well known study of this period uncovered, even amongst the adult population, the numbers of executions did not match the number of convictions (Hay 1975, p 22). It is possible, drawing upon Hay's work, to suggest that the doctrine had a more symbolic significance by contributing to the ideology of 'justice' during the 18th century. There is little doubt that its practical effect was limited.

THE IMPACT OF WELFARE REFORM

It is, in fact, only within recent history that the principle of protection has received wider recognition. From the mid-19th century onwards, concern for the welfare of young people in trouble began to influence the political agenda. Studies tracing the development of the concept of juvenile delinquency (as a social problem deserving separate consideration from adult criminality), highlight the importance of the Victorian era in marking a change of consciousness.[20] It is notable that this coincided with the perception (at least amongst the privileged classes) of childhood as an age of innocence, to be nurtured and protected.

As a result, the question of children's criminal responsibility became an issue:

> New insights into the condition of delinquents prompted a revaluation of the ancient principle of *doli capax*. [Reformers] argued that the child's 'incapacity' to distinguish between right and wrong should be more fully implemented, and 'that his age and the neglect or vice of his parents should be taken into account'.[21]

From this point at the foundation of the modern youth justice system, it is clear that the presumption of *doli incapax* was claimed to have a protective function, and it is this understanding of the legal doctrine which has informed recent debates.

In 1990, the Conservative Government's White Paper, *Crime, Justice and Protecting the Public* (Home Office 1990b), relied on this interpretation of the presumption as the reason for its continued application:

---

19 Quoted in Bingham 1997:1.
20 May 1973; Radzinowicz and Hood 1986.
21 May 1973:23.

... the criminal law is based on the principle that people understand the difference between right and wrong. Very young children cannot easily tell this difference, and the law takes account of this ... The Government does not intend to change these arrangements which make proper allowance for the fact that children's understanding, knowledge and ability to reason are still developing.[22]

While the Labour Government's White Paper, *No More Excuses*, 1997d, argued that it is no longer necessary to protect young people from a progressive youth justice process, it also identified the presumption as a key obstacle to this intervention and recommended its abolition.[23]

THE PRESUMPTION OF *DOLI INCAPAX:* IN PRACTICE

Given the supposed importance of this presumption, it is surprising that there has been no empirical research into its actual operation. When challenged for making 'sweeping assertions on the matter, based on slender evidence'[24] during the committee stage of the Crime and Disorder Bill , the Home Office Minister, Alun Michael MP, accused his questioner of being 'a woolly minded old liberal' and responded as follows: 'The lack of research is a problem only if one is not sure what the problem is. In fact, it is clear.'[25]

In fact, the weight of academic opinion suggests that this assertion is misconceived (Bandalli 1998; Cavadino 1997). The presumption could easily be rebutted (Crofts 1998) as there was no need for direct evidence relating to the child's own perception of what they had done. Knowledge that an act was seriously wrong could be inferred from the surrounding circumstances.[26] Nor was it necessary under the previous law, to introduce the evidence of a psychiatrist or a teacher, as this information could have been elicited during a police interview without difficulty.[27] Ironically, the presumption could also be rebutted by proof that a child was of normal mental capacity for his or her age,[28] and this clearly undermined any 'benevolent protection' which was attributed to the doctrine.[29]

---

22 Home Office 1990b, para 8.4

23 Home Office 1997d, paras 4.3–4.4.

24 Clappison MP (C, Hertesmere), HC Standing Committee B 12/5/98.

25 Michael MP (Lab, Cardiff South and Penarth), HC Standing Committee B 12/5/98.

26 *A v DPP* [1997] Crim LR 125.

27 *L (A Minor) v DPP* [1997] Crim LR 127; see, also, Bandalli 1998:117. The Solicitor General, during the second reading debate in the House of Commons, claimed that the impracticality of producing teachers or social workers as witnesses was used by the defence to manipulate the CPS into dropping their case (see Hudson 1998:60).

28 *JM (A Minor) v Runeckles* (1984) 79 Cr App R 255; *CC (A Minor) v DPP* [1996] 1 Cr App R 375.

29 Crofts 1998:190.

The illusory nature of this protection was openly admitted by the judiciary. Lord Lowry in *C v DPP* observed that 'the courts, lacking really cogent evidence, often treat the rebuttal as a formality' and a magistrate observed that, 'in practice, juvenile courts rarely look at the *doli incapax* requirement'.[30]

Closer consideration of the official statistics also suggests that the effect of the presumption on the prosecution of young people was limited. Although records do not separate out youth court proceedings, the high rate of guilty pleas at magistrates' courts level indicates that the prosecution had no need to overcome the presumption in the majority of youth court cases.[31] In addition, Bandalli has pointed out that the doctrine was practically irrelevant in the case of theft and handling offences, which represented the most prevalent form of youth criminality (1998, p 117). This is because the prosecution already have to prove dishonesty in these cases, a test which largely encompasses the consideration of the defendant's understanding necessary to rebut the presumption of incapacity.[32] Cavadino estimates that, even with the *doli incapax* rule in existence, more than 4,000 children aged 10–13 years were processed through the criminal courts each year (1997, p 169).

It has been argued that the presumption was of particular importance in cases of criminal damage (Bandalli 1998; Manchester 1986; Moore 1995) and strict liability, where the criminal law does not impose a requirement of subjective *mens rea*. Presumably, it was thought that children who did not intend, or foresee, the consequences of their actions deserved greater protection from the full rigours of the law.[33] It is true that the law in this area makes little allowance for incapacity; following the controversial case of *Elliot v C*, children are imputed with the foresight of a reasonable adult when committing criminal damage[34] and strict liability admits no consideration of lack of age. There is no evidence, however, to suggest that the presumption of *doli incapax* was applied with more regularity in these cases.

In *L v DPP*,[35] the defendant was convicted of possessing a canister of CS gas, an offence of strict liability. Whilst the court applied the presumption, it demonstrated a rather cavalier attitude to this requirement, robbing it of all content:

---

30 *C (A Minor) v DPP* [1995] 2 All ER 43, p 63D–F; Manchester 1986:8.

31 Crown Prosecution Service 1997:36. See, also, Bandalli 1998:116.

32 See *T (A Minor) v DPP* [1989] Crim LR 498. *R v Ghosh* [1982] QB 1053.

33 Although it should be noted that it is possible for a child to act with intent and still lack 'mischievous discretion', the presumption remains separate, in theory, from the consideration of *mens rea*.

34 *Elliot v C (A Minor)* [1983] All ER 1005. For the alternative view that *Caldwell* recklessness may incorporate notions of capacity, see Keating 1996:540; Leigh 1995:463.

35 *L (A Minor) v DPP* [1997] Crim LR 127.

This was a statutory offence of possession and did not require proof of *mens rea*. Moreover, the act of possessing a weapon was either wrong or innocent. There was no room for mere naughtiness when he was in possession of a CS gas canister which could not be legitimately (or innocently) in his possession.

As JC Smith noted in his commentary, this was 'just the kind of case in which a child might not appreciate the serious wrongness of the mere possession of the thing – where he might not necessarily know that it was 'naughty'.[36]

It is no accident that the most important authority in this area, the decision of the House of Lords in *C v DPP*, concerned a charge of criminal damage. It is, however, surprising that the case was tested this far. Donaldson[37] sees this as a failure in police interviewing skills and the prosecution's knowledge of the law, rather than as a paradigm case which the presumption should have protected. To quote Bandalli, the doctrine 'only protects the patently subnormal or beneficiaries of prosecutorial ineptitude' (1998, p 120). It is likely that most criminal damage cases would have ended at the original conviction, rather than having been challenged in this way.[38]

It is submitted that the particular difficulties raised by cases of criminal damage and strict liability stem from the contentious nature of these forms of liability within the substantive criminal law and should not be used to confuse the debate over the presumption, which applied to all offences.

Bandalli claims that, although the presumption had a limited impact in preventing the conviction of children at trial, it may have influenced prosecutorial discretion at an earlier stage 'by focusing the attention of the police and Crown Prosecution Service' on children under 14 as a 'special case' (1998, p 121). The success of diversion as a protective policy is well documented elsewhere,[39] but it is unclear to what extent the doctrine of *doli incapax* was a relevant consideration in its application. Bandalli herself recognises the erosion of this policy, from the restrictions on cautioning (HO Circular 18/1994), the omission of the presumption in favour of not prosecuting juveniles in the Home Office Guidelines and the removal of youth as a category of vulnerable offenders in the Code for Crown Prosecutors 1994 (Bandalli 1998, p 119). Given that the Crime and Disorder Act has continued this trend away from diversion with its 'final warning' provisions,[40] it is unlikely that the presumption of *doli incapax* could add anything to the operation of discretion before prosecution.

---

36 *L (A Minor) v DPP* [1997] Crim LR 127, p 129.

37 Donaldson 1995, quoted in Bandalli 1998:117.

38 See, also, below, p 71, for a more detailed consideration of the test for *doli incapax*.

39 See Newburn 1997 for references.

40 Crime and Disorder Act 1998, s 65, effectively limits the number of cautions to two – a reprimand and a final warning. See Leng *et al* 1998.

Clearly, these observations are no substitute for actual research, but they do problematise the Government's claims.[41] They also weaken the contentions of pressure groups and practitioners who advocated the retention of the doctrine as an effective form of protection from criminal liability (Cavadino 1997; Penal Affairs Consortium 1995; Moore 1995; Nichol 1995). It would appear that the practical consequences of the abolition of *doli incapax* for children above the age of criminal responsibility (that is, 10) will be negligible. This is not to trivialise the application of punishment to young people, only to recognise that the majority are in no worse a position than before.

THE SYMBOLIC IMPORTANCE OF ABOLITION: THE CRIMINALISATION OF CHILDREN

The true significance of the presumption's abolition exists at the level of theory, not practice. It represents yet another manifestation of the time honoured welfare/justice debate, a dispute over the boundaries of the principle of protection or what Loveland (1995) terms the 'frontiers of criminality'. Should children be protected from the imposition of criminal liability and, if so, when should this protection be lifted?

To its opponents, the abolition of *doli incapax* is symbolic, as it appears to lower this threshold of protection (whatever the reality) and it is, therefore, perceived as yet another attempt to undermine the important distinction between childhood and adult criminal responsibility. In the broader context, it is viewed as part of the 'pincer movement' against very young offenders, which has characterised youth justice policy in the mid-1990s (Ashworth 1994, p 176). As noted by Bandalli, above, there has been a marked retraction from the 1980s emphasis on diversionary measures. This has been replaced by the introduction of various provisions which allow for earlier and, arguably, more intrusive criminal justice interventions. Section 1 of the Sexual Offences Act 1993 abolished the irrebuttable presumption that a boy under the age of 14 was incapable of rape. The Criminal Justice and Public Order Act 1994 established the secure training order for persistent young offenders above the age of 12, doubled the ceiling on sentence length for persons under 18 to 24 months and extended long term detention under s 53(2) of the Children and Young Persons Act 1969 to include 10 year olds. Following the Crime Sentences Act 1997, convictions incurred before the age of 18 may qualify for the application of a mandatory minimum sentence imposed for an offence committed after that age and the Crime and Disorder Act 1998 contains a

---

41 Bala 1994 cites evidence that the presumption of *doli incapax* was frequently not raised in Canada before its abolition in 1984. See McLeod 1980.

range of new disposals to get tough on youth crime, some of which may be applied to children under the age of 10 (the child safety order and the child curfew).[42]

What is striking about this debate, however, is not that it has re-emerged at this time, but that this particular legal doctrine should have become the subject of such controversy. Given the lack of protection offered by the presumption, it is surprising that both sides have elevated its importance, displaying their ignorance of the actual effects of the legal provisions. Bandalli's excellent examination of the operation of the presumption is the one academic exception to this rule, clearly highlighting the issue's complexities, and yet she concludes with a call for the rejuvenation of the principle of protection and suggests that the doctrine of *doli incapax* could be strengthened to fulfil this role.

This leaves a number of questions unanswered, namely, how did this misconception of the law's function come to influence the political agenda? Why was it possible for government policy to be based on a 'fundamental misunderstanding'[43] of the presumption and still be successful? And why do the opponents of abolition continue to have faith in a doctrine which has proved to be so inadequate in protecting children from criminal liability throughout its history?

GOVERNMENT POLICY: CONVICTION AND CONTRADICTION

The Labour Party's manifesto commitment to 'tackle youth crime' was aimed at removing an 'excuse culture' which was alleged to exist within the youth justice system. It is evident that the presumption of *doli incapax* was identified as part of this culture, as it was thought to excuse young people by preventing them from being held criminally responsible for their actions. The reasons behind this inaccurate conclusion are, therefore, in need of closer examination.

The proposals for abolition were first outlined in a Labour Party consultation paper,[44] which highlighted the recent legal challenges to the doctrine. In March 1994, the Divisional Court in the case of *C v DPP* had prematurely decided that the doctrine was no longer to be regarded as part of the law.[45] This was overruled on appeal to the House of Lords a year later, on the grounds that the presumption had force of precedent. The Divisional

---

42 See, more generally, Goldson 1999; Fionda 1999; Piper 1999; Rutherford 1998:14; Leng *et al* 1998.

43 Bandalli 1998:115.

44 Labour Party 1996:11.

45 *C (A Minor) v DPP* [1994] 3 All ER 190.

Court, therefore, lacked the authority to draw such a conclusion and was straying into the realms of judicial legislation. The House of Lords, nevertheless, concluded that the current legal position was unsatisfactory and invited Parliament to clarify the issue through legislation. After the election, the Labour Government could, thus, legitimately claim to be responding to this request. During the committee stage of the Crime and Disorder Bill, Alan Michael defended the lack of research into the doctrine's operation in this way: '... there has been considerable debate for some time and the problems are clear to the courts.'[46]

This reliance on *C v DPP* as an authority for the policy of abolition is, however, unfounded. According to Lord Lowry, in the House of Lords' judgment, the issue was far from clear. He emphasised the need to study other youth justice systems' allocation of criminal responsibility, including that of Scotland and recommended that:

> Whatever change is made, it should come only after collating and considering the evidence and after taking account of the effect which a change would have on the whole law relating to children's anti-social behaviour.[47]

As previously noted, this research was not forthcoming.

The Home Office Consultation Paper[48] and White Paper also echo the sentiments of the Divisional Court in *C v DPP* in the two core arguments they present for the abolition of the doctrine. Again, this is ill advised, as it focuses on the two social assumptions which were qualified by Lord Lowry on appeal, instead of the more compelling judicial observations on the inadequacies of the legal test. The judgment of Laws LJ in the lower court has drawn strong criticism for its 'intense level of dismissive rhetoric' and emotive language (Sullivan 1994, p 2). It also demonstrated an ignorance which exists among some members of the judiciary of criminological realities, that is, what we actually do know about youth crime. Given Lord Lowry's caution about research, the use of the Divisional Court's reasoning, without more, leaves the policy open to question.[49]

The first official contention is that the presumption was contrary to common sense because 'most young people aged 10–13 are plainly capable of differentiating between right and wrong'.[50] This assertion is based on the idea that children today grow up more quickly, have the benefit of universal education and so do not require the protection of the law. Arguably, it is wrong on both counts. Walsh maintains that the youth of today have a considerably extended period of childhood due to 20th century developments

---

46 Michael MP (Lab, Cardiff South and Penarth), HC Standing Committee B 12/5/98.

47 *C (A Minor) v DPP* [1995] 2 All ER 43, p 64D.

48 Home Office 1997d.

49 See Walsh 1998 for a detailed criticism of the Government's claims.

50 Labour Party 1996:11; see, also, Home Office: 1997d, para 4.4.

in education and the juvenile justice system (1998, p 4). It does not necessarily follow that young people are free from adult responsibilities, the number of homeless teenagers, child carers and the development of *Gillick* competency in the civil law, for example, rather undermines this ideology. Nevertheless, there is evidence to suggest a link between this protracted period of adolescence and youth crime.[51] It is clear that many young offenders come from socially and economically vulnerable situations which may prevent them from 'growing up' and assuming adult roles and responsibilities.[52] There is also a proven correlation between truancy, school exclusion and youth crime, which weakens any positive influence of the education system (Allen 1996, p 30; Cavadino 1997, p 167).[53] Against such a background, it is impossible to generalise about young people's capabilities in any meaningful sense.

The second argument is that the presumption stopped appropriate interventions being made which could help prevent further offending. Thankfully, the Government did not repeat Laws LJ's misinformed observation that the law was 'divisive and perverse' because it only penalised children from 'good homes' (who presumably were more likely to know that an act was seriously wrong).[54] The same point, however, can be put in less invidious terms and the official line was closer to Glanville Williams's claim that the doctrine was paradoxical because 'the more warped the child's moral standards the safer he is from the correctional treatment of the criminal law'.[55]

It has already been suggested that the presumption does not present such an obstacle, but this contention is worthy of further comment for its characterisation of youth justice disposals as corrective measures. Unsurprisingly, this view of a rehabilitative youth justice system, where children are not punished but 'improved', is not a generally accepted description of our current arrangements. Although the Labour Government has shown some enthusiasm for such initiatives, the rationale of recent policy is more accurately characterised as punitive. Goldson argues that the Crime and Disorder Act is 'framed within a punitive context and its underpinning emphasis remains fixed around individual responsibility, re-moralisation and, in the final analysis, child incarceration' (1999, p 282). Where rehabilitative programmes are promoted, for example in the reparation order (ss 67 and 68), the action plan order (ss 69 and 70), final warning interventions and the youth offender contracts introduced in the Youth Justice and Criminal Evidence Act

---

51   See Pitts 1996:281; Rutherford 1992.

52   See Goldson 1999:279; Pitts 1996:282.

53   Crime and Disorder Act 1998, s 16, contains provisions aimed at reducing this problem by giving the police the power to round up truants, see Leng *et al* 1998:37.

54   *C (A Minor) v DPP* [1994] 3 All ER 190, p 198B–E. See Moore 1995:348 for criticism of this view.

55   Williams 1954:495.

1999 (ss 8–12), the Government's programmes are influenced by the principles of restorative justice and, hence, are focused more on the interests of victims than those of young offenders (Walsh 1998, p 5). More importantly, perhaps, it is these sections which possess the potential to widen the net of the criminal justice system in relation to young people and risk up-tariffing previous offenders.

The White Paper controversially maintains that preventing offending through youth justice interventions is in the interests of a child's welfare, but this confusion of welfare and punishment rather misses the point. There is a wealth of literature which questions the ability of the criminal law to prevent youth offending as an inappropriate medium for addressing the causes of crime.[56] It is disturbing that this opportunity to consider alternative welfare based responses outside of the youth justice system was not taken.

The second contention is also potentially undermined by the fact that the courts still have discretion in 'exceptional circumstances' to give a conditional discharge and it is, therefore, not certain that the 'appropriate interventions' will be ordered. The Government dropped its suggestion that the use of conditional discharges be restricted, after consultation, presumably as a concession to the sensitive issue of 'judicial independence' in sentencing matters. Under the previous law, convicted children were protected from more serious interventions by the judiciary themselves, as in the majority of cases an absolute or conditional discharge would be given. If this practice were to continue, it is difficult to see how it could prevent further offending:

> Unless it is maintained that the experience itself has positive elements for the under 14s, it is doubtful that it is worth the £2,500 which the Audit Commission 1996 study estimates it costs to prosecute each case.[57]

Perhaps the most remarkable feature of the Government's proposal for abolition is that its reasoning is fundamentally contradictory. Why do 10–13 year olds, who can 'obviously' tell the difference from right and wrong, require punishment to teach them that same difference? According to the Consultation Paper:

> ... a young person caught committing a crime must be challenged and a sanction must be applied to develop their sense of right and wrong, and the consequences which follow from offending.[58]

The policy is also illogical when viewed in the broader context. The Crime and Disorder Act aimed to increase the responsibility of both children and their parents. Section 8 establishes a new 'parenting order' which may require a parent to attend counselling or guidance sessions once a week for a maximum period of three months. Additional stipulations may be attached at the

---

56   See, eg, Rutherford 1992; Allen 1996.
57   Bandalli 1998:119.
58   Labour Party 1996:9.

discretion of the sentencing judge and failure to comply amounts to a summary offence.[59] It is difficult to see how both parties can be subject to punishment for the same wrongdoing. Either there was an autonomous, independent action by the child, for which they should be held responsible, or the parent has somehow contributed to the situation, and should be at fault. The child should not be blamed for inadequate parenting and the parent should not be blamed for causes of childhood criminality which are beyond their control or capabilities.[60] The Crime and Disorder Act appears to have replaced the supposed culture of excuse with a culture of conviction and blame.[61]

The arguments for abolition were, therefore, not particularly well informed and are contradictory, so why did they pass into law almost without objection?

ACCOUNTING FOR ABOLITION I:
THE POLITICS OF YOUTH JUSTICE IN THE 1990S

The most obvious reason was noted by Bandalli but not explored in any detail:

> This misunderstanding is also mirrored in much media and public comment about the subject: the view that 'any child from the age of five knows the difference between right and wrong' has wide popular appeal, as does the use of the criminal law against children.[62]

Why should this be the case? What prompted this change from the 1980s policy of diversion to the current rise in 'populist punitiveness'[63] towards children?

A combination of factors have contributed to the increase in concern about youth crime during the past decade. Political parties vying for position have re-politicised the issue of law and order, the Conservative Government retreated from the policy of its criminal justice legislation[64] with little attempt to defend its previous stance, and renewed its faith in the efficacy of custodial penalties without any supporting research. The then Prime Minister, John Major, urged us to 'condemn a little more and understand a little less' and Tony Blair pledged to be 'tough on crime and tough on the causes of crime'. This political climate was clearly influenced by supervening events. Inner city

---

59 Home Office 1997d, para 4:12; see Leng *et al* 1998:24.
60 This includes a consideration of their material context, see Goldson 1999:282.
61 See fn 71 and accompanying text where I suggest a possible explanation for this.
62 Bandalli 1998:115.
63 Newburn 1997:646 quoting Bottoms 1995.
64 Notably, the Criminal Justice Acts of 1982, 1988 and 1991.

disturbances in the summer of 1991, for example, raised the spectre of 'joyriders' and persistent young offenders, putting youth crime on the media agenda and, in 1993, the killing of James Bulger had a substantial impact. The judiciary were not isolated from these developments, but became increasingly, and publicly, embroiled in the imperative for 'tough justice' in order to stave off political intervention in their sentencing discretion, to protect their independence and credibility.[65]

Some commentators have attributed a wider significance to this escalation in the fear of youth crime, particularly following the highly publicised trial of two 10 year olds for the murder of a two year old boy:

> The death of Jamie Bulger became, in the broadest sense, a metaphor for the supposed moral decline of a society which experiences the exponential acceleration of social change in late modernity as the constant confrontation with the unfamiliar, that is, with 'risk'.[66]

Jenks's study of the culturally specific constructions of childhood seeks to explain the effect of these tragic events on public consciousness. He claims that the child has today become 'an index of civilisation' and, therefore, the health of society is reflected in the behaviour of the young. This helps to explain the punitive reaction to childhood criminality as an attempt to re-affirm social values and answers one of the contradictions inherent in this response:

> One question which needs to be addressed is why the moral degeneration of the population is readily admitted, whilst, when focusing on individual children, the difference between right and wrong becomes obvious.[67]

In committing a serious crime, children are not simply breaking the law, but are also breaching our ideal of childhood innocence; child offenders therefore become 'doubly vilified'.[68]

The Bulger killing was predominantly characterised in media discourse as a manifestation of 'evil'; a portrayal which reflected Morland J's condemnation of the crime as 'an act of unparalleled evil and barbarity'. In the extensive press coverage which followed, this 'evil nature' became separated from the act and projected onto the child actors. Curiously, therefore, this notion of evil which was originally intended to set the crime apart as an abnormal and isolated event was transposed into the debate on youth crime in general. Franklin and Petley have criticised the 'sociological naivety' of this response:

---

65 See, more generally, Dunbar and Langdon 1998; Newburn 1997.

66 Jenks 1996:127.

67 Bandalli 1998:116.

68 McDiarmid 1996 compares this response to the double bind faced by female offenders, a well documented phenomena in feminist criminology. See, also, Warner 1994:35.

> The press ... were not, on the whole, interested in any complicated social mitigation which, as far as they were concerned, served only to blur the clear lines of moral responsibility [1996, p 142].

The effect of such classification, however, is to close down any further aetiological inquiry.[69] Those who sought to provide alternative explanations became 'do-gooders' making 'excuses'.

It is relevant that the only other cause to be given any credence in subsequent media reports was inadequate parental upbringing, or more specifically, the influence of 'bad mothers'.[70] It is likely that, as a consequence of this narrow interpretation of events, both poor parents and their 'monstrous' offspring have become equally culpable in the public mind, thus accounting for the overly punitive response outlined above.[71]

A more difficult question to address is why the murder of one child by another provoked such a reaction? This was not inevitable, children who kill are not always the subjects of retribution[72] and the situation, whilst rare, is far from unique.[73]

One approach is to accept the press discourse as an accurate reflection of a nation's anxiety. As we have noted, Jenks attributes public concern to the insecurity of our current 'risk' society.[74] In many ways, the denunciation of an act as 'evil' suggests a pre-modern response to a post-modern problem – 'one emitting from a people whose cosmologies are under threat'.[75]

Franklin and Petley, on the other hand, emphasise the importance of the press construction of events in structuring the debate. They suggest that this style of coverage was motivated more by commercial imperatives and news values (1996, p 148). The sheer spectacle of the CCTV evidence made this an ideal front page story.[76]

---

69 Young 1996:111.

70 See Young 1996:117.

71 See fn 61 and accompanying text.

72 See Franklin and Petley 1996:148–53 for a comparison of the treatment of similar cases in Norway and in Britain during the last century. See, also, McDiarmid 1996:21 with respect to Scotland.

73 Cavadino 1996:9; McDiarmid 1996:13; Mitchell 1999.

74 See Beck 1992; Hudson 1996:153, drawing on the work of Feeley and Simon 1992, suggests that this change is linked to a move from a disciplinary to an actuarial society. Certainly, in relation to youth justice, there has been a clear emphasis on the efficient management of the system, from the Audit Commission Report 1996 to the re-organisation of the system in recent legislation.

75 Jenks 1996:129, with reference to the anthropological work of Douglas 1970. This could also account for the reversion to the use of overt social control in the punishment of children, which Foucault identified as a characteristic of pre-modern penality. This contradicts Foucault's assertion that more subtle forms of disciplinary power (through, for example, welfare and education), would become the norm in late modernity. See, also, Donzelot 1979.

76 See Young 1996 on the ambiguities of this visual image.

There may exist, however, a more complex relationship between public fear and media comment. Newburn, amongst others, has argued that 'the Bulger case was a 'flash-point' which ignited a new moral panic and led to the further demoralisation of young people' (1997, p 648). The term 'moral panic' was first coined by sociologist Stanley Cohen[77] to explain a punitive and, often disproportionate, response to a perceived social threat. This was alleged to be the result of the media over-reporting a phenomenon and presenting it in a stereotypical and emotional fashion. It is recognised that a recurrent focus of such 'panics' has been the issue of youth deviance.[78]

Opinions differ as to the reason for these over-reactions. Cohen argues that they mark 'boundary crises', that is:

> ... ritual confrontations between socially deviating groups and society's official agents, whose duty it is to define where the boundaries lie between right and wrong.[79]

A more radical interpretation of 'moral panics' views them as a consciously manufactured attempt to maintain government hegemony, by deliberately exploiting public fear and then intervening to provide a 'popular' solution to the problem.[80] Freeman suggests that the Bulger trial can be explained in this way, as a deliberate manipulation of images by the Government to advance a particular political agenda:

> It cannot be said that the trial threw any insight into why the crime was perpetrated. It was not intended to do so. To describe the trial as a 'show trial', as a 'political trial' almost, is hardly an exaggeration. The result was a foregone conclusion: the presence of the boys was a forensic irrelevance, though crucial in the construction of a demonology of deviance [1997, p 118].

It is unlikely, however, that the Government could cynically influence the initial reaction to the Bulger case in this way. The invocation of 'evil' was led by the judiciary and the media. King, therefore, rejects this critical notion of a moral panic and prefers to ascribe the response to 'contingency rather than causality' (1997, p 112). His conclusion, however, overlooks the fact that a government does not have to create a 'panic' to benefit from it, an awareness of the political context is central to any proper understanding of this event.[81] Arguably, in failing to counter the closure of the subsequent debate on the causes of youth crime, the Conservative administration avoided criticism and adopted a 'strategy of criminalisation'. As Lacey has observed:

---

77 Cohen 1973.

78 Pearson 1983; Boethius 1995.

79 Cohen, as quoted in Boethius 1995:46.

80 Hall 1978.

81 See Freeman 1997:115 and Minow 1997:253.

... it can be useful for government to diffuse political responsibility for certain perceived social problems by promoting their construction as a matter of individual wickedness rather than as failures of collective commitment or social policy [1995, p 11].

ACCOUNTING FOR ABOLITION II: *DOLI INCAPAX* AND THE CENSURE OF EVIL

The reader may be forgiven for asking what all this has to do with the abolition of *doli incapax*? After all, we now have a different political party in power and the doctrine of *doli incapax* did not prevent Venables and Thompson from being convicted of murder in a Crown Court. The straightforward answer is that the Bulger case raised questions about children's morality and capability, which are intimately connected with the consideration of the presumption. It also affected the wider development of policy in relation to youth crime by contributing to the climate of intolerance, which has been identified as significant in the call for abolition.[82]

There is, however, a more subtle and possibly more important factor which is often overlooked, that is, the existence of a link between legal rationality and the public coding of events. King has suggested that the legal system's 'understanding' of *doli incapax* facilitated the post-Bulger moral debate:

> The failure of the defence in the Bulger trial to rebut this presumption was a pre-condition to the subsequent moral dramatisation of the murder as the triumph of evil over innocence 1997, p 117].[83]

This is because the defendants were found to be '*doli capax*': literally, 'capable of evil'. Contrary to King's assertion, this legal decision was not a necessary pre-condition to the press and public's perception of the boys as evil (as violent reactions outside the courtroom before the trial commenced testify). It did, however, legitimise this reading of events by lending authority to its interpretation.

When the Labour Government proposed the abolition of the doctrine four years later, they deliberately recalled this emotive translation of *doli incapax*, rather than using the benign 'incapable of serious wrong' in their official literature. This is not simply a matter of semantics; just as the press continue to make reference to the Bulger case to provide an interpretative framework for contemporary discussions on youth crime, so the public relate childhood criminality to more sinister motivations. Ironically, it may be the construction

---

82   Freeman 1997:122.

83   Emphasis added. King, tellingly, misstates the legal position; it is for the prosecution and not the defence to rebut this presumption.

of the legal presumption itself which has undermined its relevance. Following Bulger, who would believe that all children were 'incapable of evil'?[84]

MISPLACED FAITH AND LEGAL CLOSURE

Given that the doctrine of *doli incapax* unwittingly legitimates the idea of an evil child who consciously commits wrongful acts, it may actually have contributed to the push for criminalisation, rather than stood in its way. Campaigners for the protection of children from criminal justice interventions overlook this paradox at their peril, by arguing in support of the presumption they may subvert their ultimate aims.

These unfortunate connotations of *doli incapax*, however, remain unrecognised. Youth justice commentators continue to express faith in the presumption and Sullivan optimistically claims that 'even post-Bulger there remains general support for the exclusion of young children from criminal trials and State punishment' (1994, p 1). Bandalli is more realistic, but, nevertheless, argues that the law could be strengthened to provide an effective test for development and maturity (1998, p 123). In particular, she suggests that the evidential requirements could have been tightened by removing the illogical 'presumption of normality', which allowed the prosecution to proceed easily on proof that the child was normal for his or her age and, therefore, must have known the nature of their actions.[85]

While it is probable that this suggested reform may have inconvenienced the prosecution, it is unlikely that it would have prevented eventual conviction. This is because the deficiencies of the doctrine are not just evidential, but result from a fundamental inability of the legal test to account adequately for lack of capacity.

The attribution of responsibility in the criminal law is premised on the principle of individual autonomy and for this reason childhood liability is problematic. If a transitional stage exists, the law is faced with the difficulty of establishing whether a young person possesses the necessary 'mischievous discretion', as otherwise the imposition of liability cannot be justified. This process is, however, selective since legal discourse only recognises certain factors as relevant to this issue and, therefore, excludes consideration of some

---

84 Franklin and Petley 1996:140 identify two competing images of childhood in the press discourse following the trial. Some journalists viewed the defendants as 'anomalous exceptions to children', thus preserving the romantic myth of childhood as an age of innocence. The majority, however, sought to redefine children as a group 'containing innate evil' and it is this changing consciousness which is referred to here. See, also, Fionda 1998 on the link between changing conceptualisations of childhood and the 'adulteration' of youth justice.

85 Crofts 1998:11.

features which may be thought by other disciplines to be significant to a child's development.

For example, Allen has identified three aspects which psychologists maintain are indicative of maturity. First, there is 'the cognitive', that is, a person's ability to know, think and reason. Secondly, there is 'the moral', concerning their ability to know right from wrong and evaluate their behaviour accordingly. The final aspect is 'the conative', that is, the individual's ability to control impulses and resist temptations (1996, p 18). Allen asserts that (contrary to popular belief) the test for *doli incapax* is primarily cognitive, it is not sufficient to determine moral capacity and does not question conative development.

This requires further explanation. To rebut the presumption of *doli incapax*, the prosecution had to prove that the child, at the time of their act, knew it to be 'seriously wrong' and 'not merely naughty or mischievous'.[86] This test has often been misinterpreted as requiring proof that a child has sufficient understanding to distinguish right from wrong.[87] Indeed, Lord Lowry has commented on the 'rather loose treatment accorded to the *doli incapax* doctrine by the textbooks'.[88] On closer examination, discernment, or the ability to tell right from wrong, is not at issue. It is enough to satisfy the legal test that the child knows that the particular act is 'seriously wrong'. They do not have to be capable of evaluating their behaviour in general. As Allen observes: 'There is a good deal more to mature moral judgment than simply knowing that certain behaviour is wrong.' He quotes Rousseau to emphasise this point:

> ... the apparent ease with which children learn is their ruin ... their shining, polished brain reflects, as in a mirror, the things you show them, but nothing sinks in. The child remembers the words and the ideas are reflected back; his hearers understand them but to him they are meaningless [1998, p 20].

In addition, this cognitive assessment does not require that children understand the consequences of their actions, or foresee why it is seriously wrong.[89] Allen notes that child offenders rarely comprehend the level of pain or distress their misbehaviour creates (1996, p 21). One example of this is given by Freeman who notes that there is an ambivalence in the thinking and

---

86 *C v DPP* [1995] 2 All ER 43.

87 See Crofts 1998:185; King 1997:117.

88 *C v DPP* [1995] 2 All ER 43, p 57F–G.

89 This contrasts with civil law competency where it is arguable that the courts do consider the child's foresight of the future consequences of their decision (see *Gillick v West Norfolk and Wisbech AHA* [1986] AC 112). This area of the law, however, can be further distinguished from the determination of criminal capacity. Competence in the civil law is concerned with the potential acquisition of 'rights', not submission to State punishment. The decision is also clearly premised on the best interests of the child (Children Act 1989, s 1), whereas the 'welfare principle' in juvenile justice is often subsumed by policy considerations (Children and Young Persons Act 1933, s 44).

reasoning of the offender in *DPP v C*, when the boy was interviewed for a BBC radio programme:

> He sees nothing wrong in lying or in offending if the peer group is also doing this. Nor does he regret attempting to steal a motorbike, only 'going to court and all that' [1997, p 125].

The law, of course, does not allow for the differing norms of right and wrong which may exist within young offenders' families or social networks. Yet, criminological knowledge has long recognised a connection between youth crime and parental criminality.[90]

This capacity to understand the consequences of their actions may also be absent even in the most serious crimes; children may claim to want to kill without any understanding of the meaning of death. When Gita Sereny asked Mary Bell whether she knew one of her victims was dead, she responded:

> Not dead, not really dead; just unconscious, unconscious like I had been unconscious ... I didn't understand the concept of death *for ever* ... I think to me it was, 'You'll come round in time for tea'.[91]

How can such a child be said to have developed an ability to make autonomous and (ir)responsible choices as the criminal law dictates?

The separation of the legal test from the question of morality was confirmed in the case of *JM (A Minor) v Runeckles*.[92] In this case, a 13 year old girl was prosecuted for stabbing another girl with a broken milk bottle. The prosecution sought to rebut the presumption of *doli incapax* with evidence that the defendant had run away from a policeman. The defence, however, argued that this only demonstrated that the girl knew her actions were against the law and not that they were morally wrong. The appeal court rejected this submission, finding that it was unnecessary to show that the child appreciated that her action was morally wrong. This stance is reflected elsewhere in the criminal law where the question of capacity is at issue. In the test for insanity, 'wrong' also means legally, and not morally, wrong,[93] although this decision has been criticised for excluding those very people who are not meaningfully responsible. As Horder explains:

> ... only the ability (even if unexercised) to evaluate conduct within the context of one's moral character gives individual (criminal) capacity and responsibility its full meaning [1993, p 302].

The problem is that liberal legal rationality cannot admit such considerations without jeopardising the integrity of the legal system. Judicial unease with the doctrine of *doli incapax* stems from its propensity to raise questions which are

---

90 See Farrington 1997:389.
91 Sereny 1998:347, italics in original.
92 (1984) 79 Cr App R 632, DC.
93 *R v Codere* (1916) 12 Cr App R 21.

not suitable for legal inquiry, involving the child's background and upbringing.[94] This could trespass on politically sensitive issues surrounding the status of law and social order. The point is not that these considerations are irrelevant in determining capacity, but that a legal test is incapable of adequately addressing them, because of the ideology which informs the Anglo-American criminal law. According to Norrie, this 'keeps the social context at bay' and, by 'presenting the question of responsibility in an apolitical, amoral and asocial form, it performs a negative and repressive political task of closure and exclusion' (1993, p 222).

CONCLUSION

Following the enactment of the Crime and Disorder Act 1998, the presumption of criminal incapacity, which applied to children between the ages of 10–14, has passed into history. Whilst the debate over its abolition has centred on the supposed protection offered by the presumption to young offenders and the extent to which their lack of maturity should be taken into account in the allocation of criminal responsibility, it would appear that both the Government and its critics have misconceived the role and function of the doctrine of *doli incapax*. It has been argued that the previous legal position perpetuated a fiction of protection which was obscured by legal forms.

It is not surprising that this fiction was overlooked: both youth justice commentators and legal authorities have displayed their ignorance of this effect. This may be due to the 'partitioning of intellectual terrain' which Lacey (1997) claims characterises Anglo-American legal culture. Criminal law, criminal justice and criminological knowledge is separated within distinct academic disciplines and, as a result, she argues: '... there is a real risk that questions which transcend the prevailing boundaries, marking off the three areas, may be lost from view.'[95]

Doli incapax is one such question. Certainly, few youth justice texts contain detailed discussions of the substantive criminal law (as opposed to the procedural implications of this change). Much has also been written by sociologists on the press construction of childhood, but few have recognised the way in which legal concepts may have contributed to this interpretation, or legitimated it *post facto*.

This disjuncture needs to be noted by those commentators who are concerned to communicate criminological insights into youth crime in order

---

94 The forensic psychologists who gave evidence in the Bulger trial have expressed their frustration at being unable to present the context of and possible causal factors in the boys offending. See BBC Documentary 1998.

95 Lacey 1997:439.

to inform critiques of the youth justice system. Just as the relevance of social theory has been acknowledged in understanding how political, cultural and economic imperatives continue to blur the policy agenda,[96] the exclusionary effects of legal culture must also be recognised. Criminologists should not ignore the insights of critical legal scholars into the operation of legal doctrine, as knowledge about crime and criminality may be reconstructed within law and its impact will be constrained by this ideological framework. King (1997, p 120) and Freeman (1997, p 130), for example, suggest that the possibility of scientific inquiry into the causes of the Bulger tragedy was limited or 'enslaved' by law. Experts were only called to testify to the boys' legal responsibility, that is, their capacity as defined by law and not the 'psy' sciences.[97] Similarly, Norrie explains how legal judgment in the Bulger case paralysed society's ability to judge the crime, by excluding alternative accounts which failed to fit the idea of an autonomous, morally and politically neutral legal subject: 'Legal judgments, in other words, still set the agenda and structure the field in which other discourses have their play' (1997, p 2).[98]

From this perspective, the abolition of the presumption of *doli incapax* has removed a legal concept which obscured the issues underlying arguments for the protection of children who commit crimes above the age of 10. Therefore, perhaps those who are concerned about the criminalisation of children should not be mourning the death of the doctrine but seizing the reconstructive moment which its removal presents. By abolishing the presumption, the arbitrary and strict age of criminal responsibility in England and Wales has become more apparent and, therefore, more difficult to justify on any principled basis.

---

96 See, eg, Sparks 1997:415.
97 See Johnstone 1997 for a more detailed discussion of the relation between substantive law, penality and psychiatry.
98 Norrie 1997:6.

CHAPTER 4

MAGISTRATES IN THE YOUTH COURT: TEACHING OLD 'BEAKS' NEW TRICKS

Stuart Vernon JP

INTRODUCTION

Lay magistrates sitting in the youth court are a central element in the administration of the youth justice system. They work within a system which has historically been characterised by tensions in policy, politics and practice. Today, magistrates appointed to the Youth Panel and sitting in the youth court are facing significant changes to their practice as a result of the implementation of the Crime and Disorder Act 1998 and the provisions of Part 1 of the Youth Justice and Criminal Evidence Act 1999. It is likely that changes in practice required by these legislative initiatives (which are to be introduced in stages until 2002), will redraw the current set of tensions experienced by youth justice magistrates. These tensions are themselves a product of the history of the youth justice system and of some more recent legislation, including the Criminal Justice Act 1991 and the Criminal Justice and Public Order Act 1994.

This chapter seeks to identify significant features of the youth justice system, both historical and contemporary, and to suggest the tensions between them. It will also point to important changes currently being encountered in the youth court as a result of the phased implementation of the Crime and Disorder Act 1998 and the likely impact of the Youth Justice and Criminal Evidence Act 1999. Particular emphasis is given to the work of youth justice magistrates, the lay element of the system, who will have to work within familiar tensions and with new policies and practices.

THE YOUTH PANEL

The Youth Panel is constituted by magistrates chosen by the whole bench of magistrates for a petty sessional area; the Panel is selected every three years. Youth Panel members are chosen for being 'particularly well qualified to deal with juveniles' and they must receive distinct induction and refresher training as members. It is recommended that justices aged over 50 should not be appointed to the youth panel for the first time. The retirement age for the Youth Panel used to be set at 65, though this was raised to 70 in 1991.

TENSIONS IN THE WORK OF YOUTH JUSTICE MAGISTRATES – LEGACIES FROM OLD AND RECENT HISTORY

The history of the youth justice system has been characterised by numerous changes in politics, policy and practice. Indeed, any description and comment on the system, if taken from the establishment of the juvenile court in 1908, frequently counterpoises the words to describe the sometime dominant characteristics of the system – treatment and punishment, justice and welfare, care and control – and suggests the tensions that exist between these characteristics.

The current youth court was established by the Criminal Justice Act 1991. Prior to this, the Children Act 1989 had abolished the old juvenile court by establishing a family proceedings court and creating a new distinct juvenile court, later to become the youth court, with an exclusively criminal jurisdiction. The family proceedings court administers the matrimonial jurisdiction of the magistrates' courts and hears public and private law matters concerning children under the provisions of the Children Act.

The model of the juvenile court ended by the Children Act 1989 had existed for most of this century, having been established by the Children Act 1908. The significance of the 1908 Act lay in its establishment of a court to deal with young offenders separately from adults. Though the court was constituted by the same justices who sat in the adult court, its existence as a distinct court reflected, at the very least, a recognition of the differing needs of juvenile and adult defendants and offenders. Importantly, the juvenile court also had jurisdiction over children and young people thought to be in need of care or supervision, and this 'joint' or 'dual' role, both a care and a criminal jurisdiction one, was a major (and often criticised) feature of the juvenile court until the two were separated by the Children Act 1989. Indeed, this feature of the old juvenile court can be seen as a dominant factor in the construction of the tensions which became a characteristic of the juvenile justice system and which, arguably, were a central concern of the numerous investigations into its principles and administration.

The Maloney Committee 1927 carried out an important review of the English juvenile courts and their conclusions were to have a significant impact on the subsequent development of the court and the nature of juvenile justice:

> The Committee viewed delinquents as responsible for their own fate; their law breaking was conscious and deliberate and, as such, the wickedness of their action had to be brought home to them by the formality of courtroom procedures. It was also, however, influenced by a further image: that of victims of social or psychological conditions beyond their control.

> What is interesting about the report is that these dual images of the delinquent were placed, not side by side, but in sequence. In the first instance (the

adjudicative stage), the offence was viewed as a conscious act of wickedness. Once the act was proved or admitted, however, it was viewed as a product of personal or external forces and dispositions were to be reached with these in mind.[1]

The recommendations of the Committee were legislated for in the Children and Young Persons Act 1932, later consolidated in the Children and Young Persons Act 1933. Though the juvenile court retained its criminal jurisdiction, s 44 of the Act specified an important welfare principle that has remained on the statute book to this day:

> Every court, in dealing with a child or young person who is brought before it, either as an offender or otherwise, shall have regard to the welfare of the child or young person and shall in a proper case take steps for removing him from undesirable surroundings, or for securing that proper provision is made for his education and training.

This tension in the philosophy and practice of the juvenile court, most frequently encapsulated in the counterpoising of 'justice' and 'welfare', is clear in the recommendations of the Maloney Committee and in the provisions of the 1933 Act. The juvenile court thus had both a care and a criminal jurisdiction; this latter jurisdiction was concerned with guilt and innocence, and then with punishment and welfare. However, this jurisdiction was discharged by magistrates who were specially trained and appointed, but who also sat and were influenced by their work in the ordinary magistrates' courts where the concerns of 'welfare' were of little concern.

Subsequent models of the juvenile court, and of the juvenile justice system, have reproduced other manifestations of this familiar tension. The 1960 report of the Children and Young Persons Committee (the Ingleby Report) supported a continuation of an established trend toward the interests of 'welfare' by recommending the retention of the juvenile court, but with a lessening of its criminal jurisdiction. The 1960s saw policy debates on juvenile crime reflecting an increased recognition of deprivation as a cause of offending and 'welfare' as a response to it. This debate culminated in the passing of the Children and Young Persons Act 1969, which provided for the abolition of a criminal jurisdiction for the offender under the age of 14, and for the restricted criminal prosecution of the older juvenile offender who would only be prosecuted in very rare circumstances. The majority of juvenile offenders were to be dealt with by local authorities and the courts (if necessary), under care and supervision proceedings. Though these provisions were never implemented, another element of the legislation, under which a care order could be imposed as a criminal sentence, did become an important feature of the juvenile justice system until its use became discredited by the early 1980s.

---

1   Morris and Giller 1987:70–71.

It has been argued that the 1969 Act was a logical extension of the underlying 'joint' or 'dual' jurisdiction philosophy of the Children Act 1908:

> The aim was to spare young offenders the stigma of criminality by dealing with them as far as possible outside the criminal law, and to support and treat them in their families and in the community.[2]

A gradual disillusionment with the provisions of the 1969 Act, and with the philosophy that underpinned it, occurred in the 1970s with a rise in youth crime and a reluctance of youth magistrates to implement the more welfare based provisions of the Act. This led, ultimately, to a re-assertion of a justice orientation within the juvenile justice system so that the juvenile court came to reflect many of the features of the adult magistrates' courts.

> The 1982 Criminal Justice Act [has] re-introduced three fundamental principles which mark a return from the welfare ethos of the 1960s to a more classical model of the administration of criminal justice. These three principles are: the appropriateness of adversarial proceedings, determinate sentences and proportionate sentences.[3]

This process was further enhanced by the changes that were occasioned by the implementation of the Children Act 1989 and the Criminal Justice Act 1991. The Children Act took non-criminal jurisdiction away from the juvenile court, and the 1991 Act established the youth court, imposing upon it a set of sentencing principles (primarily, that the seriousness of an offence was to be reflected in the severity of the sentence) which were shared with the adult court:

> The [Criminal Justice Act 1991] itself represented a shift away from 'welfare', in favour of a 'justice' or 'punishment' model for sentencing [Gibson et al 1994].

These developments should be understood as representing shifts in the balance between these two principles. They represent a 'pre-Crime and Disorder Act context' within which Youth Panel magistrates have administered the court based element of the youth justice system for the last few years.

For magistrates sitting in the youth court, sentencing provides the forum within which these tensions and shifts in policy and practice have most frequently to be encountered and negotiated. In this sense, sentencing in the youth court may be seen as an important terrain in which the tensions between welfare and justice, treatment and punishment, care and control are played out. The provisions of the Criminal Justice Act 1991, subsequently amended by the Criminal Justice Act 1993, and the secure training order provisions of the Criminal Justice and Public Order Act 1994, indicated a clear

---

2   Skryme 1994.
3   Morris and Giller 1987.

move towards a 'justice and punishment' orientation, particularly in the sentencing of persistent young offenders.

It might have been thought that the establishment of an exclusively criminal youth court in 1991 would have provided an opportunity for the development of a youth justice jurisprudence distinct from the unquestionably welfare orientated new family proceedings court. This has not proved to be the case. The tensions between welfare and justice, treatment and punishment, care and control have survived. Youth court magistrates are still required, under s 44 of the Children and Young Persons Act 1933, to be concerned with the welfare of offenders, whilst 'justice' based sentencing practices are emphasised by the 'just desserts' principle of the 1991 Act. The complexity of balancing the two is clearly evidenced by the tasks facing youth court sentencers contemplating the imposition of a community sentence. They are required to impose a sentence which, in terms of the deprivation of liberty, reflects the seriousness of the offence, whilst at the same time choosing a sentence which is the most appropriate for the offender, in the sense of being one which is most likely to prevent or deter re-offending.

The secure training order provisions of the Criminal Justice and Public Order Act 1994 represented a further shift towards a more punitive response to offending, particularly by young persistent offenders.[4] Again, youth court magistrates have to balance the clear policy direction of these provisions against the continuing influence of the s 44 welfare principle. Can it really be said that the imposition of a detention and training order is in the interests of the welfare of a 12, 13 or 14 year old offender, even if they are persistent and satisfy the custodial criteria of s 1 of the Criminal Justice Act 1991?

For youth court magistrates, the shift in policy represented by the 1991 and 1994 Acts, has to be balanced against the welfare principle enshrined in s 44 of the 1933 Act and replicated in a different jurisdiction by the welfare principle of the Children Act 1989. The challenges represented by these tensions should not be underestimated, nor should the disquiet and unease experienced by youth panel magistrates in the face of continual change within a youth justice system that was, by the end of the 1980s, becoming highly politicised.

These challenges are being further enhanced by the implementation of the Crime and Disorder Act, by the politics and policies that characterise its provisions, and by the radical changes incorporated in Pt 1 of the Youth Justice and Criminal Evidence Act 1999 which will effectively transfer first time offenders who plead guilty from the youth court to youth offender panels. The chapter will return to these matters later, after consideration of other tensions influencing the work of the youth panel.

---

4 Secure training orders were replaced by detention and training orders. These orders are provided for in the Crime and Disorder Act 1998, ss 73–79. The Act provides for the possibility of their extension to 10 and 11 year old offenders.

BEYOND WELFARE AND JUSTICE, TREATMENT AND PUNISHMENT, CARE AND CONTROL – OTHER TENSIONS

To these historically familiar tensions, others may be added. Here, mention will be made of four important features of the youth court which themselves constitute important tensions in the youth justice system in relation to both their administration and interaction.

Age related sentencing

The principle of age related sentencing is an important feature of the youth court. The principle has two elements; first, that the range of available sentences increases with the age of the offender and, secondly, that the generally more punitive and more serious sentences are available only for the older age range of juvenile or youth offenders. This principle has been a familiar feature of the youth justice system for many years. A recent articulation of a rationale for the principle came with the introduction of the Criminal Justice Act 1991:

> Courts will have more flexible sentencing arrangements for [16 and 17 year old offenders], reflecting the fact that offenders of this age are at a transitional stage between childhood and adulthood. Some will be more developed and independent than others. Bringing all offenders of this age group within the jurisdiction of the youth court, and providing the youth court with a flexible range of disposals for offenders of this age, will enable the penalty given in each case to reflect the individual's development and circumstances [Home Office 1991a].

In some respects, this rationale reflects the philosophy of the *Gillick* case[5] and of the Children Act 1989, both of which recognise a process of intellectual and emotional maturation, so that rights and responsibilities reflect maturity and independence. Though age related sentencing in the youth court does not evidence this level of sophistication, the principle is accommodated in statutory provisions which determine the age thresholds for the imposition of particular sentences.

Therefore, the complex sentencing task facing youth court magistrates involves balancing competing principles, namely, the age of the offender, the range of available sentences, the welfare of the offender, the 'just deserts' principle, and the sentencing thresholds of the Criminal Justice Act 1991 that require an assessment of offence seriousness as a determinant of the category of available sentence.

---

5   *Gillick v West Norfolk and Wisbech AHA* [1986] AC 112.

Doli incapax

The principle of *doli incapax* was a well established feature of the youth justice system for many years. Though it has now been abolished by the implementation of s 34 of the Crime and Disorder Act 1998 it incorporated an important understanding about the culpability and responsibility of very young offenders that continues to merit discussion.

Though the age of criminal responsibility in England and Wales is set at 10, the principle of *doli incapax* applied to defendants under the age of 14; it established a presumption that a defendant, within the age range of 10–14, was incapable of committing a crime. The presumption could be rebutted by the prosecution bringing evidence to establish, beyond a reasonable doubt, that the child defendant knew at the time of the offence that their criminal act was seriously wrong.

The proposal to abolish the presumption was canvassed in the Consultation Paper, *Tackling Youth Crime*, published by the Home Office in September 1997, and confirmed in the White Paper, *No More Excuses – A New Approach to Tackling Youth Crime in England and Wales*, published in November 1997:

> The Government believes that, in presuming that children of this age do not know the difference between naughtiness and serious wrongdoing, the notion of *doli incapax* is contrary to common sense. The practical difficulties, which the presumption presents for the prosecution, can stop some children who should be prosecuted and punished for their offences from being convicted or from even going to court. This is not in the interests of justice, of victims or of the young people themselves [Home Office 1997d].

With the abolition of *doli incapax*, the courts, both the youth court and the Crown Court, are unable to consider issues surrounding the maturity and development of the defendant until sentencing, unless they are such as to prevent the prosecution establishing the necessary mens rea for a conviction of the offence charged.

In this respect, the youth justice system is now the same as the adult criminal justice system; defendants of 10, 13, 17 and 27 will all be held equally culpable and responsible for their criminality. This 'universality' of culpability now stands in marked contrast to an age differentiated sentencing system which operates for sentencing young offenders.

It is difficult to judge the impact of the abolition of *doli incapax* on the work of youth court magistrates. In practice, the issue was rarely canvassed in the youth court. It is likely that decisions made by the police and the Crown Prosecution Service concerning the administration of final warnings (previously cautions) and decisions about charge and prosecution effectively filter those that appear in the youth court.[6] If this is the case, then the abolition of doli incapax will have little impact on the work of the youth court, though it represents a significant change of principle.

Parental responsibility

Parental responsibility has become an important part of youth justice policy and practice. The ability to bind over a parent to ensure the good behaviour of their child had been part of the provisions of the Children and Young Persons Act 1969 but had rarely been used by magistrates who were unconvinced that it would work. Nonetheless, the Government used the Criminal Justice Act 1991 to re-emphasise the importance of the principle:

> Crime prevention begins at home. Parents have the most influence on their children's development. From their children's earliest years, parents can, and should, help them develop as responsible, law abiding citizens. They should ensure that their children are aware of the existence of rules and laws and the need for them; and that they respect other people and their property ... when young people offend, the law has a part to play in reminding parents of their responsibilities [Home Office 1990b].

In the years since the implementation of the 1991 Act, legislation has sought to impose parental responsibility in three ways: (a) by attendance at court; (b) by the payment of fines, compensation and costs; and (c) by parental bindovers. The 1991 Act imposed a duty on the youth court to require the attendance of parents or guardians in cases involving defendants under the age of 16 'unless and to the extent that the court is satisfied that it would be unreasonable to require such attendance, having regard to the circumstances of the case' (s 34A(1)(b) of the Children and Young Persons Act 1933). In relation to defendants aged 16 and 17, the Act established a *power* to require attendance rather than a *duty*.

In relation to fines, compensation orders and costs, the youth court, when dealing with offenders under 16, is under a duty to impose the order on the parent or guardian unless it would be unreasonable to do so having regard to the circumstances of the case. Where the offender is aged 16 or 17, the court has a power rather than a duty to require the parent or guardian to pay (s 55(1) of the Children and Young Persons Act 1933).

Parental bindovers are provided for by s 58 of the Criminal Justice Act 1991. Where the offender is aged under 16, the court is under a duty to order the parent or guardian to enter into a financial recognisance to take proper care of or exercise proper control over the offender:

---

6 Cautions for youth offenders have been replaced by police reprimands and final warnings: Crime and Disorder Act 1998, ss 65 and 66.

... if it is satisfied, having regard to the circumstances of the case, that their exercise would be desirable in the interests of preventing the commission by him of further offences [s 58(1)(a) of the Criminal Justice Act 1991].

Indeed, where the court decides not to impose a bindover it must announce in open court why it has decided so to do. In relation to offenders aged 16 and 17, the court merely has a power to impose a bindover.

Parents or guardians must consent to the imposition of the bindover, but an unreasonable refusal to consent can be met with a fine of up to £1,000. Breach of a bindover may result in forfeiture of some or all of the recognisance.

The increased parental responsibility provisions of the 1991 Act, particularly those concerned with bindovers, were subject to widespread criticism:

> It is felt by a wide range of organisations, including the Magistrates' Association, that, if implemented, these proposals are not only unlikely to achieve the Government's objective, but are likely, in many instances, to damage such little cohesion as may survive in already fraught and vulnerable families. One of the most extreme of these proposals concerns the binding over of parents for their children's good behaviour. This power already exists under the Children and Young Persons Act 1969, but for good reason is rarely used ... ['Editorial' (1991) 46 The Magistrate 11].

> This is the kind of proposal that makes perfect sense to middle class ministers, who generally leave the taming of adolescence to their children's boarding schools. For, say, the single mother in Brixton, struggling against odds to keep a young person on track, they represent only a threat. Many such parents will be tempted to wash their hands of their responsibilities. Parental influence – the last, best hope of deflecting the youngster from a life of crime – will be removed. The magistrates do not want these powers. Parliament should not force them to have them ['Leader' (1990) The Times, 10 November].

Despite such criticisms, the Criminal Justice and Public Order Act 1994 extended parental bindovers to community sentencing to make parents responsible for ensuring that offenders comply with the requirements of the sentence. There is clear anecdotal evidence of significant local differences in the use of such orders and of lukewarm enthusiasm amongst youth court magistrates for them. The responsibility of parents is further emphasised by the introduction of parenting orders by the Crime and Disorder Act 1998.

Managerialism

Tensions between the interests of justice and interests in the administration of justice are not new. It is clear, however, that they are becoming an increasingly important issue for all those involved in the criminal justice system.

Magistrates in the youth courts have always been encouraged to avoid delay and they are familiar with more recent strictures against unnecessary adjournments. To the extent that these practices are in line with the equivalent Children Act principle that delay is contrary to the welfare of the child, there can be no argument. However, when they conflict with the principles of the proper interests of justice, such as adequate legal representation and time to give and take proper instructions, there must be cause for concern.

Changes in the funding of magistrates' courts now mean that the throughput and completion of cases is a factor in funding. Public expenditure restrictions have had an impact on funding for criminal legal aid. Regular guidance from the Lord Chancellor has encouraged all those involved in the youth justice system to reduce delay and establish fast track procedures for persistent offenders. These official encouragements can be seen as being directed towards increasing efficiency in the youth justice system and are well understood as such by youth court magistrates. Consequently, their work now includes the sometimes difficult task of balancing the demands of increased efficiency against the sometimes more complex and less immediate imperatives associated with the interests of justice.

RÉSUMÉ

The argument, then, is that youth court magistrates are faced with a complex set of politics, practices and provisions. Some of these result from the historical legacy of the dual care and crime jurisdiction of the original juvenile court, particularly the tensions between welfare and justice, treatment and punishment, care and control. Their work is also shaped by other principles and practices, such as age related sentencing, any remaining legacy from the presumption of doli incapax, the principle of parental responsibility (and the provisions that provide for its imposition), and the increasing significance of the imperatives of efficient and economic youth justice system administration.

WORKING WITHIN THE PRINCIPLES OF THE CRIMINAL JUSTICE ACT 1991 AND THE CRIMINAL JUSTICE AND PUBLIC ORDER ACT 1994

The point has already been made that the law and practice of the youth justice system are articulated and implemented in an increasingly politicised youth justice debate. Magistrates are not external to these debates, nor are they immune to the politics that generate changes in the law. It is also the pace and rapidity of change that is forcing youth court magistrates to rethink and change their practice with increasing frequency. The 1990s saw a disproportionate number of important legislative initiatives in the field of criminal justice and we now turn to consider the impact for the youth justice system of the principles and provisions of the Criminal Justice Act 1991, as amended by the Criminal Justice Act 1993, and the Criminal Justice and Public Order Act 1994.

THE ESTABLISHMENT OF THE YOUTH COURT

Section 70 of the 1991 Act renamed the juvenile court as the youth court to reflect the fact that 17 year olds were to be brought within its jurisdiction:

> The present juvenile court will be renamed the youth court. When the provisions of the Children Act 1989 are implemented, the juvenile court will no longer hear care cases ... The age balance of those appearing in criminal cases before the juvenile court is changing. In 1988, nearly 90% were aged 14–16. Increasingly, those under 14 are being dealt with without bringing them before a court. If the proposal for the court to hear most cases with defendants aged 17 is implemented, it is estimated that about three-quarters of the defendants appearing before it will be aged 16 or 17. The name of the court should reflect this considerable change in its responsibilities [Home Office 1990b].

The recruitment of 17 year olds into the jurisdiction of the youth court was consequent upon their inclusion, with 16 year old offenders, into a category of 'near adults', a category of offenders who were to benefit from the availability of flexible sentencing provisions available to the new court.

SENTENCING

The sentencing principles of the Criminal Justice Act 1991 apply both in the youth court and in all other criminal courts. Also, the principle of proportionality between the seriousness of the offence and the severity of the sentence applies to the whole age range of the youth court. This principle utilises three categories of sentence within two sentencing thresholds to distinguish the range of appropriate sentences and reflect offence seriousness. The Act provides that the range of community sentences applies to those offences that are 'serious enough' for such a sentence. Where this is not the case, then the court may only consider a discharge (absolute or conditional) or a fine. Custodial sentencing is reserved for circumstances specified in s 1.

Section 1(2) provides that a court shall not pass a custodial sentence unless it is of the opinion:

> (a) that the offence, or the combination of the offence and one or more offences associated with it, was so serious that only such a sentence can be justified for the offence; or

    (b) where the offence is a violent or sexual offence, that only such a sentence would be adequate to protect the public from serious harm from him.

Thus, the seriousness of an offence is the central issue for sentencing in both the adult and the youth court. A conclusion on seriousness is to be reached by magistrates after consideration of aggravating and mitigating factors concerning the offence and mitigating factors concerning the offender. Section 28(1) of the 1991 Act provides that, in mitigating a sentence, the court may take into account any matters that it considers to be relevant. Section 29 provides that, when considering seriousness, the court may take previous convictions of the offender into account and, additionally, any failure of the offender to respond to previous sentences. The court is under a duty to treat the commission of an offence whilst on bail as an aggravating factor.

Magistrates are familiar with the sentencing principles of the 1991 Act and all are trained to use a system of structured sentencing in which an assessment of the seriousness of the offence precedes any concern with offender mitigation. Youth court magistrates, however, face additional challenges. Age related sentencing has already been discussed and, in the youth court, the issue of offender mitigation is likely to assume an increased importance, because it will involve issues relating to maturity, development and welfare. Maturity and development are specifically identified as relevant when sentencing 'near adult' offenders of 16 and 17. Furthermore, the welfare of the offender is also a factor which the court is required to consider under the terms of s 44 of the Children and Young Persons Act 1933 across the whole age range.

The Criminal Justice and Public Order Act 1994 is a significant piece of legislation in relation to sentencing in the youth court. The Act introduced secure training orders (though youth court magistrates only recently had to consider such a sentencing option because of delays in implementing the relevant sections due to delays related to the building of appropriate centres). Such orders were designed as a custodial and supervisory sentence for persistent young offenders. Section 1(5) provides:

The court shall not make a secure training order unless it is satisfied –

    (a) that the offender was not less than 12 years of age when the offence for which he is to be dealt with by the court was committed;

    (b) that the offender has been convicted of three or more imprisonable offences; and

    (c) that the offender, either on this or a previous occasion –

        (i) has been found by a court to be in breach of a supervision order under the Children and Young Persons Act 1969; or

        (ii) has been convicted of an imprisonable offence committed whilst he was subject to such a supervision order.

The seriousness of the offence was also an issue in deciding whether to impose a secure training order, because the order could not be made unless the provisions of s 1(2) of the Criminal Justice Act 1991 are also satisfied (noted earlier).

Ironically, youth court magistrates began to encounter the challenges of secure training orders at a time when they knew that they were to be replaced by detention and training orders. The implementation of these orders took place in April 2000 and they constitute a new custodial sentence for youth offenders, except those convicted and sentenced for a grave offence under s 53 of the Children and Young Persons Act 1933, replacing both secure training orders and custody in a young offenders institution for those between the ages of 12 and 17 inclusive.

The 1994 Act provided for an increased use of custodial sentencing in the youth court and a downward extension of the age at which a young person could be sent to a custodial institution by youth court magistrates. It is clear, however, that the provision originated in an era in which increased punitivism appeared to have a measure of populist support. For many youth justice magistrates, such politics and provisions sit uneasily with the welfare provision of s 44.

THE CHARACTER OF THE YOUTH COURT

Prior to the Crime and Disorder Act 1998, the youth justice system was, arguably, moving towards a model that shared many characteristics with the adult court. Indeed, until very recently, it was even possible to envisage an amalgamation of the youth court and the adult magistrates' court. Though there are significant differences in sentencing powers for offenders under 16, there have been few differences in available sentences for 16 and 17 year old offenders and for adults, or in the process of the youth court when compared to the adult magistrates' court. The features which have historically characterised a distinct youth justice system were, particularly under the influence of the 1991 Act, ameliorated so that the youth and adult courts had much in common. There is little doubt that the 1998 Act has significantly altered these developments. Differences between the adult courts and the youth court have significantly increased as a result of the implementation of the 1998 Act and will be by the establishment of youth offender panels under the provisions of the Youth Justice and Criminal Evidence Act 1999.

In the tension between welfare and justice principles, the most recent balance, determined largely by the Criminal Justice Act 1991, has been firmly on the side of 'justice' in both the youth court and the adult court. Similarly, the balance between treatment and punishment has shifted firmly towards punishment under the influence of both the 1991 Act and the Criminal Justice and Public Order Act 1994. Youth court magistrates have had to work within the tensions produced by these developments. These tensions are highlighted when it is recognised that magistrates are working with a series of legislative provisions conceived largely within a justice orientation, but also in close day to day co-operation with a social work profession that has been trained in a welfare tradition and is concerned to see that the welfare principle of s 44 continues to influence sentencing decisions in the youth court.

National Standards for the Supervision of Offenders in the Community (Home Office, Department of Health and Welsh Office 1995) included the following statement in relation to the preparation of pre-sentence reports (PSR) on children or young persons:

> Where a PSR is being prepared on a child or young person, the report writer must take into account section 44 of the Children and Young Persons Act 1933 which requires the court to have regard to the welfare of the individual. The United Nations Convention on the Rights of the Child, to which the United Kingdom is a signatory, also requires that in all actions concerning children, that is, those aged below 18 years, in courts of law the best interests of the child shall be the primary consideration. The report writer should, therefore, take account of the age of the young offender, his or her family background and educational circumstances.

WORKING WITH THE CRIME AND DISORDER ACT 1998 – OLD AND NEW TENSIONS

The implementation of the Crime and Disorder Act 1998 promises yet more shifts in the philosophy, politics and practice of youth justice. Such changes are presenting youth panel magistrates with considerable challenges to the orthodoxies that have been learnt and practised in recent years.

True to the history of juvenile and youth justice, the Crime and Disorder Act is itself characterised by contradictions and tensions in provisions dealing with young offenders. This time, the balance to be drawn by youth justice practitioners, including youth court magistrates, involves consideration of offending, punishment, intervention and rehabilitation. In this new legislative regime, offending by a child or young person may trigger punishment, or intervention to prevent further offending, or both punishment and intervention.

A NEW YOUTH JUSTICE SYSTEM?

Significant changes to the youth justice system were indicated by the new Labour Government shortly after it came to power in May 1997. In the autumn of that year, the Home Office issued three consultation papers concerned with reforming the youth justice system: *Tackling Youth Crime; New National Focus on Youth Crime;* and *Tackling Delays in the Youth Justice System.*

The agenda for reform was set by an identification of problems in the youth justice system listed in *Tackling Youth Crime* as follows:

- it lacks public credibility and clear aims;
- the current system of repeat cautions is not working;
- re-offending continues on bail;
- the youth justice system is too cumbersome and slow;
- there is a lack of supervised community based interventions programmes aimed at changing the behaviour of young offenders early in their careers;
- the current system of custodial orders and facilities is disjointed and variable and needs a radical overhaul;
- there is an absence of national strategic direction.

The three consultation papers contained important proposals for changes in law, procedure and services to tackle the analysis presented. The period for consultation was very short, with a White Paper being issued in November 1997 entitled *No More Excuses – A New Approach to Tackling Youth Crime in England and Wales* (1997c). The White Paper closely reflected the proposals in the three consultation papers.

In relation to issues of responsibility for crime and punishment, the White Paper made a number of comments and proposed a series of new orders:

> To prevent offending and re-offending by young people, we must stop making excuses for youth crime. Children above the age of criminal responsibility are generally mature enough to be accountable for their actions and the law should recognise this. Chapter 4 sets out plans to abolish the English common law presumption of doli incapax and for requiring more young offenders to make reparation to their victims, including through a new reparation order.

> Parents have a crucial role in preventing their children committing criminal and anti-social acts. Chapter 4 sets out ways of reinforcing parents' responsibilities through a new parenting order to help parents turn their children away from crime [Home Office 1997d].

These provisions have all been legislated for and the two new orders are likely to have a significant impact on the work of youth court magistrates, despite continuing concerns surrounding the utility of court orders to enforce the responsibility of parents for the offences of their children.[7] The White Paper confirmed the Government's central concern to provide for earlier, more effective intervention to prevent offending:

> There will be a new focus on nipping crime in the bud – stopping children at risk from getting involved in crime and preventing early criminal behaviour from escalating into persistent or serious offending. Chapter 5 sets out new local authority, police and court powers to protect young children from being

---

7 Reparation orders are provided for in the Crime and Disorder Act 1998, ss 67 and 68. Parenting orders are set out in ss 8–10.

drawn into criminal and anti-social behaviour – the child safety order and the local child curfew.

A new police reprimand and final warning scheme will replace cautioning for young offenders. Community intervention programmes will follow for offenders receiving a final warning to address offending behaviour and try to turn them away from crime before they end up in court.

A new community punishment will be introduced to help prevent re-offending. The action plan order will combine punishment, reparation and rehabilitation.

If community intervention does not work, and for young offenders found guilty of serious crimes, custodial penalties are necessary to protect the public. Public protection is best served if punishment is combined with rehabilitation so that young offenders are equipped to lead law abiding and useful lives once they are released from custody.

A new detention and training order will combine custody and community supervision to punish and rehabilitate youngsters whose crimes require secure detention. The Government will also give courts clear powers to remand juveniles to secure accommodation where this is necessary to protect the public and prevent further offending [Home Office 1997d].

Again, all these proposals have been legislated for.[8] They provide an insight into the character of the new youth justice system in which punishment, rehabilitation, intervention and prevention are the new paramount principles. These are articulated, not in isolation from each other, but in partnership with one another. The new principles underpin all stages of the youth justice process – charge, prosecution, court appearance, sentencing and supervision. All agencies are involved in a new partnership – the police, the Crown Prosecution Service, the courts, youth court magistrates, parents, those involved in education and social work. The 'justice' orientation of the Criminal Justice Act 1991 and of the youth court is being superseded by a more complex, pro-active and interventionist model.[9] Indeed, the 1998 Act goes as far as defining a statutory aim in s 37:

37 (1) It shall be the principal aim of the youth justice system to prevent offending by children and young persons.

(2) In addition to any other duty to which they are subject, it shall be the duty of all persons and bodies carrying out functions in relation to the youth justice to have regard to the aim.

---

8   Child safety orders are set out in ss 11–13. Local child curfews are provided for in ss 14 and 15 and were implemented in September 1998. Action plan orders are set out in ss 69 and 70.

9   There is one particularly interesting return to the historical traditions of juvenile justice provided by the fact that applications for child safety orders will be made by local authority social services departments and heard in the family proceedings court. While this initiative follows logically from duties imposed on local authorities by the Children Act 1989 concerning crime prevention, it also begins to shade the boundaries drawn between the distinct jurisdictions of the youth court and the family proceedings court established by the Children Act 1989 and the Criminal Justice Act 1991.

Concerns with managing the youth justice system more efficiently were reflected in the White Paper proposals on 'faster, more efficient procedures'.

> Delays in the youth justice system can frustrate and anger victims and give young offenders the impression that they can offend with impunity. The Government's top priority is to halve the time taken for persistent young offenders to get from arrest to sentence.

> Delays will be cut by introducing streamlined procedures and better case management and by setting mandatory time limits for all criminal proceedings involving young people. Strict time limits for persistent young offenders, backed by performance targets, will ensure fast track justice and a speedy response to the offending of those individuals from whom the public most needs protection [Home Office 1997d].

The Act and other regulations have provided for these 'process' proposals. It will be interesting to see whether tensions will develop between what may be seen as largely managerialist concerns and the important imperatives of the interests of justice.

These extracts from the White Paper and the comment made upon them give some indication of the character of the new youth justice system and of the provisions that have been legislated to achieve the objectives of the Government. The Act is requiring youth court magistrates to give effect to new principles and practices. What is not clear is how much of the old principles and practices will remain. The s 44 welfare principle remains on the statute book, age related sentencing continues, parental responsibility has been increased. Tensions between welfare and justice, treatment and punishment, care and control, are having to be re-interpreted to accommodate new objectives, particularly those which involve intervention in the life of a young person and his or her family to prevent (further) offending. Clear distinctions between the adult criminal justice system and the youth justice system, and between the youth court and the adult magistrates' court, have been drawn, thereby reversing the trend towards similarity, which has been a feature of youth justice practice over the last 15 years or more.

A NEW YOUTH COURT?

In addition to these challenges for youth justice magistrates, the White Paper presented an analysis of, and an agenda for reforming the youth court. Provisions reflecting these proposals are now included in the youth offender panel provisions of the Youth Justice and Criminal Evidence Act 1999:

> A frank assessment of the current approach of the youth court must conclude that, all too often, inadequate attention is given to changing offending behaviour. This is not the fault of individuals working within the system. It is encouraged by the court's very structures and procedures. The Government is

determined to tackle these failings head on. The purpose of the youth court must change from simply deciding guilt or innocence and then issuing a sentence. In most cases, an offence should trigger a wider enquiry into the circumstances and nature of the offending behaviour. This requires in turn a fundamental change of approach within the youth court system [Home Office 1997d].

It seems, therefore, that the youth court and youth panel are to be recruited to the diverse team of agencies and profession(al)s being assembled to take on the task of preventing further and future offending. The adult magistrates' court model, in which guilt and innocence is decided and sentence passed, is criticised as inadequate for the challenges presented by youth offending.

The argument implicit in this criticism, that youth court magistrates have not been involved in tackling offending, will be resented by many magistrates. Their task of balancing proportionate, 'just deserts' sentencing with the welfare principle, and with the requirement to impose community sentences that are appropriate, in the sense of being the best chance of preventing re-offending, has been imposed by law, guidance and by national standards. Most youth court magistrates do not see themselves as being isolated from the responsibilities and objectives of youth justice teams. Indeed, in many petty sessional areas, the relationship between youth panels and youth justice teams has been close, constructive and jointly concerned to reduce youth offending.

Changing the culture of the youth court

Proposals in the White Paper were viewed by the Government as part of the task of changing the culture of the youth court. These objectives were re-emphasised in a letter from the Home Office to Justices' Chief Executives dated 2 June 1998:

> As you will know, the White Paper ... set out the Government's intention to bring about a step change in the culture of the youth court. In particular, the Government believes that changes should be directed at establishing:
>
> - a system that is more open, and which commands the confidence of victims and public;
>
> - processes which engage young offenders and their parents, and focus on their offending behaviour and how to change it; and
>
> - a stronger emphasis on using sentencing to prevent further offending.

The letter goes on to identify proposals for short term action. There is no doubt that the implementation of these proposals has helped the change in culture that the Government wishes to see. The aims are to:

- encourage training for magistrates to emphasise the value of talking directly to both the young defendant and his or her parents during court proceedings, even where the young person has legal representation and provide guidance;

- remove any obstacles in the Magistrates' Courts Rules which may prevent or discourage magistrates from questioning defendants about the reasons for their behaviour before reaching a final decision on sentencing;
- encourage youth courts to consider changing the physical environment of the courtroom to promote more informal, and less adversarial, proceedings. This might involve all participants in the case, including the magistrates, sitting around a table (except where security constraints exist);
- encourage magistrates to use their discretion over whom can attend proceedings and over the lifting of reporting restrictions ...

The final proposal is now the subject of a joint Home Office and Lord Chancellor's Department Circular published in June 1998 and this initiative can be seen as a first step in the reconstruction of the youth court.

Youth Offender Panels

The notions that underpin the White Paper proposals, the subsequent letter and Circular referred to, and the language used, reflect principles of restorative justice and the fact that the Government has accepted its major tenets for the construction of the new youth justice system:

> The Government considers that it will be necessary to reshape the criminal justice system in England and Wales to produce more constructive outcomes with young offenders. Its proposals for reform build on principles underlying the concept of restorative justice:
>
> - restoration: young offenders apologising to their victims and making amends for the harm they have done;
> - reintegration: young offenders paying their debt to society, putting their crime behind them and rejoining the law abiding community; and
> - responsibility: young offenders – and their parents – facing the consequences of their offending behaviour and taking responsibility for preventing further offending.
>
> The new approach is intended to:
> - ensure that the most serious offenders continue to be dealt with in a criminal court to provide punishment, protect the public and prevent re-offending;
> - provide an opportunity for less serious offending to be dealt with in a new non-criminal panel enforced by a criminal court;
> - involve young people more effectively in decisions about them – encouraging them to admit their guilt and face up to the consequences of their behaviour;
> - involve the victim in the proceedings, but only with their active consent and focus on preventing behaviour [Home Office 1997d].

These proposals were significant and are now catered for in measures contained in Pt 1 of the Youth Justice and Criminal Evidence Act 1999.

In this model, which owes much to the Scottish Children's Hearings, referral to a youth offender panel will be the sentence for first time offenders who plead guilty, except where the court proposes to make an absolute discharge, or the offence is one for which the sentence is fixed by law, or the court is proposing to make a custodial sentence or a hospital order under the Mental Health Act 1983. Offenders will be referred to the youth offender panel for the purpose of establishing by agreement a youth offender contract between the offender and the panel. The terms of the contract will be supervised by the youth offender team. If agreement cannot be reached, or the offender fails to sign the contract, the panel will refer the matter back to the youth court.

The panel will consist of a member of the youth offending team and two other persons who are not members of the team. The offender must attend panel meetings together with anyone else ordered to do so by the referral order. This will normally be the parents of the offender and, where the offender is aged 10–15, they must be ordered to attend. The victim of the offence may also attend.

The contract will include a programme of behaviour designed to prevent re-offending. A number of provisions have been identified as examples:

- financial or other reparation to the victim or others affected by the offence;
- attending mediation sessions with any victim or affected person;
- carrying out unpaid work in, or for, the community;
- being at home at specified times;
- attending school or other educational establishment or place of work;
- participating in specified activities (such as those designed to address offending behaviour, educational issues, or rehabilitation from misuse of drugs or alcohol);
- presenting to specified persons at times and places specified in the programme;
- staying away from specified places or persons or both;
- complying with arrangements to enable compliance with the programme to be supervised and recorded.

The panel may meet on any number of occasions, but must meet if the panel believes there has been a breach of the contract, the offender wishes to change the terms of the contract or wants the panel to refer the case back to the court.

The panel may vary the terms of the contract. A final meeting of the panel must be called to consider whether the conditions of the contract have been complied with.

The panel may refer an offender back to court in a number of circumstances:

- the offender has failed to attend a panel meeting;
- no agreement has been reached on a programme;
- the offender appears to have breached the contract;
- the offender fails to sign a variation of the contract without a sufficient reason;
- the offender has requested a referral in order to seek revocation of the order;
- at the final meeting, the panel is of the opinion that the offender has not satisfactorily complied with the contract.

Where the court is satisfied that the referral back to court by the panel was reasonable, it may decide to allow the contract to continue or to revoke the referral order. Where the order is revoked, the court may re-sentence for the original offence, but must take into account the offender's age, the extent of compliance with the contract and the circumstances of referral.

This new sentence of referral to a youth offender panel clearly reflects the principles of restorative justice and a belief in the virtue of early intervention to prevent re-offending.

Taken together with the implementation of the Crime and Disorder Act 1998, these proposals hold out the prospect of a four tier youth justice system with:

- a number of first time minor offences being dealt with by police reprimands or final warnings;
- first time court appearances where the offender pleads guilty being dealt with on the principles of restorative justice by a referral to the new youth offender panel;
- repeat offenders and not guilty pleas being dealt with in the ordinary youth court; and
- serious offences, including grave crimes as defined by s 53 of the Children and Young Persons Act 1933, being dealt with in the Crown Court.

Each element is subject to the statutory aim set out in s 37 of the Crime and Disorder Act.

CONCLUSION

The Crime and Disorder Act 1998 and the Youth Justice and Criminal Evidence Act 1999 establish a new set of principles and practices for youth court magistrates to work with. They are based upon a distinct view of youth justice that distinguishes between first time minor offenders and repeat and serious offenders. In both cases, offending will trigger a response from the State. For the former, it is likely that the State will intervene in the life of the offender and his or her family, with the objective of compensating the victim and/or the wider community and working to prevent repeat offending. For the latter category, offending will trigger punishment to provide public protection, compensation, and to seek rehabilitation. These categories are not exclusive; there will be a continuum of State intervention available as appropriate responses to various types of youth offending.

Magistrates sitting in the youth court have become familiar with an evolving youth justice system and with their role in such a system. They are now entering yet another period of significant change and development. The pace and rapidity of change in the criminal justice system became one of its dominant characteristics in the 1990s. It is clear that the Government envisages the youth court as one element in a unified but multidisciplinary system where the underlying objective is that of prevention of (re-)offending. The establishment of the new youth offender panel is one notable reflection of this objective. Youth courts are also being asked to promote a more informal, less adversarial process. Magistrates are encouraged to enter into a dialogue with those that appear in the youth court and with their parents.

These, and other changes already identified, will constitute a major challenge for youth court magistrates whose practice reflects the historical legacy of politics, principles, provisions and tensions that have shaped the current youth justice system and the youth court. They remain as a lay element in an increasingly professionalised system and there must be some doubt about the capacity of current training provisions to create a youth justice magistracy that is fully conversant with the policy objectives of the legislation, with its complexity and the sophistication required for its delivery. Current training is most often concerned with the technicalities of new provisions; there is little space for a critical discussion of the principles and policies underpinning the Crime and Disorder Act or of the new model for the youth court. It should also be remembered that these training challenges occurred at the same time as the Human Rights Act 1998 established its own training agenda for the magistracy.

The Youth Justice and Criminal Evidence Act represents a clear alternative to the youth court. The youth offender panel will deal with a significant number of those that currently appear before the youth court. These first time, guilty plea, offenders will be subject(ed) to the principles of restorative justice administered by professional youth justice practitioners. In practice, this group of offenders will be taken out of the hands of youth court magistrates; their sentencing discretion will be significantly limited.

The Act allows the Home Secretary to extend the category of offenders subject to the youth offender panels. Any such extension will inevitably further restrict the influence of youth court magistrates. The youth court is being required to change its practice at the same time as it faces a new model of youth justice in the form of the youth offender panels; a model which may indicate the future of the youth justice system.

Can 'old' magistrates be taught all these complex 'new' tricks? The significance of the changes to the youth justice system should not be underestimated. It is possible that the establishment of the new system, particularly that element which is provided by the youth court and its magistrates, will be subject to a process of interpretation and assimilation which reflects past practice. It is also entirely possible that old tensions will be reconstructed and reinterpreted to take account of the new principles of the 1998 Act, of the new model for the youth court and of the principles of restorative justice reflected in the provisions of the Youth Justice and Criminal Evidence Act. If this is the case, then the radicalism that the Government claims for its youth justice reforms may not be fully delivered.

The role of the magistracy, including those who sit on the youth panel, is to apply the law, with appropriate flexibility, as legislated by Parliament. The reform of youth justice envisaged by the Government is designed to establish a system which, although utilising a number of familiar principles, is sufficiently distinct to warrant the creation of panels of magistrates that sit only in the youth court. This model, which is already used in inner London, would ease the significant training challenge provided by the reforms and allow the development of the necessary expertise to administer a new youth justice system which declares itself to be 'a complete reform'. Without these changes, it might be very difficult to teach 'old beaks' the new tricks they need to learn in order to implement the spirit of this new legislation.

CHAPTER 5

BRINGING RIGHTS ALL THE WAY HOME: SOME ISSUES OF LAW AND POLICY IN INTERNATIONAL LAW AND JUVENILE JUSTICE

Deirdre Fottrell

Ernest, an 18 year old boy, told us that he had been detained for three months in a five by 10 foot cell with four other adults. He complained of the absence of floor space for sleeping and described being kicked in the eye by a guard on one occasion, which he said caused a gash over his eye that appeared to be infected.[1]

Once they enter the justice system of the USA, many children experience violations of their fundamental human rights. Children in custody have been subject to brutal physical force and other cruel punishments ... thousands of convicted children are sent to prisons where they are not separated from adult prisoners putting them at serious risk of physical and sexual abuse.[2]

INTRODUCTION

In spite of the fact that international law on the rights of the child has progressed immeasurably over the past decade, many States continue to view some children as more deserving of protection than others.[3] When the State takes a hierarchical approach to children's rights, inevitably, the rights of those children in conflict with the law are relegated. Consequently, in the treatment of these children, the majority of States are in violation of their international legal obligations.

In an alarmingly high number of States, juvenile offenders are stripped of their childhood status, their needs are overlooked or ignored, while the ultimate objective of the juvenile justice system is to punish the child. There is growing concern that children around the world are physically and sexually abused in custody and that they are detained or imprisoned when more appropriate action should be taken.[4] Moreover, in many countries, children are tried as adults and sent to adult prisons and, in others, children are

---

1   Human Rights Watch 1999:47.
2   Amnesty International 1998:51.
3   For an overview of the developments in children's rights on an international level over the past decade, see further, Fottrell 1999:67.
4   See, eg, Human Rights Watch 1997.

sentenced to death despite a clear and unambiguous prohibition on the imposition of such a sentence under international law.[5] Cantwell notes:

> ... there has been a widespread belief that children in conflict with the law do not constitute a high priority for most governments ... The problem has been that it [as an issue] is tackled in terms of 'fighting juvenile crime' rather than on the basis of promoting 'juvenile justice'.[6]

This chapter seeks to identify the international legal provisions on juvenile justice and to explore the extent to which international human rights law offers wider protections than the domestic law of many States. However, the chapter concludes that States are not taking their obligations seriously and that a hostile environment pervades which prevents the promotion of child orientated systems. Furthermore, where such systems do exist, they are often subverted by social, economic and political factors; thus, international mechanisms assume greater importance for the protection of children in conflict with the law.[7]

JUVENILE JUSTICE AS A HUMAN RIGHTS ISSUE

International human rights law is composed of an elaborate body of universal and regional treaties, non-binding declarations, resolutions, rules and guidelines.[8] In theory, it has always offered protection to juvenile offenders, in so far as provisions regarding detention and due process, in general human rights treaties, applied equally to children and adults. Thus, children could benefit, for example, from the extensive provisions on liberty and security in Art 5 of the European Convention on Human Rights or Art 6, under which States guarantee the right to a fair trial.

In addition, treaties such as the International Covenant on Civil and Political Rights (ICCPR) included child specific provisions within the relevant Articles on liberty and security of the person and fair trial. Article 6(5) of the ICCPR provides that '[a] sentence of death shall not be imposed for crimes committed by persons below 18 years of age'. Similarly, Art 14(4) of the same treaty provides that 'in the case of juvenile persons, the procedure shall be such as will take account of their age and the desirability of promoting their rehabilitation'.

These provisions confirm that aspects of juvenile justice have long been on the human rights agenda and this adds weight to demands that States establish

---

5   See International Covenant on Civil and Political Rights, Art 6(5), reprinted in Brownlie 1992. See, also, Report of the Special Rapporteur, E/CN 4/1998/68/Add 3, para 49.
6   See Cantwell 1998:3.
7   See, eg, (1987) 8 HRLJ 355. See, also, Amnesty International 1998.
8   For a good introduction to international human rights law, see, further, Steiner and Alston 1996.

a separate system for juveniles. However, in reality, these provisions had limited impact on the standards of juvenile justice within the domestic arena of most States Parties. Furthermore, while there was a paper commitment to promotion of an equitable system of juvenile justice, international fora did not prioritise this issue. On the rare occasions when the European Commission or Court of Human Rights considered juvenile justice and related issues prior to 1989 (when the United Nations Convention on the Rights of the Child was passed), decisions were unsympathetic to the specific needs of the children concerned.[9] An extreme example of this is *Sargin v Germany*,[10] where police removed a 10 year old girl from her school because she was suspected by her teacher of involvement in theft within the school. She was questioned by police and detained for two hours at the police station during which time her parents were not contacted and she was not provided with legal advice. She was released without charge and later claimed a violation of her right to liberty under Art 5 of the European Convention on Human Rights. The Commission found no violation, largely due to the length of her detention, but the decision is curiously absent, any acknowledgment of the age and vulnerability of the child and the reasoning is arguably flawed as a result of this oversight.

A REVOLUTION IN JUVENILE JUSTICE?

Van Bueren notes that, since the 1980s, 'there has been a silent and largely unheralded revolution taking place in the international law on the administration of juvenile justice'.[11] Indeed, in a single decade, a comprehensive framework was constructed to cover all aspects of juvenile justice in four international instruments:

- the United Nations Convention on the Rights of the Child (1989) (the Convention);
- the United Nations Rules for the Administration of Juvenile Justice (1985) (Beijing Rules);
- the United Nations Rules for the Protection of Juveniles Deprived of their Liberty (1990);
- the United Nations Guidelines for the Prevention of Juvenile Delinquency (1990) (Riyadh Guidelines).[12]

Of the four documents, by far the most significant is the Convention because of its binding character and its reach, as it has achieved near universal

---

9   See Kilkelly 1999:33–44.
10   *Sargin v Germany* (1981) 4 EHRR 276.
11   See Van Bueren 1995:169. See, also, Van Bueren 1992. See, further, Cantwell 1998.
12   See, further, Van Bueren 1993 for the text of all four documents.

ratification having been signed by 191 States.[13] Although the Rules and Guidelines contain greater detail and more substantive provisions, they are non-binding and are only persuasive, as a result of which the obligations of States are minimal thereunder. However, the Convention ameliorates this to an extent, in that it draws heavily on the other instruments and imports their underlying ethos into its provisions on juvenile justice. There is a marked shift in the approach advocated in these documents – the emphasis moves from punitive measures to advocating a child centred justice system, in which the child's interests are paramount and the inherent dignity of the child is preserved. Thus, Art 40 of the Convention provides that:

> State Parties recognise the right of every child alleged as, accused of, or recognised as having infringed the penal law to be treated in a manner consistent with the promotion of the child's sense of dignity and worth ...

That juvenile justice is an immensely complex area of law is evidenced by the sheer breadth and wide ranging nature of the content of these documents. The juvenile justice provisions are concerned with such issues as deprivation of liberty, ensuring that basic rights to food, health care and clothing are respected in that context, and the civil rights provisions enshrined in the Universal Declaration on Human Rights and other subsequent instruments. For example, Art 40 of the Convention details, *inter alia*, comprehensive, minimum due process guarantees for children including the presumption of innocence, the right to be informed promptly of the charges against him or her, to have legal assistance in the preparation of his or her defence, to be tried without delay by a competent legal authority and a range of other guarantees which are imported from other human rights treaties.

In addition, it requires the State to set a reasonable minimum age of criminal responsibility, to provide non-judicial methods of dealing with children in conflict with the law and to establish alternatives to institutional care. These provisions are supplemented by Art 37, which prohibits the death penalty and life imprisonment without the possibility of release. Article 37 also requires that imprisonment 'shall be used as a measure of last resort' and, where children are imprisoned, it must be for the shortest possible period of time. Article 39 requires the State to promote physical and psychological recovery and reintegration of child victims.

The specific provisions on juvenile justice are to be read in the light of the Convention's overarching principles, which provide that: States should be guided in all actions by the best interests of the child (Art 3); take into account the evolving capacities of the child (Art 5); give due weight to the views of the child (Art 12); and guarantee the rights to all children without discrimination

---

13 The Convention has been ratified by all States except the US and Somalia, the former has signed the Convention but there are no plans to ratify, the latter is a collapsed State, see, further, Fottrell 1999:167.

(Art 2).[14] The Convention champions an holistic approach to children's rights and, thus, these provisions form a backdrop to all other rights including those concerned with juvenile justice. Hodgkin and Newell note in that vein that the Committee, in its general discussion on juvenile justice, highlighted in particular the need for States to establish a:

> ... justice system, that recognises the child as the subject of fundamental rights and freedoms and stresses the need for all actions concerning children to be guided by the best interests of the child as a primary consideration.[15]

ADVANCING JUVENILE JUSTICE THROUGH THE CONVENTION – PROBLEMS OF LAW AND POLICY

States Parties to the Convention are required to give effect to its provisions by importing the standards into the legislative and administrative practices of the State.[16] The Convention establishes a supervisory Committee, which reviews periodic State Reports detailing their progress.[17] The Committee indicated that it regards the Guidelines and Rules to be taken together with the provisions of the Convention on juvenile justice.[18] The Committee also consistently criticises States for their record on Arts 37, 39 and 40. Indeed, Cantwell notes that:

> ... policy and practice relating to juvenile justice are among those areas most frequently criticised by the Committee on the Rights of the Child ... it has in fact made reference to problems in this sphere in relation to some two thirds of the reports it has reviewed.[19]

Definitions have proven particularly problematic in this area. Whereas Art 1 defines all persons under 18 as children, and Art 40 points to the importance of States establishing a minimum age of criminal responsibility, the diversity of practice among States indicates that there is no consensus on imputing criminal responsibility to children. Consequently, in some States, the child is criminally responsible at seven and, in others, at 18.[20] However, States are

---

14 See, further, Fottrell 2000.

15 See Hodgkin and Newell 1998:540.

16 See LeBlanc 1995.

17 States Parties submit their reports to the Committee, which then engages in a dialogue with the State in which further clarification is sought on certain issues. Thereafter, the Committee issues a set of concluding comments in which it highlights areas of concern and commends the State for progress made in achieving the standards of promotion and protection laid down in the Convention. See, further, Fottrell 2000. See, also, Van Bueren 1995:378.

18 See Hodgkin and Newell 1998:543. See, further, the Committee Report on the Ninth Session, May–June 1995, CRC/C/43, Annex VIII, p 64.

19 See Cantwell 1998 (Introduction).

20 See, further, Cantwell 1998, para 1.4.

encouraged not to set the age too low and, in its Concluding Comments on Sri Lanka, the Committee was 'deeply concerned by the low age of criminal responsibility (eight years) ... the age of criminal responsibility should not be set at too low an age ...'.[21] Similarly, in its examination of the initial report of the UK, the Committee stated:

> ... the low age of criminal responsibility and the national legislation relating to the administration of juvenile justice seem not to be compatible with the provisions of Arts 37 and 40 [of the Convention] ...[22]

The Committee has struggled to maximise its impact in this area because political motivations prevent States from taking an enlightened approach and, also, the diversity of practice among States themselves mitigates against the imposition of a uniform standard age.[23] In most countries, then, the age of criminal responsibility is much lower than the age of majority, to the detriment of children. In the Commentary to the Beijing Rules, States are encouraged to harmonise their laws and take a more child friendly approach to this issue:

> If the age of criminal responsibility is fixed too low or if there is no lower age limit at all, the notion of criminal responsibility would become meaningless. In general, there is a close relationship between the notion of criminal responsibility for delinquent or criminal behaviour and other social rights and responsibilities (such as marital status, civil majority, etc).[24]

The dilemma in the promotion and protection is in striking a balance between, on the one hand, recognising autonomous and participatory rights and, on the other, protecting children and promoting their welfare. This inherent tension causes the duplicity which is exposed in the commentary above, States which have a low age of criminal responsibility and high age for attainment of civil rights such as enfranchisement or the right to work send very mixed messages and their policies are, arguably, out of step with the Convention's overarching principles.

The Committee has also emphasised repeatedly to States the importance of preventative measures and has highlighted the social roots of offending. In particular, the Committee recommends that States regard the Riyadh Guidelines as providing the relevant standards and these should also be

---

21 See Hodgkin and Newell 1998:552.

22 See Concluding Comments of the Committee on the Rights of the Child: UK and Northern Ireland, CRC/C/11/Add 1, para 17. Since the first report, the UK Government has effectively reduced the age of criminal responsibility through the removal of the protection of doli incapax for children between 10 and 14. See, further, The Howard League for Penal Reform 1999:5.

23 There are indications that the Committee has enjoyed some success in this area, Ireland announced plans to raise the age of criminal responsibility from seven to 12 in October 1999. This followed a discussion during the Committee's examination of Ireland's first report: see (1999) *Irish Times*, 1 October.

24 See Van Bueren 1993.

implemented within the domestic arena.[25] In reviewing the UK Report, for example:

> ... The Committee also wishes to recommend that the State Party take the necessary measures to prevent juvenile delinquency as set down in the Convention and complemented by the Riyadh Guidelines.

Such a move would be both welcome and somewhat surprising. Adhering to the binding obligations which they have accepted under international law can prove a challenge, very few States will incorporate non-binding principles, although they will presumably take cognisance of the Committee's recommendation at some level.

A further issue which the Committee has consistently tackled relates to the mode of trial. In particular, the Committee encourages States to establish separate systems for children. When this is not possible for economic or political reasons, States remain under an obligation under Art 12 to ensure that children are not prohibited from participation in their own defence and that judicial hearings should be conducive to understanding and not exclude the child.[26] The Commentary to the Beijing Rules stresses the need for privacy throughout court proceedings in order to avoid the stigmatising and negative effects of labelling children criminals and delinquents.

A final issue for the Committee is the incarceration of children, which is highly questionable in its use as a practice, but which is used by most States Parties to the Convention. Cantwell notes that in the majority of countries most children deprived of their liberty are in fact on pre-trial remand for minor offences and will not in any case receive a custodial sentence if convicted. Such practices are clearly discouraged by both the Convention and the Beijing Rules, which advocate supervision, intensive care or placement with a family or in an educational setting or home in preference to detention.[27] Moreover, he argues that, although the ineffectiveness of custodial sentences for young offenders is well documented, the fact that the practice is widespread presents a challenge for the Convention. A range of alternative sentencing options are provided for in r 16 of the Beijing Rules and, to effectively adhere to their obligations under the Convention, a custodial sentence ought not to be imposed unless the sentencing objectives require incarceration. In its Comments on the Nigerian Report, the Committee reiterated the centrality of this principle when it noted that 'institutionalisation and detention of children must be avoided as much as

---

25 See Hodgkin and Newell 1998:546.

26 See Written Comments of Justice submitted to the European Court of Human Rights, *V v UK*, Application no 24888/94, 1994. Copy on file with the author.

27 See Beijing Rules, r 13, available in Van Bueren 1993:119.

possible and alternatives to such practices must be developed and implemented ... '.[28]

Nonetheless, very few States apply the Art 37 requirement that custodial sentences should be used as a 'last resort' because, as Cantwell notes, States tend to have a very limited range of sentencing options for children:

> ... often [the option] is a caution or conditional discharge, a fine or suspended sentence. Other responses may be on the statute books, but are not practical propositions because of a professed lack of financial and human resources ... so the 'last resort' becomes a commonplace solution.

Of particular concern to Cantwell is the disproportionately high percentage of ethnic minority children for whom incarceration is the only option considered.[29]

Similarly, homeless or economically disadvantaged children are more likely to be deprived of their liberty. In 1997, the Human Rights Watch reported that street children in Kenya were arbitrarily detained by police for several days and sometimes for weeks during which time they were routinely abused:

> ... Police roundups are conducted with brute force and little regard for the welfare of the children who are often taunted, manhandled, and beaten at the time of arrest ... once arrested street children are held under deplorable physical conditions in crowded police cells, often without toilets or bedding, with little food and inadequate supplies of water.[30]

Such practices were also reported by the same organisation in Jamaica[31] and Amnesty International has catalogued a series of similar offences in the US, although the latter remains beyond the reach of the Convention, at present being one of two States which has not yet ratified it.[32]

In addition to the use of imprisonment as a last resort, Art 37 also requires that, where children are incarcerated, it should be for the shortest possible period of time, which implies that a lengthy sentence should be exceptional. In the light of this provision, it is clear that the imposition of a life sentence on a young offender runs counter to the underlying ethos of the Convention, particularly because it fails to take into account the capacity of the child for change and reintegration. There are many States which provide in their laws for life sentences for children at the upper end of childhood between 16–18 and the Committee has expressed its view that such laws violate Art 37. In its examination of China's report, for example, the Committee stated

---

28 See Hodgkin and Newell 1998:498.
29 Cantwell 1998 singles out the US, Canada and Australia for particular mention in this regard, Pt V.
30 Human Rights Watch 1999:3.
31 Amnesty International 1998.
32 Amnesty International 1998.

unequivocally that a life sentence for persons under 18 is incompatible with the Convention.[33] The Committee's Concluding Comments to the UK report indicate that sentencing a child to an indeterminate period of detention is also contrary to the Convention.[34]

Article 37(c) requires that children be separated from adults, reiterating the established practice under Art 10(2)(b) of the ICCPR. The practice under the ICCPR indicates that many States overlook this provision and tend to rely on economic arguments to justify their non-compliance.[35] In the majority of States, dedicated units for children are rare and expensive and politically unattractive as an issue. Van Bueren has observed that economics explain why juvenile justice remains a marginal concern for many countries, despite good faith ratification of the Convention. She asks:

> ... how can States which regard themselves as being unable to afford universal child education and health services devote scarce resources to improving a juvenile justice system which only affects a minority of the child population.[36]

It is no surprise then that several States, including the UK, Canada, New Zealand and Australia, have entered reservations[37] on the specific issue of separation and, in its examination of State reports this matter is problematic for the Committee.

This brief survey highlights some juvenile justice issues that have arisen before the Committee and suggests that many States are playing fast and loose with their juvenile justice obligations. To assist States and the Committee in achieving the Convention principles in this area, the Economic and Social Council of the UN adopted Guidelines for Action on Children in the Juvenile Justice System, which recommends, *inter alia*, that States be given technical assistance to update their laws and practices.[38] In addition, specific targets are set on establishing a 'comprehensive juvenile justice system', setting up a panel of independent experts to review juvenile justice laws in the State, ensuring that no child under the legal age of criminal responsibility is subject

---

33 See Hodgkin and Newell 1998:491.

34 See Concluding Comments of the Committee on the Rights of the Child: UK and Northern Ireland, CRC/C/11/Add 1, para 36.

35 See General Comment 9 of the Human Rights Committee HRI/Gen/1/Rev 2, para 10. The Human Rights Committee is the body charged with supervising the ICCPR and indicated in this general comment a concern about a trend among States Parties relating to separation of juveniles and adults in detention.

36 See Van Bueren 1995:171.

37 Reservations allow the State to ratify the Convention without accepting all of its provisions. As a rule, ratifications ought to be compatible with the object and purposes of the treaty. See, generally, Gardner 1997.

38 Guidelines for Action on Children in the Criminal Justice System, resolution 1997/30 of 21 July 1997, Economic and Social Council. Technical assistance can be requested by a State from the Crime Prevention and Criminal Justice Division, the Centre for Human Rights and the UN Children's Fund: see, further, paras 30–40.

to criminal charges and the establishment of juvenile courts.[39] While these guidelines are well intentioned and even innovative in parts, the brief review of the Committee's work in this area would suggest that existing Convention provisions, rules and guidelines should be entrenched before further legislative layers are added to an already unwieldy body of law. The problem at present is a familiar one to international human rights lawyers and is basically one of implementation and enforcement. It is clear that international law offers wider protections to children in this area; moreover, States have overwhelmingly accepted a binding obligation to import these standards into their domestic practices. The problem then becomes one of strategy – how to close that gap between law and fact.

ADVANCING JUVENILE JUSTICE THROUGH OTHER INTERNATIONAL MECHANISMS

Kilkelly suggests that the potential of the Convention can be maximised through its use by other national and international judicial bodies, most particularly the European Court of Human Rights.[40] Recent case law indicates that certainly in the field of juvenile justice, cross fertilisation of the Convention standards from the universal to the regional forum opens up exciting possibilities and promises greater immediacy. Thus, the forward looking Convention provisions could prove to be singularly effective for raising standards within Council of Europe States, by plugging gaps in the substantive protections in the European Convention on Human Rights, while at the same time taking advantage of its effective implementation mechanisms.[41] The Court has referred to the Convention on a number of occasions citing its provisions with approval.[42] A recent decision, however, establishes that, not only will the Convention prove persuasive, but the Court may also have an important interpretative function vis à vis the Convention.[43] Moreover, the decisions suggest that the core principles in the rules and guidelines can also trickle down into the domestic arena via this rather circuitous route.

The potential of the Convention to fulfil this function is well illustrated in *T v UK* and *V v UK*. Two boys were convicted of the murder of a three year

---

39　See Guidelines for Action on Children in the Criminal Justice System, resolution 1997/30 of 21 July 1997, Economic and Social Council, para 14. See, also, para 28 for a checklist of practical steps the State is encouraged to undertake to improve the administration of juvenile justice.

40　See Kilkelly 2000. See, also, Kilkelly 1999.

41　See Kilkelly 1999:2–17 where she explores the potential of the European Convention on Human Rights as a mechanism for promoting the Convention provisions in some detail.

42　See, further, Van Bueren 1996:171.

43　Kilkelly 1999 argues that the Convention will benefit enormously from the interpretation of its principles by the Court and that the Court decisions have a clarity and force which the Committee concluding comments lack.

old child following a trial in an adult court and sentenced to detention at 'Her Majesty's pleasure'.[44] The Court found in both cases that there had been violations of Art 6(1) due to the unfairness of the trial procedure, most particularly, the intimidating nature of an adult trial which prevented the boys from participating in their own defence. Article 6(1) was also violated because a politician exercised a judicial function and set a tariff on the length of detention to be served. In addition, detention at Her Majesty's pleasure gave rise to a violation of Art 5(4) because there was no opportunity for the boys to challenge the continued lawfulness of their detention.[45]

What is exceptional about the case is the extensive examination of provisions in other international instruments on juvenile justice including the Convention, the Beijing Rules and Riyadh Guidelines.[46] Moreover, these principles were imported into the European Convention on Human Rights because of the acceptance of the United Nations Convention by all Council of Europe States was taken by the court to demonstrate an international consensus in favour of the application of the standards of juvenile justice in Arts 37, 39 and 40.[47]

CONCLUSION

It is clear from this overview that the potential exists within international law to advance considerably the rights of children to an equitable and enlightened criminal justice system. It is also evident that the international law provides the basis for a system which is more child centred and thus provides wider protection than the domestic law of most States. That this area has been prioritised relatively recently may account to some degree for the lacklustre attitude of States to its implementation. Moreover, as discussed above, the reluctance of governments to improve juvenile justice is exacerbated by prejudices and media moral panics on juvenile crime and a conceptualisation of children in conflict with the law as 'innocents lost'. The extent to which

---

44 *T v UK*, Application no 24724/95 and *V v UK*, Application no 24888/94, Judgments of the European Court of Human Rights, 16 December 1999. The judgments are almost identical with minor variations, see *The Times*, 17 December 1999.

45 See, further, Kilkelly 2000.

46 See *T v UK*, Application no 24724/95, paras 43–49 inclusive.

47 See *T v UK*, Application no 24724/95, para 75, where the Court notes that the principles of the UN Convention, combined with the Beijing Rules, 'demonstrates an international tendency in favour of the protection of juvenile defendants, and it notes in particular that the UN Convention is binding in international law on the United Kingdom, in common with all other member States of the Council of Europe.' While the Court rejected T's argument, that the public nature of the trial gave rise to a violation of Art 3, its willingness to be persuaded by the Convention's principles is immensely significant. The international documents were also highly influential on the decision of the House of Lords, which quashed the tariff imposed by the Secretary of State: see *www.parliament.uk* (decision of 10 November 1997).

international law can impact on the attitudinal deficiencies that have marked State practice in this area is limited. However, recent developments indicate that robust enforcement by international tribunals offers an extra layer of protection to children whose rights are ignored when they come into conflict with the law. This is likely to be an incremental process. Consequently, while it is correct to talk in terms of a revolution in this area, it is as yet an unfinished revolution.

CHAPTER 6

YOUTH CULTURE, DRUGS AND CRIMINALITY

Issy Harvey

INTRODUCTION

This chapter will address the interrelated social phenomena of youth cultures, drug use and criminality. First, however, we need to define the terms we are using. This is not a purely semantic exercise, as social sources of power reside in these definitions. 'Drug misuse' is a socially and historically defined problem.

Secondly, sociological theories of youth cultures and sub-cultures need to be reviewed in their historical context, especially social models of 'deviant behaviour' advanced through criminology as explanatory theories of drug taking behaviour. The role of the media in framing 'public opinion' and debate and in 'labelling', and indeed creating, deviance through the projection of stereotyped images of young drug users is considered. These factors need to be reconsidered in the light of evidence of changing patterns of illegal drug use among young people – such behaviour has moved from the margins to the mainstream and can no longer be considered simply as the actions of a minority, 'deviant' group in society.

Thirdly, many have now declared the 'war on drugs' to have been lost. Current public discourses about how different social agencies should intervene to control, prevent or reduce drug taking behaviour amongst the young are outlined in this paper and the contradictions within them are examined. These differences have emerged as lively debates within the field of drugs education in response to changing patterns of prevalence rates and drug use among this age group.

This chapter will then go on to consider the more specific issues faced by professionals who work with young drug users in the context of the criminal justice system. It will consider the role and impact that the new, multidisciplinary Youth Offending Teams (introduced nationwide in April 2000) might play in drugs education, in health based interventions and in the social control of such behaviours. It argues that professionals from different agency backgrounds are likely to hold conflicting philosophies and practices, largely due to the illicit nature of this activity. Despite non-punitive responses being widely acknowledged, within the research literature, to be the most successful interventions in reducing the most damaging social effects of such behaviour, it is arguably unlikely that certain professionals within the new YOTs will agree with such an approach.

In considering how professionals can most effectively intervene within this arena, this chapter will present recent research evidence which challenges the simplistic, but widely held formulation, that drug use leads to increased criminal behaviour. However, it will also be shown that studies indicate that both prevalence rates and 'problem' drug use are much higher than average among populations of young people who are also engaged in other criminal behaviour. This has given rise to arguments that interventions should, therefore, be focused on such 'high risk' groups.

This chapter presents the contention that, if we intervene with the aim of supporting and directing the young person, the multiplicity and complexity of issues facing most persistent or serious young offenders – a tiny percentage of the total age group – need to be thoroughly addressed. Traditional enquiries, which focused only upon the isolated, criminal behaviour which drew offenders to the attention of the authorities, are arguably inadequate. Even when assessments are made on this holistic basis – which, it will be argued, is 'good practice' in terms of professional interventions into children's lives – there are shockingly few health treatment resources available to the under 18s. Children who develop problems with their use of drugs tend to present with a particularly complex range of issues which don't respect professional boundaries and so require a holistic response. Professionals who deal with children and young people need training in drugs. Those who deal with drugs issues need training in dealing with young people. Given this situation, the multidisciplinary YOTs are well placed to develop such service responses. At the time of writing, it is too early to tell how the policies and practices of these teams will develop, but it will be argued that there is an opportunity to develop innovative, more appropriate services, based on evidence from the latest research.

WHAT IS A DRUG?

Before discussing specific issues of drug use among young offenders, we need to consider problems of definition. Although the term 'drug' is a familiar one, what it refers to varies in different contexts. Reaching for a dictionary, we find two uses of the term:

> **drug** (n) 1 Any synthetic or natural chemical substance used in the treatment, prevention or diagnosis of disease. Related adj: pharmaceutical. 2 A chemical substance, esp a narcotic, taken for the pleasant effects it produces [*Collins English Dictionary* 1986].

Aspirin, alcohol and even solvents could all be included in this definition but arguably caffeine and nicotine would not – they are neither used in the control of disease nor are they consumed primarily to produce pleasant effects (it could be argued that nicotine is consumed to avoid unpleasant withdrawal effects). A medical or biological working definition might be 'Any substance which when taken into the body may modify one or more of its physical or mental functions' (Cornwell and Cornwell 1993, p 7). This broader definition does not exclude any substances which are considered to be drugs, but it does perhaps include some, like water and nutrients, which are not usually thought of as being drugs. Use of the majority of drugs within this group of substances is deemed to be 'socially acceptable', even desirable, and many are manufactured and marketed. This includes substances with no real medical benefits, such as caffeine, a highly potent drug that can lead to physical dependence, and yet is given to children in 'soft drinks' such as cola.

Social policies frame the distinctions made between 'legal' and 'illegal' or 'controlled' substances. The key piece of legislation[1] in Britain is the 1971 Misuse of Drugs Act and its associated regulations that revised the maximum penalties available to the courts for those found in possession of or intending to supply certain substances. The Act groups controlled drugs into three classes – A, B and C (see table 1). Class C includes substances such as temazepam (mazzies) (a tranquilliser) and the supply (although not the consumption) of anabolic steroids; Class B are those commonly referred to as 'soft' drugs, the primary ones in this category being cannabis and its derivatives and amphetamines (speed); Class A – 'hard' drugs – include hallucinogens (LSD (acid)), MDMA (ecstasy), cocaine and heroin. It is not the use of any drug that is unlawful but their possession or intended supply. Some of these substances are 'socially acceptable' within the medical field, but illegal to possess without a prescription. For example, many diet pills available from doctors on prescription include amphetamine (which is an appetite suppressant and acts to increase the body's metabolic rate) and large numbers of people are addicted to tranquilisers (for example, Valium, Ativan, Mogadon) commonly prescribed by GPs for the treatment of anxiety, depression and sleep problems.

---

1   Other relevant legislation for the control of drugs includes the Medicines Act 1968, the Drug Trafficking Act 1994, the Criminal Justice (International Co-operation) Act 1990 and the Crime and Disorder Act 1998.

Table 1: substances controlled by the Misuse of Drugs Act 1971

Class	Substances included	Max penalty possession	Max penalty supply
Class A	cocaine crack MDMA heroin LSD magic mushrooms *if prepared for use* amphetamines *if prepared for injection*	seven years' imprisonment and/or fine	life imprisonment and/or fine
Class B	cannabis amphetamines	five years' imprisonment and/or fine	14 years' imprisonment and/or fine
Class C	temazepam supply of anabolic steroids and other tranquilisers	two years' imprisonment and/or fine	five years' imprisonment and/or fine

Social policies designed to control the use of certain drugs cannot be explained by an examination of the relative effects of such substances on an individual's health or bank balance. Relatively uncontrolled or socially sanctioned substances such as tobacco and alcohol have very high associated social and individual costs. Addiction to nicotine underlies the compulsive smoking of tobacco, which is estimated to cause up to 2,000 limb amputations and 110,000 premature deaths per year in Britain alone. The consumption of alcohol contributes to a wide range of social problems. Medically it is linked to the damage of vital organs, particularly the liver, heart and stomach, as well as brain damage and the onset of serious psychiatric disorders. More than 4,000 deaths in the UK each year are directly attributable to alcohol. Its consumption is also a salient factor in domestic violence, child abuse, violent crime, serious fatal driving accidents and elevated rates of depression and suicide. It is widely accepted that alcohol is implicated in 28,000–33,000 deaths per year. In comparison, in the last 10 years, there have been approximately 60 ecstasy related deaths in the UK.[2]

The consumption of these two substances, alcohol and nicotine, can lead to addiction and dependency and can be damaging to users' health and, indeed, the communities in which they live; but social policies in relation to nicotine and alcohol seek to educate not prohibit. Cigarette advertising continues to target young people even though it is now well known that more than 90% of

2   Figures supplied by the Health Education Authority 1998 and Alcohol Concern.

teenagers who smoke five or more cigarettes a day will become adult smokers. Alcopops, with an alcohol content higher than that of many beers, lager or cider, are marketed to appeal primarily to the young. These anomalies in society which appear to sanction or condone the individuals' consumption of drugs are apparent to young people and need to be addressed if drugs education is to be effective (a point which will be returned to later).

Table 2: definition of common terms[3]

Tolerance	The body adapts to the repeated presence of a substance, requiring increasing doses to achieve the desired effect.
Withdrawal	A physiological or psychological reaction to the reduction or complete withdrawal of a substance. A repeated dose will alleviate the symptoms.
Addiction	Describes a situation where the individual uses the substance to prevent withdrawal symptoms. The word has to some extent been replaced by the term 'dependence'.
Abuse and misuse	This is unclear terminology. Some specialists are now arguing for a move to the term 'use'. Some observers believe that drug taking is harmful (abuse) or an unacceptable way of using that substance (misuse).

Until the 1970s, most drugs which were 'misused' (that is, taken for recreational and not medical purposes) in Britain were diverted from legitimate sources. The definition of 'misuse' or 'problem use' or 'abuse' is usually presented as a consensus view, related in some way to perceived and agreed negative or damaging effects to health and to the wider society and is defined in opposition to 'normal' or 'legitimate' use. Among drug service professionals today, such terms are more likely to be applied in a more direct way in relation to difficulties an individual may be experiencing as a direct result of their consumption of certain substances – although such problems may, in themselves, be a manifestation of legal controls rather than the substance use alone.[4] Much of the research literature now focuses upon either prevalence rates of drug use – usually specifying illegal drug use – or social policy interventions to reduce 'problem' drug use or drug misuse (which American literature refers to as 'drug abuse'). 'Problem' drug use, then, is in part determined by who defines the 'problem'. As will be discussed in the section addressing young offenders (see below), one of the difficulties in intervening with this group can be that the young people who are targeted as the recipients of such 'help' may often not accept the professional's view that

---

3   These definitions are taken from the medical literature. Eg, Cooper 1995.

4   The prescription of methadone to heroin addicts is a social/medical policy in part related to reducing the greater risks posed by individuals maintaining their dependency by securing drugs from the black market.

their drug use is in any way 'problematic'. This in turn has obvious implications for how successful any intervention might be considered to be.

Social policy and strategies of social control are framed as 'natural' political and social responses to social problems. A brief look at the history of such 'problems' can reveal the wider social issues that are considered to be at stake.

THE HISTORY OF PROHIBITION

Every known culture has included the ritualistic use of mind altering substances such as peyote, cocoa, alcohol and hallucinogenic fungi.[5] Throughout history, there have also been numerous attempts to prohibit or regulate the use of certain drugs. Although it is generally assumed that such measures are taken for humanitarian reasons, behind the rhetoric lurk economic and ideological vested interests. Much of the wealth Britain accumulated during the 19th century was through the nation's control of the world's biggest opium growing areas in its largest colony, India, and its trade of this drug across the world.[6] Throughout the 19th century, there were no legal constrictions on the sale of opium or opiate based medicines such as laudanum. Although addiction to the medicines' pleasant side effects was quite common, it wasn't considered a problem. The smoking of opium was almost exclusively practised by the Chinese. When America was hit by an economic recession in 1875, the Chinese – being a more recent immigrant group – were scapegoated for taking scarce jobs and all aspects of their culture, including smoking opium, came under attack. The first anti-narcotic laws were introduced in that year and this culminated in the Harrison Narcotics Act which came into effect in 1915. By 1918, the number of addicts in America had risen dramatically and the illegal opiates market was as large as the legal trafficking (Inglis 1975). What had been a medical problem had now become a law enforcement problem. In Britain, in 1914, a Ministry of Health Commission set up to review the American experience concluded that heroin addiction should remain a medical issue with doctors able to prescribe maintenance doses. A significant heroin problem did not begin here until 1967, when Britain, under pressure from the UN (an organisation dominated by America), adopted a prohibition stance.

The histories in Britain and America of tobacco and alcohol regulation reveal a tension between the prohibitionist arguments that consumption of such substances made working people less productive and unmanageable and

---

5   See Williamson 1997 for a list of further books covering the use of potent plants throughout history.

6   The infamous Opium Wars saw British ships sailing down the Yangtse River shelling the Chinese in order to force them into buying British opium in the name of free trade! For more information on this history, see Berridge and Edwards 1998 which traces the development of opium from an everyday remedy to its classification as a 'dangerous drug'.

the economic interests of both the suppliers and the State (who could only levy taxes on legally imported goods). Any society's acceptance of drugs is culturally and historically specific and, although prevailing attitudes change, there are no examples of drugs, once built into the fabric of society, being completely eliminated (Cornwell and Cornwell 1993, p 8). The banning of recreational substances has often gone hand in hand with an attack on the culture in which they were taken.[7] Drug prohibition has always been used as the cutting edge of social control.[8]

SOCIAL PROBLEMS PRODUCE
SOCIAL POLICIES – AND VICE VERSA

Rose defined 'social problems' as 'practices significantly out of harmony with the society. But it is only when the society decides to do something about it that it can become termed a social problem' (1971, p 3). In other words, it is not what people do that makes a social problem, but the society's reaction to it – how it is defined, responded to and reacted to.

Traditional criminology had located blame in the individual person. In the 1970s, radical criminologists[9] undertook a sociological critique of criminology, creating a fully social theory of 'deviance'. Labelling theory had shifted analysis from the examination of individuals to historically specific issues of social control. Such theories propose that, if the consensus values of a society are perceived to be 'at risk' from certain behaviour which challenges or undermines them, then such behaviours become defined as 'deviant'. Deviant behaviour is, therefore, defined in relation to social norms and is not, in itself, synonymous with definitions of social problems. However, if such behaviour is responded to by social policies which act to reinforce social norms through the responses and practices of powerful institutions (government, police, education, social services, etc), then they become defined as a social problem.

Young's (1974) seminal analysis of the consequences of drug control strategies in Notting Hill, West London between 1967 and 1969 examined the social mechanisms by which certain groups in society became labelled as a 'social problem'. Key features which he identified as needing to be present included a conflict of interests between the values held by the deviant group and those of the dominant order, producing moral indignation at the

---

7　See Williamson 1997:23 for illustrations of this point from throughout this century.

8　For a fuller description of the various prohibition movements throughout history see Williamson 1997. Eg, the prophet Mohammed (circa 570–632AD) outlawed the use of alcohol among his followers to differentiate them from the early Christians who had adopted alcohol as the official drug of their religion. It also served to create a unifying social factor among Mohammed's people. Such policies towards the drug use of other cultures continued over the centuries of European expansion with the imposition of Christianity on conquered peoples. The outlawing of drugs which had played a central role in these societies 'pagan' rituals was a central means of repressing native cultures.

9　Such as Taylor, Walton and Young 1971.

perceived protagonists' which led to policies being framed in the language of protectionism and aimed at limiting the growth of such social groups. Such a description characterises the terms on which the 'war against drugs' has been played out in the public arena for the last 30 years.

THE ROLE OF THE MEDIA IN SHAPING SOCIAL PROBLEMS

The media commands a central ideological role in modern, urban societies. Agencies which represent the dominant class have privileged access to the media but their views and interests are 'disguised' as the interests of everyone in society. Hall 1981 argues that it is these agencies, through the media, that are the primary definers of what is and what is not presented as a social problem. It has been shown how media reporting of events can not only change an audience's views of 'social problems' but can in fact define what social problems are.

'The new epidemic. Drugs: heroin, cocaine and ecstasy are now purer, cheaper and more widely available than ever before. And demand is rising', screamed the front page headlines with a six column colour photograph of two 'prepared' syringes. The associated article inside was headlined: 'Blighted children who find hope in heroin' ((1999) *The Guardian*, 26 May). Although this press article stems from recent official figures about an increase in heroin use among some children, it speaks in the language of moral panic and reduces a complex social phenomena to a simple, causal relation – 'serious' drugs are cheaper so more children are taking them.

The media plays a key role in influencing public perceptions of crime, and of specific drug taking behaviour, as a 'social problem'. There are key features of the mass media (which generally includes newspapers, magazines, film, television and radio) that distinguish it from earlier, pre-industrial forms of communication and which are considered salient in every model concerning its influence as a source of ideological production and dissemination. The media is a primary source of information in urban societies, which have, as a feature, extreme social segregation between different groups, so that the media's influence is not often counteracted by its audience's direct experience of the social problems presented (Young 1971, 1974). Through the mass media, information and opinions are disseminated with authority to a large, atomised and heterogeneous audience. This requires the involvement of complex organisations, technical machinery and skilled personnel. The means of production – for example, the printing presses or television studios – are owned or controlled by members of the capitalist class (that minority in society with individual wealth and power), although the necessary resources for production and distribution usually extend beyond the capacity of private individuals. Oligopolisation of the media has occurred in ownership and control over the last 60 years.

There are three basic types of theory about the relationship between the mass media and the opinions held by the general population or 'public opinion' (Young 1974). In historical order, these are 'the mass manipulative', the 'commercial *laissez faire*' and the 'consensus-paradigm' models. Those who subscribe to 'mass manipulative' theories view the media as a powerful agent in the manipulation of the opinions of the public – a mass audience which is both passive and atomised. Different political stances have been taken around this model. On the Marxist Left it has been argued that the media is the source of a 'false ideology' that represents the class interests of the capitalist class. The Right see the media as the propagator of permissiveness and 'left wing' ideas (recall the continual complaints by the Thatcher Government that the BBC had become politicised and representative of left wing ideology), while the Centre promote it as a 'potent force for cohesion in a divided society' (Young 1974, p 229).

The 'commercial *laissez faire*' theory emerged from a critique of this first 'mass manipulative' model. It does not regard the media's influence as absolute, or evenly applied, but minimised by certain factors. The media is not homogenous in its ideological standpoint because 'market forces' produce a diversification of opinions presented in the media to cater for the heterogeneity of a mass audience. The consumer exerts a 'choice' and selects those media products which agree with the attitudes he or she already holds. This model claims that attitudes or opinions, if strongly held, cannot be changed by the media, only reinforced. Personal experience or the experience and views of someone whose opinion is highly valued have a much greater influence on people's ideas about the world in which they live. Thus, the mass media is taken to have very little impact on 'shaping' perceptions or opinions about social issues and is seen as having a more benign role in the transmission and diffusion of knowledge in complex, industrial (urbanised) societies. The media is seen as the means by which events and information can be shared in an open and democratic society to create social (public) awareness and an agreed 'social reality'.

Within this model, it has been argued that the process by which crime news (which includes reports of drug taking) is selected by the press results in a constructed and distorted view of the 'real' picture and that these distortions then influence the public's reporting of crime or the police's prioritising of specific types of crime and, hence, the 'official' (statistical) picture to 'amplify' specific aspects of drug taking (Wilkins 1964). This process has been termed 'deviance amplification'. Other studies have questioned the validity of the amplification hypothesis as a simple process of feedback. Roshier 1981 found that although more serious types of crime, including drug incidents, were over-reported by newspapers, such distortions between the picture of crime presented in newspapers and that conveyed by official statistics were not reflected in reader's views, which more closely resembled the 'true' picture. He therefore concluded that people use the media selectively to reinforce attitudes they already hold.

The consensual-paradigm model, which was developed to more accurately account for the findings of such studies, proposes that the range of opinions or positions seemingly represented in the various media remain 'within certain distinct ideological limits' (Hall 1981, p 345). Different (competing) papers code selected crime stories into a product specific style of language that Hall calls the 'mode of address'. This gears the paper towards its target audience (Roshier's 'give the public what they want' criteria) and gives a surface appearance of presenting different political positions (for example, *The Mirror* and *The Sun*), but all reporting remains couched in the 'public idiom' of the media. Consumer 'choice' is of a limited nature. The consensus view of society that the media helps to construct assumes an homogenous audience. Everyone is seen to be an equal part of one society with not only a common cultural knowledge but also shared interests, values and concerns. Economic inequalities and opposing class interests in society are submerged and the ideological standpoint constructed through the media helps to present the values of the capitalist and professional classes as the universal values of society. The 'public idiom' expects there to be differences and disagreements within society, but it assumes that everyone has equal access to power and decision making and that conflicts of interest should be resolved by discussion, through recourse to official institutions and without violence or confrontation. Society's normative values are constantly re-asserted through the labelling (and over-reporting) of deviant behaviour and its association, through the public idiom of the media, with concomitant negative effects (that is, deviance is either meaningless, unpleasurable, regrettable, or depraved). There is a significant distinction between the way the press handles day to day crime reporting and the way it reports areas 'of particular topical concern' (such as drugs or football hooliganism), which are dramatised with regard to their seriousness and extent in order to publicise 'get tough' statements from 'experts' (Roshier 1981). These primary definers (for example, officials, politicians) have a 'news making power to channel the coverage of social problems into a definite direction: news of the problem becomes news of how the system is working to remedy the situation' (Fishman 1981, p 112). The Government appointed 'drugs tsar', Keith Hellawell, is a recent example of such an 'expert spokesman'.

Another aspect of this public idiom is the language of 'objectivity' (Hall et al 1981). Journalism is underwritten by notions of impartiality and objectivity which is confirmed by reference to 'accredited' sources – institutional representatives or 'experts'. Police sources report crimes that reflect the areas in which police resources are focused (for example, street crimes). They do not, for example, have information about tax evasion, environmental pollution, consumer fraud or political bribery – so such areas are less likely to be reported as crime news. Aware of the salience of certain 'newsworthy' factors, police agencies tend not to report 'uninteresting' common crimes such as thefts, wife beating, child abuse within the home (stranger abuse is more likely to be reported), rapes, race attacks, etc. In urban areas, particularly, the police are known to report only a summary of the crime dealt with, not the total picture, but news workers have no way of knowing what the police have not detected or reported. Or, as Fishman puts it, 'crime news is really police news' (1981, p 108). This produces 'a systematically structured over-accessing to media of those in powerful and privileged institutional positions' (Hall *et al* 1981, p 341). Unlike the representation of other social issues, police 'experts' are not usually 'balanced', because the criminal is seen as participating in illegitimate behaviour and, therefore, has no right to an equal part in the debate. These 'spokesmen' become the primary definers of topics. In other words, they set the terms of reference for the subsequent debate – they can define what is at issue and what is relevant or irrelevant. When a statement or viewpoint of a 'primary definer' is reported as evidence of a social concern, it gets translated into the public idiom which naturalises this viewpoint.

The media is, therefore, central in setting the social agenda, because its attention lends objectivity to a topic or 'concern' and confers the status of high public concern on the issues highlighted. By transforming the item into the public idiom, it has 'a reality-confirming effect' (Hall *et al* 1981, p 346). This process becomes linked to public opinion through the relationship between the 'public idiom' and a paper's editorial voice (Hall *et al* 1981). Sometimes, the language in the editorial is just in the same mode of address as the rest of the paper, so it is taken to represent a valid (because it is ostensibly based on 'objective' fact) press opinion. Often, though, an editorial will go beyond this and take a campaigning role in which it claims to actively speak for the public (for example 'We believe ...' or 'The public believes ...'). In this way, the media aims to actively shape public opinion. It provides a crucial mediating link between the apparatus of social control (for example, police and courts) and the public and, as such, can be used either to justify official action or to mobilise 'public opinion'.

Throughout the 1980s, the police provided 'evidence' to the press of concerns about new patterns of drug use, thus giving the stories legitimacy. Fears about 'new heroin users' were superseded by a series of moral panics over the use and abuse of crack cocaine (black male youth – 'yardies' – were stereotyped as the 'folk devils' responsible for causing this moral threat to society, making the object of 'public concern' concrete), rave drugs and amphetamines. The press 'responded' to the concerns of the police agency and, through their use of the public idiom and campaigning editorial voices, they proclaimed these drug 'epidemics' an issue of public concern. New police powers were introduced to respond to the new social crisis (for example, the Criminal Justice and Public Order Act 1994 was a direct response to the 'rave' culture and forced its move into regulated spaces – clubs with licences).

The role of the media in our society can, therefore, be understood as a major factor influencing the nature of any public discussion about how drug use should be responded to. Fears that such behaviour is implicitly threatening to the maintenance of the social order frame the debate. Those who wish to argue for changes in social policies to take account of the changing nature of drug use at the close of the century have to contend with the silencing power of powerful agencies – principally, the police and medical lobbies – who have a vested interest in resisting any attempts to 'modernise' drug control policies. Yet, the same processes can also be seen to exacerbate the problem. Young has argued that the process of labelling has the consequence of 'deviancy amplification' whereby the label increases the individual's isolation from the norm and, therefore, acts to encourage identification with others similarly labelled. The association of certain behaviours with values and attitudes that oppose the 'conventional' status quo may add to their appeal, particularly for the young.[10] Young people may choose not to read newspapers or watch the BBC through which this dominant discourse is disseminated. Other media texts, which hold more appeal for a youth market – magazines, music, books such as Junk and films such as *Trainspotting* – present alternative representations of drug taking.

The mainstream media, therefore, presents us with a paradox: it is the only forum for 'public debate' and yet it simultaneously represses informed discussion on topics which include illegal activities. Concerns about drug use among the young, expressed through the dominant media, coalesce around two major themes: first, that we all have a social responsibility to protect 'innocent' children from the corrupting and negative effects that contact with such substances is assumed to produce; and, secondly, in framing debates about how society should respond to those individuals who have become 'victims' or, even worse, 'perpetrators', of this social problem.

THE STUDY OF ADOLESCENCE AND YOUTH CULTURES

In our society, 'adolescence' is thought of as a transient phase which typically involves conflict with the parent culture. As such, it is an age which, particularly for boys, is sometimes viewed as a 'social problem' in itself. The study of youth as a distinct social category arose in response to the changing social landscapes of Britain and the US following the end of the Second World War. In the 1950s and 1960s, economic conditions in the US and Western Europe meant that for the first time 'teenagers' became a powerful consumer group whose tastes were targeted and catered for by commodity capitalism. During the late 1960s in America, the anti-Vietnam War movement and the widespread growth of the 'hippies' culture challenged the adult or 'parent' social order. Unprecedentedly large numbers of young people spoke both articulately and vociferously against many of the institutions, traditions and values of the establishment. Within one generation, adolescents' and young

---

10 Eg, one famous campaign from the mid-1980s of billboard posters showing a teenage boy suffering the effects of withdrawal with the slogan 'heroin screws you up' had unexpected consequences – it had been designed to shock and repel but it also appealed to some youth who contacted the campaign in unprecedented numbers, asking for copies of the poster to put up on their bedroom walls alongside those of popstars and movie idols!

adults' styles of dress and music, political affiliations, attitudes towards sexuality and drugs suddenly became so radically different from those of their parents that the effect on the latter was profoundly disturbing. The use of cannabis and LSD among members of these social movements were, therefore, linked from the start to their categorisation as 'problem' groups exhibiting 'problem' behaviour. Drug use has been linked with the occurrence of youth sub-cultures since their inception and has aided their categorisation as 'problem' social groups requiring and justifying the development of methods of social control and containment as 'social problems'.

This conflict between the values held by large sections of youth and the parent culture placed considerable pressure on social psychologists and sociologists to produce theories to explain this modern phenomena. Jessor and Jessor 1977 undertook a large scale longitudinal study of American high school and college students which resulted in the development of the hugely influential 'problem behaviour theory' (PBT) which is still widely used today. 'Problem behaviour' was viewed in relation to activism, drug use, sexual intercourse, alcohol use and misuse and what they termed 'general deviant behaviour', meaning stealing, lying, vandalism, disruptive behaviour and aggression. Conventional behaviour ('the values, norms and practices of the larger society') was considered only superficially by the theory, but was assessed in terms of church attendance, militarism, academic involvement and achievement. PBT considers activities, such as smoking and drug and alcohol use, to be the product of three major systems. These are *the personality system* comprising motivational attitudes, personal beliefs and personal control; the *perceived environment system* in which salient factors are the adolescent's orientation towards parents or peers; and the *behaviour system*, especially the prevalence of, and support for, problem behaviour in an individual's environment. All these components are seen by the theory to interrelate and work with or against each other to produce problem or conventional behaviour. The result of this work is the proposition that such socially undesirable behaviour forms a 'syndrome'. In the 1990s, PBT continues to be mobilised to address concerns about teenage behaviour, attitudes and social development. Recent conceptual developments of PBT concern the reciprocal relationship between what are termed risk factors and protective factors in adolescents who engage in drug taking behaviours.

An alternative but not wholly unrelated theory for the clustering of certain behaviours in adolescence was proposed by Zuckerman 1979 in his 'sensation seeking theory'. The causes of sensation seeking behaviours are thought to be complex and multifaceted, based on individual differences in psychology, personality, physiology and genetics. Again, these behaviours include smoking, drinking, drug use and sexual activity and are more likely to be engaged in by those individuals who score highly on a sensation seeking scale (SSS). Since these early studies, sensation seeking has been demonstrated to be associated with adolescent alcohol use and misuse, marijuana use, with the use of amphetamines, barbiturates, cocaine and opiates and with multiple drug usage as well as with delinquency (Zuckerman 1994).

The evidence in support of problem behaviour theory has also been thought to have been strengthened over recent years with a high degree of concurrency being reported between delinquency, school failure, substance misuse and high risk sexual behaviour reported in American teenagers (Barone *et al* 1995). Yet, much of the work produced in support of both theories has been correlational in nature. Although factors may be seen to co-exist or predict one another, a *correlational* relationship is not the same as a causal one.

It should be noted that all these studies are concerned with adolescents engaging in behaviour defined *by adults* as risky. It assumes a consensus view of the 'risk' attached to different types of behaviour and denies the possibility that youth cultures, in differing from adult values, might be producing a healthy response to social discrepancies. Smoking, drinking and sexual activity are strongly associated in our culture with normative, desirable, fun-loving adult behaviour – an association often glamourised further by advertising copy. The 'social identity' of the smoker or drug user may be very attractive to those who want to be seen as 'grown up' but who do not accept the conformist values of adult society and who do not wish to see themselves as 'conventional'. Furthermore, it has been assumed that the consequences of engaging in certain behaviour are psychologically complementary to the benefits of not doing so, but recent studies have suggested that this is a false premise (Lloyd *et al* 1998). Both theories have been highly influential, not only in social science research into drug use, but also in the approaches used by professionals in intervention with offending behaviour. Since the 1970s, there have also been theories which seek to explain drug use among certain youth sub-cultures not just in terms of their pharmaceutical effects, but also in relation to the cultural and social significance of such behaviour to other values and features of a chosen lifestyle.[11] Theories of sub-cultural style as a form of symbolic resistance arose as an alternative to theories developed within sociology and social psychology, which pathologised drug taking behaviour. A critical examination of these theories will be put forward later when discussing their contemporary application today in the responses of social welfare agencies to drug taking among young people today.

YOUTH IN BRITAIN TODAY

The social position of young people is constantly changing, making 'youth' an expanding social category. In the last 10 years, changes in the benefits system, high rates of youth unemployment, fewer work opportunities and changes in higher education funding (for example, the virtual removal of student grants)

---

11   The development of sociological theories by the Birmingham Centre for Cultural Studies has been central to this area of academic debate.

have all contributed to young people remaining dependent on others for longer (for example, continuing to live in the parental home). This extension of the social category 'youth' has been further highlighted by commodity markets which target this section of the population as having a large and expanding disposable income. The costs of maintaining independent living accommodation are often prohibitively high for the under 25s whose rates of pay can be much lower than those of older employees (there is no minimum wage for those under 18 years, for the 18–25 year olds it is £3.30 per hour while for 'adults' it is £3.60). Living at home, however, often means that any wages earned, however exploitative the pay rates, are largely available as disposable income for the young person. The growth in 1990s Britain of the club scene, with its spin-off merchandise, alongside the designer brand labels that have hit the high street, are all signs of this trend towards consumerism amongst young people.

However, 'youth' is not a homogenous group. The gap in society between the richest and poorest has been widening steadily throughout the 1980s and 1990s. Twenty-five per cent of children in Britain are born into poverty.[12] Many young people grow up in homes that for many different reasons cannot continue to offer them a supportive environment. It may be overcrowded, there may be family tensions, adults in the home may suffer from depression, mental ill health, alcohol related problems or other conditions which are well documented in their negative effects on effective parenting. For some young people, their relationship with their parent(s) may be abusive. The social environment in which any individual young person is located will have an impact upon their opportunities and choices and consequently upon their behaviour. Those who have experienced multiple social difficulties and inequalities are arguably more likely to be attracted to the use of drugs.

EXTENT AND NATURE OF DRUG USE AMONG YOUNG PEOPLE

Social policies in relation to drug use in this country have begun to be re-assessed in recent years in the light of new evidence which indicates widespread drug taking behaviour among young people. The illicit nature of most recreational or compulsive drug use presents obvious difficulties in producing accurate figures for the prevalence and nature of this activity. Until the late 1980s, the only official figures were based on police reports, drug seizure rates and the Addict Index – a system whereby the Home Office was 'notified' of those drug users who contacted health services for treatment. Attempts were made to extrapolate from these figures of primarily heroin (then methadone and cocaine) addicts to

---

12 Where 'poverty' is defined as those living in households with incomes below the national average.

produce estimates of 'undetected' drug use, but these varied widely for obvious reasons. Those under the age of 21 represent less than 10% of the total number of addicts notified to the Home Office. Agencies of treatment and control have, therefore, historically focused on the problems of adult heroin addicts – and those with alcohol dependency problems. Since then, a number of surveys have sought to augment the notifications data, many of them specifically focusing on young people as a social group whose involvement in these behaviours is officially viewed with special interest. Survey data needs to be treated with caution and the variation in prevalence rates reflects differences in sample design, response rates and methodologies.

Most of the resulting evidence suggests that drug use among young people has been steadily rising over the last decade. Although most surveys suggest that drug use is rare among children and young teenagers, it increases markedly after the ages of 14 or 15, with the highest incidence of drug use being found among the 16–29 age group (ISDD 1994 and 1997). It is as yet unclear whether this peak age category of drug use amongst those in their mid-teens and early 20s is the result of risktaking or experimentation behaviour that is later grown out of, or if it is an indication of a permanent shift in social behaviour.

In relation to cannabis, which is universally shown by all surveys to be the most widely used illicit drug in the UK, somewhere in the region of one-third or even one-half of 16–19 year olds report having tried it (ISDD 1994 and 1997). Regular use, defined in most surveys as within the last month, is also relatively high with a third continuing their use on a regular basis. The researchers calculated that this amounts to at least 8 million people aged between 16 and 59 having taken cannabis in England and Wales alone, with 1.5 million using it at least once a month. Such a mainstream activity – one which many people will obviously either have direct personal experience of or will know someone who has – is difficult to label as a social problem. Its frequency of occurrence and acceptability to large sections of the population 'normalises' its use (Measham et al 1994). We can see this effect in perennial debates in the public sphere which question the rationale for devoting so many resources to the enforcement of a ban on a behaviour perceived by many to be benign – or no worse than the two lethal and legal drugs, tobacco and alcohol. Yet, 82% of drug convictions continue to be related to cannabis use.[13]

Commercial enterprise has been quick to recognise and openly acknowledge the influence of drug culture among the young. Many drinks marketed at this age group are advertised as if they had the properties of MDMA, LSD or cocaine.[14] Figure 1 shows a promotional campaign for the Princes' Youth Trust Volunteers scheme which was designed on commission by a magazine produced in North London by young people for young

13   Home Office Statistical Bulletins 1985; 1995.
14   Eg, alcopops such as 'Hooch' have been given an 'acid house' image in terms of marketing and packaging.

people.[15] The fleur-de-lis has been manipulated to connote a marijuana leaf and the accompanying text clearly makes references to phrases more commonly associated with drugs parlance. This design and distribution policy resulted in the greatest response to date for the volunteer organisation. Contrary to stereotypes, it suggests that young people who identify with this culture are also interested in making positive social contributions.

Figure 1: advert for the Prince's Youth Trust Volunteers, from (1999)
Exposure, **April**

---

15 Reproduced by kind permission of *Exposure* magazine. The editorial team and contributors are all under 25 years and the magazine is distributed monthly, free, to all secondary aged children in the borough through schools, libraries, sports centres and other networks.

The popular assumption that 'soft drugs lead to hard drugs', otherwise known as 'the gateway theory', has been the much quoted rationale behind the authorities' continued repression of cannabis. This 'public idiom' tends to assume that use of 'hard drugs' leads to physical dependence or premature death. It is an argument that has largely, and falsely, been perpetrated by the medical authorities and it represents a 'contagion' model of drug use.

Figure 2: billboard in North London 1999[16]

Conflating figures for occasional cannabis use (40%) with injecting behaviours (less than 1%) serves to fuel a moral panic among the 'parent' population, whose own experience is less likely to have informed them of the vast difference between these two levels of drug taking. Concerns about the social and health risks of injecting a substance – behaviour often accompanied by the problems of addiction – are misplaced onto a far wider group in society (see figure 2). Amphetamines are self-reported as the second most popular drug with estimates of around 20% of young people having used it. The 'hard' drugs – the Class As – are only reported to have been tried by a much smaller number of young people (see table 3). Of those, hallucinogens and ecstasy are not generally considered to be addictive – which is not to say that their use does not have other associated health risks, but physical dependence is not one of them. Crack and heroin are used by no more than 1% of the population (and are not necessarily injected) and cocaine by 2%. The potential population of young people at risk of developing 'problem' drug use is, therefore, a small proportion of those who have 'experimented' with, or continued to use, other illegal substances. Correlational studies clearly show that those who take 'hard' drugs

16 Produced for the charity Action on Addiction.

have also used cannabis, cigarettes and alcohol (although regular drinking is not associated with elevated levels of cannabis consumption (Powis *et al* 1998)). However, such studies can not provide evidence of causal relationships. This is not to argue that the consumption of cannabis is without associated health risks. There is evidence to suggest that regular use can effect short term memory and the ability to concentrate. It can induce temporary anxiety and paranoia. It impairs co-ordination and response rates, thus increasing the risk of accidents in operating machinery (including cars). Perhaps the greatest risk is posed by the cultural practise of smoking cannabis with unfiltered tobacco, which can lead to nicotine addiction and lung cancer. But the 'war on drugs' and the 'public idiom' expressed by the press in focusing on its illegal status makes it indistinguishable from the more potent and dangerous drugs and arguably precludes the possibility of reasoned debate about its use.

Table 3 gives average prevalence rates compiled from a number of studies. In reality, the picture nationwide is uneven and prevalence rates vary by region and within particular groups of young people who are usually discussed in the literature as 'high risk'. There is a much smaller population of young people who are defined as 'problem', regular and/or multiple drug users. The associated social and medical risks of drug use increase with increased frequency or multiple use. Multiple drug use is considered to be a higher risk activity in health terms and has been seen to increase in relation to the rise of the dance club scene and the greater distribution of drug choices. However, although the North of England has the lowest prevalence figures for Britain, this region also has the highest problem use rates. There is no simple, causal relationship between recreational drug use and the development of problem use (ISDD 1999).

Table 3: drug prevalence rates among young people

Drug	Percentage of young people who report having tried this drug[17]	Percentage of young people estimated to use this drug regularly[18]
Cannabis	40%	16% (of under 20s)
Amphetamines	21% (of 20–24 year olds)	6%
Hallucinogens (LSD, magic mushrooms)	10–20%	1%
Ecstasy	10%	3%
Solvents (legal)	4–8% (peak age is 13–15)	1%
Cocaine	3%	1%
Crack	2%	<1%
Heroin		

17 Definitions of 'young people' vary between different studies.
18 Definitions of 'regular' use and, therefore, of their estimated frequency vary widely in different surveys

DRUGS AND SOCIAL CONTROL POLICIES

For the past 38 years, following the UN agreement which declared that all the UN Member States would follow America's lead on drug prohibition, the 'war on drugs' has consisted of focusing resources in three areas: international drug trafficking; the criminalisation of drug users; and education. Priority has been given to law enforcement agencies – the police, customs and excise and international intelligence forces. This policy stems from the rationale that drugs can be stopped from reaching the general population, which in turn rests on the assumption that their production and use is not widespread and could be cut out like a cancer in society. In the US alone, it is conservatively estimated that $15 billion a year is spent by the Government on financing 57 different departments and agencies involved in their anti-drug strategy (Williamson 1997, p 26). In 1997, The World Drug report compiled by the UN estimated that the world trade in illicit drugs now stands at $400 billion (£250 billion) per annum – greater than the international trade in motor vehicles! In the UK, drug seizures have been increasing yearly, although HM Customs estimate that only around 10% of total imports are intercepted.[19]

The second strategy complements the first and is based on the deterrent model of 'justice'. As table 1 shows, maximum penalties for drug offences are severe, especially if compared with those for other offences. This reflects the fact that social policies in respect of drug use frame this phenomena as a criminal rather than a medical issue. The focus is on the criminalisation and marginalisation of such individuals more than it is on treatment. The number of people processed by the criminal justice system for drug offences in 1995 was 93,631 compared to 6,911 in 1969. Removing a drug offender from society does not remove the individual from contact with drugs and serves merely to temporarily contain the problem. It is well known that, despite security measures, drugs continue to be readily available in Britain's prisons. A recent study found that, not only is the prison environment not a supportive one for those individuals who want to abstain from drug use, it actually encourages drug use (Swann and James 1998). Since the introduction of random drug testing, there is an incentive for prisoners to favour heroin, as this substance clears from the body (and is, therefore, less easily detected) at a much quicker rate than cannabis or hallucinogens. Drug treatment strategies have not been given the same priority, resources or co-ordinated systems as the criminal justice system and, until recently, were exclusively focused upon those individuals who had already developed an unmanageable addiction.

---

19   See Home Office Statistical Bulletins 1975–95 for further facts and figures.

DRUG CONTROLS AND THE
LEGITIMISATION OF RACIST POLICIES

The policy of 'zero tolerance' or 'three strikes and you're out' introduced by the Clinton administration in America has been verbally ascribed to by politicians in this country. In America, this led to the incarceration of a further 5,000 people, the majority of whom were charged with low level, non-violent drug offences. Policing of drug taking behaviour is not evenly applied but focused around specific populations. Today, in the US official statistics show that whites are five times more likely than blacks to use drugs – blacks make up just 13% of drug users. Yet, blacks make up 37% of those arrested on drugs charges, 55% of those convicted and 74% of all those sentenced to prison for drug offences (Smith 1999). Punishments for selling crack cocaine – a form of the drug associated with African-American communities – attract sentences 100 times greater than for selling powdered cocaine which is more commonly associated with high society (mainly white) users. The police have a policy known as 'racial profiling' based on the racist premise that 'most drug offences are committed by minorities' despite the lack of factual evidence for this proposition. The American Civil Liberties Union (ACLU) issued a report called *Driving While Black – Racial Profiling on our Nation's Highways* (1999), which documents police policies of stopping and searching vehicles driven by blacks, in search of drugs. In 1997 alone, California's highway patrol, in pursuit of this enforcement strategy, stopped and searched 34,000 cars using drug sniffer dogs, but found that less than 2% of them were actually carrying drugs.

In this country, powers to stop and search people on the street on the suspicion that a crime has been committed have long been criticised for their targeting of black male youth on the assumption that this social group is synonymous with drug users. In 1997–98, 40% of all those stopped and searched by the Metropolitan Police were from 'ethnic minorities'. Nationally, black people are five times more likely than white people to be stopped by the police.[20] Institutional racism has been thinly cloaked by the 'public idiom' surrounding drug control policies. The Prison Service continues to refuse to recognise Rastafarianism as a religion represented among inmates. Many Rasta prisoners choose not to declare their religion for fear of increased repression by the authorities on the assumption that they would be more likely than their peers to be hiding drugs in their cells.[21]

---

20 (1999) *The Guardian*, 14 July.
21 The only other unrecognised religions are the Nation of Islam, whose most notorious representative was Malcolm X, and the Scientologists.

DRUGS EDUCATION

The third strategy has been 'primary prevention' through drugs education, which has traditionally been seen as a form of 'inoculation' against the temptation that allegedly takes place in schools. Within the public discourse, there has always been a core policy advocating abstinence – or the 'just say no' approach – to educating young people about drugs. This is based on the assumption that, if you tell young people how bad drugs are for their health and warn them that to ignore such advice would be criminal behaviour, then they will not want to 'experiment' with them. The prevalence rates show that this is a largely ineffective strategy and illustrate the impossibility of an approach based upon the premise that drugs can be eradicated from society. Such figures paint a social picture of drug use – particularly the casual use of cannabis – being widely accepted among the 15–25 age group. Recreational drug use exists at levels among the youth that indicate that this is a mainstream activity and not one on the margins. Recognition of this social fact has recently been reflected in government policy:

> In 1993, in response to growing concerns at the increasing evidence of illegal drug use, particularly among young people, and increases in drug related crime, the Government decided to review its existing drugs strategies. In all four countries of the UK, it was recognised that as well as focusing on supply reduction there was a need to put a new emphasis on demand reduction [ISDD 1999].

> This reflects a slight shift in focus away from law enforcement and drug control strategies, towards educational initiatives based on harm minimisation rather than the shock tactics of previous eras. The aim of 'educating' young people not to use drugs (that is, of reducing demand) has in the past been based more on propaganda than education, in that it ignores research evidence and the prevalence of drug use among young people (Cohen 1996). Some have even argued that current models of drugs education actually make matters worse by revealing adult ignorance of the world that youths inhabit – the intervention shines a spotlight on the gap between the two. Young people who do experience problems or concerns are, therefore, less likely to ask for advice or help from what they perceive to be judgmental and ill informed adults (Cohen 1996). In many areas, the problem is further exacerbated by schools using the police to deliver the prevention message. Police officers have themselves questioned whether they are the appropriate agency for this role. Given the illegal nature of this activity, the presence of the police makes frank discussion of their experiences, doubts and questions highly unlikely among teenagers. Officers involved in delivering such drugs education programmes have also been critical of the quality of training and materials on which it was based (Superintendent Green 1996, Greater Manchester Police, quoted in Keene and Williams 1996)

Traditionally, drugs education has been based on information giving, rational approaches. It is now known that increased knowledge about health risks does not necessarily lead to changes in attitude or behaviour (Lloyd et al 1998). Attitude surveys reveal that younger children are reasonably well informed about the negative dangers of smoking, alcohol and drugs. If questioned, most will give the 'right' answer and say that they have no intention of trying these substances. Yet, a few years later, over half of them will have done so. The issue is not, therefore, one of lack of information.

This social fact has led to calls for 'effective and realistic' drugs education in schools that enables informed choices and harm minimisation (Cohen 1996) and a move away from simply 'imparting facts' to more discussion based education. A Health Education Authority survey on drug prevalence and youth attitudes (*Druglink News* 1996) found that very few knew of any associated health risks – although those who reported recent use were more knowledgable. More of these young people were able to describe what they liked about drugs than any problems associated with their use. Since the early 1990s, health education authorities are increasingly adopting more proactive 'harm minimisation' strategies to drug intervention. This has shown signs of successfully reducing the number of fatalities per year associated with occasional or 'recreational' drug users.

DRUGS EDUCATION V HARM REDUCTION

New research suggests that intervention strategies must take account of the positive effects young people who have tried drugs might have experienced (Lloyd *et al* 1998). Teenage heroes, such as James Dean in the 1950s, Jimi Hendrix in the 1960s, Sid Vicious in the 1970s and Kurt Cobain in the 1990s, have exhibited 'unhealthy', risk taking, annihilistic behaviour. Across nearly five decades of teenage culture, appearing 'fashionably wrecked' has been associated with desirable lifestyles that are non-conformist, glamourous and exciting. Being beyond the rules and dying young has a certain appeal. Education about drugs needs to be based on information that is accurate and acknowledges both the risks and benefits of drug use (Cohen 1996). Pleasure has never previously been considered as a reason for drug use and neither has young people's curiosity and need to experiment, to take risks and define their own boundaries (Cohen 1996).

Table 4: reasons given by young people for using drugs[22]

Reasons given	Number	Percentage
Pleasure and enjoyment: the buzz	353	46%
Sociability: relax with friends	155	20%
Negative life circumstances: escape from problems	83	11%
Peer pressure: all my friends do it	52	7%
Experimentation: to see what it was like	35	5%
Anti-alcohol: better than drinking	29	4%
Don't know: never thought about it	26	3%
Other: because illegal	15	2%
Physical circumstances: due to operation	10	1%
Problem usage: I need them	10	1%
Total	**768**	**100%**

Another of the criticisms levelled at drugs education programmes is the lack of data evaluating their effectiveness. The illegality of drug use makes such evaluations highly problematic for obvious reasons. Studies of health education approaches towards teenage cigarette smoking are therefore a valuable source of relevant research findings. Published meta-analysis of school based smoking prevention strategies in the 1970s and 1980s provide a useful starting point. Bruvold 1993 has identified that interventions are based on four different theoretical approaches:

(1) *Rational approaches* seek to provide information on smoking, its effects and consequences, which underpins health promotion activities. This tends to be based on lectures and demonstration materials, worksheets and question and answer sessions.

(2) *Developmental approaches* aim to increase self-esteem and self-reliance, reducing alienation and developing interpersonal and decision making skills. This supplements the information given with discussions, group problem solving and sometimes role play.

(3) *Social norms approaches* based on Jessor and Jessor's work (PBT) seek to provide alternatives to smoking, increase self-esteem and reduce alienation and boredom. This can involve providing opportunities for young people's participation in community improvement projects or recreational activities.

---

22 Maslanka 1994. Survey conducted in Edinburgh by a peer education scheme.

(4) *Social reinforcement approaches*, through discussion, modelling behaviour and role play focus on social pressures, such as peer pressure, with the aim of enabling the identification and resistance to such pressures.

Although approaches can overlap or be combined, Bruvold established that traditional, information giving approaches in (1) produced larger changes in adolescents' knowledge about smoking than did the newer approaches, but that the newer interventions in (2)–(4), had a greater effect upon *attitudes* and *behaviour*. Others have begun to develop approaches to drugs education within other areas of the curricula, such as media studies, that encourage active critical thinking (Kelly 1997). An innovative conference in Bristol initiated by the education authority and planned collaboratively by teachers, media workers, drugs advice workers and further education students aimed to critically discuss students' ideas and opinions on drugs related issues, through a critical appraisal of media portrayals of the topic. Feedback from students was overwhelmingly positive in both knowledge and attitudes (Kelly 1997).

However, there remains a conflict at the heart of public discourse about drug use between the health needs of the individual and the control and criminalisation of those who take drugs. In 1998, a new strategy was set out in the document *Tackling Drugs to Build a Better Britain: The Government's 10 Year Strategy for Tackling Drug Misuse.* This has four key objectives:

(1) young people are to be helped to resist drug use in order to achieve their full potential in society;

(2) communities are to be protected from drug related anti-social and criminal behaviour;

(3) treatment should enable people with drug problems to overcome them and live healthy and crime free lives; and

(4) the availability of illegal drugs on the street should be reduced.

The strategies for achieving these objectives of supply and demand reduction are based on re-affirming the need for drugs education that 'works'; identifying new treatment responses and developing multi-agency interventions.

By 1996, 105 Drug Action Teams (DATs) had been established nationally to assess local services and co-ordinate further initiatives. Each team has a minimum of seven bodies represented on it and each has different principles and priorities (for example, police enforcement targets v health authority treatment targets) and different perspectives on 'the drug problem' and the most appropriate response to it (Mounteney 1996). DATs have, for the first time, contributed to a review of existing services and strategies, but the results have so far confirmed that, in many areas, service delivery is unevaluated, unco-ordinated and failing to reflect the treatment needs of the local populations. In relation to interagency drugs work with young people, they have produced evidence of diminished success rates because of the absence of common aims, the existence of a divergent ethos and competition over scarce resources (Newburn 1998).

The 1998 Crime and Disorder Act has a particular focus on youth justice and on reducing drug related crime. Local authorities are required, in co-operation with the police, the probation service and the health authority, to establish Youth Offending Teams (YOTs) by April 2000, to co-ordinate the provision of youth justice services that reflect local needs. There is some official recognition that the 'problems' associated with the widespread recreational use of cannabis need to be separated from those associated with addictive drug use, but the equally illicit status of both substances presents policy difficulties. Far from being complementary, the two discourses – health and control – view the drug user very differently. Current government strategies are attempting to straddle both approaches. These include less judgmental 'education' that acknowledges the attractions of recreational drug use for the young and improved more responsive treatment services for those who develop problems – combined with 'get tough' statements on dealing with those who are caught, new legislation that makes 'treatment' compulsory and multi-agency teams in which both control (police, probation) and welfare (health, social work) agencies are expected to pull in the same direction. Those who work with young offenders will be caught at the heart of this storm.

Figure 3: Crimestoppers campaign[23]

23 London Underground 1999.

Figure 3 shows an image from a recent campaign by Crimestoppers on the London Underground. This reflects a Home Office report in 1997 in which it was calculated that property worth £1.3 billion is stolen annually to pay for heroin addiction. The image is one of a criminal not an addict. The 'message' is that the 'innocent' public is at risk from the activities of these offenders, not that the individual's addiction reflects complex social problems requiring medical care and treatment. The police, media and, probably, the general public take as an indisputable fact the association of drugs with crime. Yet, the picture from research is more complex. Distinctions need to be drawn between different types of drug use and different types of crime. On one level, the illegal nature of drug use makes the link between drugs and crime indisputable. Anyone who possesses a drug controlled by the Misuse of Drugs Act 1971 has committed a crime – a 'victimless' crime, but enough of a crime to end your career if you are a celebrity, politician or sports personality. Public disclosure of this type of individual engaging in 'deviant' behaviour has to be followed by public reaction castigating the transgression and re-asserting the normative values of the society. Such behaviour must be publicly shown to be detrimental to the perpetrator, otherwise consensus values are undermined. One of the most common accompanying attitudes is that such behaviour sets a bad example to the young. Usually, today, such 'personality' figures are not criminalised but are publicly castigated and then allowed to send themselves for (expensive, private) treatment.

There is also an undisputed link between organised crime and the import of illegal drugs. This is the law of supply and demand. The history of alcohol prohibition in the US is a clear example of how this method of social control creates an insatiable 'black market' with massive profits for those ruthless enough to exploit them. The 'war on drugs' by the authorities includes expenditure per year on attempting to cut off the supply of drugs that exceeds the £69 billion spent on development aid each year (Williamson 1997). Until recently, figures of drug seizures by custom and excise were quoted as evidence of who was winning this war. The surveys in the 1990s that, for the first time, have revealed the scale of drug use within the general population and the under 30s, in particular, have consequently undermined the confidence with which such figures are now reported. Whatever the annual tally in the amount of drugs seized, evidence suggests it has had little impact on stemming supplies to an expanding market with increasing demands.

THE LINK BETWEEN DRUG USE AND CRIME?

Many research studies have found evidence for a strong association between substance abuse and anti-social behaviour in young people (Farrington and West 1990; Howard and Zibert 1990; Huizinga *et al* 1994). However, although there is an association, this does not prove a causal link and the precise relationship is still far from clear. Much of the research on the links between crime and drug use focuses on individuals with drug dependence – usually heroin or crack – that motivates users to commit criminal acts (as alluded to in the Crimestoppers campaign, see figure 3), but the links between non-dependant users and criminal behaviour has not been clearly shown (Williamson *et al* 1996). Despite the debates about the relationship between drug use and crime, there is very little research exploring this. However, prevalence rates among the young offending population and levels of drug use by individual offenders are high, with young offenders at greater risk of developing harmful patterns of drug use (Newburn 1998).

Addiction to an illegal drug substance can lead to highly anti-social behaviour and, in some working class housing estates, the presence of drug addicts can cause much misery to the whole community. This is a very real social problem for some sections of society. Heroin and crack cocaine are the two drugs most commonly associated with such problems. Much of the anti-social behaviour associated with their use is connected to their illegality – the high costs of feeding such an addiction and the unreliable nature of the supply.

The risks of adolescent substance abuse are not spread uniformly throughout the general youth population (Gilvarry 1998); this has led to new arguments for targeting resources at 'high risk' groups. Surveys of prevalence rates among young offenders and excluded pupils present a picture of much higher levels of drug taking (including cocaine and crack cocaine use) among these groups, but such evidence does not show that drug use causes offending (Powis *et al* 1998, p 254). Most studies indicate that delinquent behaviour typically pre-dates drug use, even though the drug use may subsequently influence delinquent behaviour (Newburn 1998). Simple causal explanations – drug use causes crime so crack down on individual drug users – fails to account for the complexity of the picture. But it is clear that young offenders and young drug users are overlapping populations. Young people whose social and psychological problems put them at risk of drug and alcohol abuse often have multiple and complex difficulties ranging from depression and suicidal behaviour, poor school attendance or school failure, delinquency, current or past history of abuse, family dysfunction or parental substance abuse (Gilvarry 1998). Thirty per cent of young people in Britain continue to leave education without any GCSEs above grade C. Structural changes to the education system have resulted in a massive increase in the number of under 16s being excluded from school and from the opportunities associated with education. In the five years between 1991 and 1996 permanent exclusions rose from 2,910 per year to a staggering 13,581 with estimates of another 100,000 being temporarily excluded from receiving an education (Pearce and Hillman 1998). 'Emotional and behavioural difficulties' is the most often cited reason for excluding pupils – in other words, the system penalises those whose development has already been afflicted with stress and difficulties. Again, race is an issue here, as African-Caribbean boys suffer disproportionately high rates of permanent exclusion (approximately five times higher than for the population as a whole), although the precise reasons for this are unclear (Pearce and Hillman 1998). For some young people, the informal economy of the drug markets will offer an alternative, entrepreneurial route to financial success – or at least the hope of one. For others, the rejection of the values of a society that has rejected them may hold a certain annihilistic appeal. Or simply taking substances that make the user feel good and help the user to (momentarily) forget his or her boredom, lack of direction and powerlessness over his or her circumstances may appear to be a rational (individual) solution. Within the medical field, there is beginning to be a recognition that drug use can often be a form of self-medication for other emotional difficulties and that treatment, therefore, needs to include ways of providing individuals with other coping strategies.

Yet, there is the possibility of drug use also causing many difficulties in the life of the user. 'Drug misuse' can be defined in relation to the young person's own perception of their consumption and its consequent benefits and costs. Instead of being a label which the young person experiences as reflecting someone else's values, values that may have already been consciously rejected, it is then a description of their own concerns about habitual use. Unless the young person can agree that their drug use is problematic on some level, any intervention is unlikely to be successful.

THE CHALLENGE FOR YOUTH OFFENDING TEAMS

The current view that the criminal justice system provides a means of identifying a 'target population' for drug interventions has been enshrined in the Crime and Disorder Act 1998 and its introduction of multi-agency YOTs. Intervention could potentially occur at three stages: before sentence; as an element in community penalties; or within prison (Hough 1996). Initiatives targeted at the pre-court stage have tended to take the form of drug referral schemes upon arrest (at police stations) or at court. In practice, though, such schemes again focus on those individuals whose substance abuse is directly related to their reason for arrest and are, therefore, primarily concerned with addiction and alcohol abuse. The treatment services to which drug users are referred continue to reflect the concerns of the past and tend to have been designed to meet the needs of opiate addicts (for example, needle exchange schemes). Research has shown that these agencies are perceived as being 'run by white people, for white people' (Awiah et al 1992). Services for young drug users, particularly those from ethnic minorities, are generally absent. The current situation is one in which there are few specific drug service initiatives aimed at young offenders within the youth justice system (Newburn 1998) and even fewer treatment services orientated to the needs of the under 18s:

> For those who present with agreed and recognised drug dependency
> problems, the insistence on abstinence in those rehabilitation services with
> places for under 18s that do exist may discourage engagement and retention of
> the young person in the services [Gilvarry 1998, p 284].

There is concern that new compulsory drug treatment orders, particularly in
the absence of services sensitive to the very specific needs of young people,
may serve merely to further criminalise sections of the population already
excluded from many social opportunities. The danger with the control
discourse dominating this new approach is that it places the blame for what
are primarily social inequalities (poverty, poor housing, exclusion from
education, etc) solely on the shoulders of individuals, who are then punished
further if they fail to find more positive ways of living.

A key issue here is the need to embed a drugs input into work already
being delivered by responsible agencies (Lloyd 1998, p 217). Youth justice
officers have experience of working with individual young people to develop
their self-esteem and maturity. A focus of the work, for some years, has been
to encourage young people to develop their ability to make informed and
appropriate choices and decisions about their future. This often happens in
conjunction with attempts to secure other welfare services to address unmet
needs. YOTs should, therefore, develop policies which are, as far as possible,
based upon an holistic assessment of young offenders' needs and not those
which focus solely on their anti-social behaviour as an isolated element. Many
youth justice workers have received little training in connection with drug use
and drugs prevention and are, therefore, sometimes unsure or uncomfortable
talking to their clients about their substance use (Newburn 1998). Yet, the
widespread influence of PBT and sensation seeking theory means that
intervention strategies for delinquency and drug misuse have much in
common. Therefore, the youth justice officer's approach to helping a young
person to assess their offending behaviour will be similar to the drugs
worker's approach to addressing drug misuse and vice versa. Specific
information and materials for discussing drugs with young people have been
developed by other agencies and could be used more widely by those
employed in YOTs.[24]

A report on two innovative schemes initiated by the Home Office Drugs
Prevention Initiative has found that:

> ... the majority of young drug using offenders seen so far have not had prior
> contact with drugs agencies, confirming the importance of the criminal justice
> system as a site for targeting drugs prevention and treatment. This is
> reinforced by the fact that very few of the young people referred have
> convictions for drug offences [Newburn 1998].

---

24 Sources of such materials are given at the end of this book.

However, philosophies of minimum intervention among social workers means that uncovering the type of information about drug use which might lead to referrals to drug agencies typically occurs only when young people are on a supervision order rather than at arrest and caution. Youth justice workers appear to feel more comfortable making a referral when there is already a statutory involvement with a social worker (Newburn 1998). Such tensions are, arguably, an inevitable consequence of the contradictory policies of health and control, which are always likely to surface in multi-agency teams which straddle both camps. Attention will also, therefore, need to be paid within these teams to establishing codes of practice relating to confidentiality and the sharing of information about individuals between agencies with very different objectives.

There are signs that new initiatives are currently being developed in an attempt to redress gaps in existing services. For example, in North London a new voluntary agency, 'Uplift', has been set up to address the specific needs of black drug users and their families. Their approach is holistic (for example, it includes providing hot meals, alternative therapies, housing and benefit advice and counselling), and aims to individually tailor their intervention plans in consultation with the recipient. YOTs could aim to develop closer links with such services, while retaining their separation from them (and thus avoiding compromising the confidentiality of information disclosed during counselling, for example).

CONCLUSION

The Crime and Disorder Act 1998 seeks to address issues of drug use and drug motivated or related crime through multi-agency partnerships. Although 'working together' to reduce crime in the community is a laudable aim, it assumes that different social agencies have not previously pooled their expertise, services and information through a lack of shared vision, organisation or co-ordination. It therefore seeks to resolve these structural gaps through legislation that compels the agencies of health, police, criminal justice and welfare to become located within the same physical space. It assumes that professionals can then exchange information and resources more efficiently, develop joint approaches towards drug users and respond more effectively to reduce this social problem together.

What it fails to acknowledge is that different social agencies have different histories, agendas and responsibilities – reflected in very different cultures and discourses. Policy developments that promote their convergence often gloss over their incongruent philosophies. For example, discourses within health aim to encourage young people to adopt lifestyles which do not undermine their physical well being. They therefore place importance on the non-judgmental education of the individual (in which tobacco addiction can be understood to be the greatest risk associated with cannabis consumption by the young), self-referral (that is, voluntary as opposed to coerced) and a strict professional-client confidentiality. The criminal justice system, on the other hand, is based on a discourse that places paramount importance on the benefits to the 'wider community' of curbing or reducing certain individual behaviour. The 40–50% of 'recreational' drug users are as 'illegal' as the 1% 'problem' drug users and the two categories are often conflated. Controlling or 'treating' the behaviour of individuals is seen to be as much for the benefit of the public as for the individual. Punishment can be a consequence of disclosure or non-compliance.

Youth justice officers and other professionals who are due to come together in the new Youth Offending Teams (YOTs) in April 2000 need to be aware that issues of social control underlie both their work and the public debates about young people's use of drugs. The media plays a pivotal role in the generation of moral panics about drugs and professionals have a duty to be more informed than the simplistic notions on which media articles tend to be based. Although drug use is now known to be widespread among young people, particularly those who are likely to come into contact with the criminal justice system (that is, boys, the 15–18 age group, black and ethnic minorities, excluded pupils, those with multiple social difficulties), it is not considered problematic by the majority of those who take them. Much drug use is no more 'harmful' than individual choices related to diet, exercise, smoking, drinking or participating in dangerous sports, and this needs to be acknowledged by those who seek to engage young people in discussion. However, young people are often ill informed about the associated health risks of drug taking, particularly multiple drug use, and are entitled to accurate and relevant information in an atmosphere that encourages discussion and problem solving. Condemnation will not encourage young people to talk about the difficulties they face – which are specific and very different to those faced by the generation before them.

Some drug use is problematic, and research suggests that a disproportionately high number of those in the criminal justice system are at risk of developing problem or addictive use. This reflects the fact that those in the criminal justice system are often facing multiple disadvantages and many, as a consequence, have emotional and behavioural difficulties. Youth offending services need to recognise that some young people who develop drug misuse problems may also have experienced highly traumatic life events. Further criminalisation of the individual is unlikely to do more than 'contain' the problem. To avoid further criminalisation of individual youth, professionals may continue to avoid proactively addressing drug use among their client base, except in those circumstances where it is already known to the authorities and is clearly linked to their offending behaviour. This would, however, mean refusing to recognise the complex needs of young people who typically have few other sources of support or education and are known to be vulnerable to developing problem drug using habits.

YOTs should, therefore, consider taking a lead in developing harm minimisation education programmes for all those who come into contact with them, based on the best available evidence of which approaches effect attitudes and behaviour, as well as levels of knowledge. Drug and alcohol consumption should be considered and incorporated into assessment procedures of young people whose behaviour has brought them to the attention of youth justice agencies. Issues of confidentiality, disclosure and referral between different agencies within these new, multidisciplinary teams need to be addressed explicitly through policy documents and these should be made available to those who use the service. Strategies for supporting the parents of drug misusing teenagers also need to be developed as well as treatment programmes for those who want to access them. When working with young people, it is important not to over-react to drug use which incurs little apparent risk of harm, whilst nevertheless being ready to mobilise a range of responses to more serious threats to the health and safety of the young person. Professionals, therefore, need to develop the skills necessary for assessing how and when to intervene. Where complex problems, especially mental health problems, are identified, then appropriate, child centred services need to be accessed. Although treatment options are currently severely limited, DAT and YOT plans for this target group should aim to provide a range of holistic community services that aim to keep the welfare of the child as the paramount concern. In recognition of the conflict that exists between the discourses of criminal justice and health promotion, YOTs may need to develop closer working links with specialist, voluntary sector agencies who are better placed to provide a non-judgmental, child centred and holistic response to the young person experiencing problems with their drug use.

CHAPTER 7

PRACTICAL IMPLICATIONS OF THE CRIME AND DISORDER ACT FOR YOUTH OFFENDING TEAMS – A YOUTH OFFENDING TEAM'S PERSPECTIVE

Susannah Hancock

High on diesel and gasoline, psycho for drum machine ...

Drag act, drug acts, suicides ...

Cracked up, stacked up ... lost it to Bostik yeah,

Shaved heads, raved heads. On the pill, got too much time to kill

get into bands and gangs

Oh here they come, the beautiful ones, the beautiful ones

Loved up, doved up, lost in a lonely town

Oh here they come, the beautiful ones,

Just don't think about

Just don't think about it ...[1]

The old system has allowed young offenders to wreck their lives as well as disrupting families and communities. Young offenders have escaped facing up to their crimes for too long.[2]

INTRODUCTION

The pace of activity, innovation and change within the youth justice system on the cusp of the next millennium is incredible. Keeping up with all the current changes in the youth justice system feels a little like climbing that elusive mountain and never quite making it to the top – every time you reach the peak, another one looms up ahead. Or, if you prefer football analogies (as I must confess I do), it is all a bit like making it to the top of your Sunday football league, only to find that a whole new division has been created ahead of you. However, as someone once said about football, 'It's a game of two halves'. So perhaps it is with youth justice. We've all emerged from the first half that was the old youth justice system, several goals down – with rising youth crime rates, lengthy court processes and high rates of youth custody – and some of them, let's face it, are own goals. But we now have the second half ahead of us and it is already looking like a completely different ball game.

---

1   Suede, 'The beautiful ones', from the album *Coming Up*, 1998, Nude.
2   Michael MP (Lab), then Home Office Minister, June 1998 Home Office News.

For a start, the team has got a new name – the Youth Offending Team (YOT). There is a new manager – the Youth Justice Board. There are new funding opportunities and we are in a far stronger position to be proactive about tackling youth crime. It is challenging stuff, but it is also an incredibly exciting time to be involved in the youth justice system.

For too many years, the youth justice system had remained the poor relative of the criminal justice system. Even the Prison Service seemed to get better press and, whenever there was a spate of youth crime, the papers had a field day, usually at the expense of the Youth Justice Service. Whether it was Safari Boy, Rat Boy, the Bulger murder – all added fuel to an already volatile bonfire. In many cases, quite rightly so. In some areas, the Youth Justice System was just not equipped, resourced or qualified enough to effectively tackle youth crime. And, with monitoring and evaluation systems rarely operating, there was little hard evidence to demonstrate whether community interventions with young offenders actually made a difference.

In 1996, the youth justice system was turned upside down with the publication of one key report, *Misspent Youth*. Commissioned by the Government and produced by the National Audit Commission in June 1996, the report exposed a range of deficiencies in the youth justice system at both national and local levels and made for disturbing reading, particularly in light of the growing national levels of youth crime (in 1994, offenders under 18 committed about seven million offences a year and cost the pubic about £1 billion a year dealing with them). *Misspent Youth* was to prove instrumental in instigating systematic change at every level of the youth justice system.

Despite being commissioned whilst the Conservative Party were in power, the recommendations of the report were quickly picked up as a key election manifesto theme by every one of the three major parties in the lead up to the 1997 General Election. It was in this climate that the Labour Party came to power in May 1997, bringing with them radical plans for sweeping changes across the whole spectrum of youth justice.

This chapter will look at some of these changes from a largely practical perspective, examining specifically how they impact on the now newly formed YOTs. The chapter will first explore the nature and development of multi-agency YOTs, examining their make up, their developing role in addressing youth crime and the challenges that have been encountered to date in their evolution. It will then move on to something of a whistle stop tour of the new crime and disorder legislation as it impacts on YOTs, beginning with pre-court disposals, the new final warning schemes, child safety orders, parenting orders and other diversionary initiates. It will then explore the new referral order bought in via the Youth Justice and Criminal Evidence Act 1999, before looking at the other new orders – action plan order, reparation order, etc and the recent shift towards evidence based practice. It will, furthermore, explore changes around bail, remands and custody, and finally focus on the increasing use of Management Information Systems in YOTs as well as key future developments.

To try to cover the brave new world of youth justice in just one chapter is, of course, impossible. However, this chapter represents at least a start in exploring some of the salient issues for YOTs emerging from the new legislation. It is also imperative to raise the issue of tackling inequalities within the youth justice system. This is a key development area and, until we get it right, the system will continue to fail young people. As such, I will seek to address issues of discrimination and equalities throughout this chapter, rather than keeping them to one section. Issues such as the McPherson Report into the death of Stephen Lawrence, the new provisions on racially aggravated offences and the continuous over-representation of young black offenders in the criminal justice system all point to the fact that the youth justice system must get its house in order. YOTs can and must use the new legislation to make a difference.

YOUTH OFFENDING TEAMS – SALAD, SOUP OR FRUITCAKE?[3]

An excuse culture has developed in the youth justice system. It excuses itself for its inefficiency, and too often excuses the young offenders before it, implying that they cannot help themselves ... rarely are they confronted with their behaviour and helped to take more personal responsibility for their actions. The system allows them to go on wrecking their own lives as well as disrupting their families and communities ... All those working in the youth justice system must now have a principle aim – to prevent offending. That will be the new statutory aim of the new Crime and Disorder Act.[4]

In 1998, the Crime and Disorder Act gave the entire youth justice system one principle aim: to prevent offending. Pivotal to this aim has been the establishment of multidisciplinary YOTs:

It shall be the duty of each local authority to establish for their area one or more youth offending teams – a Youth Offending Team shall include one of each of the following, namely –

– a probation officer/a social worker

– a police officer/a person nominated by the Health Authority

– a person nominated by the chief education officer

– any other such persons as the local authority thinks appropriate.[5]

3   Finegan 1998, Lewisham YOT Manager.
4   Straw 1997.
5   Crime and Disorder Act 1998, Pt 3, s 30(4).

YOTs are a whole new animal. Prior to the 1998 legislation, the Youth Justice Service had remained largely in the hands of small Social Service Teams with little interaction with other professionals. Communication between statutory and voluntary agencies around working with young offenders was often poor and youth justice staff were often unqualified.

There were, nevertheless, examples of good practice in the field. Projects such as the Northamptonshire Diversion Project demonstrated the real benefits of multi-agency work in reducing offending behaviour. The advent of YOTs represented a significant shift away from isolated, reactive working, towards the Blair ethos of joined-up thinking and joined-up action. For the first time, innovation and motivation were being actively encouraged and rewarded within the youth justice system.

YOTs are essentially the key to making much of the Government's new agenda on youth crime work. In establishing YOTs, local authorities have been given the responsibility to consult and involve all key professional agencies in the formation of the YOT. This is a radical shift, not just at practitioner level. At senior management level Chief Executives, Directors of Social Services and Education, Chief Probation Officers, Chief Superintendents, Directors of Health Authorities and so on must now meet regularly to develop and review the progress of YOTs, to ensure targets are met, and to pool staff and resources towards a common and effective youth justice strategy. In the London Borough of Lewisham where I work, the council and its partners moved fast. The Crime and Disorder Act was passed in the summer of 1998, the Lewisham YOT Manager was appointed in June and the Lewisham YOT pilot was live by October. This was policy very swiftly becoming practice.

The multi-agency YOT experience in Lewisham continues to be challenging. The make up of a YOT is in fact not completely prescribed by the Home Office, although some key agencies do have to be involved (social services, probation, police, education and health). This makes for increased flexibility at a local level and means that the staff make up of each YOT can respond to the needs of the local community in different and innovative ways. Perhaps one of the slower partners within YOTs nationally has been that of health. This raises the key question as to what is the most appropriate and effective contribution for health to play within a YOT? Is it through the provision of a substance misuse worker, a mental health nurse, a psychologist, or access to GPs? Different YOTs are exploring diverse approaches to this issue, often undertaking a health audit of a sample group of their young offender population in order to establish need and appropriate provision.

In Lewisham, the multi-agency model initially proved quite complex, with different members coming into the team wearing often quite diverse professional hats and acclimatised to very different professional environments. Youth workers were unused to working side by side with police officers. Social workers felt threatened by the more rigorous approach of probation officers. Probation officers felt threatened by the more relaxed style of social workers, education staff were baffled by the complexities of the criminal justice system. And everyone was concerned that the YOT could mean losing something of their professional identity. It was here that the Lewisham YOT manager had some insightful approaches to tackling the thorny issue of multi-agency work with the question 'salad, soup or fruitcake?'. It was this little metaphor that provided both a language and some answers to many of the YOT staff's initial concerns:

(a) Was the YOT to be a 'soup' with all individual professional identities and expertise 'slopped' together into one big melting pot, everyone undertaking the same tasks and adopting the same roles? Everyone writing reports, supervising young people, going to court, and so on regardless of profession? Everyone losing their professional identifies and becoming something of a YOT robot?

(b) Was the YOT to be a 'salad' with everyone maintaining strict individual roles and jobs? With professional cultures sacred and each YOT member only doing the very specific task that their parent agency engaged in?

(c) Was the YOT to be a 'fruitcake' with each YOT member preserving their identity and specialisms, but at the same time using their skills and experience within a partnership framework – working together, being in the same cake, but not ending up as identical?

The fruitcake model provided a vital vernacular for the Lewisham YOT to develop effective work in such a new area – an area where there were few signposts and instruction manuals. In the article 'Team spirit' 1999, Mark Hunter presents some interesting early discussions around multi-agency working. He writes:

> Charlie Beaumont from the Youth Justice Board also stresses that it is important for YOT members to retain their individual professional identities. He sees little point in seconding staff with specialist skills if, in time, they all merge into generic YOT officers carrying out identical tasks:
>
> > There is always a danger that once they have joined the team they can become isolated from their parent agencies, which in the long run defeats the whole object of having seconded professionals in the first place.[6]

The fruitcake analogy was particularly useful in the early days when the spilt between core/current work and future/development work was quite marked. When pre-sentence reports were piling high and court duties need-ed to be covered, it was tempting to want all staff to simply cover tasks that were seen as core youth justice tasks. However, what had to be acknowl-edged was that this was a new way of working and not simply a re-run of

---

6   Hunter 1999.

the old system with more staff to help out. Education staff needed time to develop their work areas and explore new and innovative ways of encouraging young offenders back into the education system, as well as encouraging schools to accept them back. Police and other staff needed time to develop the new work around restorative justice and working with victims. These new areas soon became 'core work' and we are now seeing a far more even split between work areas.

EVIDENCE BASED PRACTICE

> While we need to do everything we can to protect the public from offenders, we need to be as creative and effective as possible in dealing with the problem of the young offenders themselves. We need to provide a clear evidence base to inform policy and practice.[7]

Alongside radical changes within youth justice teams, came a new emphasis on evidence based, effective practice with young offenders. This had been emerging via the 'what works' models of the Probation Service in working with adult offenders. From the early to mid-1990s, the Probation Service had been developing both individual and group work programmes for addressing offending behaviour using specific cognitive behavioural models of working based on research. This was largely new to the Youth Justice Service who, often for quite legitimate reasons (lack of resources, lack of training, lack of appropriate programmes for this age group), had rarely employed evidence based practice, and had continued with more youth work models of working. Whilst much of this still plays an important role in tackling youth crime, of itself, it was demonstrably not working in reducing the increasing levels of youth crime across the country. The 1997 District Audit resulting from the National Audit, *Misspent Youth*, revealed Lewisham to have one of the highest rates of youth crime in inner London and it was perhaps no coincidence that only 14% of youth justice time was at that time spent directly addressing offending behaviour. Whilst the high rates of youth crime could be put down to many factors, it was evident that new and proactive approaches were needed to tackle the problem.

Effective practice involves all YOT staff focusing on the emerging evidence base of effective models of working with young offenders. It means a shift away from the older intermediate treatment models of working and a move towards more structured and individually targeted interventions for addressing offending behaviour. Based on social learning theory, cognitive behavioural practice draws on a range of established cognitive and behavioural techniques to help offenders face up to the consequences of their actions and develop new skills and techniques for controlling their behaviour.

---

7   Boateng 1998, then Under-Secretary of State for Health.

By developing problem solving, thinking skills and value enhancement techniques, this approach recognises that behaviour cannot be changed without first changing the way young people think about and understand their environment. In their chapter 'Effective interventions with offenders', Vennard and Hedderman conclude:

> Cognitive behavioural approaches ... are more successful than techniques such as unfocused group work, individual counselling or unstructured therapy ... When delivered non-selectively to a broad range of offenders, cognitive behavioural programmes achieve a 10–15% lower reconviction rate than reported for similar offenders who did not attend such programmes [1998, p 105].

It was vital to know that interventions were being delivered to all young people consistently and effectively regardless of the individual staff member delivering them. The importance of joint staff training for all members of the YOT became increasingly apparent. Alongside this, issues of anti-discriminatory practice also emerged. If interventions with young offenders are to be effective, they must also be delivered within a framework that is both equal and culturally sensitive. This is also a key YOT training issue, particularly due to staff coming from different professional backgrounds with possibly different understandings of issues of difference. Key to a successful YOT, therefore, must be training at the earliest opportunity around team building, evidence based practice and working with difference.

PRE-COURT DISPOSALS

I want some help to help myself.[8]

Final warnings

The old police cautioning scheme had fallen into disrepute for some years. Young people were notching up as many as six or seven cautions a piece and very little was being done about it. However, in some areas, examples of good practice were developing via what became known as caution plus schemes. Again, the Northamptonshire Diversion Unit and the Milton Keynes Retail Theft Initiatives were examples of proactive work at the caution stage. The effectiveness of these schemes in reducing offending behaviour (only three per cent re-offended in the Milton Keynes Programme) led on to the proposed final warning schemes of the new Crime and Disorder Act 1998 (Pt 4, s 52). The Act stipulated that, at the first offence, a young person should receive a reprimand and, at the second, a final warning. At this stage, the young person

---

8   Nirvana, 'Polly', from the album *Nevermind*, 1991, Geffen.

would be immediately referred to the YOT for an assessment. YOT staff would assess both the young person and their family with a view to exploring the reasons behind their offending. Intervention programmes would then be offered on the basis of this assessment, with due regard to the seriousness of the offence, proportionality, etc. However, all interventions within the caution plus scheme remain voluntary and, whilst YOTs are engaged in following up families who do not attend, there is no compulsion by law that they are present. However, if the young person does re-offend, then they will be sent to court and the court will be informed of their attendance (or lack of it) at the final warning stage.

This is the primary pre-court diversionary aspect of the Crime and Disorder Act 1998. It ensures that all young people and their families are given the opportunity to receive support and intervention at the earliest possible opportunity before offending becomes entrenched and the young person acquires a criminal record. This represents a whole new client group for YOT staff – a group who previously would have received little more than a ticking off by the police. Many YOTs will be looking at significant numbers of final warnings per week and this necessitates creative and innovative ways of working. In Lewisham, the YOT is delivering joined-up approaches to working with young people at the pre-court stage through the funding of staff in the local Social Services Family and Adolescent Support Team, to deliver interventions in conjunction with YOT police officers. Evidence based practice has demonstrated that, if young people are offered intensive interventions too early in their offending careers, this can do more harm than good and actually encourage them into further offending. Levels of intervention must be based on thorough assessments, with local family support services having a key role to play in this area. The multi-agency YOT programme must also embrace partnership and work with other associated teams and agencies outside the actual YOT itself. Achieving this balance is vital. However well resourced, individual YOTs cannot and must not attempt the whole youth crime prevention agenda singlehanded.

CHILD SAFETY ORDERS

Child safety orders represent another diversionary tool introduced by the 1998 Crime and Disorder Act. These orders are for children under the age of 10 who are beneath the age of criminal responsibility. A child safety order can be made if a child is felt to be at risk of offending, or involved in offending which, if they were over 10, would constitute an offence. On the application of the local authority, the magistrates' court can make a child safety order which places the child under the supervision of a responsible officer and requires the child to comply with specific requirements (Pt 1, s 2 of the Crime and Disorder Act 1998). Children may be referred to the YOT from the police, housing and/or social services. Once this information has been received, the YOT calls together a panel of all key professionals to explore the nature of the referral, what interventions, if any, are already being offered and whether a child safety order is necessary to prevent further offending. To date, only one child safety order has been made in the whole of the country (in Sunderland). Certainly, in Lewisham, whilst we have had several referrals to date, we have as yet had no orders. This is largely because other interventions such as care proceedings are already being enforced, predominantly via social services, or other such interventions are in the pipeline. As a result, a child safety order would not be appropriate. It is interesting that this reflects the general mood of the rest of the country. At the time of writing, in fact, both Tony Blair and Jack Straw have raised concerns at the low numbers of such orders being introduced.

ANTI-SOCIAL BEHAVIOUR ORDERS

Another important piece of legislation affecting YOTs, perhaps more indirectly than directly, is that of the anti-social behaviour order (ASBO) which came into effect in early 1999. The ASBO is primarily aimed at reducing anti-social behaviour and nuisance by adults and young people. It allows local authorities, in partnership with the police, to take out such orders on individuals who, 'act in an anti-social manner that causes harassment, harm or distress'. It demands that, when such an order is applied for, comprehensive inter-agency consultation takes place between all agencies involved with the individual or families concerned. ASBOs can be taken out against any individual over the age of 10 years, and it is not difficult to predict that a considerable percentage of candidates for ASBOs will be young people. This means a key role for the YOT. ASBOs serve to prohibit the individual from doing specific things – such as the anti-social behaviour itself, having contact with the victim, being in a certain area at a certain time, etc. It is, to date, largely a tool at the disposal of the local authority housing department in resolving problems in local neighbourhoods and estates. However, YOTs will be involved as a significant partner. In Lewisham, the housing department calls a review meeting at every case being considered for an ASBO with the YOT invited to provide information, sharing the consideration of a parenting orders, etc. ASBOs have already led to increased levels of inter-departmental and inter-agency working, and to better understandings of connections between the work of housing, the police and other key agencies. This could represent a real catalyst for the beginning of highly effective joint working around youth crime prevention.[9]

---

9   Other orders not addressed in this chapter, but linked to YOT activity, are: child curfew (s 14), sex offender (s 2) and racially aggravated offences (Pt 2, ss 22–25).

PARENTING ORDERS

> Gravity keeps me down, or maybe it's just shame, at being so young and so vain ... and if you tolerate this your children will be next.[10]

> None of us should evade our responsibilities to our children. You have to get parents to accept their responsibilities. The earlier you get to these parents and children the better.[11]

A controversial piece of legislation within the Crime and Disorder Act 1998 is that of the parenting order. This order is aimed at parents and carers of young offenders, and is seen as part of the Government's wider plan of action for families. The Government believes that parents have a pivotal role to play in terms of reducing the offending behaviour of their children and that they must take an increasing responsibility with regard to this. As a result, the parenting order has been introduced, stipulating that the parents or carers of young offenders and young people not attending school could be made subject to such an order by the local youth court, the family proceedings court or magistrates' court.

The primary aim of the parenting order is to prevent the problematic/offending behaviour of the young person. Parents made subject to such an order have to:

- comply for a period not exceeding 12 months with requirements specified in the order; and/or

- attend for a period not exceeding three months and not more than once a week, counselling or guidance sessions as specified by the responsible officer (Crime and Disorder Act 1998, Pt 1, s 8).

The first component, regarding the specific requirements, is discretionary and need not be part of every order. It could involve the parents ensuring that their children attend school for a specified period, or attend drugs counselling, for example. However, the second component is compulsory and means that the parents must attend for parenting skills and guidance support sessions for a maximum of a three-month period. The parenting order itself is not a criminal conviction for the parent/carer. However, if they breach the order, this does constitute an offence and the parents must then appear before the court to answer the breach. If found guilty, they could receive up to a level 3 fine (£1,000) and a criminal record. Breach proceedings are complex and time consuming, involving police interviews and CPS decisions over prosecutions. Already, this is an area that the YOT pilots are hoping will be amended over time.

---

10   Manic Street Preachers, 'If you tolerate this your children will be next', from the album *This Is My Truth, Tell Me Yours*, 1998, Sony.

11   Straw (1998) *The Guardian*, 26 September.

The parenting orders have been greeted with a mixture of interest and scepticism not only in this country but also across Europe and the US. Whilst, studies as far back as the 1970s were being undertaken with parents of young offenders, training them in basic parenting skills, negotiation, rule and boundaries setting, etc and meeting with considerable success, these were nevertheless voluntary and little had been tried with parents on a more mandatory basis. As a result, the introduction of the parenting order is not just a new criminal justice intervention – it is also an experiment in new ways of working with parents, with the YOTs acting as something of a guinea pig.

Across the country, pilot YOTs have adopted very different models in the delivery of parenting order programmes. In Lewisham, we approached local voluntary sector parenting groups who were already providing support and skills-based programmes to parents on a voluntary basis. We felt that parenting order programmes could be delivered more sensitively and effectively via the voluntary sector in that there would be less social services stigma attached to parents attending, and the groups would be more connected to the local community. We commissioned two different voluntary providers to deliver our group work programmes, with a view to evaluating both models in order to develop an evidence base of 'what works'. A 10 week programme, covering areas such as active listening, boundary setting, coping strategies, issues around substance misuse, communication and listening, anger management and problem solving, was delivered to all parents on orders. There was also the option of one to one sessions for those parents who were felt to be in need of more individual support. Another key issue was that of ensuring that programmes were sensitive to different cultural and religious dimensions. Parents and carers from different ethnic groups often have different needs and concerns around parenting. These must be acknowledged and addressed at the assessment stage, and YOTs must then ensure that a comprehensive and flexible menu of options is available for parents in order that all needs are addressed. In Lewisham, we have appointed a parenting order co-ordinator to develop work with all parents and carers, as well as devising assessment tools for work within pre-sentence reports.

From the beginning, the Lewisham YOT prepared itself to be inundated with parenting orders. We assumed the courts would love them and would dish out orders like confetti; and there was reason for our prediction. The Crime and Disorder Act 1998 stipulates that parenting orders can be made on all parents/carers of young people aged 15 years or under. (Once a young person reaches 16, a parenting order can still be made, but only in exceptional circumstances, having regard to the young person's level of maturity, etc).

However, we were wrong. At the time of writing, numbers of parenting orders remain relatively low.[12] The possible reasons behind this are

---

12 Although other YOTs, such as Sunderland, have had higher numbers.

interesting. First, the courts seem far more cautious about using the new parenting orders than we had anticipated. In almost all cases, they seem ready to be guided by the YOT assessment report. Secondly, the issue of getting education social workers on board in order to address parenting orders in magistrates' courts is complex. Training and joint assessment is vital here if magistrates' courts are to not be left behind. Initially, we did try to refer parents as much as possible to attend support groups on a voluntary rather than statutory order basis. However, take up remained low, and we are now more proactive in proposing parent orders in court where appropriate. As yet, our local data is not extensive enough to gauge how successful the parenting orders have been, although the national data from research carried out at Sheffield University should answer some of these questions. However, initial observations suggest that programmes are presenting parents with a new and valuable opportunity for help and support that had not previously been available. Some parents are asking: 'Why did this take so long?' Maybe we need to ask the same question.

REFERRAL ORDER

Lord Longford: 'What kind of people could help young offenders?'

Anthony (persistent offender): 'Multidisciplinary. But the most important thing is that they actually care about us – are interested in us. Some of them maybe don't need qualifications apart from their humanity.'[13]

Just when YOTs thought they were beginning to get their heads around the new crime and disorder legislation, just when they thought it was safe to go outside and take a quick breather, the new Youth Justice and Criminal Evidence Act 1999 was introduced. This was yet another new piece of legislation to get to grips with. This received royal assent in the summer of 1999 and, amongst other things, provided for the introduction of the referral order. First outlined in the final chapters of the initial Government White Paper, *No More Excuses*, this introduced a whole new framework for working with first time offenders and hailed a significant shift towards restorative justice models of practice.

The impact of the referral order on the youth justice system is as yet impossible to gauge. But its sheer scope, potential and philosophical shift will certainly have enormous implications for YOT practitioners and, indeed, the whole of the youth justice system. Due for piloting from April 2000, the referral order will constitute the standard sentence for all first time young offenders under 18. A referral order is a sentence of the court, not a pre-court disposal, but is not, however, a community penalty and does not require a

---

13   Longford 1993.

pre-sentence report. All young offenders appearing before the court on a first offence (many of whom will have been through the final warning scheme) will be made subject to a referral order by the court regardless of their offence, exceptions being where the court chooses to make an absolute discharge, or where the offence is so serious that only a custodial sentence or hospital order can be made.

The court must make a referral order if the young person has:

- pleaded guilty to the offence;
- no previous convictions (a previous conditional discharge or binding over is treated as a previous conviction).

There is also scope for discretionary referrals if:

- the young person has no previous convictions and is being dealt with by the court for more than one associated offence and, although he or she has pleaded guilty to at least one of the offences, he or she has also pleaded not guilty to at least one of them.

A referral order is for no less than three months and no more than 12 months. Once a referral order has been made, the young person is referred to a Youth Offender Panel, which is organised by the local YOT. The panel must consist of one YOT member and at least two other persons. These must be recruited from the local community, and could be local residents, members of community organisations, business people, etc, who will have received appropriate training from the YOT and associated partners. The parents/carers of the young person can be ordered by the court to attend the panel. Other people such as the victim, the victim's supporter, anyone else over 18 years who is felt to exert a positive influence on the young person, as well as other key players can also attend. The panel must then meet to seek an agreement about an appropriate course of action and intervention programme for the young person. When an agreement is reached between the panel and the young person, a contract is drawn up and signed by the young person and panel members. It could include elements such as:

- reparation to the victim;
- counselling and support for the family / young person;
- help around substance misuse;
- education attendance;
- addressing offending behaviour;
- use of leisure time, etc.

Interventions can include any of the elements that appear in both final warning, reparation orders and other community penalty programmes. The panel must meet again to review the progress of the order and, finally, to ensure the order has been completed. If a young person fails to agree to the proposed contract, or agrees but later fails to comply with the contract, they will be returned to court. At this stage, the court can choose to: (a) allow the order to continue if appropriate; or (b) revoke the order and re-sentence. If the young person re-offends whilst subject to a referral order, the court can choose to extend the compliance period of the initial order. However, this is only on the basis of a report from the panel where it is felt that there are exceptional circumstances indicating that a further compliance period could help reduce offending. This cannot, however, take the period of the order beyond 12 months. If the court does not or cannot make an extension order then it can revoke the order and re-sentence.

This is very close to the approach adopted and delivered for the past 10 years in Scotland via Scottish Youth Panels. Such a model is also employed in Australia, New Zealand (where it was originally developed with the Maori communities) and other European countries. However, in these cases, the panel process keeps the young person entirely out of the youth court system. If they complete their contract, they do not receive a criminal record. The British model is distinctly different in that the referral order is an order of the court and the young person *does* effectively receive a criminal record. It is this aspect that has raised the concern for many YOT practitioners that the referral order represents a significant watering down of the excellent restorative justice models developed in Scotland and beyond.

Of course, the issues emerging from this as regards YOTs are considerable. First, there is the sheer volume of young people coming through the referral order process. YOTs will now have contact with a large number of young people referred for intervention programmes who, under the old system, would probably have only received a conditional discharge or fine. The sheer range of young people and offences will be enormous – anything from stealing their third packet of crisps at Tescos to seriously assaulting a victim. All will now need different levels of intervention delivered by the YOTs. In Lewisham, we estimate approximately 250 referral orders a year. Not only will this mean increased workloads, but there is also the considerable task of developing, recruiting and training local volunteers to sit on referral panels. This will be no mean feat in the current climate when almost every organisation is pilfering keen members of the local community to act as volunteers in mentoring schemes, appropriate adult schemes, and so on.

For panels to run effectively and receive the confidence of the court, they must be seen to be both professional in approach and consistent in delivery and, above all to demonstrate effectiveness in reducing offending. Issues of impartiality and continuity will be vital, and there are already questions as to who will provide legal guidance to panels. Effective delivery will mean a strong training programme and excellent organisational skills on the part of the YOT who must both administer and monitor the panels. And there is, of course, the added question of costs. YOTs are already running to tight budgets, but the Home Office has made it clear that no new money will be made available for implementing the referral orders.

However, if this all sounds rather negative, I certainly do not mean it to. The introduction of the referral order marks an exciting and significant shift in the youth justice system away from the former restricted processes of the court, towards:

- the restorative justice model of working with real possibilities for family group conferencing models to develop;
- greater involvement of families;
- greater say for young people in their intervention programmes;
- greater involvement for victims, and also for the local community, in preventing re-offending; and
- getting young people out of the courts into a more real life, interactive forum where they can begin to take more responsibility for their actions.

Issues for concern may be:

- possible increased use of custody for young people before the court on more serious first offences if the court does not have confidence in panels;
- high levels of interventions for very minor offences – not commensurate with the seriousness of the offence and often not necessarily a good use of resources when time is scarce;
- many young people may have received some form of similar programme at caution plus level. If these are introduced again at referral order stage, and the young person again re-offends, the court may be unlikely to try an action plan/reparation order where similar interventions may be offered. The young person may be seen to have ruined their chance to change and may then be treated more seriously. However, we know that with young people it is often more about when they are ready to change, as well as what intervention can be offered. Opportunities for change need to be offered at all points in the system;
- ensuring the panel receives the confidence of the court – will the court feel their power is being removed in that they cannot stipulate the content of an order?

Evaluation and monitoring of the pilot sites will prove vital in order to demonstrate the effectiveness of the referral order. It is likely that, if successful, the Government may roll out the programme to include other groups of young offenders within the youth justice system. Whilst it is unlikely that we will ever move young offenders entirely outside of the court process, this at least marks the beginning of a more restorative and diversionary approach to youth crime.

OTHER NEW ORDERS

It's a bitter sweet symphony, that's life.[14]

The new menu of orders that can be now served up by the courts is extensive and often confusing.

A colleague from another YOT told me of a young man who had presented at their team in some distress. He said that he had just got a 'reproduction order' and could they help him out? Another young man from Lewisham told me that his mate had got an 'Action Man Order' and, as this sounded like a reasonable sentence, could he have one? It seems that these new orders can be as much a minefield for the young people we work with as they can be for us.

Action plan order

The Action Plan Order (Pt 4, s 56) constitutes a new community penalty. It is short (three months in duration), focused and intended for relatively serious offending. However, it also offers an early opportunity for targeted intervention to help prevent further offending. Pitching the action plan at the right level is key here in terms of assessments and pre-sentence report recommendations. For some young people, where offending is serious enough to justify a community sentence, the action plan order should be considered as the first option. It offers the court a new disposal which is designed to provide a short but individually tailored response to offending behaviour which tackles the causes of offending as well as the offending behaviour itself. The programmes can include a number of components, such as reparation, work to address offending behaviour, education, victim empathy, drugs counselling, etc. The order aims to deliver focused and intensive work over a short period, recognising that lengthy supervision orders can often be inappropriate when what is needed is short, focused programmes of work to tackle the causes of offending immediately.

Key issues for YOTs seem to be that:

- Young people may receive three or more interventions per week during the action plan order. This will mean more focused and targeted work for YOT staff.
- YOTs will need to develop co-ordinated programmes of work, working closely with voluntary and statutory partners who may well be responsible for delivering on aspects of the order.
- It will be interesting to observe whether, with the advent of the referral order, fewer action plan orders are made by courts who may well feel that

---

14   Verve, 'Bitter sweet symphony', from the album *Urban Hymns*, 1997, Virgin.

the interventions offered within an action plan order have alre
tried via the earlier disposal of the referral order.

Reparation order/restorative justice

An essential part of healing and reconciliation is encounter.[15]

A good deal of detail and discussion on this subject has already been covered
in Chapter One by Dr Wayne Morrison. However, I will briefly explore how
new developments around reparation may impact on YOT work.

The move towards restorative justice and reparation was clearly indicated
by Jack Straw within the Crime and Disorder Act 1998. For too long, the youth
justice system had largely excluded the victim from the justice process, and
certainly most youth justice practitioners had had little experience of
including victims in their work with young offenders. Research from the US,
Scotland and New Zealand dating back to the 1970s, and use of restorative
justice in mainstream practice in Germany, Poland, New Zealand and the
Czech Republic (amongst others) had all demonstrated the value and
effectiveness of using restorative justice models in working with young
offenders. This body of evidence could no longer be ignored. However, the
new British system did not entirely remain true to the rationale of restorative
justice models being developed abroad. As already outlined in the section on
Referral Orders, whilst other countries (including Scotland) employed
restorative justice to keep young people out of the youth court system, the
Crime and Disorder Act sought to implement restorative justice models
within the youth court system.

The reparation order is just one of the new areas encompassing principles
of restorative justice, with the expectation being that most orders will contain
elements of reparation. The reparation order itself requires an offender to
carry out a maximum of 24 hours reparation activity over a period of three
months. The reparation should either be carried out directly to the victim or to
the community at large. reparation orders are court disposals and not
community penalties. They are intended for lower level offending behaviour,
where previously a conditional discharge or fine may have been made. No
pre-sentence report is needed, but some form of stand down report, or short
report should be prepared for the court to assess the young person and the
victim's response.

For YOTs, developments in reparation marked a major shift towards
listening to the voice of the victim, and raised key questions about victim
consultation. Certainly, in London, the Metropolitan Police were clear that
they would not divulge victims' details without the victims' consent. This
ensured that the job of initially consulting the victim lay clearly with the police

---

15   New Zealand Maori Priest, Father Henare Tate.

officers seconded to the YOT. For the police, this was quite a task, considering the large numbers of victims involved. Victim consultation means giving the victim the opportunity to decide: (a) whether or not they wish to be involved in either direct or indirect mediation with the young offender – this could be victim/offender mediation or family group conferencing; or (b) whether they wish to see the young offender involved in a particular reparation activity. Indirect community reparation could mean some form of reparative work undertaken within the community that would recompense the victim/community, help the young person take more responsibility for their actions and prove to be a positive and developmental programme for the young person.

Difficulties are already arising in terms of timescale. Courts are requesting either stand down reports in court regarding suitability for a reparation order, or are requesting pre-sentence reports to assess the suitability of other orders. Both can give very little time for YOTs to contact victims and, consequently, give victims very little time to make decisions as regards mediation or otherwise with the young offenders. When approached, many victims are still in shock and can often only consider involvement at a later stage. As a result, timescales need to be flexible enough to cater for victim consultation. But, in the arena of 'speeding up the youth justice system', courts are understandably wary of any form of delay. This continues to be an issue that many YOTs are grappling with. Some courts are being innovative and are willing to make a reparation order/other community sentence without exact details as to the nature of reparation/mediation involved. This then gives the YOT scope to have further contact with the victim and develop a programme around this. However, other courts are insisting that they stipulate the exact nature of reparation/mediation undertaken at the sentencing stage. This reduces considerably opportunities for developing more flexible approaches to reparation. Either way, YOTs need to be considering innovative ways of approaching the new arena of restorative justice. Opportunities for partnership work with local mediation projects and victim support will be key in determining the success of these projects.

CUSTODY

While national standards for the through care of offenders do exist, these minimum levels of provision are just not being met ... large numbers of children and young people are left unsupported while in prison and are ill prepared for their return to the community. The standard supervision provided by youth justice teams after release is a low priority for practitioners.[16]

---

16   (1998) The Guardian, 8 July.

> In recent years, the massively increased numbers of children sent to custody have been dumped in Prison Service establishments, in a prison system that has not, traditionally, recognised that it has a role in caring for children in need of care, development and control. Within this system children are, quite frankly, lost.[17]

Another significant change for YOTs has been in the arena of youth custody. With the Government committed to seeing reductions in the numbers of young people remanded and sentenced to custody, the Crime and Disorder Act 1998 heralded new ways of tackling the thorny issue of youth custody. Alongside this, came increasing evidence that, once sentenced, little if any effective work was undertaken with young people inside custodial institutions. Both the rising suicide rates and re-offending rates suggested that often damaging experiences in custody led to increased risks of harm to both young people themselves and to the public. There was little effective communication between Young Offender Institutions and youth justice teams – young people would begin employment or substance misuse programmes whilst in custody, which would then not be sustained once back in the community, education would often stop, school places and accommodation would be lost, and vital family links would be severed without any communication taking place. Research undertaken by the Howard League in 1998, showed that only 50% of youth justice teams had any input into the sentence planning process for young offenders and two-thirds of young offenders were unaware of having any form of sentence plan at all. It seemed that the Blairite vision of joined-up thinking was just not happening.

The new strategy regarding juvenile custody is far reaching, although some feel not far reaching enough. It involves work at both the pre-sentence and post-sentence ends of the youth justice system. Pre-sentence, the Government, via the Youth Justice Board, has been releasing development fund money for bail support and remand fostering programmes in order to reduce the use of remands. In recent research undertaken by the Children's Society 'Remand Rescue' Project, some 25% of young people remanded were in custody without the knowledge of their local youth justice team. It is clear that proactive work needs to be implemented by YOTs at the remand stage. For many YOTs this has meant/will mean the introduction of dedicated bail support workers whose roles involve developing robust bail support packages for young offenders, many of whom would otherwise have been remanded in custody. However, further changes have come via the introduction of court ordered secure remands. Introduced in the summer of 1999, these built on the provision that was initially established in the 1991 Criminal Justice Act where s 60 was primarily intended to abolish remands to prison custody for 15–16 year old males. Implementation was, however,

---

17   Ramsbotham 1997.

delayed pending the provision of sufficient additional places in secure accommodation. The new 1999 arrangements build on this, with the addition that they also apply to girls. Court ordered secure remands will be available for 12–14 year old boys or 12–16 year old girls who:

> ... are charged or convicted with violent or sexual offences/have a recent history of absconding while remanded to local authority accommodation and are charged with or convicted of an imprisonable offence and the court believes that only a secure remand would be adequate to protect the public from serious harm from that young person.

However, the crunch comes with 15–16 year old males. For, whilst younger males and all females are now no longer at risk of remands to prison custody, the age old problems of 15–16 year old boys continues. For the YOT, this means that they now must prove to the court the 'physical or emotional vulnerability, or propensity for self-harm' of young men in order to ensure a place in secure remand accommodation. This is no easy task, particularly with low numbers of secure beds available. Assessing vulnerability will be an issue of prime importance and, whilst the Home Office have released guidance for vulnerability criteria (Home Office Guidance Paper 1999) based on issues of levels of maturity and risk of self-harm, along with other key indicators such as mental health, substance misuse, minority ethnic groups, sexuality, etc, many YOT practitioners nevertheless continue to feel that all 15–16 year olds meet this vulnerability criteria. Whilst the Government has pledged to increase the numbers of secure beds available, there currently remains the perennial problem of few secure bed spaces. So it is that, even with the new legislation, we still have the age old issue of YOT staff with tight deadlines battling in frantic courtrooms to find secure beds for vulnerable young people.

Some of this may be addressed via organisational changes afoot. The Youth Justice Board, established by the Government in October 1998 to deliver and monitor youth justice services more effectively, will be taking over both budgetary and managerial responsibility for all the juvenile secure estates. This means that they will be in a position to ensure more cost effective regimes, managed within a framework of national standards and effective practice.

The new juvenile secure estate regimes will be significantly different from the regimes that existed in the 1990s, not least because they will have a principle aim of preventing rather than containment. They must also offer a 'structured and caring environment, address individual needs of young people, offer continuity in work both inside and out side of secure facilities and have a health and education priority' (see Youth Justice Board 1998).

This is a significant area of reform, as is the introduction of the new detention and training order (Pt 4, s 60). This came into effect in April 2000. All juvenile prison service establishments will now be known as Detention and Training Centres, although some Local Authority Secure Units may well maintain their original names in that they also hold welfare cases. Sentenced young people will be accommodated separately from those on remand, and young offenders will only be kept in adult prisons in 'exceptional circumstances'. Detention and training orders will become the generic custodial sentence for 12–17 years olds, replacing the secure training order and youth offender institutions sentence. They can be served in a variety of places – in local authority secure accommodation, in secure training centres or in youth offender institutions, depending on age and need. But what will this mean for both YOTs? With regimes now changing from containment to 'preventing offending' and with only half the sentence served in custody, the need for joined-up working and effective sentence planning between detention and training units and YOT supervising officers becomes vital. Indeed, the role of the YOT supervising officer is increased in that they will have overall responsibility for drafting and implementing the sentence/post-sentence plan. They will develop sentence plans, attend regular review meetings at the unit and contribute to personnel development programmes based on effective practice principles.

Links to new prison CARAT (substance misuse) programmes, as well as education and training programmes (at least 15 hours per week education for young people of school age, with governors instructed to provide out of cell programmes for at least 14 hours a day) should mean that young people will now have far better access to more effective rehabilitation and change programmes whilst in custody. However, the challenges remain enormous. Key issues emerging would seem to be:

- there is still insufficient provision for juvenile secure estate provision. Whilst the Youth Justice Board is working on this issue, it may be some time before significant change is apparent;

- many schools remain reluctant to hold places for young offenders whilst they serve a custodial sentence. So whilst detention and training centres may now be delivering stronger education programmes, when the young person emerges from prison, the challenge will be how best to build on this back in the community;

- managing and maintaining consistent programmes in and outside of the detention and training centres.

There also remains the disturbing issue of the large numbers of black young men incarcerated in British custodial institutions. At the time of writing, some 30% of the juvenile remand population are from minority ethnic groups. Action must be taken throughout the youth justice system, via remand and sentencing monitoring, as well as through specifically developed programmes, to ensure that this issue is addressed at the earliest opportunity. YOT staff can play a crucial role in this and in ensuring that they remain abreast of key resource opportunities for all young people in order to ensure that young people are no longer sentenced to fail in our youth justice system.

ASSESSMENT, MONITORING AND EVALUATION

> Considering the importance of evaluation and monitoring, it is striking how few programmes are currently being evaluated. Out of 210 probation programmes surveyed by Underdown in 1996, only 16% showed evidence of evaluation in terms of measurable change and effectiveness ... However, there is no doubt that the importance of evaluation is gradually being recognised ... there is at the present time what must be described as an evaluation movement.[18]

The arrival of the Youth Justice Board's *Planning and Performance Management – A Guide for YOTs* (summer 1999), the developments around a common assessment tool (ASSET), the increasing move towards delivering evidence based programmes, and the considerable changes in the fields of information sharing and management information systems, all came as a much needed wake up call for YOTs. They were going to have to get their acts together as regards monitoring and evaluation. The *Misspent Youth* Audit 1996, along with the subsequent regional audits, found that most youth justice services had little if any consistent data collecting systems in operation. Few knew if the interventions they were offering worked, let alone had a detailed breakdown of their workload. *Misspent Youth* demanded that 'good quality information systems should be established to allow sharing of information between all key agencies'. It stressed that those with computerised systems would find the data collection considerably easier.

In what seemed like a parallel universe, other agencies had already been addressing these imbalances for several years. Since the early 1990s, the Probation Service had been developing their own Management Information System (CRAMS) and spending time and money on evaluating offending behaviour programmes to demonstrate what works. The police service had also been working on comprehensive information and monitoring systems, and work was already afoot via the Home Office Integrated Business Information Systems (IBIS) on linking these and other key systems together. It was not impossible, therefore, to ask the same of YOTs. The Youth Justice Board took a proactive stance with the publication of their *Planning and Performance Management* where they requested quarterly data collections relating to approximately 20 work areas, alongside a yearly Youth Justice Plan, outlining both local and national objectives and links to local Crime and Disorder Plans/other key local audits and plans. This could also have a real impact on issues of discrimination. With robust monitoring systems in place, issues such as the over-representation of young black males on remand and in custody, differences in sentencing between young men and young women, access to secure beds, mental health concerns, suicides in custody can all be

---

18 Merrington 1998.

monitored with local and national figures and then scrutinised with a view to immediate action being taken across the whole youth justice system to address inequalities.

This represents a significant development for most YOTs, many of whom had been using a paper system of data collection for years. YOT staff were often not computer trained and YOT managers had quickly to negotiate the minefield of computer software sales pitches that were battering on their doors for business. Alongside this was work already being developed by the Probation Service around both a common assessment tool (ACE) and a common risk assessment model. Both were being employed with considerable effect. This constituted a whole new landscape for many youth justice teams who had been using localised, and often ad hoc, assessment tools, with little consistency between teams. Work began on developing a similar tool for YOTs (ASSET) which is now being used within all YOTs as of summer 2000. This represents a comprehensive common assessment tool employed by all YOTs in initial assessments of all young offenders, ensuring consistency of practice, evaluation/change measurements and a further step towards joined-up working between agencies as they shared assessment and referral mechanisms. ASSET marks a considerable shift for YOT staff practice and certainly a huge step forward in the development of effective, evidence based practice.

CONCLUSION

Talking in a YOT team meeting the other day, someone commented that 'youth crime has just got sexy again' and they had a point. It does seem that, whilst for years the Youth Justice Service was relegated to the bottom division of the criminal justice system, YOTs are now premier division stuff. But as with all change, you never know how long the momentum – both external and internal will last. Next year, another equally vital issue may have risen to claim the Government's attention, and YOTs need to be in a fighting position to ensure that we are able to demonstrate both the effectiveness of what we deliver as well as our ability to offer a cost effective, best value service to both young offenders, their victims and the wider community. Unless we are able to achieve this, we may find that some other body or organisation is brought in to deliver. However, this will not happen because YOTs are in a prime position to develop and deliver innovative and effective programmes for preventing and addressing youth crime. No other national or indeed international agency has developed such a comprehensive and joined-up approach to tackling youth offending and it is up to us, along with our other partners in the youth justice system, to make it work.

A final thought. Just the other day we had a visit from a principal youth court judge from New Zealand. He visited the YOT, spoke with the staff and summed up in a way that speaks volumes for the potential future of YOTs:

> I was enormously impressed with the YOT concept and the work that was being done. I was also impressed with the calibre of staff who are doing it ... It seems to me that [YOTs] are a pioneering model which could become a world best if all the support and resources are made available.

CHAPTER 8

YOUTH JUSTICE IN SCOTLAND

Bill Whyte

INTRODUCTION

A conventional way of looking at developments in youth justice policy and practice is to see them as a reflection of changing perceptions of crime and young offenders. This, however, provides only a superficial picture. It can be better argued that the varied and different legal structures developed by modern States reflect different assumptions about the nature and value of youth and the value of property held by those States. Developments in legislation and systems of response to youth crime often reflect social and political debates that are inextricably bound up with changes in social and economic order as each society tries to develop its own pattern of response to troublesome young people (Gelsthorpe and Morris 1994). A society's response will reflect its conceptualisation of the phenomenon of youth crime, which is related to its understanding of the roles children and young people have in that society.

Policies in many Western countries during much of the 20th century sought to create systems that eroded the distinction between the young person in need and the delinquent youth. In the latter part of the century, many countries have reviewed their youth justice systems, some to bring their practices within the framework set by the UN Convention on the Rights of the Child 1989, which all Western countries, other than the US, have now ratified. However, a greater emphasis on legal rights, responsibility, due process and 'just deserts' seems to have been associated with a retreat from welfare and the use of non-criminal and extra-judicial processes. In some countries, child-orientated reforms have been superseded by punitive law and order ideologies, driven by politicians under pressure to be seen to be tough on crime. The combination of two concepts – special responses to children and young people; and equal rights and value – creates tension in practice. The basic conflict for any system is how best to reconcile the competing claims of the law, judicial process and punishment with the need to consider the best interests and rights of the child.

The debate has tended to be classified, rather simplistically and unhelpfully, as justice versus welfare. This has, until recently, taken little account of other paradigms, including non-adversarial problem resolution, restorative and reparative approaches, or of the validity, in practice, of maximising the strengths of different approaches within one system. Commentators have tended to evaluate systems against ideal types of welfare or justice. The push has often been for a coherence of approach rather than one that best meets the needs of young people. As one commentator suggests, it is perhaps misguided to attempt to squeeze the facts of childhood into a unified theory and any system dealing with young offenders needs 'to be sufficiently flexible to accommodate conflicting theories to achieve justice for children, instead of denying the conflicts of childhood to achieve a coherent philosophy'.[1]

The Scottish youth justice system attempts to achieve flexibility by bringing together a range of approaches which cannot be said to be either exclusively welfare or justice orientated in approach. The system is concerned to act in the best interests of the young person by reducing and preventing crime through a process of social education (Bruce 1985) on the assumption that acting with regard to such interests will, in the long run, be beneficial to the victims and the public at large. As Parsloe 1975 observes, 'It is not a weakness of the system that it contains different approaches but rather the very purpose for which it exists' (p 27).

Policy paradigms are a curious mixture of psychological assumptions, scientific concepts, value commitments, social aspirations, personal beliefs and administrative constraints.[2] A wide variety of factors contributed to the paradigmatic change in Scotland. The only real issue on which there was complete consensus at the time concerned the inadequacy of the existing arrangements, which reflected disillusionment with the dominant justice paradigm. The existing system was considered unsuccessful in its attempts to compromise between crime, responsibility and punishment, on the one hand, and the welfare and best interests of the young person on the other. It was also agreed that a new approach was needed. The development of Scotland's Children's Hearing System, its aims and processes, strengths and weakness, have to be understood within the social policy context of the time and against the principles on which it was constructed. These principles were based on specific assumptions about the nature of childhood and adolescence, social disadvantage and the role of State intervention.

Scotland's system aims neither at punishment nor welfare *per se*, but focuses on assessing needs and solving problems. The underpinning values of the radically new 'solution' to youth crime were not in themselves very radical in concept. Indeed, the success in overcoming the muted objections to the proposals from the Law Society of Scotland and the Police and the

---

1   Adler 1985:2.
2   Marris and Rein 1974.

Sheriff's Association was because the proposals were cast in a language that reflected legal tradition and sentiment in Scotland (Cowperthwaite 1988). The concept of social education found favour because it appealed to the strong Scottish identity with educational processes. Education was particularly highly rated in Scottish circles and conveyed a sense of rigour and discipline. The role of lay people in decision making reflected the generally favourable view of volunteering to help with social problems. In any case, a double track system was planned which, in principle, allowed retention by the court of serious young offenders.

The following discussion outlines the nature and structure of the Scottish system, its strengths and limitations and the author's view of its compatibility with current research on effective intervention with youth offenders. The initial discussion draws heavily on the Report of the Kilbrandon Committee 1964, not to imply biblical qualities to it, or to suggest that the principles are beyond question, but simply to outline the values and practice assumptions made in designing the Scottish system.

THE CHILDREN'S HEARING SYSTEM

Scotland's Children's Hearing System is based on the philosophy of justice advocated by the Kilbrandon Report which made recommendations resulting not only in the introduction of a distinctively new system for dealing with children and young people in difficulty, but also, consequentially, in the re-organisation of all social work services under the umbrella of local authority all purpose social work departments (including probation work) – an equally distinctive Scottish arrangement.

Scottish law has always been separate from English law. Although the adversarial system of prosecution prevails in the higher courts, it never dominated juvenile procedures (Bruce 1985). Before the introduction of the current system for dealing with young people in trouble by the Social Work (Scotland) Act 1968, Scotland had never had a systematic or uniform juvenile court structure as England had, a fact that may, in part, account for the development of its unique system. There were few specialist courts in Scotland for dealing with juvenile offenders (that is, offenders under 16 years) and little uniformity in the type of court attended. Procedures were often considered unintelligible to the offender and family.[3] Where action was taken, the traditional Scottish response was either boarding out (that is, the placement of children, on a voluntary basis, with private families, mainly in rural areas deliberately remote from family and community) or placement in large residential institutions (Murphy 1992).

---

3   Lockyer and Stone 1998:4.

The Kilbrandon Committee was chaired by one of Scotland's senior judges, Lord Kilbrandon. It probably needed someone of this status and experience to question the role and expertise of the court in dealing with children and young people who offend and to propose an alternative extra-judicial system. The committee viewed the court as having two fundamental roles: first, in the adjudication of the legal facts – whether or not an offence had been established beyond reasonable doubt – and, secondly, in deciding on disposal, or what should be done once the facts are established. The Report made the assertion that the two roles require 'quite different skills and qualities' and that attempting to combine them 'within the present juvenile court system' was a source of 'dissatisfaction' (para 71). This logic was influenced by the practice in Scandinavia of separating these roles completely.

A central aim of the children's hearings was to spare young people the rigours of the criminal justice system, since the perceived objective was to make decisions that could have a positive effect on the young person. The intention was to deal with them and their parents in a setting which, by its informality and allocation of time, would ensure, as far as practically possible, effective participation by the young person and adults in resolving problems.[4]

The proposal to separate adjudication from disposal was strengthened by experience which suggested that, no matter how much they are modified, adversarial criminal proceedings affect the nature of communication and seem incompatible with the effective participation of young people and adults in reaching a decision that is in the best interests of the young person. Courts were considered to be an inappropriate setting to promote discussion with families. Lawyers and judges were thought to be ill equipped for this task (paras 99–101). In any case, evidence at the time indicated that the vast majority of young people coming before Scottish courts did not dispute the facts and so the function for which the court was best equipped, the adjudication of the legal facts, was seldom actually required.

A children's hearing has no power to determine questions of innocence or guilt. This remains the essential role for the court in Scotland. Access to due process with legal representation is available to all young people and their parents who dispute the facts or appeal against the outcome of a hearing; or, where children are considered, for whatever reason, unable to understand the evidence against them. This is intended to be a safeguard of their legal rights and a check against over-enthusiastic interventionism. In practice, the vast majority of children and young people brought before hearings in Scotland accept the facts and, therefore, are dealt with in this non-criminal setting.

Children's hearings have a jurisdiction which encompasses, not only young people who are alleged to have committed criminal offences, but, also, those deemed to be in need of care and protection and those regarded as being too young (legally speaking) to form the necessary intention to commit a

4   Lockyer and Stone 1998:3.

criminal act. Indeed, it was a contention of the Kilbrandon Committee that the 'similarities in the underlying situation' of young offenders and children in need of care and protection 'far outweigh the differences' (para 15). Difficulties were felt to arise from a failure in the upbringing process in the home, the family environment and school. It was argued that, in principle, they should be dealt with in similar ways within an integrated system, since both groups were in need of help to address their needs and not solely their deeds. The emphasis on preventative intervention was quite remarkable for its time and is not without its tensions philosophically and in practice.[5]

Developments in psychology and behavioural sciences suggested, at the time, that emotional deprivation associated with disorganised families, separation and poor parenting could have a major impact on the subsequent behaviour of the young. More recent studies[6] tend to support a similar view that a commonality among young persistent offenders is less to do with the nature of their criminality than their history of social adversity. Similarly, current research continues to emphasise the important role of schooling and education (Rutter *et al* 1979) and the crucial role of parental supervision in preventing delinquency (Farrington 1997; Laybourn 1985).

While poverty and disadvantage are important factors in delinquency, they do not represent its simple underlying cause. The committee observed (as have British crime surveys in the last 20 years) that it is not all of the poor nor only the poor who commit crime. Equal in emphasis to the social environment should be an emphasis on individual and family factors, particularly with regard to the role of parenting. Consequently, measures aimed at strengthening families in adversity were seen as an essential means of combating delinquency.

Young offenders were not to be viewed primarily as criminals, but as young people whose upbringing had been unsatisfactory and where responsibility for their supervision and education should be shared between the young person, the family, the community and the State. Parents should be involved in a non-coercive way, which the Kilbrandon Report described as a process of social education intended to 'strengthen, support and supplement ... the natural beneficial influences of the home and family' (para 35). Consequently, the report asserted that 'coercive powers in relation to parents ... are ultimately incompatible with the nature of the educational process itself ... particularly in the context of the parent-child relationship' (para 35). Children's hearings have no power over parents directly.

The focus on individual responses or treatment has given rise to criticism that the philosophy of the system is one of individual pathology (Morris and McIsaac 1978). While medical analogies were used within the report, overall, the term 'treatment' was generally used in a broad social sense and always in

---

5   See Adler 1985.
6   See Hagell and Newburn 1994; Graham and Bowling 1995; Waterhouse *et al* 1999.

the context of the concept of social education, which, while not well defined, seemed intended to encapsulate the combination of individual, family and community responses. It was to this end that the report recommended, as an essential component of the system, the establishment of integrated local authority services to provide early multi-agency and multidisciplinary responses to individual, family and community concerns. Social work legislation currently places a statutory duty on the local authority to promote welfare. The concept of co-ordinated planning and provision is one that has continued to be problematic and is again subject to much debate within the context of the current Government's strategy of social inclusion.

Many proponents of the Scottish system suggest that there is no place for punishment within it. This is to misunderstand the paradigm of social education. A philosophical discourse on the nature of punishment and the distinction between State punishment within a 'just deserts' framework as a discrete end in itself, and the control and sanction of young people as a constructive means of addressing factors associated with criminality, is beyond the scope of this chapter. The Kilbrandon Report, however, is clear 'that punishment might be good treatment' (para 53) – but could only be so (and, therefore, rarely would be so) if imposed for the purpose of help and effecting positive change in the young person, not as a retributive end in itself.

It is naive and unsustainable to suggest that the Children's Hearing System is not concerned with control as an important element in a young person's welfare. Consequently, while the offence does not provide the exclusive rationale for intervention, it is intended to be a central issue in the problem resolution work to be undertaken and it is one of the explicit objectives of the system to try to help young people stop offending.

In principle, the system is structured as one of diversion and early intervention aimed at addressing the needs of the young person in partnership with parents, where possible. It does not exclusively focus on offending and it is not the intention of the system to simply separate out 'offending' and 'non-offending' children. Consequently, young people dealt with by the children's hearings are not convicted, (except for the purpose of s 3 of the Rehabilitation of Offenders Act 1974) and do not attract a criminal record for their appearances before hearings.

Part III of the Social Work (Scotland) Act 1968, replaced the former system of criminal courts dealing with juveniles with a system of hearings for children, young people and their families, which became known as 'children's hearings'. Part III of the 1968 Act was subsequently replaced by the Children (Scotland) Act 1995 which now provides the legal basis for the operation of the system. The system came into operation in 1971 following the implementation of the statutory instruments.[7]

---

7   For a more detailed discussion on the Children's Hearing System, see Lockyer and Stone 1998; Moore and Whyte 1998, Chapter 6; and Norrie 1997.

THE REPORTER

A key figure in the youth justice system in Scotland is the Reporter. The office is intended to be free from administrative and political interference to give the office holder security in exercising discretion and decision making without fear or favour. The Local Government (Scotland) Act 1994 established the Scottish Children's Reporter Administration (SCRA) and from 1 April 1996 created, for the first time, a national non-departmental Government service under a Principal Reporter (see Finlayson 1992). Prior to this, Reporters had been employed by local authorities.

The duties of the Principal Reporter (a term which covers all Reporters since they act under powers delegated to them by the Principal Reporter) are set out in the Children (Scotland) Act 1995 in various statutory instruments and, in particular, The Children's Hearings (Scotland) Rules 1996. All Reporters have legal training, but are drawn from a range of professional backgrounds including law, education and social work on the assumption that they need an amalgam of skills to make decisions that are in the best interests of young people.

The Reporter is the official to whom all referrals regarding young people considered to be in need of compulsory supervision must be made. He or she has a number of functions. These are:

- to act as a gatekeeper and filter in respect of young people referred to the system;
- to be the administrative arm of the system;
- to act as the community watchdog in respect of the observance of the statutory rules governing the workings of the system;
- to act as legal representative of the hearings when matters have to be referred to the courts for various reasons.[8]

The Reporter has no power to make formal disposals, such as supervision, but has the statutory discretion to decide on how to process the matter and has a duty to make an initial investigation before deciding on what action to take. The Reporter's task is to decide whether or not the young person may be in need of 'compulsory measures of supervision' (the legal criterion). When considering whether to send a young person to a hearing in respect of an alleged offence, the Reporter has to be satisfied on two counts:

(a) that on the evidence available, there is, in law, a *prima facie* case to answer; *and*

(b) that on the evidence available, the young person may be in need of compulsory measures of supervision.

---

8   Moore and Whyte 1998:131.

The existence of a ground or reason for referral of an offence does not in itself indicate that a young person may be in need of compulsory measures of supervision. The Reporter has a crucial role in minimising the risk of net widening associated with welfare orientated systems. The most common outcome of a referral to the Reporter is 'no formal action'. This administrative term masks a range of informal action undertaken by the Reporter as part of his or her role in diversion and early intervention. The young person and parents may be seen informally; information might be sought from the social work authority or any other appropriate source; and various arrangements might be made with the agreement of parents and the young person, for example, for the confiscation of weapons; for a written apology to the victim or for making restitution with the assistance of a voluntary agency. The Reporter may decide to refer the young person to the local authority for 'advice, guidance and assistance' which can include a programme of assistance under a 'voluntary agreement'.

Anyone who has 'reasonable cause' to think a young person may require compulsory measures of supervision *may* (and in the case of the police shall) give that information to the Reporter. Not only are the police obliged to pass information to the Reporter to assist in any decision to arrange a hearing, but the criminal prosecuting authorities are also obliged to pass on any evidence they hold when the Reporter is trying to establish a ground (reason) of referral before the sheriff court. In practice, most referrals on youth offenders come from the police. In reality, police practice seems to vary across the country and they often exercise the kind of discretion found in most jurisdictions, ranging from a 'quiet word' of warning through to a more formal caution, before passing information to the Reporter.

When information is passed, the Reporter is then in a position to take a more holistic view of the young person's circumstances in deciding what action to take, which may include informal action to facilitate early assistance from the local authority or elsewhere to avoid the need for compulsion or to request a hearing. In practice, about 60–70% of offence related referrals to the Reporter result in no formal action. These young people are diverted by Reporters not only from criminal procedures, but also from any formal procedures, unless no further action is taken because the young person is currently subject to compulsory measures.

To assist in the investigation, the Reporter can request reports from the local authority (routinely, social work and education reports) or from any other source to provide information on the young person and their social circumstances. The local authority and the police have a legal duty to provide information. The scope of the investigation at this initial stage can be very wide ranging. The legislation simply indicates that the report may contain 'such information, from any person whomsoever, as the Principal Reporter thinks or the local authority think, fit'. This investigation stage can provide an opportunity for social workers to consider early preventative or restorative intervention.

In the early years of the system, initial investigation by social workers was often undertaken to assist Reporters in determining the need for formal action and could involve voluntary restorative measures. These kinds of imaginative responses largely disappeared with local authority cuts in the 1980s and re-appeared in the late 1990s along with a renewed interest in family conferences. Research (Hallett *et al* 1998) suggests that Reporters' practices vary across Scotland and anecdotal evidence suggests that, because of resource constraints, many Reporters may have low expectations of early intervention at the initial investigation stage.

Panel members

A panel of lay people is responsible for decision making and disposals in children's hearings. Panel members are volunteers and are intended to be ordinary members of the community who are chosen because of their special qualities. The proposals for placing decision making in the hands of lay panel members were received with some enthusiasm from politicians at the time; less because of a particular preference for 'lay' as opposed to professional decision making and more because of enthusiasm for community involvement in addressing young people's difficulties (Cowperthwaite 1988). Nonetheless, the proposal to allow ordinary men and women to replace the judiciary in this way was a radical departure from what existed before.

The White Paper, *Social Work in the Community* (1966), which developed the idea of community lay involvement recognised that, in practice, the success or failure of the system would hinge on identifying suitable members of the community who were willing and able to serve on the panels in adequate numbers. In general, this has proved to be one of the overwhelming successes of the system in its 28 years of existence. Research carried out at the time indicated that many professionals viewed lay decision makers as an 'invaluable source of strength to the system'.[9] Currently, there are over 2,200 panel members across Scotland.

Panel members between the ages of 18 and 60 are recruited by open advertisement in newspapers, TV campaigns and through the internet. In practice, most are aged between 20 and 50 and, as a result, are often closer to the age of young people and their parents than decision makers in other jurisdictions. Panel members are appointed (and re-appointed) by the Secretary of State for Scotland[10] initially for up to five years. Selection, which

---

9   Hallett *et al* 1998:88.

10   Following the re-establishment of Scotland's Parliament in 1999, the many functions of the Secretary of State for Scotland have been transferred to the First Minister.

is the task of local authority Children's Panel Advisory Committees, is by written application, interview and group discussion. Panel members must undergo initial training of between 70 and 85 hours (Rose 1994), which is a local authority responsibility. A national curriculum is provided by government financed trainers based in four of Scotland's Universities. Additional training is required before undertaking responsibility for chairing a hearing. Panel members have a statutory entitlement to time off work to sit on hearings. In practice, most have to rely on a great deal of good will from their employers.

Inevitably, 'selection' brings with it the risk of bias. A major debate at the time, which is still pertinent today, was the tension between the 'suitability' of panel members to carry out the disposal functions of a hearing and their 'representativeness' in terms of local communities. The ideal of community had to be balanced with the best interests of young people. The Government of the day decided that, while representativeness of the community should be sought as far as possible, suitability to deal with children and young people in difficulty must remain the overarching criterion for the selection of panel members and this has to be supported by the provision of adequate training (Raeburn 1994). The White Paper did not define suitability, nor did the legislation provide guidance, but indicated that panel members should be drawn from a wide variety of occupations, neighbourhoods, ages and income groups.

Early research on the occupational class of panel members (Mapstone 1973; Moody 1976) suggested that a relatively high proportion of panel members were drawn from white collar occupations and that manual workers constituted a minority of panel members. More recent studies (for example, Lockyer 1992) have suggested that a better balance in social class membership has been achieved since the 1970s, while still remaining somewhat problematic.

THE HEARING

A hearing is a tribunal consisting of three lay panel members (at least one man and one woman). The aim is that decisions on how to deal with a particular young person should be taken by members who have 'personal knowledge of the community to which the child belongs'.[11]

A hearing is usually held at a place in the young person's home area. The whole procedure is conducted in front of all the participants, usually in the form of a round table discussion and decisions are reached in public. A majority decision is sufficient and families can hear debates, doubts and

11   SHHD 1966.

difficulties discussed before them. The chairperson is required by law to share the substance of and the reasons for all decisions with the family. These reasons are given in writing. Normally, the young person must attend and the attendance of parents (or relevant persons) is compulsory. A local authority social worker will normally also be present. Others may attend, for example, a school teacher or residential staff member with the permission of the chairperson and agreement of the family. Social work reports and school reports are routinely available to the hearing (in principle three days in advance) to allow the panel to examine and understand the young person's circumstances and any proposals for action. Additional professional reports, such as medical, psychological or psychiatric assessments can be requested by the hearing and the young person is often encouraged to put his or her views in writing.

Representation for the young person is encouraged, but this need not be legal representation since the role is a non-adversarial one. Legal aid and legal representation is available to young people and their parents in the event of the matter going before the sheriff court, when legal facts are disputed or disposals challenged. Young people and their families also have the right to be represented in a hearing. However, no legal aid is available for representation. This is an issue that Norrie 1997 considers unacceptable in a signatory country to the UN Convention on the Rights of the Child 1989. Research has indicated that many families and young people prefer non-legal representation (Martin *et al* 1981). This, of course, may be influenced by the legal aid situation. It does seem incongruous to allow the right of representation on the one hand, but to restrict the family's choice, in practice, on the other. There is concern that, if lawyers routinely appeared, they would undermine the non-adversarial nature of the process.

The hearing has the power to appoint a safeguarder to protect the interests of the young person. However, safeguarders do not act as independent advocates for the young person or take instruction from the young person and are not frequently used for young offenders. It has been suggested that this issue could be addressed by making lay advocates available who are trained in non-adversarial processes, should young people and families wish to use them, without destroying the ethos of the system (Duquette 1994). Legal aid is available, however, for legal advice prior to a hearing and some lawyers will offer advice in the waiting room and then attend the hearing to assist the family.

The young person, as well as the parent, has the right to express his or her views as intended by the non-adversarial nature of the proceedings and promoted by the UN Convention on the Rights of the Child 1989. In practice, the success or otherwise of this intention varies greatly, depending on how well the family and young person have been prepared for the hearing and how willing and confident they are in expressing their views. Recent research[12] reported that the participation of young people and their families was often brief. Nonetheless, family members considered that their participation was important. Similarly, parents and young people considered the system fair and felt that their views were listened to by Reporters and in hearings. Despite feeling nervous, families spoke positively of the informality and relative ease of communication in hearings.

The research findings suggest that, while hearings do not necessarily result in relaxed open debate between young people, their family and decision makers, the family seem to understand what is going on, believe they are treated fairly and listened to, and feel they have an opportunity to participate in the hearing and in decision making, whether or not they actually do so or agree with the outcome. One important area related to rights and representation highlighted by the research is that the understanding of young people and families of the procedural aspects, rights of appeal, etc, are often partial. While access to written material is normally available, this does not ensure understanding and more has to be done to ensure both young people and their families clearly comprehend their rights within the system, particularly where young people are made subject to supervision away from home.

Young people dealt with by the children's hearings are not convicted (except for the purpose of s 3 of the Rehabilitation of Offenders Act 1974) and do not attract a criminal record for appearances at hearings. A hearing has no power to imprison, fine, order compensation or impose a community sentence. Disposals are restricted to powers of compulsory supervision, albeit with the ability to attach conditions (for example, involving reparation and mediation), particularly of residence, including secure accommodation.

The diversionary nature of the system has always been underpinned by a notion of minimum intervention now expressed in law as the 'non-intervention' principle. The Children (Scotland) Act (s 16(3)) is clear that no intervention should be embarked on unless the hearing is satisfied that the action will have a positive effect on the young person. However, the same section (s 16(5)), introduced in 1996, in the face of much opposition from panel members, gave powers for the first time to override the best interests of the young person should this be required in the public interest. The operational assumption of panel members seems to be that acting in the best interests of the young person will be in the public interest and this section remains unused.

Because the hearing is empowered to take sweeping measures for the welfare of the young person, the hearing has to review all supervision orders it makes, regularly and systematically, and can set a review date at the time of decision making. The young person, and indeed others involved, can also

---

12 See Hallett *et al* 1998; Waterhouse *et al* 1999.

apply for a review. All orders must be reviewed within a year or they will automatically lapse. The legislation intends, however, that reviews should take place regularly and the hearing can require a review at any future date when making its decision; the Reporter and the local authority have the right to call a review at any time. In addition to rights of appeal, the young person and parents have specified rights to call a review, generally, three months after the decision. A review can mean that the supervising authority must account for intervention in open session, since the young person and parents must be present. Reviews can result from a desire to terminate a supervision requirement on the grounds of good progress, to have further conditions imposed, to delete existing conditions or to vary a requirement in more substantial ways, for example, by substituting a residential condition.

All decisions are subject to appeal to the court. Until 1996, the court could only adjudicate on the facts, confirm a hearing decision or question it and return the young person to the hearing to reconsider their decision. Because of government concerns that there should always be a court based forum available to make final decisions about young people and to allay anticipated criticisms in relation to the European Convention on Human Rights, the Children (Scotland) Act 1995 introduced a provision for the court to overturn a hearing decision and substitute the court's own decision. This was a major departure from the original principle of separating adjudication from disposal with the potential of undermining the balance between hearings and the courts. As Norrie put it:

> ... if judicial decision making is seriously considered to be more appropriate than letting a children's hearing make decisions then the whole children's hearing system ought to be abolished forthwith and all children in need of compulsory measures of supervision given the 'benefit' of a judicial determination ... Not only is the provision bad in principle but it is likely to prove bad in practice [1997, p 90].

It was stated in Parliament that this power '... should be used sparingly and that a sheriff should think carefully before interfering with the decision of a children's hearing' (Clelland 1995, p 28). To date, there have been no cases where sheriffs have substituted the decision of a hearing.

Criminal responsibility and age thresholds

Social work/children's legislation makes provision for young offenders under 16 years of age. Those already within the system can continue to be referred up to the age of 18. The Criminal Procedures (Scotland) Act, 1995 contains provisions for summary courts to refer most young people under 17 years and six months to a hearing, either to provide advice or for disposal. Thus, the Scottish youth justice legal framework provides for most young people up to the age of 18 to be diverted from criminal procedures completely. In practice, most young people aged 16–18 continue to be dealt with in adult criminal proceedings.

The age of criminal responsibility is much debated in modern States. The UN Convention on the Rights of the Child 1989 recommends the age of 18 as an appropriate age but countries vary greatly on this issue. At the time of the Kilbrandon Committee, the age of criminal responsibility in Scotland was eight years, primarily to protect children from 'the rigours of the criminal law applicable in earlier times' (para 62). The committee noted that any age between 8 and 21 could be justified. However:

> ... no witness who gave evidence was prepared to say that by clinical observation or otherwise it was possible to come to a conclusion that chronological age as such had any direct bearing on the capacity to form a criminal intent and to commit a crime [para 64].

Consequently, no change was made to the age of criminal responsibility based on the assumption that most children and young people would not be brought before a criminal court for disposal.

In practice, this has the advantage that any child aged eight or over coming the attention of the non-criminal hearing system because of offending can have the legal facts established or challenged before a professional judge in a criminal court 'beyond reasonable doubt', with the same representation rights and legal aid as any other citizen. If the 'grounds' are proven, the young person returns, with few exceptions, to a hearing for disposal. The weakness of such a low age becomes apparent if and when the system brings young people before the criminal courts. In recent years, the appearance of relatively young children in England and Scotland before criminal courts for disposal because of serious offences has again opened the debate on whether any child or young person, even for very serious offences, should be 'disposed of' in a criminal court.[13]

The existence of machinery for criminal courts to deal with some young people under 16 years on the instruction of the Lord Advocate (the Crown Prosecutor) is a weakness which, to some extent, undermines the logic of the system. The Lord Advocate retains the power to prosecute all children between the ages of eight and 16 in the criminal courts and has issued instructions on which categories of offences are to be considered for prosecution in the courts. Generally, this relates to the gravity of the offence (for example, cases of murder, rape and armed robbery); but also covers some offences under road traffic legislation for those over 14 years when conviction can result in disqualification; offences which permit forfeiture; and offences committed by a child acting along with an adult.

---

13 The Scottish Executive has accepted the recommendation of a recent review to raise the age of criminal minority from eight to 12 years and to pilot removing most 16–17 year olds from criminal proceedings.

While these categories of young people around the age of 16 are reported to the procurator fiscal (local prosecutors) in the first instance, directions from the Lord Advocate ensure that they are ordinarily also reported to the Principal Children's Reporter as 'jointly reported' young people. The two officers liaise, either generally, or on a case by case basis, as to whether the young person in question should be dealt with in the criminal justice system or referred to the Children's Hearing System. In general, the prosecuting authorities observe the basic spirit and intention of social work/children's legislation, and only prosecute young people before the criminal courts if a special reason exists; the authority for the decision nonetheless lies with the prosecutor and not with the Reporter. The existence of this double track system, where prosecutors have the power of decision over some young people, can operate to undermine the integrity of the Children's Hearing System.

THE INTERFACE BETWEEN THE CHILDREN'S HEARING SYSTEM AND THE CRIMINAL JUSTICE SYSTEM

Few young people under 16 years are dealt with in criminal proceedings in Scotland. In 1997, only 148 young people under 16 years had a charge proved against them in a criminal court (Statistical Bulletin 1999, table 12) compared with over 40,000 referrals to the Children's Hearing System resulting in no criminal proceedings at all. However, most young offenders aged 16–18 are routinely dealt with in adult criminal courts.

Policy statements indicate that tackling youth crime is a priority area for the Government and for the Children's Hearing System, in particular, young offenders aged 16–17:

> Tackling offending behaviour among young people is a central part of tackling crime as a whole and the children's hearing has a vital role within this process [SOED 1993, para 7.8].

> ... there are ... young offenders who are immature and for whom a programme of care and supervision under existing powers through the hearing system might be a more effective way of changing their behaviour and reducing the risk of future offending [SOED 1993, para 7.29].

National objectives for criminal justice social work equally recognise the issue:

> Because of their lack of maturity or particular factors in their social background and experience of life it may be preferable to continue to deal with some 16 and 17 year old offenders in the children's hearings and to make greater use of the opportunities for doing this which are contained in the current legislation ... Experience has shown a tendency for offenders in this category to progress fairly rapidly to custody once they enter the criminal justice system [SWSG 1996, para 134].

There is no guidance or criteria for assessing 'immaturity'. Nonetheless, it is clear that both youth and criminal justice policy support diverting persistent young offenders aged 16–17 from the criminal justice system.

Few social work reports (or social enquiry reports) seem to recommend this course of action to the courts (Johnstone 1995). In 1997, only 219 remits from the criminal court to children's hearings were recorded (Statistical Bulletin 1999, table 12). Commentators have suggested that social work agency practices have resulted in the routine termination of supervision around the age of 16 with very negative consequences for the young people (Save the Children 1992). This apparent failure of the criminal justice system to utilise fully the provisions within Scottish legislation lies partly with the Crown Office. Procurators fiscal seem to deal with 16 and 17 year olds routinely in the criminal justice system unless special circumstances indicate that they should be dealt with by the hearings, rather than approach decision making from the standpoint that no young person aged 16–17 should be dealt with in the criminal justice system unless there is a very strong public interest in doing so. The arrangements for liaison between Reporters and procurators fiscal seem to vary across the country, resulting in quite different rates of retention for jointly reported young people in the hearing system ranging from 20–66% of referrals (Hallett *et al* 1998, p 109).

Research suggests that these young people show characteristics of severe social adversity; may quickly exhaust disposals in the adult court; and are at high risk of custody before the age of 18 – an important indicator of a future criminal career (Waterhouse *et al* 1999). Research also suggests that procurators fiscal have little background information on the social circumstances of young people under 18 years which would allow them to apply any test of maturity or to assist them in making an appropriate decision when balancing public interest with the welfare of the young person.

Scottish research suggests that the hearing system often fails either to recognise that such young people continue to be in need of compulsory measures or considers that they cannot be helped within it. It is equally possible that some professionals and panel members hold a view that troublesome and difficult young people are better dealt with through the more punitive processes of the adult court. Lack of resources for youth offenders within the system and a lack of confidence in the ability of child care social workers (who service the Children's Hearing System) to provide effective offence focused intervention has also been cited as a reason for not retaining young people aged 16–18 within the hearing system (Hallett *et al* 1998, p 115).

Each local authority social work service contains specialist criminal justice social workers as part of their provision to the criminal justice system. Their expertise is seldom available to the hearing system, partly because of separate funding arrangements; poor strategic planning; the problems many local authorities have in establishing co-ordinated provision; and, anecdotally, because of a lack of recognition by many child care social work managers of the need to involve their criminal justice colleagues early to prevent young people progressing to the criminal justice system.

PREVENTION AND EFFECTIVE INTERVENTION

The view that only large scale economic and social arrangements can prevent crime co-exists with the view that the greatest prevention possibilities lie in changing the hearts and minds of those who offend. There is a limited, but growing, consensus that crime as an activity involves moral choices in certain restricting circumstances, seldom totally determined or fully rational. 'Realist' theories, right and left (Wilson and Herrnstein 1985; Young 1994), acknowledge to varying degrees that the individual and the social context are relevant to crime prevention. Early intervention can assist children, families and communities to develop personal and cultural norms of social control through primary, secondary and tertiary preventative measures (Hope and Shaw 1988).

Research suggests that the major factors fostering anti-social tendencies are long term ones and include impulsivity; poor ability to manipulate abstract concepts (cognition); low empathy; weak conscience; poor internalised norms and attitudes supporting offending; in addition to influences such as desire for material gain and status with peers. Factors influencing whether or not anti-social behaviour leads to offending are often short term situational influences such as boredom; frustration; alcohol or drug misuse; opportunities to offend; and the perceived costs and benefits of delinquency (Farrington 1992).

Methods of prevention need to be based on theories developed from empirical data on the nature of offending behaviour. Those concerned with young offenders, in addition to understanding the developmental needs of young people, must also develop an understanding of the nature of crime itself. Understanding the young offender requires a knowledge of the background of crime; the significance of its form (the relationship of offender and victim); the social and moral context of opting for criminal behaviour; the situation of committing crime, that is, its enactment in time and space; the processes of detection; and the system's response to the offender and to the victim (Young 1997).

Most young people who come to a hearing on offence related grounds are heavily under-achieving, educationally and socially. Supervision requirements ought to be positive, designed to enhance social skills and adult/parent-child relations; improve educational performance; control deviant behaviour and associations; and provide opportunities for socially acceptable leisure activity. Opportunities should be available for young people to make good any wrong that they have done, where this is possible, for example, by direct reparation or mediation, or simply by writing a letter of apology, as an important stage in supervision. Many of these services should be available to young people at risk of offending before they come to be in need of compulsory measures of supervision.

Research indicates that effectiveness is greatest where there is:

- good communication directly with the young person and the family;
- a focus on the nature and consequences of the offending behaviour;
- a planned programme of intervention carried out in a systematic way;
- an emphasis on problem solving and behaviour change, cognitive development, personal or social skills;
- a diversity of methods of intervention and a multidisciplinary approach;
- use of positive authority;
- an emphasis on community integration;
- access to a wide range of resources (Andrews *et al* 1990).

In addition to focusing on the environment, the most effective methods of supervision include social learning or social education techniques aimed at having an impact on behaviour. This includes a focus on the thinking (cognition) and attitudes of the young offender intended to improve critical reasoning; and improving problem solving skills, to help develop alternative interpretations of social rules and obligations and to comprehend the thoughts and feelings of other people, in particular, victims (Izzo and Ross 1990).

Research findings on effectiveness stress the importance of cognitive behaviour and social learning that are consistent with the social education approach promoted by the hearing system in Scotland. The aim, in many instances, should be to teach the skills we might have expected offenders to develop as young people in the home, in school and in their communities. It is questionable if this knowledge of 'criminogenic need' (Andrews *et al* 1990) and the so called 'what works' research is familiar to many social workers supervising persistent young offenders in the Children's Hearing System in Scotland.

THROUGH CARE AND AFTER CARE

Research indicates that many young people looked after away from home experience difficulties in re-integration (Stein 1997). It is now well recognised that those who, for example, have experienced secure care because of their offending, will have particular difficulties returning to the community and making a successful transition to independence. Preparation for young people leaving care is particularly important if a career of crime is to be avoided.

All young people subject to a supervision requirement beyond school leaving age because of their offending are 'looked after' children, eligible in law for assistance until they are 18 and, under certain circumstances, until they are 21 and beyond. After care duties and responsibilities for young people lie with the local authority as a whole and not with one particular department. Central government guidance makes specific reference to young people who are 'looked after' as a consequence of their offending and suggests that to 'make the best use of the flexible provisions in the law, local authority children's and criminal justice services should be co-ordinated' to address young people's needs. Despite the impressive legal provisions and well intentioned sentiments of the policy, there is little evidence to suggest that resources are available to young offenders under these provisions.

A recent report by the National Planning Group 1999 recommended that the annual review of Children's Services Plans by each local authority should include a strategy to address offending for those up to 18 years in consultation with other relevant local authority services and external agencies. The report questions whether the criminal justice system is appropriate to respond to the needs, or be effective in changing the behaviour of, young people aged 16–17. It suggests that better resourcing is needed, along with greater co-operation within social work sections and between those working in the fields of social work, education and health, the police and local communities.

CONCLUDING COMMENT

The Children's Hearing System is based on key assumptions about the nature of youth offending and about shared responsibility between young person, family, community and the State. Its principles and philosophy are expressed in its diversionary and extra-judicial approach to tackling offending. There are no simple or ideal solutions to the problem of youth crime and the model provides no miracle cure. It does demonstrate, however, that action taken in the best interests of the young person are not necessarily counter to the interests of victims or the community; and that, for most young people, its positive, non-punitive strategies are consistent with research on effective intervention. Any system that emphasises needs as much as deeds runs the risk of unnecessary interventionism and restricting the rights of young people. The hearing system exists within a legal framework with checks and balances that give the young person and their parents access to due process and legal adjudication at all stages. Nonetheless, without adequate understanding and representation, these safeguards can be compromised.

The principles on which the hearing system are founded seem sound. Research emphasises the importance of community based and social education approaches. It supports a view that attempting to define young people in criminal terms alone is an ineffective form of classification with limited predictive validity in terms of getting positive results. The key to helping young people address and change their offending behaviour lies in providing, primarily, community based services focused on the individual, the family and the community. The design relies on the availability of adequate resources and integrated local authority and multidisciplinary provisions and has a resonance with a policy of social inclusion, though these are not within its control.

In practice, Scottish data supports a view that the Children's Hearing System operates reasonably effectively as a method of diversion for most youth offenders, in that between 60–70% of such referrals are not brought even before a hearing, with no obvious negative effects on the general picture of offending within the country as compared to other jurisdictions. The picture in relation to serious or persistent offenders is much less satisfactory and the full potential of legislative provisions and policy directives is yet to be realised.

CHAPTER 9

AN ENGLISH MAGISTRATE'S VIEW OF SCOTTISH YOUTH JUSTICE

Malcolm Bentley JP[1]

If a Home Secretary announced that it was the intention of the Government to scrap the youth court, that a young offender could not be prosecuted for any but the most serious offences, but instead would be dealt with by a tribunal that could not imprison, fine, order compensation or community service and could only make an order for some form of social work intervention in the life of that offender, what might be the reaction of an English magistrate? Surprise? Disbelief? Apoplexy? Perhaps a combination of all three and a feeling that the end of civilisation is near. In one part of the UK such a system exists. In Scotland, at the beginning of the 1970s, as a result of law enacted in 1968, the Scottish youth justice system was radically changed. Despite some criticism, it gained the confidence of the Scottish people and retains it to the present day.

In 1964, a committee under the chairmanship of Lord Kilbrandon, a senior Scottish judge, issued a report (*Children and Young Persons: Scotland* (the Kilbrandon Report) 1964) and made recommendations which were to form the basis of the Social Work (Scotland) Act 1968. This Act was one of the most revolutionary pieces of legislation in the field of criminal justice within the UK and resulted in Scotland taking a path in respect of youth justice that went in a very different direction to that in England. It largely removed the young offender from the jurisdiction of the criminal courts and thereafter treated him or her on the same basis as other young people in trouble and in need of help for non-criminal reasons.

How could such proposals obtain approval and get onto the statute book? The background to the report, the passage of the legislation and its subsequent implementation, was examined by Cowperthwaite 1988. He compared the success of the Scottish reforms with the relative failure to achieve similar changes in England and Wales as had been intended in the initial White Papers and Bill which subsequently became the Children and Young Persons Act 1969. There were complex reasons behind the successful enactment of the Scottish legislation. At that time, there was a greater political

---

1 I am grateful to the following people for their help in preparing this chapter: Mike Pride, Richard Howard, Robin Wright (Clerk to the Justices, Barking and Dagenham), Elaine Cassidy and Jackie Robeson (Reporters with the Scottish Children's Reporters Administration, Glasgow), Chris Stanley (NACRO), Mary Mason (formerly Director of Social Services, Bolton, and also Chair of the Manchester Juvenile Panel) and my supervisor Jane Pickford, University of East London. Any opinions and errors are mine.

consensus than in later years; but the persuasiveness of the Kilbrandon Report, luck in timing, a bi-partisan approach, distinctive social values in Scotland and the acquiescence of the Scottish judiciary to the proposed legislation were all important elements. The aims of the reformers were diluted in the English Act of 1969 and even this Act was not fully and effectively activated. Had those aims been realised, the English youth justice system might have been very similar to that in Scotland. The idea of a family court to replace the juvenile court was dropped in England in the face of opposition, the provision of the Act for raising the age of criminal responsibility was not acted upon and the care order fell into disuse.

Cowperthwaite summarised the grounds on which the changes proposed in the two White Papers and the Bill preceding the Children and Young Persons Act 1969 were opposed. The first was that there would be a lack of due process, in that it would be unsafe to treat a young person as guilty of an offence before that offence has been formally admitted in a court of law; essentially, it confused the guilty with the innocent by dealing with them under the same welfare umbrella. The second was that there was a potential lack of equality before the law in that, allowing such a breadth of discretion in the disposal of cases would mean that different offenders might be dealt with in different ways for the same offence. The third ground of opposition was that the proposals underestimated the constructive work of the juvenile courts and the final ground was that the reforms would interfere with the work of the police.

This chapter gives a short account of the main features of the Scottish approach to youth justice, particularly its central focus on the hearing system. It highlights those practices that might seem most surprising to those working within the English youth justice system.

A NOTE ON THE PHILOSOPHY OF THE KILBRANDON REPORT, THE SOCIAL WORK (SCOTLAND) ACT 1968 AND THE CHILDREN'S HEARING

The Kilbrandon Report is a remarkable document for several reasons. Its proposals for dealing with young offenders, as has been stated, were, arguably, revolutionary. The reasons given for the proposals and the underlying philosophy seem almost commonplace, as though they were no more than self-evident and amounted to nothing more than a rationalisation of what was already the practice in Scottish youth justice. It is remarkable for what it did not say. It contained little theoretical explanation of the causes and treatment of youth crime but, instead, appeared to regard offenders as the victims of their circumstances. It merely noted that, in practical terms, young offenders and children in trouble were, historically and culturally, mainly dealt with by 'social education', yet it made little effort to define social education. The majority of offenders pleaded guilty to the offence and, therefore, it did not require the full procedures of a court of law to deal with the offender. The committee felt that there were tensions in pursuing the objectives of social education within the adversarial atmosphere of the court. Those tensions could be avoided largely by removing the process of sentencing and disposing of offenders from the jurisdiction of the courts, placing it instead in the hands of a lay, non-criminal tribunal, which came to be called the children's hearing.

The main principles of the Children's Hearing System were to be social education, care in the local community and the support of parents, who are viewed as the most important formative influence in the development of young people. These principles are seen as key elements in what has been described as a welfare system of dealing with young persons in difficulty. The hearing was not given the power, for example, to fine, award compensation, impose community sentences, etc, that had previously been within the power of the criminal court (Kearney 1987).

A BRIEF OVERVIEW OF THE CHILDREN'S HEARING SYSTEM

The children's hearing consists of a panel of lay members drawn from the local community. The area served by the panel is coterminus with the local authority area within which it is located. For each hearing, there is a permanent paid official called the Reporter who has administrative, legal and quasi-judicial duties. Cases are referred to the hearing by, among others, the police, social workers, or the Royal Scottish Society for the Prevention of Cruelty to Children, when there are grounds for believing that a child, that is, a young person under the age of 16, has committed an offence or is in need of care and protection. Frequently, the same child will fall under both categories, and both are dealt with within the same forum. If the grounds for the referral are accepted, the case will be disposed of within the hearing system. This may be by the formal imposition of compulsory supervision, by the hearing or by informal measures, such as a warning, given by the Reporter instead of, or prior to, a hearing. If the grounds are not accepted, the case is referred to the sheriff court for proof.

The procedures in the sheriff court are adversarial, but give rise to a decision that is civil rather than criminal, even in a case where an offence is alleged. Notwithstanding this, in offence cases, the criminal standard of proof applies. If the grounds are proved, then the case is referred back to the hearing for disposal. Cases where the grounds are accepted or proved may be discharged, no further action may be taken or supervision by social workers may be arranged or ordered, on a voluntary or compulsory basis. Cases are brought back to the hearing for review within stated time limits and under stated circumstances. If an appeal is made against the disposal of the panel, then the sheriff, following the implementation of the Children (Scotland) Act 1995, may substitute his or her own disposal.

THE SELECTION AND TRAINING OF PANEL MEMBERS

If an English magistrate moved to Scotland and applied to become a member of a hearing panel would the application be successful? There is the possibility that it might not. Panel members in the Scottish system are not elected from the members of a magistrates' court bench as in England and Wales, but are selected and appointed directly to the panel specifically for qualities that are relevant to working with young persons in difficulty. The choice of members of the youth and family courts in England and Wales is made from a pool of magistrates who were not chosen specifically for this kind of work. In any event, the number of persons offering themselves for election by their peers to the youth court may be so small that, in fact, there is no choice. By contrast, appointments to the Scottish panel are made by the Secretary of State, acting on the recommendation of an advisory committee, after a demanding and rigorous selection process which includes group exercises and interviews and in which use is sometimes made of independent professional advisers.

What are the qualities required in a panel member?

Kelly 1996 describes the qualities sought in prospective hearing panel members; they should be representative of the community in which the hearing is located and should be sensitive as to what is acceptable to that community. Group discussions form part of the selection process in which the candidate is expected to be able to make effective and intelligent contributions. Any candidate with a strong predisposition to punishment would be excluded. He or she should show common sense that should be exercised in a kindly, considerate and sympathetic manner. Curran 1977, quoting Higgins amongst others, reviewed research on the composition of panels that seemed to indicate that the criteria for the selection of members were not achieved in practice. At that time, there was an over-representation of teachers, of the middle class and persons who were inclined to seek the approval of their colleagues rather than take an independent view. It was suggested, however, that persons in the upper middle class were less likely to be authoritarian than those in other classes. Subsequently, the problems have been addressed.

Appointments to the panel are made by the Secretary of State on the advice of the children's panel advisory committee for the relevant hearing. The committee is not drawn from present panel members, but past members may be included, as well as local authority representatives and individuals appointed by the Secretary of State. Prospective panel members are recruited in the autumn by a national advertising campaign in the local and national press and on television. There are usually more candidates than the vacancies to be filled. It would seem that, although there is a need to ensure that the panel reflects the community that it serves, the advisory committee does not feel the need to strive to achieve the same kind of 'balance' sought on a bench in England and Wales where, for example, political orientation, gender, ethnicity, or social background can be an issue.

Mapstone 1973 researched the selection of persons for appointment to the children's panel in Fife. The Fife Children's Panel Advisory Committee, at that time, identified the following qualities as important for prospective panel members:

- freedom from excessive bias, rigidity or interest in power;
- ability to communicate and evaluate advice;
- commitment;
- self-knowledge;
- willingness to tolerate criticism;
- capacity to withstand stress;
- ability to reach a fair and reasoned conclusion.

No doubt, other committees have adopted their own criteria and those of Fife may have developed since the research took place, but such a systematic evaluation would not seem possible in England and Wales in relation to the appointment of youth court members which is by election. The only stage at which such an evaluation could be possible would be when the magistrate is first appointed.

The training of the panel member is rigorous and is spread over several months before he or she is formally appointed and can take part in meetings of the hearing. The training programme is, in a sense, a part of the selection process. If a candidate does not achieve a satisfactory standard, or reveals characteristics that would make him or her unsuitable to be a panel member, then the appointment would not be confirmed.

The Scottish Office funds posts of training organisers in four universities, each of whom is responsible for training panel members in a group of local authorities. The training of new panel members is based on a national curriculum. In service training is planned in conjunction with a local training committee. The syllabus covers, not only the legal structure of the hearing, but also the principles of welfare or social education that are a critical part of the hearing philosophy. The methods of training are discussions, group work, lectures, reading, visits of observation and meetings with people who work within the hearings system. There is a continuing commitment to training, including attendance at a yearly national school for panel members from all parts of Scotland. An account is given of the training of a panel member in the Stair Memorial Encyclopedia of the Laws of Scotland (Black ed. 1987). The panel member is appointed for a period of up to five years and is then re-appointed for further limited periods after an appraisal by members of the advisory committee. The upper age limit for service on the panel is 65. At a later date, the member may become a panel chairman, being appointed by the Secretary of State, not by election by fellow panel members.

THE GROUNDS FOR REFERRAL TO THE HEARING

Unlike the youth court in England, the hearing has jurisdiction not only over young offenders, but also over young persons experiencing other forms of difficulty. In this respect, its jurisdiction is similar to that of of the juvenile court in England before the Children Act 1989 and the Criminal Justice Act 1991. Both Acts endeavoured to eradicate any overlap between justice and welfare issues and to prevent care issues being dealt with in a criminal court forum.

The grounds for referral are to be found in s 52 of the Children (Scotland) Act 1995 and are that the child:

(a) is beyond the control of any relevant person;

(b) is falling into bad associations or is exposed to moral danger;

(c) is likely –

(i) to suffer unnecessarily; or

(ii) to be seriously impaired in his health or development, due to lack of parental care;

(d) is a child in respect of whom any of the offences in Sched 1 to the Criminal Procedure (Scotland) Act 1975 (offences against children to which special provisions apply) has been committed;

(e) is, or is likely to be become, a member of the same household as a child in respect of whom any of the offences referred to in para (d) above has been committed;

(f) that the child is, or is likely to become, a member of the same household as a person who has committed a scheduled offence;

(g) is, or is likely to become, a member of the same household as a person in respect of whom an offence under ss 2A to 2C of the Sexual Offences (Scotland) Act 1976 (incest and intercourse with a child by stepparent or person in a position of trust) has been committed by a member of that household;

(h) has failed to attend school regularly without reasonable excuse;

(i) has committed an offence;

(j) has misused alcohol or any drug, whether or not a controlled drug within the meaning of the Misuse of Drugs Act 1971;

(k) has misused a volatile substance by deliberately inhaling its vapour, other than for medical purposes;

(l) is being provided with accommodation by a local authority under s 25, or is the subject of a parental responsibilities order obtained under s 86, of this Act and, in either case, his behaviour is such that special measures are necessary for his adequate supervision in his interest or the interest of others.

The grounds for offence referral do not appear to give rise to a potential difference to those that apply in England. It is interesting to contrast, however, the non-offence grounds with the more generalised grounds for the referral of children to the family panel in England.

A family court may make a care and supervision order if it is satisfied:

(a) that the child is suffering, or is likely to suffer, significant harm; and

(b) that the harm, or the likelihood of harm, is attributable to –

(i) the care given to the child, or likely to be given to him if the order were not made, not being what it would be reasonable to expect a parent to give to him; or

(ii) the child's being beyond parental control [s 31 of the Children and Young Persons Act 1933].

In England, there must be a lack of care of the kind that it would be reasonable to expect a parent to give to a child. In Scotland, there is no such criterion and, presumably, intervention can be made even when that care is present. It would seem that the law in Scotland enables intervention to be made in a much wider range of circumstances when compared with those that apply in England.

The grounds for the referral have to be accepted by the child and parents and, if they are not, then they have to be proved in the sheriff court before the hearing can make a disposal.

WHO MAKES REFERRALS AND WHY?

As magistrates know, the youth courts deal with only a minority of the known young offenders in England and Wales. According to the Audit Commission 1996, 60% are dealt with by a police caution, although other sources put the figure higher. There is no reason to think that the new final warning system introduced by the Crime and Disorder Act 1998 will be used any more sparingly. The caution may be given immediately by the police or after reference to a local multi-agency panel at which the police, social workers, the probation service and education services may be represented. The panel is able to gather information about the offender and, if appropriate, recommend a social work intervention which, if accepted by the offender, is arranged on a voluntary basis. Of the remainder, 10% of cases are discontinued and 30% are sentenced by the courts. The youth court does not deal with non-criminal cases where children are in need of care or protection; these are within the jurisdiction of the family court.

In Scotland, the pattern is very different. Formal police warnings play a very much smaller part in the criminal justice system as, for example, on average between different police authorities, only 11% of known young offenders were cautioned in 1989. Of referrals made by the police, 13% were directly to the procurator fiscal, reflecting the fact that the most serious offences and some traffic cases are still dealt with in the criminal court although some of these might then be referred by the procurator fiscal to the Reporter (Scottish Office Statistical Bulletin 1991). Seventy-six per cent were referred to the Reporter of a children's hearing. Thus, the Reporter and the hearing together deal with many of the offenders that would be dealt with by the police or multi-agency panels in England.

Any person is entitled to pass information to the Reporter if they believe that compulsory supervision of a child may be required. The police and local authorities have a duty to do so (Norrie 1997). Scottish Office statistics (Social Work Series 1997) suggest that, in 1995, 78% of referrals to the Reporter were made by law enforcement agencies; 19% were made by Social Work Departments or from educational sources and 2% were made by parents, relatives or neighbours. For boys, the grounds for referral were related to offences in 69% of cases and 31% for non-offence cases. For girls, the percentages are almost exactly reversed.

THE REPORTER

The pivotal figure in the Scottish youth justice system is the Reporter. He or she has no counterpart in England. The functions of the Reporter embody a much wider range than those of the justices' clerk; they are administrative, investigatory, advisory, quasi-judicial and also those of advocate. They are closer to those of the procurator fiscal, who has more wide ranging powers than a Crown Prosecutor or court clerk, and who has very broad discretionary powers. Cowperthwaite 1989 felt that it was because these wide powers were already a familiar element in the Scottish legal process that it was acceptable that similar powers should be given to the Reporter. The qualifications required for a Reporter may be determined by the Secretary of State for Scotland, although, so far, this power has not been exercised. He or she need not be legally qualified and may have a social work background that would be in keeping with the nature of the Reporter's work and the welfare based practice and philosophy of the hearing. In practice, however, because of the increased legal complexity of the law relating to children, it is increasingly likely that the Reporter is legally qualified.

All referrals on offence or non-offence grounds are initially made to the Reporter who is the gatekeeper to the Children's Hearing System. He or she can take various courses of action. The first is to seek further information to supplement that supplied in the referral. This may be obtained by seeking reports from any person who is able to give useful information about the child, for example, from the police, social work departments, teachers or voluntary organisations concerned with child welfare. In offence cases, she may ask the police to make a further investigation of the offence, but will not take formal control of the conduct of the case in the same manner as the procurator fiscal.

He or she can then decide to deal with the child informally; the majority of cases are dealt with in this way. In 1995, there were 45,878 referrals to Reporters of which only 14,620 (32%) were submitted to the hearing; 25,867 referrals (56%) resulted in no further action being taken by the Reporter. The balance was dealt with by informal action. A reason for taking no further action might be, for example, that the Reporter feels that there is insufficient evidence to support the establishment of an offence. If the child is already under supervision, then the Reporter may decide to do no more than allow the existing order to continue. However, Curran 1977 indicated that there might have been, in practice, some kind of informal action. The Reporter may give a warning to the child and parents by letter or at an interview. He or she may invite the child and parents to an informal meeting at which the consequences of the child's actions will be discussed. He or she can arrange for a social work intervention to be made on a voluntary basis or he or she may refer the case to the police for a warning to be administered.

Finally, the case may be referred to the hearing to decide whether some compulsory measure of supervision should be imposed. When the case is submitted to the hearing, the Reporter is present and has an advisory role, but does not participate in the decisions. As at all stages, he or she will call for any necessary reports, prepare papers and keep records. If the case has to be referred to the sheriff court, either because the grounds for referral are not accepted or there is an appeal against disposal, then the Reporter is responsible for presenting the case before the court.

THE HEARING

Those cases that have not been disposed of by the Reporter are submitted by him or her to the hearing and it is at this stage that the panel member participates in the youth justice system. The hearing is not a court of law and, unlike the youth court, is not concerned with the establishment of the grounds for the referral. Its function is to assess the needs of the child in both offence and non-offence cases and it has the power to order compulsory measures of supervision or care for the child when they are thought to be necessary in the child's interest.

The hearing takes place before three members of the panel, including at least one woman and one man. The grounds for the referral must have been accepted or proved before the sheriff court. The hearing is sometimes described as informal in relation to the nature of its proceedings. It might be better described as non-adversarial and less legalistic than the magistrates' court. The hearing works within a detailed framework of legislation and cannot be regarded, in that sense, as truly informal. Norrie states:

> ... though the system contains some informality, that informality is seen only in the discussion of the case which lies at the heart of the procedure; other elements of the procedure are as formal and as mandatory as the procedure in a court of law [Norrie 1997, p 3].

He goes on to comment that the hearing is a quasi-judicial tribunal having many of the powers of a court and must, therefore, observe the requirements of procedural fairness required by natural justice and international obligations.

The hearing takes place in premises that vary in their standards and facilities but which are intended to be less intimidating than those of a courthouse. The child and his or her parents have an appointment, by time and date, for the hearing. On arrival, they should be met by a Reporter. At the beginning and end of the proceedings, there are formalities to be observed in that the purpose and need of the hearing is explained as is the decision of the hearing. In contrast to the youth court, however, the atmosphere is that of a discussion between the members of the panel and the child and his or her parents in which a consensus of views is sought. An English magistrate who has sat in the family court might feel that there is a lack of structure in the proceedings, for example, there is no welfare 'checklist'. One of the skills expected of a panel member, particularly the chairman, is the ability to put the parents, and especially the child, at ease that they are able to take part in the discussion. The extent to which they do so, in practice, varies and must depend on the personalities of those present. No matter how informal the panel members and others feel the proceedings to be, the child of a (relatively) younger age, in the presence of adults and faced with the possibility of an unwelcome order in respect of his or her future, may not see it the same way. He or she will be asked for his or her views and, in offence cases, may be asked to explain his or her actions and think of their consequences for him or herself and others. Some young people who have experience of both the court and the hearing do not regard the hearing as a soft option.

Others present are the Reporter, social workers and, on occasion, a representative of the education services. These may add up to a daunting array to a young person. As in the youth court, the public are not allowed to be present. Those who may be present are the child, the parents, a representative, the safeguarder, a social worker and the press. The press is not permitted to publish anything that will identify the child. This was the case in England until s 45 of the Crime (Sentences) Act 1997 gave discretion to magistrates to lift reporting restrictions. In exceptional circumstances, the chairman may permit the presence of observers.

An English magistrate might also be struck by the absence of a legal representative at the hearing to speak on behalf of the young person. Legal aid is not available and, if the child is represented, it is at his or her own expense, or that of the family. Where an advocate is present it is not usually the case that it inhibits the informal atmosphere of the hearing. A magistrate with long experience, however, would recall the time in the juvenile court when it was less common for an offender to be represented and when it was more usual to converse directly with the juvenile. Today, it is unusual for a young person not to be represented in the youth court and the atmosphere is that of a mini adult court. This difference between the two systems gives rise to an issue to be discussed later which is the possible conflict between the absence of formality at the hearing and a lack of 'due process'.

All three members of the hearing, in turn, engage in discussion with the young person and parents; questions are not put through the chair. At the conclusion of the hearing, the panel members (there must be three sitting) will discuss the case in front of those present without retiring and each member gives his or her decision. Any disagreement is apparent to those present. The hearing, of course, does not need to be concerned with findings of fact or guilt and has a much more restricted range of disposal options and criteria to be considered than arise in the youth court. The reasons for the decision are recorded by the chairperson or Reporter.

The panel member will have had to do a considerable amount of 'homework' prior to the hearing, such as, reading reports in preparation for the meeting with the child that will have taken considerably longer than the 40 minutes or so that the discussion lasts. (This has been eased by the Children (Scotland) Act 1995 which permits earlier reports to be summarised. Since October 1996, the family has had a right of access to the same papers as the panel.) This will be familiar to members of the family panel, but less so to other members of the bench in England who may often sentence with much less preparation. The magistrate, in sentencing, is mainly concerned with the offence that has been committed. He or she is aware of the welfare principle stated in the Children and Young Person Act 1933:

> Every court in dealing with a child or young person who is brought before it either as an offender or otherwise, shall have regard to the welfare of the child

or young person, and shall in a proper case take steps for removing him from undesirable surroundings and for securing that proper provision is made for his education and training.

What does this statement amount to in practice? Does it amount to more than empty rhetoric? (Ball *et al* 1995.) How often is it considered in the youth court? The principle cannot be used to order a sentence in a criminal court that could only be justified on the grounds of welfare. In other words, even if the court would like to help the offender by giving a social work order because it sees such a need, this cannot be done if the offence does not justify it. In the family court, the welfare principle is more strongly stated. In s 1(1) of the Children Act 1989, the welfare principle is paramount. In the English system, those dealing with young persons have to apply different welfare standards in criminal and civil cases and, in the former, may subordinate the welfare principle to punishment and other philosophies of sentencing.

In Scotland, a young offender can be prosecuted in the criminal court for a serious offence and certain other offences, but the proportion of these to total offences is relatively small. If there is a prosecution, then the welfare principle in point is that in the Criminal Procedure (Scotland) Act 1995, which is not dissimilar to that in the English criminal courts.

The great majority of young offenders are dealt with by the hearing. The legislation in the Children (Scotland) Act 1995, which partly replaced the 1968 Act, provides that in criminal as well as civil matters the welfare of the child is the paramount concern of the hearing. There is an exception. Section 16(5) of the Act allows the paramount character of the welfare principle to be overridden for the purpose of protecting the public from serious harm. Norrie 1995 states that this sub-section should not be used lightly. It follows that the hearing does not need to concern itself, in the main, with punishment or any of the other sentencing objectives of the youth court. The primacy of the welfare principle is reinforced by, and reflected in, the type of disposal that is available to the hearing. As has been noted, it cannot imprison, fine, order compensation or impose community sentences. The disposals available are restricted to powers of compulsory supervision, albeit with the ability to attach conditions, particularly of residence, of which one form may be that it should be in secure accommodation. For a secure accommodation order to be made, certain criteria have to be met. These are that the child has already absconded and must be likely to abscond if not in secure accommodation; that his physical, moral or mental welfare will be at risk; or that he is likely to injure himself or some other person.

There are two other main principles that the hearing must observe. First, the views of the child should be heard and taken into account in any intervention ordered by the hearing. Secondly, any intervention should be the minimum that is appropriate, but some intervention is better than no intervention at all.

If the child or his or her family disagree with the order made by the panel then they may appeal against it to the sheriff court. One of the changes that was made by the 1995 Act to the original 1968 legislation is that the sheriff is now able to substitute his or her own order for that of the panel. Prior to this, he or she could only return the case asking the panel to reconsider its order. Some panel members regard this alteration as undermining the status and philosophy of the hearing. The sheriff is trained in the law. The Reporter and the panel members are more likely to be trained in the philosophies of social work and social education, the principles that underpin the hearing system.

The youth court, once having passed sentence, very rarely hears the outcome unless the child commits another offence or is in breach of an order of the court. The hearing, on the other hand, must review its cases where a compulsory supervision order has been made. This must be done at least at yearly intervals, or earlier in certain circumstances, such as at the request of certain stated persons including the child or young person. Various options are open to the hearing on review. The order may be continued, terminated or continued but with changed conditions. Contrast these powers with those of the youth court, where this degree of flexibility has been slightly improved by recent legislation, but is nevertheless still virtually non-existent.

THE SAFEGUARDER

The magistrate who sits in the family court is familiar with the role of the guardian ad litem who is appointed to protect the interests of the child in public proceedings where some measure of care or protection may be required. The court is required to appoint a guardian, unless it is satisfied that it is not necessary to do so; it is unusual for one not to be appointed (White *et al* 1995). The office of the guardian was created by the Children Act 1975 but was not activated in opposed proceedings until 27 May 1984. Jasmine Beckford died in 1984; a guardian had not been appointed in her case. Blom-Cooper *et al* 1985, in the report of the panel of enquiry into her death, stated that they could not say that, if a guardian had been appointed, there would have been a different outcome to the care proceedings. The report does state, however:

> We should like to highlight the value of the guardian ad litem in care proceedings. The essential feature of that role is that for the first time there is someone, other than a legal representative, whose concern is exclusively the welfare of the child independent of the child's parents and of the local authority which has the duty to protect the child.

The safeguarder might be regarded as the counterpart, in the Scottish system, of the guardian. Their terms of reference are not defined by statute and Norrie 1997 states that he or she has discretion regarding the role that he or she plays.

Scotland introduced the safeguarder to the hearing system in the Children (Scotland) Act 1975, but the legislation was not activated until 1985. The safeguarder is appointed to a panel, formed under the aegis of the local authority, which determines the qualifications and experience that are required of an appointee. He or she acts in an individual case, at the request of the chairman of the hearing, and provides a contribution to the procedure that ensures that the interests of the child are protected at the hearing, at the proof of an offence and on appeal at the sheriff court against an order of the hearing. It is intended that the safeguarder should prevent the dilution of the focus of the hearing process on the welfare of the child when there might be conflict of interests with, for example, the parents.

It is, therefore, strange that safeguarders are only appointed in a very small number of cases referred to hearings, that is, in only 1% of offence and 8% of non-offence cases. This, together with the lack of legal representation at the hearing, is referred to later.

THE ADVANTAGES AND DISADVANTAGES OF THE SCOTTISH CHILDREN'S HEARING SYSTEM

Having outlined the origins of the hearing, its philosophy and methods, there are some general issues to be considered. These are:

(a) the continuity and cohesion of the system and the degree of change;

(b) whether the hearing lacks adequate safeguards for the offender and whether it realises the welfare objective; and

(c) is it successful and a better system than that in England?

The hearing, although it has acceptance in Scotland and even acclaim at home and abroad, is not free from weaknesses nor, consequently, from criticism. Each of the above issues will be covered in turn.

Continuity and cohesion in the Scottish youth justice system

For those who deal with youth justice in England and Wales, the three decades preceding 1998 were years of substantial changes of policy and practice with, at times, a seemingly never ending flood of legislation. In the early post-war period, there was much in common in the views of the two major political parties. At a time when there was growing concern at the upward trend in crime and particularly youth crime there was also a bi-partisan feeling that there should be a new look at the youth justice system. In Scotland, a new approach succeeded; in England, it failed. What followed in England has been a history of U-turns, inconsistencies and ambiguities in a system which is fragmented between the agencies that operate it and is bifurcated in its philosophy. There has been a welfare approach of diversion and treatment on the one hand and punishment and non-welfare sentencing policies on the other.

The Children and Young Persons Act 1969 that was to be the flagship of welfare foundered. The age of criminal responsibility was to be raised, the intention that family courts should take over much of the work of the juvenile court in criminal matters had been abandoned and the juvenile court was retained. The main disposal was to be a care order rather than a punitive disposal, but this approach fell into disuse. The proposals for legislation in discussion and White Papers, the Bill and the Act came under attack from many sides and its provisions, which eventually came into being, only in a severely mauled form, were never fully implemented. Thereafter, welfarism never fully regained the ground lost. Between 1969 and 1998, there were eight major items of legislation of relevance to young offenders, quite apart from Home Office Directives, in which the sentencing options became more severe, but the ability to use custodial sentences was constrained. More recently, the political and popular climate has been summed up in the phrase that 'prison works' and the idea that some young offenders should be committed to military style prisons or 'boot camps'.

Paradoxically, at the same time as the courts were becoming more punitive, moves were afoot to divert the offender from the courts and the prisons. The practice of police cautioning was officially encouraged by the Home Office; the creation of multi-agency panels, in some parts of the country, assisted this practice and, where appropriate, a welfare intervention on a voluntary basis and alternatives to imprisonment were introduced by way of community sentences associated with supervision.

In Scotland, there has been greater consistency and continuity. There were only two fundamental pieces of legislation in the comparable period and there has been no major change in the underlying approach to young persons in difficulty. It was, and remains, a welfare orientated system. The 1995 Act sticks to the main principles of the 1968 Act. Supervision, within the framework of the philosophy of social education, remains the main disposal of the hearing. A significant change, however, is that on appeal against an order of the hearing, the sheriff can substitute his or her own order, although still within the same range as that available to the hearing. Previously, he or she could only refer the case back to the hearing with a request that, if appropriate, the disposal should be reconsidered. The argument against this change is that the sheriff does not have the social work background of the hearing and is, therefore, arguably less likely to make an effective disposal. Thus, the U-turns and changes of direction experienced in England and Wales have largely bypassed Scotland. The major seismic shocks to the Scottish system came, not from changes of perspective of criminal justice for young offender, but from matters that would be dealt with in the family court in England and Wales. As a result of some high profile cases, such as the Orkney child abuse case, the Children's Hearing System was put in the spotlight and the need for reform considered. Although the 1995 Act made significant changes to the law in non-offence matters of private law, it left the hearing fundamentally unchanged in its philosophy and practice (Norrie 1995).

What is apparent is that the hearing encompasses jurisdictions exercised by the police, the diversion panel, social services departments and, to some extent, the courts in England. In most cases dealt with by the hearing, the underlying principle is that the welfare of the child is paramount and the disposal options are limited to those that are consistent with the welfare principle. Children who are at risk, or in need of care for reasons other than having committed an offence, are mainly dealt with within the same system, but the practices of social work can vary between different local authority regions, in that intervention is sometimes made without referral to the hearing. The Scottish system does not need, therefore, to be concerned with any tension between welfare issues and offence issues, whereas it is arguable that such tensions are a major feature of the youth justice system in England and Wales.

Due process, welfare and informality

What is due process? *The Oxford Companion to Law* 1980 gives the following definition:

> The conduct of legal proceedings according to established principles and rules which *safeguard the position of the person charged* [Walker, p 381, emphasis added].

This should be extended to include stages of a judicial process prior to charge and to a system, such as the Scottish one, where a charge will not be brought but where some compulsory order may be made.

The hearing system has not been beyond criticism – most fundamentally that it does not have sufficient procedural and legal safeguards to ensure due process for an alleged offender. The magistrate is familiar with the adversarial system in court, the presence of advocates, the rules of evidence, the formalities of procedure and the deference of those in the court to the bench. These are all the trappings of due process in evidence at a magistrates' court. The essential elements are, according to King 1981, equality between the parties, rules protecting the defendant against error, restraint of arbitrary power and a presumption of innocence.

A key protection for the young offender is the age at which the law determines whether he or she has the capacity to commit an offence. In most European countries, the age is higher than in England and Wales or Scotland.

The age of criminal responsibility in Scotland, at the age of eight, is lower than in England and Wales. There is no doctrine of *doli incapax* in Scotland, the rebuttable presumption of incapacity of a child up to the age of 14 to commit a crime which, in England, until 1998, gave further protection beyond the age of criminal responsibility at 10. This presumption has now disappeared in England, by virtue of the Crime and Disorder Act 1998. However, a child below the age of 16 is, generally, not prosecuted in Scotland for an offence and, therefore, avoids the consequences of a criminal sentence. But the young person can be dealt with by the hearing in a way that may seem like punishment to him or her. As noted, the hearing should have the interests of the child as its paramount concern. However, is this sufficient to safeguard the young person's civil rights? The hearing does not determine the correctness of the referral, which is either admitted or, if necessary, proved in the sheriff court. Legal aid is granted in cases that are heard before the sheriff court, but are these offences, which are admitted in the absence of legal advice, ones which, arguably, could not always be proved if taken to court? If an offence is admitted, but the facts of the referral are disputed, then the matter can be resolved in the sheriff court. Disputes on ancillary facts, which are not part of the referral, have to be resolved by the hearing at which there may be no legal representation. These facts may be more important in determining the disposal made by the hearing than those in the referral itself.

At the hearing, the young person is, in many ways, at a disadvantage. He or she is unlikely to have legal representation (unless the family feel that it is appropriate and can afford to pay for it) or the help of a safeguarder. The young person, or his or her parents, may not have the ability or confidence to speak on his or her behalf. Both Norrie 1997 and Kelly 1996 argue that it is in contravention of the UN Convention on the Rights of the Child 1989 that there is no right to legal aid at the hearing stage. It has been noted previously that a safeguarder is appointed in only a small number of cases. As has been seen from the statistics considered earlier, the majority of referrals are dealt with by the Reporter without reference to the panel and may be discharged for lack of evidence. Is this, together with the right to take issues to the sheriff court for proof or on appeal, sufficient protection? Arguably, it is not. Are the weaknesses in the system that arise from this any worse than those that exist in the English system? It would seem that there is greater protection for the young person in the youth court, but the majority of criminal cases are dealt with outside the courts, for example, traditionally by cautioning, where there may be a similar lack of legal representation. This trend for offenders to be dealt with outside the formal court system in England and Wales has been extended by the provisions of the Crime and Disorder Act 1998 and the Youth Justice and Criminal Evidence Act 1999, particularly the latter, which introduces the Youth Offender Panels (YOPs) to deal with referral orders.

Is this weakness in the system a price that is worth paying for the benefits? It is arguable that the presence of lawyers would erode the informality of the hearing and might inhibit the ability of the panel members to speak directly with the child and family, as has happened in the juvenile and youth court in England and Wales. It is possible, of course, that, with appropriate training for advocates and sound procedures, the informality of the hearing could be maintained. There is, after all, some legal representation and, when present, this does not seem to adversely affect the atmosphere of the hearing. Legal representation is not barred; it is just uncommon because of the lack of legal aid.

The main perceived benefit of the Scottish system is that it is essentially a welfare system and it can be said that, as a system in which the majority of offenders are dealt with outside the criminal courts, it avoids stigmatising them as criminals. What does this amount to in practice and what are the consequences? The English system contains within it an uncertain mixture of philosophies if, indeed, it can be said to have any philosophies at all. Punishment, incapacitation, deterrence, as well as welfare and rehabilitation can all be said to be part of the system and there is no clear framework or logic within which decisions are taken regarding which objective should be preferred. The emphasis and priorities may alter and shift and, therefore, be uncertain at different stages in the system.

Is police cautioning a welfare approach? It may appear to be so since it avoids the offender being brought before the courts and given a criminal record and, arguably, there is no punishment. But does it offer any constructive help to those that may need it? The number of cases where some form of helpful intervention is made as well as a caution is, according to the Audit Commission, relatively small. Of 12 study sites examined by the Commission, at only two did local agencies address the behaviour of offenders in significant numbers. In all cases, the number was less than 10% of the total number of offenders. The comments of Ball *et al* 1995 on the welfare principle in the English youth justice system have been noted earlier. How often is the welfare principle considered as a separate element when sentence is considered in the retiring room? Magistrates are more likely to focus on the offence rather than the offender; a sentence is more likely to be passed by reference to the particular offence rather than the welfare and needs of the offender.

In Scotland, because the welfare principle is paramount, the focus of the hearing is on the child, although note is taken of any offence or victim; thus, there are not the same tensions that exist in the English system. The hearing can individualise the disposal and does not need to be concerned with any of the other sentencing objectives and parity of sentencing – issues that the magistrate might need to consider. Potentially, this would seem to give rise to the difficulties over parity of sentencing or equality before the law that had been a major criticism of the reforms of the English system proposed in the 1960s. It can only make a range of supervisory orders that involve a social work programme albeit, where appropriate, with conditions of residence.

What, however, is the objective of the welfare principle? A difficulty is that 'welfare' is not defined in the statutes, neither English nor Scottish. It may be appropriate to refer to the UN Convention on the Rights of the Child 1989. Article 40(1) states:

> State parties recognise the right of every child alleged as, accused of, or recognised as having infringed the penal law to be treated in a manner consistent with the promotion of the child's sense of dignity and worth, which reinforces the child's respect for the human rights and fundamental freedom of others and which take into account the child's age and the desirability of promoting the child's reintegration and the child's assuming a constructive role in society.

The UK is a signatory to the Convention but there is no mechanism by which a failure to implement or observe it can be taken to appeal in the same way that there can be an appeal to the European Court of Human Rights on a point arising from the European Convention on Human Rights. The UN clause seems more easily accommodated within the Scottish system than within the English, although it is not formally adopted within the Children (Scotland) Act 1995. The welfare orientation of the hearing, the absence of the criminal orientation of the youth courts and the nature of the supervisory disposals of the hearing, all point to an objective consistent with Art 40 of the Convention – even though it has not been formally adopted.

Is the Scottish hearing really a welfare system? It has been argued, by some critics, that in reality it differs very little from the system it replaced. Under the old system, most young offenders were dealt with in a manner that was hardly different to the way in which they are now dealt with by the hearing. Because the disposal made by the hearing can be compulsory, it is, perhaps, just as much a means of social control over children as that exercised by the courts, based on the idea of 'crime-responsibility-punishment'. But is punishment incompatible with the welfare principle? Kearney 1987 quoted the views of Baroness Wootton, a sociologist and magistrate, that individuals respond to different stimuli and that deprivation of privileges may be justified on welfare grounds providing that the aim is to secure the welfare of the child. Does it matter that there is compulsion in some elements of the supervision? There is compulsion in early academic education, but it would not generally be thought of as punishment. It can inculcate into children the values of society but it is not generally thought to be a method of social control.

The distinguishing feature of a welfare system is not, perhaps, the sentencing options that are used or available, but the purpose for which they are used. Under the English system, the objectives of sentencing can be various and complex. Sentences of the youth court may not, perhaps, be individualised but imposed on a tariff basis, reflecting the perceived seriousness of the offence or the offending history of the person concerned. In some circumstances, for example, where diversion from the courts is being attempted, or where the court imposes a supervision order with some form of social work intervention, there may be individualisation with the purpose of achieving welfare objectives. In Scotland, the same tensions should, theoretically, not exist. The welfare of the child is paramount and, therefore, whatever disposals are available should, in theory, be used to achieve that purpose. In practice, the disposals that are available to the hearing are restricted to some form of supervision which reduces the risk that the hearing may become confused about its objectives and drift into a punishment regime. Even when supervision is imposed in its most draconian form, with a condition that the offender should be placed in secure accommodation, this can only be done by reference to criteria that are not related to the offence.

Which is the better system, English or Scottish?

There is probably no way to give a definitive answer to this question. The best answer that may be possible is some generalised statement which must depend upon a variety of values, criteria and objectives which may be difficult to define and even more difficult to measure. Some of these may be in harmony, others may be in contradiction with each other. If the objectives are the control of crime and the punishment of the offender, then the means of achieving them are likely to be very different to a system where the aim is the rehabilitation of the offender. The Scottish and the English systems seem to have very different objectives. In the former, they are mainly those of rehabilitation; the latter is mainly a system which emphasises due process but with undertones of crime control and punishment; however, rehabilitation can also be an element. As to which factor is dominant, this may change according to the stage of the justice process. The diversion panel, for example, is likely to have different objectives to those of the court. Given these differences, can you assess the success of one system according to whether it achieves the objectives of the other? It would seem fair to do so if one system has the secondary or incidental objectives of the other.

If the objectives of a system are crime control and deterrence, then the English system might be thought to be more capable of achieving them than the Scottish, in that it has a greater range of sentencing powers. It is open to question whether it in fact does succeed in achieving these aims, however. There is some evidence that the amount of youth crime as measured by the number of known young male offenders has declined. In the period 1985–93 the number of known young male offenders fell by 39% (Home Office 1993). Newburn (in Maguire *et al* 1997) quotes Farrington, who doubts whether this fall is real, but adds that the information available is insufficient to be sure whether or not the pattern of offending had changed. The Audit Commission 1996 strongly questions the effectiveness of the youth justice system, describing how the same persons appear before the court time and again without, apparently, any benefit either to the offender or the community. It seems that the system is costly and slow in its processes. It cannot be said that deterrence never works or indeed that it always does work. This is, perhaps, no more than self-evident and the answer must be at an uncertain point between these two positions. We do not know enough about how individuals react to sentences and whether they will be deterred by the possibility of punishment. What may be more important than the severity of punishment is the perceived risk of detection; where this is thought to be low, the severity of punishment may be relatively unimportant.

If there are successful features to be found in the English system, perhaps these can be more readily seen in areas concerned with rehabilitation rather than those which are concerned with punishment and which are either located outside the courts or where the court adopts a non-punitive stance. Police cautioning seemed to be successful in dealing with offenders, in that 85% did not re-offend within two years after caution (NACRO February 1997). According to the Audit Commission 1996 analysis, a conditional discharge is less likely to be followed by a reconviction than any disposal other than a caution. However, a conditional discharge is more likely to be given to a person who has not been previously convicted. Conditional discharges may not be so successful when given to a more hardened offender.

The English magistrate might then end up being confused, uncertain and frustrated as to what he or she should do for the best and whether anything he or she does has any beneficial effect. It might be of small consolation for him or her to know that the majority of young offenders do grow out of their offending behaviour, but probably because of influences that have nothing to do with the work of the court, for example, finding employment or settling down with a partner.

What of the Scottish system? There are difficulties for the English magistrate in comparing it with his or her own. The statistics on young offenders are differently based to those in Scotland and, as the hearing is a non-criminal tribunal, they may not appear in the criminal statistics at all. If youth crime had gone through the roof in Scotland because of a weakness in a punishment focus, then it could be argued that, in this respect, the Scottish system does not perform as well as the English and that the defect should be corrected. What evidence is there of this though? On the face of it, this does not appear to have happened. The Scottish Office Statistical Bulletin 1991 on initial police action in respect of young offenders shows that reports made by the police fell from 33,578 in 1981 to 26,336 in 1989. However, expressed in terms of a rate per 1,000 children, it has fluctuated narrowly between 50 in 1981 and 52 in 1989 due to demographic changes. Young 1997 examines the evidence from crime surveys and other sources and, whilst acknowledging the difficulty in interpreting the data, suggests that crime rates in Scotland are lower per head of the population than in England and Wales and that the rate of increase in crime is lower.

In addition, although it is circumstantial, it may be powerful evidence that the hearing system has remained largely unchanged in 27 years. In 1980, a consultative memorandum was issued by the Government which canvassed the views of interested parties as to whether the system should be changed and whether powers of punishing offenders should be introduced. The general view, including that of the police, was that change was neither needed nor desirable.

In a research report, Asquith *et al* 1998 quote Pickles J:

Scotland has the highest number of people in prison per head of population in the UK which, in turn, has the highest overall prison population within western Europe. Within these figures lie the disturbing statistic that in Scotland 16–21 year olds receive the highest rate of custodial sentencing. A major concern for this age group is, therefore, to reduce the number of young people receiving custodial sentences. There is also widespread concern about the difficulties faced by 16 and 17 year olds in the interface between the Children's Hearing System and the adult Criminal Justice System [p 111].

Difficult child abuse cases in the early 1990s put the hearing system under the microscope; but the legislation in 1995 left it unchanged in its underlying principles and, indeed, strengthened them by making the welfare of the child the paramount concern of the hearing. The welfare orientation of the hearing is strengthened by the selection methods and the training and practice of panel members that tend to be antipathetic to punishment. It has been argued earlier that, in practice, a disposal by the hearing may seem like a punishment to the child and that punishment is not necessarily inconsistent with the welfare principle, providing that it is in the interests of the child. In addition, the Lord Advocate retains the power to give leave for an offender to be prosecuted, either because of the nature of the offence, or because the hearing can do no more with the child (Norrie 1995, pp 36–85). The main aims of the system are social education and the supervision of young persons to enable them to overcome their difficulties. The Audit Commission 1996 commented on the effectiveness of different sentences in England. Literature seems to be largely silent on re-offending rates under the hearing system, but research is proceeding in this area. Mary Hartnoll (Howard League 1995) comments on the absence of published research on the Scottish system and is cautious in making comparisons with that in England. She has, however, considerable experience of working within both systems up to the most senior levels and, from that experience, concludes that the hearing is a far better system than the youth court.

From an administrative aspect, the hearing seems to have some advantages when compared with the youth court. For example, the appearance of the child and parents at the hearing are carefully timed to avoid the stress of an unknown waiting period. The cost of dealing with a case in the hearing system, according to Audit Commission 1996, based on information drawn from Strathclyde Reporter's Department in 1994, was £183 for each referral or £880 for each panel hearing. According to the Commission, the cost of successfully prosecuting an offender in the English system is £2,500. This is not to say that those cases that are prosecuted in Scotland cost any less than those in England, nor that those cases that are not brought to the youth court, but are dealt with by caution (now reprimand and final warning) or diversion in England, cost any more than in Scotland. It is likely, however, that a system that avoids the courts will be less expensive. Delay, however, is a concern for the hearing just as much as for the youth court. The average number of days taken to deal with a case from the offence to the disposal was 166 days in 1995. In non-offence cases, the time span was 191 days from the event that gave rise to the referral to the date of disposal of the case (Scottish Children's Reporter Administration 1997). In England and Wales, the average time taken to deal with offenders was 131 days in 1996 (Lord Chancellor's Department 1997).

WHAT CAN THE ENGLISH LEARN FROM THE SCOTTISH YOUTH JUSTICE SYSTEM?

Despite differences that exist between England and Scotland in culture, education, religion and law, there is still much in common between them. The English magistrate might ponder that, within a society that is not so very different from his or her own, a radically different youth justice system can flourish. The welfare principle, which is paramount in Scotland, has an uncertain place in England and often receives only token consideration. The Scottish system might be seen as more compassionate than that in England and Wales and more in accord with international standards in its objectives. The English magistrate might reflect on the fact that the youth court plays only a relatively small part in dealing with known offenders and that it is possible for much of the most constructive and effective work in dealing with young offenders to take place outside the youth court.

With the change of government in 1997 came a root and branch review of the English and Welsh youth justice system. The proposals for change were deep and far reaching. If there were lessons to be learned from the Scottish system, did the proposals reflect them? Whilst in Opposition, the Labour Party produced a Consultation Paper, *Tackling Youth Crime: Reforming Youth Justice* (Home Office 1997c) (see NACRO September 1997), that pointed to the tensions that exist between welfare and punishment in the English system and the need to strike a new balance between them. This was an echo of the views of the Kilbrandon Committee over 30 years before. The solution of Kilbrandon to this tension was to remove young people from the jurisdiction of the criminal courts. To attempt such a change south of the border would, perhaps, be an act of political suicide for some members of the Government. There is an impression, however, that the proposed changes point to some regard having been paid to the Scottish system. Do they incorporate elements of the hearing system? The White Paper *No More Excuses – A New Approach to Tackling Youth Crime in England and Wales* (Home Office 1997d) contained proposals that are now included in the Crime and Disorder Act 1998 and the Youth Justice and Criminal Evidence Act 1999. The White Paper also proposed reform of the youth court and invited discussion before further change is made.

What was the underlying philosophy of the White Paper for dealing with young offenders?

The White Paper did not seem to have the social education, welfare philosophy emphasis of the hearing. It did not propose that the welfare of the child should be paramount in criminal as in family court cases. On the other hand, it did not adopt a purely punitive position. The philosophy might be seen in the adoption of the three Rs as the basis of youth justice, a blend of:

(a) responsibility;

(b) restoration; and

(c) reintegration.

The proposals envisaged that both the young offender and his parents should be made more responsible for offending behaviour. An aspect of this was the abolition of the presumption of *doli incapax*. The arguments for the abolition, presented in *Tackling Youth Crime* (Home Office 1997c) seemed one sided when compared with the analysis made by Lord Lowry in the House of Lords appeal in the case of *C v DPP*.[2] Andrew Nicol QC, writing in a Howard League report (Howard League 1995), reviewed the concept of *doli incapax* and the judgments in the courts. He concluded by saying that it allowed individualisation in deciding whether a child is responsible for his or her actions, a principle that is in accord with the UN Convention on the Rights of the Child 1989. The Kilbrandon Report was inclined to the view that the young offender was, to a large extent, a victim of misfortune in the same way as other children in difficulty. The report went further by saying that:

> ... a child's capacity to distinguish right and wrong, that is, his intellectual knowledge of moral standards, may, although well developed at an early age, not be accompanied by a corresponding degree of emotional maturity that would enable him to act on that knowledge [Kilbrandon 1964, p 31].

The restorative element in the philosophy consists of an apology to the victim, the possible presence of the victim in the court and reparation, either to the victim personally or to the community at large. This seems to be drawn, not from the hearing, but rather the family group conference to be found within the Australian and New Zealand systems. (For an overview of the Australian

---

2   *C (A Minor) v DPP* [1995] 2 All ER 43.

youth justice system, see Winterdyke 1997.) The element of the reintegration of the offender to become a useful member of society seems consistent with that of the hearing and also, of course, with the UN Convention on the Rights of the Child 1989.

The methods by which this philosophy is to be put into effect are described in detail in the White Paper, although they are modified in legislation. They include measures to co-ordinate, standardise and improve the work of the agencies that have responsibility for work with young offenders which may do much to overcome the criticism of fragmentation and variable quality of the existing system. This involves the formation, under the Crime and Disorder Act 1998, of Youth Offending Teams (YOTs) by local authorities to be overseen by the Youth Justice Board for England and Wales. The YOTs are to be made up of representatives from the professional groups working with young people, for example, police, social workers, probation officers and perhaps representatives from the voluntary sector that work with young people in difficulty.

Although not included in the Crime and Disorder Act, there were proposals in the White Paper for the reform of the youth court that seemed to have been influenced by the hearing system and by the family group conferences. An important aspect of this is the creation of a climate in which there may be more direct engagement between the magistrate and the young person. This would be achieved by reviewing any obstacles in the Magistrates' Court Rules, altering the physical environment of the courtroom and giving training for magistrates to emphasise the importance of talking to the young person and his parents, even with the presence of an advocate.

Under the Youth Justice and Criminal Evidence Act 1999, it is also proposed to create YOPs to deal with juveniles who have been made the subject of a referral order by the youth court. The panel would be made up of three persons, one of whom would be a member of the YOT; the others would be made up of persons appointed in accordance with criteria laid down by the Secretary of State. It would be formed and serviced under the aegis of the YOT rather than the magistrates' court. The offender would be required to attend together with any other person specified in the order. The panel may allow the victim to attend, together with any person over the age of 18 who may be able to exercise a good influence on the young person.

How does this panel compare with the hearing?

It plainly does not have an identical philosophy. The welfare of the offender is not paramount. The panel would, possibly, include a youth justice practitioner. Compare this with the hearing panel made up of lay representatives of the local community. The criteria that may be established by the Secretary of State for the appointment of the other panel members have not yet been promulgated. Children are not usually legally represented before the hearing because legal aid is not granted for this purpose. The child may have representation, but the child or family must pay for it. Before the YOP, legal representation will not be allowed at all. It could be argued that, in this respect, both systems are, or would be, in contravention of the UN Convention on the Rights of the Child 1989. It remains to be seen whether this view of how the panel is to operate will be sustained. The criteria for referral orders will be, broadly, that the offender:

(a) has no previous convictions;

(b) has pleaded guilty to the offence;

(c) has never been bound over.

If these criteria are satisfied, then it is mandatory that a referral should be made with some exceptions by nature of sentence, for example, custody. If, in addition, the offender has committed several offences, some of which he or she has pleaded guilty to and some not guilty to, the youth court has discretion as to whether to make a referral order.

However, a person might deny guilt on advice, for perfectly good reasons. In any event, the intended objectives and methods of the panel might be equally valid for such a person or for a second time offender. In Scotland, a re-offender, even if persistent, is generally still dealt with by the hearing, which may do no more than confirm the existing supervision order, thus allowing time for the social work interventions to take effect.

Without reviewing in detail the statute relating to the referral order, it would seem that the powers of the YOP and the youth court, in relation to referral orders, will contain some of the features of the hearing system in Scotland in that:

(a) as part of a contract between the offender and the panel a social work supervision programme will be agreed with the offender at the first meeting;

(b) progress review meetings can be called either by the panel or the offender. There must be at least one;

(c) a final review will be held when the compliance period is at an end;

(d) the terms of the contract agreed between the offender and the panel can be renegotiated. The order can be referred back to the youth court either by the panel or at the request of the offender; and

(e) if further offences are proved after the order has been made, or if further offences come to light that were committed before the order was made, it does not automatically bring the order to an end. The youth court has discretion as to whether to continue, terminate or extend the referral order.

In general, these features include some of the elements of flexibility, reviews and protection for the young person that are to be found in the hearing system.

Had the philosophy of the hearing been adopted in the changes, it would not only have simplified the English youth justice system, but it would have been revolutionary. What of the three Rs? Do they supplement or replace existing sentencing principles? Stuart Vernon, in Chapter 4 of this book, has highlighted the possibility that the changes in the youth justice system may create tensions in addition to those that already exist and poses the question whether old magistrates can be taught new tricks.

CONCLUSION

It has been argued above that the reforms to the English system are not strongly based on the Scottish system with regard to philosophy. Nevertheless, are there lessons to be learned for the way in which the changed system is to be operated? Both the new youth court and the new youth panel may require a major change in the culture of youth justice.

It has been argued here, in its favour, that the Scottish hearing has a clear agenda. It is focused on the child and has his or her welfare as its objective. If the reformed English system is in danger of creating new tensions between the possible objectives of punishment, deterrence, welfare, incapacitation and the three Rs, then there is a need for clear guidance for magistrates as to how they select their objectives. Should there be a requirement for the youth court and the proposed new youth panel to formally consider the objective of the sentence to be made? A difficulty is the constraint that exists in the English system (but not in the Scottish) of individualising sentences.

Also going in the Scottish system's favour is the fact that the process of disposing of an offence case in the hearing system appears to be more painstaking than sentencing in the youth court. Reports are read before the date of the hearing. The hearing itself lasts for about 45 minutes. If, in order to reconcile the tensions that already exist, and may increase, in the English system the youth court and the panel have to be analytical and deliberative in deciding their objectives and the means by which they are achieved, then the time allowed for sentencing and disposal will need to be greater than is often the case at present. Sentencing (as opposed to trial) sometimes takes place in the court as part of a heavy list of cases. An offender might be given a criminal sentence in less time than it takes to check out at a supermarket. The youth court will have complex decisions to take as to whether to continue or vary a referral order when there has been a lack of compliance or further offences have been committed. There is a potential for tension between the YOP and the youth court if the former is following a restorative justice philosophy and the latter is more inclined to punishment.

Although it might be difficult to teach old magistrates new tricks, it should be easy to get some new magistrates to deal with young offenders. The hearing panel is not drawn from magistrates. Why should it be relatively easy to recruit panel members in Scotland but difficult to recruit magistrates in England? Do youth court magistrates need to be drawn exclusively from an existing bench? There may be persons who would be willing to work with young offenders in the youth court and on the YOP in a constructive way who are not willing to do general magistrates' court work.

Following on from this it can be asked whether there are lessons to be learned from Scotland in the selection of magistrates that deal with young offenders. The methods of selection in Scotland for appointing members of the hearing panel are specific as to the qualities needed for dealing with young people in difficulty, and more painstaking in method. Should all prospective members of the youth court, including existing youth magistrates and the proposed YOP members, be interviewed before appointment within the reformed youth justice system? The Youth Justice and Criminal Evidence Act 1999 enables the Secretary of State to lay down criteria for the appointment of YOP members.

The new approach will undoubtedly require a new culture in the youth justice system. Stuart Vernon, in Chapter 4 of this book, highlights the relatively narrow basis of the training of magistrates and the difficulties that may arise from lay magistrates working in an increasingly professionalised system. The culture of the hearing is derived not only from the Kilbrandon Report, but also from the selection and training of members by psychiatrists, sociologists and universities. The basic training is more broadly based than in England and Wales.

Scotland had the advantage of starting with a clean sheet, they did not need to reform an existing system or bring to it the intellectual luggage and practices of the past. Changes to the present system in England and Wales are likely to be achieved at a cost.

But, if the Audit Commission 1996 is right, the cost of not changing is even higher.

CHAPTER 10

POLICING YOUTH CRIME: PICKING UP THE BILL FOR OUR KIDS?

Matt Long

CONTEXTUALISING THE LEGISLATION

The Report of the Morgan Inquiry (Home Office 1991b) argued that local authority involvement in the delivery of effective programmes of crime prevention should be prioritised. This report encouraged a shift away from law enforcement and crime control towards a crime reduction approach. It basically drew attention to the fact that the police service could no longer deliver community safety on its own. The seeds of the crime and disorder legislation were sown in this report in that it recognised that the forming of partnerships with other agencies (which would come to be referred to as 'responsible authorities') was the way forward. The legislation itself is underpinned by the replacement of the terminology of 'crime prevention' with the more all encompassing notion of 'community safety'. It is important that account be taken of this notion of community safety because it incorporates wider quality of life issues such as the fear of crime, as well as criminal activity itself.

The belief that community safety should not be the sole responsibility of the police acting alone was reiterated by the Audit Commission in *Misspent Youth: Young People and Crime* (1996). This report arguably vindicated the existing youth justice system, arguing that recidivist offending was almost bound to occur because the roots of offending behaviour were simply not challenged. It furthermore pointed to the need for youth crime in particular to be seen as a problem which should be tackled with the co-operation of the police, community groups, youth services, schools and social services. Certainly, the Act is underpinned by an implicit recognition that the police acting alone simply cannot be expected to address crime problems, but rather the active participation of other public service agencies is required.

Tony Blair's now famous statement about being 'tough on crime – tough on the causes of crime', was articulated particularly in New Labour's strategy paper *Tackling Youth Crime* (1996) which spoke about reconciling the conflicting demands of 'welfare' on the one hand and 'punishment' on the other. This was clearly a pre-election attempt by New Labour to challenge the traditional monopoly held by the Conservative Party on being seen to be tough on law and order issues. The acknowledgment that causes of crime may be social, and not simply reducible to individual pathology, gave New Labour the opportunity to make the links between crime, unemployment and wider social exclusion, hence the creation of the Social Exclusion Unit and investment in education and training for marginalised youngsters as part of the 'New Deal' initiative. Upon its election in 1997, the New Labour administration began to speak of the necessity of 'joined-up government' in order to achieve the provision of 'joined-up services' and a holistic approach to community safety. In practical terms, this was to imply the development of 'joint strategies' to be initiated and co-ordinated by the local authority and the police to reduce crime in designated areas.

THE CRIME AND DISORDER ACT

The introduction of the Crime and Disorder Act 1998 placed a statutory obligation on the police as one of a number of 'responsible authorities' who were tasked, alongside other public services and voluntary agencies, with working with local authorities to implement effective crime reduction strategies. Section 37(1) of the Act states that 'it shall be the principal aim of the youth justice system to prevent offending by children and young persons'. Section 38(1) of the legislation requires the co-operation of every local authority, chief police officer and probation committee in terms of provision into a common fund for youth justice services. The legislation itself clearly requires that the police must seek crime reduction, rather than the simple processing of offenders by means of arrest and charge, as their primary aim.

Under the legislation, the chief officer of police sits down with the other chief executives of the district and county councils to take strategic decisions. As well as this level, a seconded police officer will be heavily involved in local Young Offender Teams (YOTs) in terms of implementing the overall youth offending strategy devised at the local level. In practical terms, this often means that they have to decide whether a charge or a final warning is appropriate for an offender and police officers who are themselves part of these teams may find themselves greatly involved in reparation, supervision and action planning work with young offenders.

Under the Act, a 'relevant authority' (which is the local council or chief officer of police) can make an application for an *anti-social behaviour order*, should it be demonstrated that a person aged 10 or over has acted in an 'anti-social manner' by behaving or there being a likelihood of him or her behaving in a manner which would cause 'harassment, alarm or distress' to one or more persons 'not of the same household' as that person. An application for an order can be made to a magistrates' court. This prohibits a defendant from behaving in any way that contravenes the order and has effect for at least two years. Should the order be breached, the defendant is subject, on summary conviction, to up to six months' imprisonment plus the possibility of a financial penalty. The period of imprisonment for conviction on indictment may be up to five years.

Where it can be demonstrated that a child has committed an act which would have constituted a criminal offence had he or she been over the age of 10,[1] then a local authority may apply to a magistrates' court for a *child safety order* which places a child under the supervision of a 'responsible officer' (a social worker or member of a YOT), requiring the child to comply with 'such requirements as are specified'. Unless exceptional circumstances can be cited, child safety orders run for three months, with breaches of the orders subjecting the child to a care order whose conditions have to be set by a magistrates' court. Closely linked with child safety orders are parenting orders which are made to attempt to prevent repetition of the breaking of original orders. These place a three month requirement on parents to attend counselling sessions which are provided by either probation officers, social workers or members of a YOT (otherwise referred to as 'responsible officers'). Failure to comply with an order leaves the parent subject to a fine on summary conviction.

The Home Secretary has the power to confirm or to refuse the creation of local *child curfew schemes* (which run for 90 days and can be renewable) that can be introduced by local authorities in order to ban children under 10 years of age being in a public place within specified areas between certain hours,[2] unless they are in the company of a parent or other party deemed to be a 'responsible person'. Where there is evidence that a curfew has been broken, a child may be taken from his or her place of residence and put into care. Where breach of a curfew has occurred, police are heavily involved in terms of making the decision as to whether to return the child to his or her place of residence under s 15 of the Act.

The philosophy of joined-up services can be evidenced in relation to youth justice by the fact that YOTs have been created which require the police and probation services[3] to work in co-operation with each other, rather than autonomously, in order to co-ordinate the provision of all youth justice services in the area. The YOT is tasked with putting into practice the Youth Justice Plan which is formulated by the local authority. These plans are submitted annually to a national Youth Justice Board, which is itself accountable to the Home Secretary in the form of the publication of annual reports.

---

1   Or that an order is necessary to prevent the commission of an offence.
2   Between 9 pm and 6 am.
3   The YOT contains a police officer and probation officer seconded to the team on a full time basis, as well as a social worker and a person with a background in health and education.

As a means of diverting young offenders from the courts and attempting to address the underlying causes of offending, the legislation introduces a system of police reprimands and final warnings to replace the standard police caution. Where an officer believes an offence has been committed, but the offender has no previous convictions, then a warning along with a reprimand may be given by the officer at a station in the presence of an 'appropriate adult'. Any subsequent re-offending results in a final warning which can then lead to referral to a YOT. Unlike the previous system where offenders built up multiple cautions, where a first offence receives a final warning, any further offence should automatically lead to the instigation of criminal charges. The aim of this 'diversionary system' is to facilitate behavioural change through such programmes as supervised community activities, action plan orders and reparation to victims. This is a clear development from the approach previously adopted by Thames Valley Police under the leadership of Chief Constable Charles Pollard, which introduced restorative justice conferences for the whole force, whereby victims and offenders were given the opportunity to confront each other with a 'restorative caution'.

The philosophy of restorative justice and reparation to the victim is clearly evidenced by *reparation orders* which require YOT members to take into account the attitude of the victim under ss 67–68 of the Act, before deciding on the suitability of the type of work for the victim which has to be supervised by a 'responsible officer'. *Action plan orders* can also be made which bind the offender to a particular programme for a three month period, whilst being accountable to a responsible officer. Under ss 69–70 of the Act, the attitude of the parents of the offender must be taken into account by the member of the YOT making the written report for the order.

Under the legislation, detention and training orders can be made for convicted offenders under the age of 15 where it is decided that they are persistent offenders.[4] Detention and training orders involve custodial sentences which either have to be spent in a secure training centre or young offender institution. The Crime and Disorder Act 1998 defines a persistent young offender as someone aged between 10 and 17 years who has been sentenced for one or more recordable offence(s) on three or more separate occasions, and who is furthermore arrested again within three years of last being sentenced. In these cases, whilst bail with conditions is an option, the Home Office 1997b has maintained that secure accommodation may be necessary in order to prevent recidivism. The Act aims to put into practice the recommendations of the Glidewell and Narey Reports in terms of attempting to fast track files on all youth offenders, particularly recidivist offenders. It was, in fact, one of New Labour's election pledges to halve the time taken to

---

4   Under s 73, offenders under the age of 12 years may be subject to similar detention and training orders where the court is of the view that the public need to be 'protected from further offending'.

deal with young offenders from arrest to sentence via the introduction of statutory time limits for processing cases. Again, due to the philosophy of restorative justice in terms of making reparation to the victim and society in general, the shorter the delay between arrest and sentence, then the more meaningful the punishment should be to the offender.

These orders mentioned above effectively give responsible authorities the powers to 'get tough' on juvenile offending where it is felt to be necessary. It has to be said, however, that, despite the wishes of Home Office ministers, only a relatively few anti-social behaviour orders have been applied for by the courts to this date. This is in order to attempt to curtail the very worst excesses of youth offending behaviour. On the other hand, the future may see the issuing of more orders than at present and it may well be that the police have an increasingly difficult role to perform in attempting to ensure that compliance with these orders is maintained. Whether or not these orders are actually issued in practice is dependant on an agreement between the police and the local authority as to what action to take.

PERFORMANCE TRANSPARENCY: LOCAL CRIME REDUCTION STRATEGIES

The legislation provides a statutory requirement for the carrying out of a regional audit of crime and disorder in the local authority area, as well as a crime strategy with objectives and targets, which has to be formulated by a 'leadership group', made up of the local police chief and chief executive of the local authority. The crime and disorder strategy is expected to be based on extensive public consultation with the idea that the 'customer' should have a major say in determining local crime and disorder priorities. Crime and disorder strategies tended to highlight and prioritise certain common themes such as burglary, violent crime and racial incidents. The police are expected to take the strategy on board in terms of the local policing plan, which includes the determination of local policing priorities.

Monitoring the application of the strategy is again the joint responsibility of the police and the local authority. In relation to the evaluation of strategies based on the local crime audit, there is now a concerted political will aimed at being able to calculate the financial costs and social consequences of crime on a national level. The problem with this is that the level of variation in the way in which audits are conducted is so great, that one has to question the gathering, comparison and integrity of data. This in turn leads to the additional problem of not being able to ascertain reliable and accurate costings of crime.

YOUTH JUSTICE IN PRACTICE

The following three areas need to be addressed when attempting to assess how the ideology and policy of the crime and disorder legislation actually translates into practice:

(a) The ideology of the Crime and Disorder Act 1998 encourages the police to see their role as one of facilitating behavioural change rather than being satisfied merely with the processing of young offenders. Whilst seconded members of the YOT will have been briefed on this matter, for genuine change to occur, this would have to translate into whole police forces changing conventional working practices. One has to question whether the police can escape so called 'traditional' approaches to the arrest, charge and, ultimately, conviction of young offenders. Until fairly recently there has been little research about what actually works in terms of the use of joined-up services in order to attempt to achieve better social outcomes.

(b) In terms of multi-agency co-operation, tensions between the different criminal justice agencies are to be expected. The work of Gilling 1994 demonstrates the different assumptions and starting points which different agencies work from and consequently it is possible for practitioners from different agencies to unwittingly 'talk past each other'.

(c) In practice, it is questionable whether the information which is needed from all agencies in order to produce crime audits is actually available. What are referred to as 'incivilities' or minor disorders often go unrecorded and are extremely difficult to assess in terms of how they actually impact on the quality of life in local areas. This raises wider questions about how performance is measured. It is worth considering whether the partnership approach to solving youth crime, advocated by the Government, is centred around a return to the idea of local agents being empowered to solve problems themselves in their own 'communities', without too much interference from outside. The fact that bodies like the Audit Commission and Her Majesty's Inspectorate of Constabulary require the calculation of standardised performance indicators for police forces throughout England and Wales inevitably leads to a tension between serving local needs and meeting national standards where the 'success' of local partnerships has to be measured.

THEORISING YOUTH JUSTICE

At the heart of the Crime and Disorder Act 1998 is the belief in joined-up services to allow for ease of access for the 'consumers' of welfare services. This is where the crime and disorder legislation is inextricably linked with the 'best value' initiative in the sense that the focus on the customer can be traced to the

White Paper *Modernising Government: In Touch with the People* (1998) which emphasised the need to improve both productivity and performance in the public sector so that rapid and measurable improvements in both cost effectiveness and quality of public services could be secured. The emphasis on local approaches to problem solving under the Crime and Disorder Act 1998, and the focus on BCU performance delivery as part of the best value initiative, is indicative of a political elite which legitimates managerial change on the basis that users or consumers of welfare should be able to exercise choice.

It is not just in the field of crime, but also in the context of public housing, education, health and community care, that the notion of the 'consumer' or customer has emerged. This goes back to the initiation of the Citizens Charter and was something which the then Prime Minister, John Major, spoke about back in the early 1990s. Major stated that consultation with service users would take place in relation to 'their views about the services they use [which] should be sought regularly and systematically to inform decisions about what services should be provided'.[5] According to Clarke and Newman, the rise of the customer as a reference point in political discourse cannot simply be reduced to party politics:

> Despite its political character as part of the New Right assault on the old Welfare State, the consumerist challenge to the dominance of the professional bureaucracies has drawn on sources of support based in a variety of oppositions to the institutionalised power which they represented. Views of the user as more than a passive (and supposedly grateful) recipient of the services granted by a benevolent State have been championed by a range of different groups – in particular, disaffected professionals and user groups themselves. Consumerist innovations – both locally and nationally – were thus able to mobilise support because of their capacity to address issues of "needs led services" and greater responsiveness to the diversity of users.[6]

This focus on the customer is part and parcel of the New Labour Government's attempt to present itself as being committed to a more participatory style of public sector governance through a variety of tools such as consultative forums, focus groups and referenda, all of which, it argues, are designed to put community needs and choice at the heart of public service provision. For some, this consultative approach is clearly distinctive from the approach undertaken by previous Thatcher administrations in particular. According to *The Guardian*:

> ... unlike Margaret Thatcher, Tony Blair signalled yesterday [that] he would be consulting widely and openly with all interested parties – professionals, patients and community groups. Not for him the secret conclave of five people who dreamed up Margaret Thatcher's 'internal market' without even

---

5   Barnes and Prior 1995:53.
6   Clarke and Newman 1997: 122.

consulting fellow ministers, let alone the health service ['Health service failures face hit squads' (2000) *The Guardian*, 23 March].

The belief in joined-up services has been presented as the way in which organisations can break out of working in traditional 'silos' whereby they become preoccupied with their own outputs rather than with the pursuit of wider social outcomes. By dismantling the monolithic silos of traditional organisational working practices, it is believed that the needs of customers can be serviced by integrating services. Again, there is a link here with the best value initiative which encourages forces to think about business process mapping as a way of taking a 'systems' or 'whole organisation' approach to service delivery. This is where the European Foundation for Quality Management (EFQM)[7] model attempts to measure 'quality' of service delivery by cutting holistically across departments to enable the genuine comparison of business processes.

The move away from measures of 'output' towards ones of social 'outcome' is, however, difficult to achieve in practice. This was highlighted by the Audit Commission who acknowledged that:

... for most services, it is easier to set output targets than outcome targets. Nevertheless, setting targets for the outcomes of a service is especially important, because they tell you whether the service is achieving its purpose, rather than whether it is running efficiently.[8]

It is, furthermore, well established that there are negative unintended consequences when organisations pursue their own self-interest in the desire to demonstrate the achievement of 'outputs'. In the context of education, for example, some schools have, in the past, expelled students labelled as being 'difficult' in an attempt to raise their own performance against a narrow band of indicators. By individual schools focusing on what was best for their own performance, the wider social outcomes in terms of dealing with social exclusion, drug abuse and unwanted pregnancies and so on can be forgotten.

The complex issue of assessing and measuring social outcomes was raised by Brodie 1996 who pointed out that, since the introduction of indicators concerning school exclusions were introduced, the number of actual exclusions had risen markedly. It is quite possible to argue that a rise in school exclusions may mean more disaffected pupils who are not attending school and who are more likely to turn to crime, which in turn could adversely affect the crime figures, thus altering the perception of police performance. This would be an example of where 'unintended consequences' would make it virtually impossible to assess outcome based performance.

The idea of multi-agency partnerships working in practice is dependent

---

7   Often referred to more simply as the Business Excellence Model.
8   Audit Commission 1998:82.

upon re-discovering the notion of community. This re-discovery of community paradoxically arrived at precisely the time that New Right ideology and policy impoverished much of the 'public', the 'collective' and the 'social' in Britain. Multi-agency crime prevention strategies are underpinned by a belief in community and consequently New Labour communitarianism has to 'buy into' the type of imagery associated with the ethics and values instilled by traditional working class communities whose industries were typically localised and built up around mining, shipbuilding and steel work. We can see an alliance in party political thinking by looking at the similarity of John Major's 'back to basics' movement and Tony Blair's focus on 'responsible citizens' in the run up to the 1997 General Election. This is a far cry from the politics of Margaret Thatcher, who vehemently argued that society did not really exist, believing instead that geographical communities were made up of no more than the aggregate of individuals and their families.

The idea of restorative justice is underpinned by New Labour's attempt to present the idea that localised social relationships in terms of neighbourhoods, where people share the same identities, really can exist (again). There is a belief that such ideological attachments will translate into policies that actually mobilise people to act in the interests of the social rather than as self-motivated individuals. This is very much in line with Tony Blair's belief that communitarianism can offer us a 'third way', rather than returning to the ideology of the 'old left', which prioritised the State, or the New Right, who focused on marketisation.

The Crime and Disorder Act 1998, with its emphasis on attempting to change offending behaviour rather than simply punishing it, attempts to instill into disaffected youth the idea that communities really do exist and that there is a moral code within these communities. This is consistent with New Labour's ideology of stakeholding which was articulated in the following way by Will Hutton 1996 who argued that:

> The unifying idea is inclusion; the individual is a member, a citizen and a potential partner. But inclusion is not a one way street; it places reciprocal obligations on the individual as well as rights – and in every domain and in every social class.[9]

The idea is that there is a need to increase the number of people who have a stake in society to prevent further decay of the social fabric. In relation to youth justice, this implies that those who are given rights, in terms of the 'justice' they receive, should also accept responsibility for the consequences of their actions.

---

9   1996:2.

CONCLUSION

In an age of rampant individualism, we should, perhaps, try to look positively at the renewed emphasis on multi-agency approaches to the policing of youth because, without ideologies of social co-operation, genuine social progress is impossible. We do, however, have to ask ourselves whether multi-agency partnerships, which aim to reintegrate those with a 'stake' in society, are going to be successful in the context of the dismantling of the post-war welfare settlement and the Keynesian pursuit of full employment. There is nowadays the acknowledgment that full employment, which is surely the most effective means of reintegration, cannot be achieved.

CHAPTER 11

IN THE COUNTRY OF THE BLIND: YOUTH STUDIES AND CULTURAL STUDIES IN BRITAIN

Phil Cohen and Dr Patrick Ainley

INTRODUCTION

In this chapter, we look at the history of youth research and cultural studies in Britain and consider the relationship between these two very different intellectual trajectories and traditions. We argue that the youth question is potentially at the cutting edge of interdisciplinary enquiry in the human sciences, that it has an important role to play in reconstituting the problematics of identity and modernity and that it serves to focus policy debates around a strategic nexus of social contradiction in post-colonial Britain. But we also suggest that, until we transcend the narrow empiricism of most youth transition studies, and the theoreticism that continues to characterise the study of cultural texts, the youth question will continue to be a sideshow. The article concludes by outlining one possible approach that may help build bridges between youth studies and cultural studies in order to advance research beyond these limitations.

The marginality of youth research in British academic life has often been regarded as reflecting the marginalised position of young people in our society. This is reflected in the low status of youth policy (as opposed to child and family centred or education centred policy) within the discourses of governance. The youth service remains a poor relation and youth workers have developed a culture of client advocacy that underwrites a populist and 'youthist' perspective hostile to more theoretically grounded approach to the youth question (Cohen 1997).

In the rest of Europe, in Germany, in the Scandinavian countries in Italy, in many of the ex-communist bloc countries, and to a lesser extent in France, it seems to be a rather different story. Issues of youth policy cover the whole extent of social, cultural, educational and psychological formation, and are addressed as important topics by mainstream politicians and engage the interest of major intellectuals (Hazenkamp 1998; Levi and Schmidt 1996).

The reason for this high profile is not difficult to discern. In all these countries, youth movements, student movements, young worker movements, or youth political organisations have at some time or another played a decisive role in shaping the history of the nation and have helped to bring about, directly or indirectly, some basic shift in power or ideology (Mitterauer 1992). As a result, and however long ago this may have happened, youth is regarded, in bio-political terms, as a potential threat to the equilibrium of governance. In Britain, this is simply not the case. No one would seriously argue that Disraeli's Young England Movement brought about a fundamental shift in Victorian values! In this country, it is youth cultures rather than youth movements which have played a crucial role in reconfiguring elements of the social imaginary without, for all that, posing a real threat to the political elite (Hebdige 1984).

As a result, the youth question in Britain has primarily been about moral or aesthetic issues rather than political or economic ones. Moral panics about drugs, delinquency, sexual promiscuity and street violence are our forte; complacent self-congratulation about the creative dynamism of Britpop are all the rage. Even when given a quasi-political edge, as with the current debate over lawless and unemployed masculinities associated with the so called youth underclass, no one seriously thinks that youth mobs are going to combine into some revolutionary force capable of challenging the power of the State! But the spectacle of this threat – as opposed to its actuality – does make exceedingly good ammunition for various kinds of political propaganda about the breakdown of family and community values. Ironically, it is precisely because they pose no real threat to the body politic that these unemployed young people are made to carry the enormous burden of symbolising the moral crisis of civil society, framed here in terms of its ungovernability by the State (Keith and Cross 1993).

YOUTH RESEARCH: FROM ECONOMISM TO CULTURALISM

It could also be argued that the intellectual marginality of youth research is partly the fault of youth researchers themselves. In the world of academic 'official knowledge', youth studies have become cramped into an all pervasive economism (Mizen 1997). The youth-as-transition approach not only implies a linear teleological model of psycho-social development, it is premised upon the availability of waged labour as the 'ultimate goal'. The consequent emphasis on production has led to a limited research paradigm focused on 'transition' as a rite of passage between developmental stages of psychological maturity and immaturity, complemented by a sociological transition narrowly restricted to (vocational) maturity and (nuclear) family formation. Such was the conceptual 'coherence' of the first of the ESRC's youth programmes, the 16–19 Initiative (Bates and Riseborough 1993; Banks et al 1991).

The youth studies to which this research paradigm has given rise operate within conventionally understood notions of social class for which educational qualifications are taken as proxies and, thus, take no account of current processes of class displacement and recomposition (Furlong 1993). Social exclusion from successful transition is seen in terms of a so called 'underclass' and taken as a 'dysfunction' to be overcome by individual efforts combined with ameliorative reform, rather than being seen as integral to and generated by the system of social categories that the research paradigm itself accepts as given.

The same economistic approach was trotted out once again in the rewriting of the proposal for the ESRC's new 15–25 Programme, only this time spiced with flavour-of-the-month reflexive and risk sociology. That transition had become 'reflexively risky' merely added to the succession of qualifying adjectives in this series of repetitive and redundant 'long', 'extended', 'fragmented', 'fractured', 'disrupted', etc, transition studies.

What has actually been delivered by the ESRC in the form of its latest 15–25: Youth, Citizenship and Social Change Programme, is an incoherent mix that, sadly, is becoming standard for ESRC programmes whatever their focus. While some of these 15 unrelated studies at least compensate for the lack of attention to minority ethnic young people, gay and lesbian youth and drug users in the previous 16–19 Initiative, the lack of an integrated research design means that the sum is much less than the parts. The previous 16–19 Initiative, whatever its shortcomings, at least allowed for a comparison of its findings with the wilder claims that the Manpower Services Commission was then making for the quality of the Youth Training Scheme as a new institutionalised 'transition' from school to work (Ainley and Corney 1990). By comparison, the new 15–25 Programme will not provide any purchase upon the success or failure of the Government's New Deal since it lacks the coherence to touch upon it more than tangentially.

Empiricist youth research, as exemplified by the ESRC's programmes, did, however, occupy the terrain vacated by cultural studies in the 1980s. By insisting on the persistence of class divisions (even if only as conventionally defined), tracking the gendered patterns of adolescent transition strategies and (to some extent) documenting racial inequalities in educational outcomes, this body of work provided a skeletal picture of social realities that were airbrushed out of most of the pictures drawn within the post-modern frame. What this genre of youth studies did not do was locate this evidence within any culturally textured account of social structural change in Britain (Phoenix and Rattansi 1998).

Such an account would have to comprehend the meanings that the transformation in post-school provision have had for school-leavers as they have grown older. As the 'transition studies' discussed above indicate, school leavers enter an extended period of transition in the labour market – even if not in work. This has raised the threshold of adulthood and lengthened what is regarded as 'youth', 'adolescence', or even the 'permanent adolescence', or 'post-adolescence', in which many young men are allegedly trapped

(Adamski and Grootings 1989). The shake up of life stage definitions as a result of economic restructuring has put in question the idea (or ideal) of adult status as a completed state of psychological identity and/or vocational maturity, replacing it with the notion of continuous and provisional development or becoming (Wallace and Grootings 1996; Jeffs 1998). But we still do not know enough about how this change is negotiated by young people themselves, especially by those whose life scripts and self-narratives continue to be shaped by customary codes of apprenticeship and inheritance (Cohen 1999b).

Changes in the cultures and boundaries of childhood and youth also, of course, impact upon older people. Images of youth and adulthood have become blurred and confused because, for example, whilst students become older, many adults engage in activities previously associated with younger people, not least by enrolling as students. They also stay single for longer so that the average age of a first marriage has risen from its all time low of 20 for women and 22 for men in 1971 to 26 and 27 respectively today (Irwin 1996). At the same time, there is a simultaneous lowering of the formal adult threshold; for example, the lowering of the age for legal consensual homosexual relations as well as for undertaking hire-purchase agreements. So, the various phases of life in which age was linked to status have become uncoupled. Despite the vocational emphasis in schools and colleges, education no longer relates necessarily to work, nor home making to marriage or marriage to child rearing.

The State, which plays a large part in defining age statuses, also contributes to confusing them by its successive attempts to meet the deepening crisis of structural unemployment. Employment, training and education policies, backed by social security policy, have moved towards constructing just two groups of young people: trainees or students (Jones and Wallace 1992). During the 'high period' of vocationalist optimism from 1976–87, the target was for a ratio of 2:8 as between academic schooling and vocational training, based on the German model (Finn 1987). This scenario was subsequently drastically revised towards a goal of 8:2 as between continuing education and drop-out/residual training, based on the US model. This latest phase of 'Learning Policy', marked by the 1988 Education Act and the 1992 Further and Higher Education Act, may be called one of 'education without jobs' (Ainley 1994).

There has, however, been a partial revival of vocational training for a minority, with the introduction of Modern Apprenticeships in 1993 as an alternative to the provision of a general education for all (Ainley and Rainbird 1999). This shift was signalled by Sir Ron Dearing's first review of *The National Curriculum and its Assessment* in 1993, in which he made room in schools for a work based route at 14 plus linked to further education, and then, by his second *Review of Qualifications for 16–19 Year Olds* in 1996, in which he sought to establish sixth forms as the royal road to higher education and to associate further education with school failure.

Accompanying these shifting learning policies since the end of the long boom has been a move away from the social insurance principle of dependency on the old Welfare State towards an encouragement of individual self-reliance and enterprise. With the advent of New Labour we have arrived at a new Workfare State run on the contracting principle (Harden 1992; Jones 1996). Just as youth unemployment was officially abolished by the guarantee of youth training for all 16–18 year olds, so the new knowledge policy for full employability moves towards constituting all adults as either being in direct employment or engaged in some kind of learning, whether on or off the job; no one, however economically inactive is to be regarded as actually unemployed or even job seeking. In both cases institutionalised learning is now related to the cultural meanings of employment and unemployment.

What these transformations in work, learning and leisure might mean for young people can be most clearly seen if we compare the situation facing most 16 year olds completing compulsory schooling today with the position of 14 and 15 year old school leavers under the ancien regime of the post-war Welfare State. Then, for most people, employers as well as employees, a key feature of life was its age graded predictability. For the majority (including 'dependent' women), future prospects were predicated upon guaranteed full-time male employment from the age of 15 to 65. This was despite the fact that it was only with the introduction of CSEs in 1959 that the majority of English and Welsh school leavers came to possess any educational certification at all, as compared with only one in 12 without any certification today (Ainley 1999).

Even without formal qualifications, a young person growing up in the 1960s could look forward to leaving school, entering employment, leaving home, marrying and setting up home, followed by early patterns of child bearing and rearing. These predictable patterns of the life course underwrote customary forms of apprenticeship, occupational succession, and adolescent identity work (Anderson 1983). None of this is now relevant as most of us – not only young people – find ourselves catapulted into conditions of post-industrial insecurity that carry echoes of earlier pre-war and even Victorian times.

Yet, this is not a case of returning to Victorian values. The loss of old certainties has also entailed the overcoming of certain restrictive limitations. In place of reliance upon a male breadwinner, women are gaining at least relative economic equality in the labour market. The pay gap between female and male 16–24 year-olds has narrowed to a negligible 4.3% (Deakin 1996). However, this has been at the expense of a fall in the relative value of male income, so that wages for the same age group have fallen as a proportion of average wages by 10 per cent over the decade to 1995 (Deakin 1996). What has been called 'the feminisation of male labour' means that more and more men are coming to share the conditions of part time, intermittent working that most women were long used to. In fact, with the decline of heavy industry and the rise of the service based economy, the sexual division of labour is no longer anchored to material differences in the work process or the musculatures of the labouring body. In this context, the persistence of the distinction between so called 'men's and women's work is now open to question along with the whole social construction of gender.

These transformations have occurred as the collapse of traditional manufacturing industry removed the economic underpinning of full employment. Those born into this new world are pioneering a life cycle paradigm which entails moving from education to part time work, interspersed with periods of education and training. Many young people find themselves moving from one scheme and training course to another without ever entering full time, secure employment. This pattern of life is rising steadily up the age range to include wider social groups beyond those for whom it has long been habitual.

Even in the inner city, it is not unusual for young people to intersperse periodic education and training with periods of casual work and/or travel, especially to relatives abroad (Ainley and Bailey 1997).

As employment – and especially the prospect of one occupation for the whole of a working life – becomes increasingly less relevant for defining social identities, consumer and leisure identities become more important. At the same time, conventional consumer and leisure identities are harder to sustain without regular income and this partly accounts for the proliferation of counter-cultures amongst the young. Despite the relentless vocational pressures for conformity, to which education at all levels now subjects students, youth cultures generally oppose the whole work ethic which derives identity from occupation (Aronowitz and DiFazio 1994).

Such reactions are part of a new typology of life patterns, which are putting in question the prevailing imagery of transitional 'pathways' (Dwyer and Wyn 1997). The pathways metaphor displays a preoccupation with a career paradigm based on a definition of labour market participation as a *consequence* of participation in various forms of post-compulsory education. This construction masks a significant overlap between study and work. Young people simply do not view work and study in the linear way implied by the conventional career paradigm and by the policy formulations based upon it. Images about 'pathways' and linear transitions *from* school *via* further study and *then into* the world of work and an independent adult way of life do not reflect the actual experience of growing up. Young people are establishing different patterns of response which involve complicated mixtures of leaving and returning to the parental home, of part time work and part time study, of full time work and part time study and even of full time work and full time study (Ainley 1991).

This shift of focus from transitional pathways to a typology of discontinuous life patterns thus brings conventional youth research very close to the theory of life cycle paradigms and reproduction codes which has been developed within that branch of cultural studies that has devoted itself to a consideration of informal processes of schooling, adolescent identity formation and the autobiographical grammars through which subject positions are articulated (Cohen 1997). The shift from economism to culturalism opens up a whole new perspective on the youth question, albeit one which, as we will see, has its own form of reductionism, its own repressed objects of the desire to know.

MODS AND SHOCKERS:
CULTURAL STUDIES AND THE YOUTH QUESTION

Within the trajectory of British cultural studies, the youth question was first taken up in the late 1960s in the early work of the Birmingham School as a means of challenging the economistic theories of class that have subsequently come to dominate empirical youth research. The emergence of highly visible youth cultures – Teds, Mods, Rockers and Skinheads – in the 1960s, and the erosion of customary transitions from school to work, provided key sites for both ethnographic and theoretical investigation, inspired by a Gramscian analysis of popular culture (Jefferson and Hall 1978; Hall 1992). The detailed analysis of these new cultural forms was a way of looking afresh at dislocations in the post-war British social structure; at the same time, it enabled cultural studies to distance itself both from the English literary tradition of condescension towards popular culture and the Fabian perspective of social reform associated with English settlement sociology (Bennett 1997; Grossberg 1997).

The early Centre on Contemporary Cultural Studies work often proceeded from an identification with the marginal and the outsider, influenced by notions of sub-culture and counter-culture derived from West Coast deviancy theory; this was often grafted onto a more home-grown concern with issues of popular literacy and working class education raised by the New Left. The youth question brought these two sides of the story rather neatly together (Willis 1977; Robins and Cohen 1978).

Yet, if cultural studies, in the beginning, used (white male working class) youth culture as a sounding board from which to create its own distinctive voice, the field quickly expanded to include questions of gender and race. By the early 1980s girls' cultures and black youth cultures had become the site of important new work both theoretically and substantively (McRobbie 1991; Gilroy 1987). *En route* questions of class (trans)formation were rather left to one side. This was quite understandable given their association with the white 'malestream'. Yet this displacement of the class problematic was to have some unfortunate repercussions for the subsequent development of the field (Willis 1990).

More immediately, the linguistic and semiotic turn in the human sciences provided cultural studies with its main chance to put itself at the cutting edge of research. The study of cultural codes of every kind could now, it seemed, be put on a properly scientific basis. Teenage fashion, music, films, magazines and fiction would henceforth be treated as seriously as their more supposedly 'adult' counterparts.

In retrospect, this move seems more like a false dawn than a fresh start for youth cultural analysis, but it did have the effect of encouraging more detailed studies of stylistic practices than had hitherto been possible (Hebdige 1981). Clash lyrics and trainer ads, bedroom walls and shopping malls, scarf rituals on the soccer terraces and mating rituals on the dance floor, all were subjected to exhaustive scrutiny for what they might reveal about the process of 'revolt into style' (Melly 1989; Brake 1986). One, perhaps inevitable, result of these close up 'storm and dress' youth studies was that the social contexts of family, school, work and community life that gave these practices their life historical depth and meaning were pushed ever further into the background. But there was a socio-logic to this move.

With the demise of Punk, it was no longer enough to focus on the 'spectacular'- visible and audible – forms of youth culture (Frith 1983). As the 1980s went on and signs of resistance became ever more subliminal, the quest for subtexts pushed researchers into ever more sophisticated ways of reading between the lines. Ethnography, with its realist epistemology and naive commitment to the naturalistic observation of everyday social interaction, was clearly not up to the task. The practice was virtually abandoned. At the same time, the limitations of semiology, and structuralism more generally, had become apparent once the play of substitutions within the code yielded evidence of processes of representation that could not be explained in purely linguistic terms. Just as the pleasure principles of much popular cultural practice remained incomprehensible (or a sign of 'false consciousness') to rationalistic forms of 'ideology critique' so they proved irreducible to the analysis of binary oppositions. What was unsaid, unthought, unconscious, increasingly demanded the right to be spoken, thought and made articulate on its own terms (Zizek 1998).

Enter psychoanalysis as handmaiden to a 'new new' art, film and literary criticism. Cultural critics could now study the covert and disavowed strategies of authorisation at work in the image/text as symptomatic of everything that escaped the author's own conscious intentionality: from the genealogy of signatures; to the epistemic zeitgeist; from the archaeology of knowledge, to the most secret and perverse pleasures of the text, it was all grist to the deconstructive mill.

The advent of post-structuralism was singularly good news for armchair critics of popular culture. They no longer had to leave the security of the university bookstacks in order to perform Hegelian headstands on the high wire of Grand Theory. If there was no reality outside its representation, and no referent beyond the internal play of signification, if meaning was continually deferred, every reading supplementary, and intertextuality ruled ok, then the work of cultural criticism became a never ending quest to avoid the temptations of foreclosure by appealing to the social or the real (McRobbie 1997).

Yet, if all the world was a text and all the people in it merely quotations, some way had still to be found to tackle what was nominally outside the text but very much in the substance of what discourses of race, gender and sexuality insisted upon as their central reference point, namely, the body. Courtesy of Foucault, the formation of a corpus of texts into an institutionalised discourse of power might be related to a particular 'bio-political' strategy. With Lacan, it seemed that, conversely, bodies might be read as if they were texts and, hence, subjected to a purely linguistic form of psychoanalysis operating behind, as well as between, the lines of desire.

Throughout the 1980s, cultural texts of every kind were thus laid out on the analyst's couch, not in order to be dissected according to the old methods of moral anatomy (the good and important distinguished from the bad and trivial), nor to be cured of their prosodic ills or 'reintegrated back into society' as the old style Modernists and Marxists preferred, but to be taken apart around the fault lines of unconscious identification which they provoked in the reader. By the bias of this new approach, students of cultural studies embarked on the toils of decentred subjectivity and en route wrote themselves back into their PhDs as narrators of their own intellectual enterprise. But where would it lead them?

It might have indirectly provided a point of re-entry into the youth question. Post-structuralism drew attention to the effect of non-rationalised structures of feeling, associated with the assumption of fully sexualised and sometimes racialised bodies split down the line of their desires for the Other. The discursive construction – and social performance – of adolescence as a nexus of imaginary identifications thus came more fully into focus as a discrete object of analysis. If this set of object relations went largely unexplored, it was because the lure of identity politics pulled in another direction (Fuss 1989).

Feminist and black cultural studies developed styles of autobiographical and memory work designed to explore more dramatic claims of historical injustice than the frustrations and impasses of growing up. In these highly politicised forms of self-narration adolescence itself was often portrayed as little more than a rite of passage from primary (and hence unconscious) oppression to a state of greater political enlightenment (hooks 1992). From this vantage point, the insistence of the British school of psychoanalysis on the subterfuges of the false self, (not to mention the primacy of the mother/child dyad) were all too politically suspect. In particular, Kleinian theory was bad news for anyone who wanted to celebrate the socially transgressive nature of pre-Oedipal object choices mandated by some versions of sexual politics, just as it had a lot of uncomfortable things to say about the conservative structures of Oedipal revolt to those radical feminists whose attack on patriarchy took just this form (Alford 1989).

By the early 1990s, the textualisation of cultural studies was all but complete. The gains were manifest and multiple. It permitted cultural studies to install itself as a powerful intellectual force within university humanities departments and art schools, as well as to set up in business on its own account. The technique of deconstruction spearheaded an internal critique of the human and social sciences for their complicity in the tyrannies of Western Reason and, hence, indirectly helped cultural studies to establish its claims as a pioneer of post-colonial theory (Moore-Gilbert 1997).

Yet the cult of textuality had its downside. For one thing it failed to equip cultural studies with the intellectual tools or motivation to engage in the profound culturalisation of polity and economy that was taking place during this period. The growth of cultural industries, and their deployment as part of a new strategy of urban regeneration, was at the cutting edge of structural change in the 1980s. As cultural capitalism went global, helping to cement post-Fordist regimes into the remaining workplaces, the local State was left to pick up the pieces; the fragments of labour history or ethnography that were left behind on the doorstep were converted into cultural flagship projects, the post-colonial city dressed up in drag for the tourist trade (Sassen 1991; Cohen 1999b).

The deeper implications of these changes for the class structure were for a long time ignored by cultural theorists. Despite the advent of informatics, labour processes were still too unlike textual ones to be considered a suitable case for treatment. The fact that labouring bodies became increasingly sexualised and racialised in the iconography of popular culture also went largely unremarked (Cohen 1997b).

At a time when the mainstream political culture in Britain was firmly dominated by the agendas of the New Right, an alternative 'cultural politics' emerged in which key issues of structural change affecting working class communities – the decline of manual labourism and the crisis of its masculinities, the transformation of schooling and training systems into a simulacrum of post-Fordist work processes the dismantling of the Welfare State – were all strictly off limits (O'Shea 1998). In their place, eco-feminism, gay politics and black perspective anti-racism made a virtue out of a necessity and celebrated their respective marginalities as a site of transcendence from the oppressive constraints of a more or less monolithic white, heterosexist power structure. *En route*, 'race' and 'gender' were made equivalent to 'class' as identity constructs, despite their very different ontological status, not to mention their disparate provenance as analytic categories and sites of inequality. The payoff, of course, was that these instances could either be stacked up to constitute a hierarchy of oppression, or rendered down into a 'play of difference'.

Cultural studies promised to provide an intellectual space within which these new social movements and identity politics as a whole might be critically assessed and even 'deconstructed'. Yet, in practice, the institutionalisation of the field as a distinct department of academic knowledge tended to militate against making this remit part of any wider political project (O'Shea 1998). Many of the leading lights concentrated on developing a unifying field theory in the shape of post-modernism, whilst ignoring the impact of Thatcherism on the political culture as a whole. But this apparent retreat from the wider political agenda has to be understood in context.

Even though culture wars have not occurred in British universities, at least not on the North American scale, there is no doubt that much cultural theory in this country has been devoted, directly or indirectly, to what student identity politics has put on the campus agenda. This process of political involution intensified as the cultural studies jargonaut began to roll; throughout the 1980s, the academic journals multiplied, along with accretions of theoretical vocabulary and hierarchies of knowledge allied to their mastery; the development of an internal star system, fights over the canon and border disputes with cognate disciplines fuelling personal and professional rivalries within the field all took their toll. Academic politicking increasingly took the place of more exogenous pursuits. By the end of the decade, it seemed as if the main preoccupations of the early phase of British cultural studies – changes in working class life and labour, the methods of ethnographic case study, the engagement with structural inequalities through initiatives in popular education – had all been definitively surpassed (O'Shea 1998). Cultural studies had shed its roots in these parochial and peculiarly English concerns and become a properly transnational and travelling theory, fit to explore and rule a post-colonial universe of discourse that was as fully hybrid as itself.

That, however, proved to be only one side of the story. In the 1990s, the narrative turn in the human sciences, coupled with the rise of cultural geography in place of a discredited historicism, meant a renewed interest in the everyday discourses regulating social interactions, with the local as a site of multiple contestation in and against the global city. In addition, the advent of cultural flagship projects and the building of whole 'cultural quarters' in many downtown areas has alerted many university administrators to the potential of cultural industries as a source of postgraduate employment. By extension, cultural studies might now become a vocational subject, leading to jobs not only for those leaving university, but for young people who had missed out on higher education but were in the vanguard of innovation in popular music, fashion and general youth style. For purely practical reasons to do with student recruitment, and in order to survive in an increasingly competitive academic marketplace, cultural studies has been forced to look beyond itself to the very questions of youth and labour formation that it had theoretically repressed as a condition of its initial academic success.

Meanwhile, on the 'po-mo' Left, it was time to rediscover youth as the site of newly fascinating multi-cultures on the front lines of a transgressive body politics, struggling to assert autonomy against the disciplinary structures of schooling, the homogenising powers of capital and bureaucratic governance by the State (Giroux 1996; Rutherford 1997). Youth cultures were 'cool places' where young people could come out of the various closets imposed by repressive normalisation, if only by hiding in the light (Valentine 1996). For some, the seductive power of ethnography to add a little 'local colour' to the bare bones of sociological analysis proved a compelling motivation for its re-introduction, albeit in a naturalistic rather than a critical mode (Blackman 1986; Bates and Riseborough 1993). For the more entrepreneurially minded, adolescent ethnicities provided a golden opportunity to lay claim to what was valuable in enterprise culture and carve out their own niche in the global marketing of youth culture (Redhead 1993). From both points of view, new lines of battle were drawn between those youth identities regarded as examples of healthy happy hybridity and those which clung to pathological purities.

There was, however, an alternative tradition, largely ignored in both cultural studies and in mainstream youth studies, which attempted to challenge these new dichotomies and to rework the youth question in the light of the larger theoretical debates, whilst at the same time struggling to create an alternative space of representation through direct interventions in the cultures of schooling, training and youth provision around issues of gender, race and class (Cockburn 1987; Hollands 1990; Back 1997; Hewitt 1981; Sewell 1997). In many cases, this also involved the development of a more sophisticated and reflexive approach to ethnographic work; the use of audio and video diaries, photo-mapping, story making and guided fantasy have been variously tried as a means of developing a more dialogic and interactive approach to research with young people (Cohen 1997 and 1999b; Walkerdine 1998). In this way, some links between cultural studies and social policy were, however tenuously, maintained.

IN THE COUNTRY OF THE BLIND

Youth research clearly has to find a way forward beyond economism and culturalism, to create a third space between a narrow empiricist focus on transitions and a quasi-anthropological concern with exotic instances of youthful deviance and difference.

One possible strategy, but one which so far has not been much taken up, is to stake a claim for the youth question as being a strategic site of theoretical and methodological innovation because of the terms of investigation imposed by the peculiar object, or subject, of research (Levi and Schmidt 1996). Here, the multiple articulations of class, gender and ethnicity find an immediate site of engagement with social policy. Here, too, the specific concerns of psychoanalysis and history, cultural geography and political economy, comparative sociology and cognitive psychology meet on otherwise uncommon ground. The argument is about more than these necessary coincidences. What makes the youth question so central to debates in the social and human sciences, and gives it a much wider public resonance, is the fact that it is a question about tradition and modernity (Fornas 1995).

The question of tradition and modernity gave birth to the original problematics of social science at the end of the 19th century. The issue was posed as a question of generations and was intimately bound up with constructing a binary opposition between age and youth. As Marx put it:

> History is nothing but the succession of the separate generations, each of which exploits the materials, the capital funds, the productive forces handed down to it by all the proceeding generations. And this, on the one hand, continues the traditional activity in completely changed circumstances, and on the other modifies the old circumstances with completely changed activity [1985].

Marx, typically, counterpoises the notions of tradition and modernity, without, for all that, abandoning the problematics of generation. Certainly, the idea that youth is a unitary, and hence unifying, category has a history as long as that of modernity, and the two are closely linked. The invention of adolescence as a distinctive stage of the life cycle was part of the same discourse that challenged the 'dead hand of tradition' braking the 'engines of progress'. As a result, young people have had to carry a peculiar burden of representation; everything they do, say, think, or feel, is scrutinised by an army of professional commentators for signs of the times. Over the last century, the 'condition of youth question' has assumed increasing importance as being symptomatic of the health of the nation or the future of the race, the welfare of the family, or the state of civilisation as we know it.

Today, the relation between invented traditions of youth and what is sometimes called post-modernity has overthrown many of the categorical assumptions of both classical Marxist and non-Marxist sociology, including the associations between youth and the new, age and traditionalism (Phoenix and Rattansi 1998). In the 'old' societies of the West, within which we must now include the USA, the great fear of ageing and the search for 'eternal youth' has produced an apparently unquenchable desire to keep up with new times amongst all age groups, but especially those over 40 who can afford it. Post-modernism provides this 'new old' middle class with a ready made template for an ironic plagiarism that enables them to pursue a masquerade of youthfulness with a semblance of style. In order to stake out their privileged claim on 'youth', young people – especially those who are not able to enter into the middle class world of studenthood – have thus to continually improvise fresh ways of asserting difference from their elders as well as from their more advantaged peers. They increasingly do this by adopting an implicit rhetoric of progress and modernity, through forms of mimesis that are now entirely disconnected from the sphere of social production. The trick is to be seen to be growing up faster, doing things sooner and going one bigger and better than those on the other side of the tracks. This 'first past the post' logic both deconstructs youth culture as a unitary phenomenon and, of course, fuels the recycling of its commodity forms.

Turning exotic forms of marginality into marketable lifestyles is all grist to the mill of today's global multicultural capitalism; trading off cultural cross-overs, fusions, ethnic diversities and hybridities of every kind is where the action is and where the profits are to be made (Cohen 1999). Of course, this does little for the self-esteem of young people locked into structural unemployment, the casual labour market and the hidden economy of drugs and petty crime. But it does make exceedingly good advertising copy and provides the stuff of teenage magazine journalism (Lewis 1997)

The enlargement of adolescence, its encroachment on childhood and prolongation into what used to be adulthood is thus both culturally driven and required by the economic collapse of earlier strategies of generational replacement for all but the most privileged. For the disadvantaged, chronic prematurity in the realm of sexual 'body politics' has gone along with the retardation of skills required to stake out claims to public amenity and resources in wider and more civic terms.

The classic contradiction between the symbolic power of the adolescent body associated with its sexuality, looks and style and the political/economic powerlessness of youth as a socio-legal category has thus to be reformulated. The binarisms that hitherto assigned family, community and peer groups to the side of 'tradition'; and school, labour process, State and mass media to the province of 'modernity' no longer apply and explanations of the youth question that depend on them dissolve into incoherence. This conceptual transformation of the youth question highlighted by recent work in the theoretical sociology of culture thus begins to address the phenomenology of youth restructuring mapped by empirical transition studies.

The recent attempt to construct a post-modern sociology has profound implications for both theorisation and empirical research into the youth question. Whether or not this project actually goes beyond the tradition/modernity distinction, or the essentialised categories of structure and agency which derive from it, remains open to doubt. However, for present purposes, it is enough to note the significant conjuncture between social theory and cultural studies. Whether inspired by cyborgery, dance multi-culture or the virtual communities of the internet, or a concern with the 'other scenes' of gender, race and class politics played out in the school yard, a new generation of youth researchers is making waves.

The work of the German sociologist Ulrich Beck, as elaborated by Anthony Giddens in Britain, has been one influential factor in this renaissance (Beck 1992; Beck, Giddens and Scott-Lash 1994). Beck and Giddens argue that individualisation and reflexivity are all pervasive characteristics of 'late modernity', and that we are seeing the emergence of new forms of inequality based on the uneven distribution of risks, rather than resources.

This analysis has provided youth researchers with a conceptual peg on which to hang a new generation of empirical transition studies (Furlong and Cartmel 1997). The attempt to connect issues of citizenship, cultural entitlement and educational stakeholding in this new literature certainly represents a very significant advance over previous work in the field. Hopefully, this work will be sustained in some of the new areas mapped out by recent work in cultural studies around the local and global dimensions of metropolitan change.

The danger of this approach, however, is that bio-political categories of populations 'at risk' are applied to those young people who conspicuously fail to adapt to the kinds of flexible specialisation and individualised self-reflexivity demanded by post-Fordist work discipline (Sennett 1998). For example, Scott-Lash, one of the chief protagonists of the reflexive modernity thesis writes:

> ... in the white ghettoes of British council estates in Liverpool, Glasgow, Newcastle, working class fathers breed underclass sons, fathers who worked in the mines or the docks, in the steel mills and large chemical and machine building plants, have sons who leave school at 16 without an apprenticeship, fail to find anything in the way of steady employment until they are 25; unable to find the industrial labouring jobs they were brought up to do, they wind up behind the counter at Dixons, or as cleaners at the local supermarkets or porters in the local college [Becks, Giddens and Scott-Lash 1994].

This post-industrial 'youth underclass' is then castigated for its racism, violence and general lack of reflexive self-monitoring or civility. This new residuum bears a suspicious resemblance to the old one as far as its distinguishing pre-industrial features are concerned! In place of bad time keeping, sabotage, and lack of productivity, these young people are accused of failing to master the arts of public impression management, multi-tasking and flexitime. The underlying principle of indiscipline remains the same.

The current complication of structural inequalities, and of the forms of self-narration through which they are actively contested and reproduced, clearly requires more sophisticated and empirically grounded accounts than this. If we are to do justice to what is at stake in young people's lives, we have to find new ways of integrating empirically grounded and dialogical strategies of youth research within interdisciplinary and theoretically sophisticated frameworks of comparative analysis (Back, Cohen and Keith 1999).

A THIRD WAY?

This article has looked at two main approaches to youth research in Britain. For the past 20 years, these schools of thought have entertained relations of mutual disinterest or distrust vis à vis each other's accomplishments. You have only to look at the bibliographies of *Rethinking Youth* and *Rethinking the Youth Question* to see how little cross referencing there has been, despite so many potential points of convergence (Wyn and White 1997; Cohen 1997a). We think it is time that youth research grew up to take its rightful 'adult' place as a major site of theoretical and empirical research in the human sciences; but this will only happen if there is a more productive dialogue than hitherto between these different perspectives. The advent of New Labour's so called 'third way' with its constant mantra about 'joined up thinking' provides both a critical focus and space of intervention where these two agendas can fruitfully converge. In conclusion, we would like to indicate a few possible points of common engagement with the present youth political conjuncture.

One of the key aporia in cultural studies is an adequate theory of cultural learning that is, a theory of the cultural processes and practices through which subjects of learning are articulated as objects of the desire to know. In principle, the elements of such a theory are there. Cultural studies spends a lot of time demonstrating that the social designations of identity are becoming much more fluid, fractured and contested; yet very little of this work is applied to the task of following up what such a theory of identity formation might imply about the way children and young people actually learn (Buckingham 1998).

Until very recently, educational researchers with an empiricist cast of mind were not much help because they were only looking at what goes on in classrooms, in the process of academic (dis)qualification, in curriculum development and formal pedagogies. They were not looking at how, what and where people actually learn, in families, through friendships, in peer groups; they were not looking at the locally situated knowledge that is acquired and transmitted in these settings, or at the kinds of identity work this entails. Above all, they were looking at the problem of educability from the vantage point of cultural capital rather than cultural labour.

Once we change our standpoint, a new set of questions open up as a focus of empirical enquiry (Ainley and Rainbird 1999). How do people learn to culturally labour – how do they learn to dance, knit, make love, ride bicycles or horses, or play football, or write graffiti or poetry, or tell jokes, or tall stories, practice safe sex, use computers, play musical instruments, conduct experiments, or learn a foreign language.

Recently, some educationalists have been trying to develop a theory of learning as cultural practice which suggests that whatever the difference in content, or modality, at a formal level, in terms of how people learn to learn, there are some common denominators (Lave and Wenger 1991). They suggest first, that any kind of learning involves investment in personal meanings which in turn shape the sense of self. What is learnt is not just a skill but an identity, or rather a form of identity work. If you can't manage the identity work entailed, you won't manage to succeed in doing the activity. If you cannot see yourself as a budding chemist or rock musician, then you are not going to get your head and your hands round a Bunsen burner or a guitar. But, secondly, until you take the first step into an actual community of practice where that potential identity is plausibly available, you are not going to do more than play at 'Walter Mitty' fantasy games. Thirdly, unless you can tolerate the initial beginner's position, with its association of peripheral participation, then, especially if you come from a group already marginalised in the wider society, you will be likely to drop out into a sub-culture of defiant outsiderdom. Fourthly, unless you can move on from an initial position of mimetic mastery over surface procedures to a position of creative engagement with the underlying grammars of practice, then you will never properly learn the tricks of your particular trade. Finally, unless there are institutional structures to support progression from informal to formal cultures of learning, then a lot of people are never going to take any of these steps.

Some young people are clearly better at handling this kind of progression than others, and some have both more options and more conflicts to work through in reconciling the different identities they take up en route. We need to pinpoint those structures or processes which either facilitate or militate against young people making the transition from imagined to real communities of practice; and we need more context sensitive studies of the cultures of destructive conformity and rebellion that they may become involved. Once we have this kind of locally situated knowledge, we may be in a better position to develop strategies of educational intervention and support that make sense to young people because they address their own narratives of aspiration, and provide a meaningful supplement to the stories they tell themselves about the ways their lives should go. The advent of Educational Action Zones clearly provides an immediate point of reference for such a project.

Another strand of New Labour thinking concerns the role of creative industry and youth culture in 'capacity building'. How some young people learn to culturally labour more productively than others, why some are more able than others to turn their cultural labour into realisable forms of cultural capital and how this relates to 'social capital' formation and peer networks thus becomes the heart of the new youth policy research agenda.

This leads us straight into another cognate area where there is clearly much to be gained from interdisciplinary collaboration. There is a lot of general discussion about changing narrative identities and styles of performativity in the period of 'late modernity', but precious little of this theorising is grounded in thick description of youth practices. How far do the new habits of schooling and working provide principles of periodisation and predicament that can make sense of life transitions no longer organised around the dramatic unities of time and place? How far does visual culture, in both its analogue and digital media modes, provide an alternative vocabulary for describing these shifting positions. And how does this pan out in Moss Side, or Liverpool 8 compared with Bath and Melton Mowbray?

Here are a set of questions around which educationalists, youth researchers and social policy analysts are converging and where the various research trades – cultural geographers, visual ethnographers, narratologists, clinical psychologists, etc – all have their own story to tell. To address these issues properly through empirical research, we are certainly going to have to extend our methodologies into new and largely uncharted regions. Social scientists are going to have to learn to grapple with the emotional intricacies of the 'interview transference' if they are going to put some biographical flesh on the bare bones of youth policy analysis, just as hardened number crunchers are going to have to experiment with the internet to develop new sampling strategies in which high response rates are predicated on respondents having access to the questionnaire findings and the right of reply.

Increasingly, youth researchers will not be academics in the traditional sense but young people who have been trained in new interactive and dialogic modes of social investigation and who apply these fieldwork methods to investigating topics defined by their peers. Teachers and youth workers will need to play a key role in defining and implementing this research process, especially by working it into the curriculum of cultural studies and sociology at 'A' level. Increasingly, public workshops at which research findings are presented and evaluated by the so called 'research subjects' will become a standard feature of good research practice. More accessible forms of dissemination involving the making of video programmes, interactive multi-media exhibitions and online archives will also become more important. Youth researchers are likely to be at the forefront of these new developments. Equally, the new universities, with their strong school and community links, are well placed to become the leaders of this new kind of open access research culture. It is important, then, that both the ESRC and the European Union support youth research initiatives that take full advantage of these new possibilities to widen young people's participation in the production and dissemination of social scientific knowledge .

This does not mean that there will be no place in the future for original or independent scholarship. Quite the contrary: greater interdisciplinarity and a wider comparative database will require strenuous intellectual engagement to effect some kind of sustainable creative synthesis. It is just that challenge that makes the youth question such an important and potentially productive site of theoretical innovation.

CHAPTER 12

ALTERNATIVE SANCTIONS: AN AMERICAN EXPERIMENT INCORPORATING YOUTH RIGHTS – AN APPROACH FOR THE 21ST CENTURY

Caroline Hunt

INTRODUCTION

This chapter is a micro analysis of an experiment entitled 'The Delaware Juvenile Advocacy Project', conducted in the early 1990s by the National Centre on Institutions and Alternatives (NCIA), in partnership with the State of Delaware. It was an experiment dedicated to the protection of youth and the promotion and advocacy of their rights in the context of community based alternative sanctions. This philosophy was spearheaded by Dr Jerome Miller and Herb Hoelter, President and Director of the National Center on Institutions and Alternatives, Virginia, USA, respected criminal justice reformers and tireless advocates for decency in juvenile justice. The project was significant for its focus upon the practical application of international juvenile justice standards.

The project concept grew from an initiative by the Delaware Department for Children, Youth and their Families (DCYF) to de-institutionalise an overcrowded juvenile prison, namely, the Ferris Secure Institution. This chapter provides an analysis of the various stages or parts of the project, including: the criteria for selection of appropriate youth, the placement process, post-placement recidivism and comparative experiments and their results. Finally, it will reflect on systemic problems encountered and the lessons learned from this groundbreaking project.

JUVENILE JUSTICE: A CYCLE OF PARADIGMS

The history of juvenile justice in the US can be characterised as cyclical (Rothman 1984). Rehabilitative justice was introduced at the turn of this century with great hopes, considerable investment and scientific expertise. Indeed, Tulkens 1993 commented that 'resorting to penal justice was regarded as a sign of failure and powerlessness' (p 489). In the 1960s, against a background of rapidly increasing juvenile arrests and the perceived failure of the juvenile court to stem the rising crime rate, the community corrections movement created optional placements within the juvenile justice system. In the 1970s, for the first time, empirical analysis took place, contributing to a shift of theoretical focus in the 1980s from rehabilitation to accountability and sanctioning.

The cycle of paradigms within youth justice in the US begins with the introduction of policy innovations, central to this being the search for effective alternatives to prison. Intrinsic to this process is the 'illusion' (Bloomberg 1983) that such advances will contain and even deter crime and delinquency. In time, dissatisfaction with such an approach grows and unintended consequences develop. There is little understanding of the reasons behind the disparity between the rhetoric and reality, largely as a result of the lack of post-implementation research in the field.[1]

The year 1972 marked a turning point in the cycle of US juvenile justice paradigms when Dr Jerome Miller pioneered an alternative strategy for dealing with serious juvenile offenders by closing Massachusetts's largest training schools.[2] This model has been both praised and criticised. A 10 year study by the Harvard Center for Criminal Justice concluded that the:

> ... regions that most adequately implemented the reform measures with a diversity of programs did produce decreases in recidivism on the institutionalization-normalization continuum.[3]

Additionally, it was found that rates of serious juvenile crime declined in Massachusetts; the number of juveniles that ended up in the adult State prison system dropped significantly and fewer juveniles were placed out of State.[4] The States of Massachusetts and Utah[5] successfully restructured their juvenile correctional systems by defining which youths were appropriate for secure placement and reinvesting available resources in order to fund a better and more efficient delivery system for adjudicated youth. The alternative sanctions delivery system included the development of a comprehensive classification process and placement system. This in turn created the demand for a wider spectrum of appropriate interventions for delinquent youth. This was the model upon which the Delaware experiment was conceived and it is to this that we now turn.

---

1   The increasing trend of juvenile justice to become the subject of social and emotional pressure is a matter of concern to the Committee on the Rights of the Child (Report on the 10th Session, Oct–Nov 1995, CRC/C46, para 20).

2   The 1972 experiment remains subject to case study at Harvard University School of Government, due to its unique qualities and vision.

3   Coates, Miller and Ohlin 1978:177.

4   Schwartz 1989:53.

5   Schwartz 1989:53.

BACKGROUND

Experiment mandate and context

A 1988 US Justice Department Survey reported that there were over 53,000 youths confined in public juvenile correctional facilities nationwide.[6] This was the highest number in US history.[7] In 1989, the Ferris Secure Institution for Juveniles was one such chronically overcrowded correctional facility and litigation in this regard was pending by the Prison Project of the American Civil Liberties Union (ACLU).[8]

In response to the law suit, the Governor of Delaware requested that the Delaware DCYF and, more specifically, the Division of Youth Rehabilitative Services (DYRS) reduce the number of youth incarcerated in the institution as a precondition to settlement of the law suit. In response to this political pressure, the Secretary of DYRS appointed a working committee, comprising two senior members of DYRS, a member of the Foster Care Review Board,[9] a juvenile justice expert and two members of the Delaware criminal justice system, to determine a strategy to address the law suit.

Review and consultation and the development of a risk assessment instrument

The Governors Committee began their task by reviewing all existing reports, memos and plans concerning the youth incarcerated in the State of Delaware. Independent consultants[10] were appointed to the Governors Committee to enhance its credibility and neutrality. Following the review, a State wide consultation took place with members of the judiciary, the law enforcement community and child care professionals. A source of controversy emerged during this process as to how many secure places were needed to accommodate the needs of the State. An earlier study by Krisberg and Schwartz 1983 indicated that individual States varied in their admissions to

---

6   Allen-Hagen 1988.

7   The number of youths incarcerated was increasing even though the teenage population and volume of arrests were declining. However, juvenile violent crime had increased in certain areas: US Sourcebook of Criminal Justice Statistics 1992.

8   ACLU investigations concluded that violations of youths' eighth amendment rights were occurring at the Ferris Secure Institution and were being exacerbated by the overcrowded conditions.

9   The Foster Care Review Board is an independent legal entity appointed by the State legislature to review the placement of youth by the DCYF. It had a watchdog role and power to make recommendations but implementation is discretionary.

10 Paul De Muro, a national expert in the field of juvenile justice, and Barry Krisberg of the National Council on Crime and Delinquency, co-authored the initial risk assessment, *Adjudicated Youth in Delaware Who Need Secure Care* (1987).

secure facilities; in essence, there was little correlation between the chronicity of the youth's offence, their record, their potential danger to the community and their incarceration. Delaware had one of the highest placement rates of youth in secure facilities in the country.

In order to determine the number of secure places needed by the State, a risk assessment instrument (RAI) was developed by the consultants to the DYRS working committee of the youth incarcerated at the Ferris Secure Institution, so as to determine which youths were appropriate for community based placement.[11]

Application of the RAI criteria to youths in secure care in Delaware

The population of the Ferris Secure Institution at the time of the assessment was approximately 140 youths. The population was to be divided into three distinct groups: those requiring secure care because of the nature of the instant offence and/or offence history scored 10 or above (which totalled six youths of the cohort); those youths clearly eligible for direct community placement who scored between one and five (95 youths); and those youths requiring special consideration and placement work before deciding on secure or alternative placement. The latter group scored between six and nine and were the group from which the NCIA experiment cohort was primarily drawn. The number of youths fitting into this category was 32 at the date of the assessment. At the commencement of the NCIA project, the cohort comprised 38 youths.[12] It may seem surprising, therefore, that these youths were incarcerated at the Ferris Secure Institution in the first place. However, this is because they had simply exhausted all placement options; family court judges

---

11   The model used for the instrument was the National Council on Crime and Delinquency's (NCCD) Oregon model, but customised to the needs of Delaware. The instrument assigned points to various factors relevant to the severity of the instant offence and chronicity of the youth's prior record. In reviewing Delaware class A and class B felonies, the committee made two important decisions. First, although an adjudication for an escape would count as a felony adjudication, the committee decided not to count an instant adjudication for escape as a heavily weighted item. Most youth adjudicated for escape simply walk away from open, non-secure placements. When escape was accompanied by violent offences, the latter was considered. Secondly, the committee decided to reduce the risk factor for youth convicted of first degree burglary, although offenders guilty of repeated burglaries would be given higher scores and thus would be eligible for a secure placement. Finally, aggravating and mitigating criteria were used to help make the initial placement for those youth who were neither clearly nor easily identifiable as low risk youth who should be directly placed in community programmes.

12   De Muro and Krisberg 1987:6.

had to commit youths to the Ferris Secure Institution because there simply were not any viable alternatives available.[13]

Findings of the Governors Working Committee

The preliminary findings of the Working Committee Report confirmed that the State of Delaware was clearly over-incarcerating youth, especially black youth. Two-thirds of the population in the institution were black, many having committed, in the most part, minor offences. Moreover, a recommendation was made to close the secure programme for females and provide alternative programming, as it was alleged that young females were inappropriately securely committed. The overriding recommendation of the report was that the population of the Ferris Secure Institution should be reduced. Shortly after the publication of the report in August 1989, NCIA were retained by DYRS to address the unwarranted incarceration of 38 youths.[14]

Characteristics of the cohort[15]

The NCIA cohort, in addition to serious records of offending, unanimously had a chronic record of failure in community placements. All eight girls and most of the 25 male cohort had challenged other systems and exhausted the State's ability to provide appropriate programmes for them (Child Protective Services, residential treatment centres, etc). The NCIA cohort could be categorised as repeat offenders. Two youth profiles of the NCIA cohort are outlined in the following, the profile of the male youth being typical of the cohort of 38 males, the profile of the female being the outlier of the sample.

Profile 1 – an NCIA cohort female (outlier): M's mother was incarcerated and had been for most of her life. M had been passed from relative to relative, seeing her mother for short interim spells between incarceration. M committed mostly theft and burglary, as had her mother. She had been discharged from every treatment facility in which she was placed after

---

13 These youths had simply exhausted all their other options, their parents had given up on them or were not interested. Many youths lived with a grandparent or relative as their parent was incarcerated or living elsewhere. The problem facing family court judges is having to commit youths to the Ferris Secure Institution because there are no viable alternatives available.

14 The State of Delaware decided to retain an independent agency to conduct the experiment as it was acknowledged that de-institutionalisation meant job cuts which could cause resistance to the experiment if conducted by State employees.

15 The cohort comprised 30 males (seven Caucasian and 23 black); eight females (three Caucasian and five black) all of whom scored between six and nine on the risk assessment instrument and who had been committed at an early age, usually between 11 and 14.

displaying an aptitude for 'testing limits'. While M was placed in Maryland's most secure facility for youth, she organised a mass escape and then ate a glass sandwich. The latter was grounds for discharge and placement into a psychiatric facility. In the psychiatric facility, she behaved perfectly and earned a discharge from that facility. Maryland, however, would not accept her back into their facility, as the escape had embarrassing consequences for the administration. Her next placement was in a foster home where she seduced the foster father and was removed from placement. The pattern continued. She became pregnant during her last placement.

Profile 2 – a typical NCIA cohort male (mode): D was 18, he was known to the system since the age of 10 and was committed to the Ferris Institution at 14. He was a victim of sexual abuse and from an incestuous family. He had escaped from Ferris and residential placements on several occasions.

THE PROJECT

The emergence of the rights perspective via the 'client specific planning' tool[16]

The methodology used to develop the alternative sanctions, the so called client specific planning (CSP) treatment model, was central to the experiment. The approach used to develop a community treatment plan was based on fundamental principles which were consistent with international juvenile justice standards, namely:

(a) the principle of 'best interests' contained in the Beijing Rules;[17]

(b) the importance of listening to the youth;[18]

(c) allowance for the young person's right to development;

(d) inclusion of the family in decisions relating to the youth's life;

---

16 CSP, created by NCIA, is an integrated approach comprising a recommendation, implementation and tracking strategy designed following extensive background research and consultation with the youth and his or her family, significant others, employers, psychologists and educational specialists. This, with its tracking component, improves the success of placement in the community.

17 The Beijing Rules require 'the furtherance of the well being of the juvenile and his or her family' (r 1(1)), and that 'the juvenile justice system shall emphasize the well being of the juvenile' (r 5(1)). Also, 'proceedings shall be conducive to the best interests of the juvenile ...' (r 14(2)), and the well being of the juvenile 'shall be the guiding factor in the consideration of his or her case' (r 17(1)(d)).

18 The active obligation to listen to the child's views and to take them seriously is drawn from the CRC, Art 12(2), which states that 'the child who is capable of forming his or her own views has the right to express those views freely in all matters affecting the child, the views of the child being given due weight in accordance with the age and maturity of the child freely in all matters affecting the child. For this purpose, the child shall in particular be provided with the opportunity to be heard in any judicial and administrative proceedings affecting the child ...'.

(e) the young person's freedom to enjoy his or her rights without discrimination;[19]

(f) balancing the youth's interests with the needs of the community;[20] and

(g) victim[21] impact and loss caused (taken into account as elements in their own right).[22]

Built into each comprehensive client specific plan was a victim compensation component, with full victim participation monitored, where appropriate, by the NCIA tracker.

Furthermore, the CSP approach closely monitored the actual development and implementation of the programme and its effect on each young person, as well as the tracking of the youth one year after placement in the community. The tracking component of the CSP tool throughout its implementation period and the consequential ability to individually tailor, modify and adapt it by anticipating, supporting and advocating for the youth, was the hallmark of the Delaware experiment.

---

19 The CRC was passed by the General Assembly of the UN on 20 November 1989 and has been ratified by all Member States of the UN except the US. A child for the purposes of the CRC is defined in Art 1 as 'every human being below the age of 18, unless, under the law applicable to the child, majority is attained earlier'.

20 The UN Rules for the Protection of Juveniles Deprived of their Liberty include a section on 'Return to the community'. All juveniles should benefit from arrangements designed to assist them in returning to society, family life, education or employment after release. Procedures, including early release and special courses, should be devised to this end (para 79). Moreover, competent authorities should provide or ensure services to assist juveniles in re-establishing themselves in society and lessen prejudice against such juveniles (para 80).

21 The Declaration of Basic Principles of Justice for Victims of Crime and Abuse of Power 1985 calls upon States to provide remedies, including restitution and/or compensation and necessary material, medical, psychological and social assistance to victims, and ensure justice to the extent to which such abuse is a violation of national law (General Assembly Resolution 40/34 November 1985, Annex).

22 CRC, Art 40(4): 'A variety of dispositions such as care, guidance and supervision orders; counselling, probation, foster care, educational and vocational training programs and other alternatives to institutional care shall be available to ensure that children are dealt with in a manner appropriate to their well being and proportionate both to their circumstances and offence.'

Consistent with the approach advocated by the CRC were the UN Riyadh Guidelines on the prevention of juvenile delinquency. More specifically, the Guidelines propose that a comprehensive development plan should include victim compensation and assistance programmes, with full victim participation (para 9). The Riyadh Guidelines state that: 'Communities should provide or strengthen, where they exist, a wide range of community based support measures for young persons, including development centers, recreational facilities and services to respond to the special problems of children at social risk. Government agencies should take special responsibility in this regard' (paras 33, 34, 38).

CSP implementation and development of the alternative sanctions

The experiment was called the 'NCIA Delaware Juvenile Advocacy Project' and was set up in an office at the Ferris Secure Institution in August 1989. It had a small staff: a project director,[23] four caseworkers and an administrative assistant. The staff were local Delawareans, hired for their expertise in child advocacy and trained under the NCIA-CSP model.

Each of the NCIA cohort offenders were interviewed and assigned to an NCIA caseworker/tracker, who in turn initiated an inter-agency review of files and commenced a consultation process with all other case managers from various agencies[24] with knowledge of the youth, so as to establish a comprehensive overview of the youth's history, while utilising the expertise of other professionals on innovative programming for chronic juvenile offenders. In addition, all relatives and significant others were consulted during the development of the plan, a component notably lacking in the discharge planning for youth leaving the secure facility.[25]

Following the identification of a suitable community placement, additional components were added to the plan, for example, a private tutor would be used in school if the young person was deemed to be under-achieving; the sponsorship of a local sports celebrity would be sought in order to support the youth after discharge; or a tracker would be appointed to supervise a positive recreational activity. Usually, additional funding was required to pay for the alternatives and such needs were met from a State budget.[26]

Once the plan/placement had been developed[27] and endorsed by all divisions of DYRS, an exit meeting took place prior to discharge, with the youth, his or her family, the service provider, the probation officer and the NCIA caseworker. This meeting reinforced the parameters of the plan.

---

23 The author of this article.

24 These agencies would include the other divisions of the department such as Child Protective Services and Child Mental Health as well as the caseworker responsible for managing the youth in the Ferris Secure Institution and the school authorities in the community the youth resided in.

25 The Ferris Secure Institution case managers responsible for discharge planning frequently did not have the time or the energy to create a CSP. Their duties included managing the youth in the institution and attending court on behalf of the youth; they had little time to devote to discharge planning.

26 To facilitate the placement, the NCIA project director would submit a proposal to the DYRS with the justification as to why the State should include the requisite services in its continuum of community placements. The proposal would also approach the State bureaucracy to secure a new contract with an appropriate service provider. This was an unusually time consuming activity and would have placed unreasonable demands on State workers responsible for discharge planning.

27 'Developed' in this context, means identifying a programme in tandem with the youth's needs, securing placement in the programme. This often required advocacy and adding additional components to programmes as our youths were usually considered to be 'too deep end' for most placements in the community.

Thereafter, arrangements were made for transportation, and the youth was discharged from the institution under the legal supervision of the aftercare or probation department.

The role of the NCIA caseworker provided continuity for the youth as they made the transition from the institution into the community. The NCIA tracker who had developed the plan was charged with adapting it if this became necessary and dealing with arrests or placement problems. This holistic case management approach combated the fragmentation of the existing system, where case managers and probation officers were not invested in keeping the youth out of the institution. The commitment to keep the youth out of the institution underpinned the NCIA-CSP philosophy of the experiment.

Imparting information about the particular features and methodology of the experiment and generally promoting the alternative sanctions approach was important for the State workers charged with the responsibility for the youth after the experiment. To this end, formal training sessions of Delaware State officials were conducted by NCIA's head office throughout the duration of the experiment.

The alternative sanctions

In the 12 months following de-institutionalisation, 22 youths were settled in home based placements,[28] receiving home based services such as intensive probation, family therapy, the assignment of a youth advocate[29] and an individualised work or education programme. One youth was placed in an independent living programme, one in specialised foster care, one in an in-patient psychiatric facility,[30] three youths were in group homes, three in residential treatment centres, five in secure institutional care[31] and two were in interim detention pending replacement.

---

28 CRC, Art 20 applies principally to social work or welfare departments of government. It implies, but does not spell out, that placement in 'suitable institutions for care of children' is a last resort that is second best to placement in an alternative family. Institutionalisation is deemed to be a last resort often because the State has failed to put resources into keeping children with their families or finding and maintaining foster families.

29 A youth advocate is an individual who supports the youth for 30 hours a week. The youth advocate structures the youth's recreational, cultural and employment resources, helps to mediate problem situations and plays the role of a big brother or sister.

30 CRC, Art 23(2) addresses the international obligations of a child suffering from mental illness. It advocates 'the right of the youth to special care' and encourages and ensures 'the extension, subject to available resources, to the eligible child and to those responsible for his or her care, of assistance for which application is made and which is appropriate to the child's condition and to the circumstances of the parents or others caring for the child'.

31 The youth in this category had failed in placement and been re-arrested and recommitted to the institution.

Home based placement, whenever possible, was integral to the CSP approach. Placement types were ranked in order of preference: first, family options were considered; secondly, substitute family; and, lastly, an appropriate institution (in line with Art 4 of the 1986 Declaration on Social and Legal Principles relating to the Protection and Welfare of Children).[32] NCIA recognised that the loss to the youth of family attachments and identity, together with the instabilities and disruption of their replacement, impeded their physical, intellectual and emotional development, thereby potentially perpetuating 'abuse' of the youngster and exacerbating the chance of further offending behaviour.

EVALUATION

Post-placement analysis: defence based advocacy, 24 hour trackers and unconditional care – the Key rights approach[33]

Keeping a youth in the placement was adaptive work. It was the joint charge of the probation officer and service provider to provide support and supervision for the youth in placement. The NCIA cohort had frequently alienated their probation officer[34] on previous occasions under the old system and relationships were often tense. The NCIA tracker was an additional resource and advocate for the youth. For example, in the event of a behavioural incident in school, the NCIA tracker would mediate a situation (as would a parent in a normal situation), as soon as this was practicable. However, if expulsion from a placement was pending, NCIA would attempt to provide an extra component so as to support the service provider and adapt the programme to the youth's particular needs.[35] Special visits to loved ones were made to help with behaviour modification, for example, visiting a parent in prison. A youth may, for example, have had a parent relapse into drug addiction and start to exhibit behavioural problems as an expression of anxiety or frustration ('act out') due to a fear that they would be removed from the home. NCIA's philosophy of unconditional care included anticipating, supporting and advocating for the youth by creating innovative

---

32 When care by the child's own parents is unavailable or inappropriate care is being given by relatives of the child's parents, or by another substitute foster or adoptive family or, if necessary, by an appropriate institution (Declaration on Social and Legal Principles relating to the Protection and Welfare of Children 1986, Art 4).

33 The Key Program was the model for the tracking system, a programme set up following the Massachusetts reforms of 1972.

34 The probation caseload allocation system was such that a probation officer would always have the same youth. While consistency was good, it could be a double edged sword.

35 Eg, NCIA arranged for a youth to be chauffeured between school and her residential treatment centre as the youth was 'acting out' on the way back from school.

solutions to accommodate the youth and their support system. For example, if a parent required treatment or placement in a detoxification centre, respite supervision for the youth, rather than removing the youth from home was preferred.

If the youth was arrested during a placement, the NCIA case manager would advocate in court for the youth, usually recommending adapting the placement,[36] while ensuring that the youth took responsibility for his or her actions. On occasions, this was at cross purposes with the youths' aftercare/probation officer who may have wanted to revoke aftercare status/probation and have the youth returned to the Ferris Secure Institution.

Returning the youth to Ferris was an entrenched practice in the aftercare/probation department when complications arose with the youth. This practice had become entrenched mainly because many of the aftercare workers had previously worked at the Ferris Institution and were of the mindset that locking up the juvenile was appropriate for the youth's 'acting out' behaviour problems. There was little incentive for probation officers to keep the youth out of the institution. Changing this mindset was one of the principal challenges of the experiment.

NCIA caseworkers were available to the young person via a beeper system on a 24 hour a day basis. One of the problems with existing supervisory services for youth was that supervisors were available between 9 am and 5 pm while most delinquency took place during periods of unstructured time, usually during the night. The 24 hour facility meant that the NCIA tracker could mediate a volatile situation when it occurred. Central to this process was the relationship of trust that had built up between the NCIA caseworker and the youth. Without this essential element of trust, the youth would not even call the NCIA worker. On average, an NCIA caseworker received between four and 16 calls per day. The experiment process was conducive to building strong bonds between the NCIA tracker and the youth primarily because NCIA was perceived by the youth as responsible for their release into the community. The relationship often inevitably led to limit-testing with certain youths, for many of them had never experienced an advocate acting specifically on their behalf.[37] However, that advocacy component was seen as a model for good probation work.

Finally, the tracking system provided for a periodic review of the treatment and services being provided to the youth during their community placement. It was a standard which allowed the youth to be heard, to be in touch with the outside world and to have access to an independent person to

---

36 This may mean adding an intensive supervision component or moving the youth from one placement to another within a community based range of alternative placements rather than returning them to Ferris.

37 Additionally, NCIA was not charged with the legal responsibilities of a probation officer and, therefore, the NCIA aftercare role was similar to one of an advocate for the youth.

complain to – arguably, an important check and balance in any rights based approach to juvenile justice.

Tracking reports for decision makers – an innovation in accountability

The accountability of this project was through a monthly tracking status report produced by the NCIA director. The report was distributed to DYRS and family court judges, allowing them, for the first time in the history of the system, to monitor progress in placements. The monthly tracking status report provided an alphabetical list of the youths and their locations. Each placement was coded by type. Most importantly, this report indicated the current performance of the youth within the placement. The categories were as follows: 'Absolute compliance', 'AWOL', 'Committed', 'Detained', 'Meeting requirements', 'Needs assistance', 'Pending replacement' and 'Very good'. For ease of interpretation, the monthly data was summarised graphically. The arrest disposition component of the report summarised post-placement arrests for all youths in the project. The type of offence, the current disposition and the effect on the placement was also included. A cumulative chart illustrated arrests per month and the number of re-commitment or transfers to the adult system. This data provided valuable at a glance information about recidivism for decision makers.

Recidivism

It is understood that one of the principal tests of any rehabilitation programme is its effect on the criminal behaviour of youths after they leave the programme, that is, their recidivism rate compared with that of similar youths outside the programme. There is, however, no standard measure of recidivism. Studies measuring the success of juvenile correctional efforts have employed a number of different indicators to gauge subsequent criminality. The most widely used and accepted recidivism measures record the proportion of youths who are crime free during a specified follow-up period and the incidence or frequency of re-offending before and after commitment. Because each of these measures has certain limitations, it appears best to examine multiple indicators of subsequent law violations. The follow-up period covers the time when the youth is in the community and therefore 'at risk' of committing new crimes.[38]

---

38 Krisberg, Austin and Steel 1989. Although a school of thought, including Charles Murray and Louis Cox, demonstrated that using an absolute standard of 'cure', ie, complete desistence from offending, may actually mask significant reductions in the number and severity of crimes committed by programme clients.

It has been argued that arrest is an imperfect indicator because so many youths (particularly those from minority ethnic groups) get arrested. Approximately 47% of all males and 21% of all females have juvenile court careers.[39] Wolfgang, in his Philadelphia cohort of youth, found that as many as one-third of all black youth were arrested at some time during their adolescent years. Elliott et al 1978 found that, for example, one-third of all youth residing within the jurisdiction of a south western urban juvenile court's were referred to a juvenile court for a delinquency or status offence before their 18th birthday. Arrest figures, however, can understate as well as overstate criminal offending. Many youths who commit offences do not get arrested. Problems faced in calculating recidivism rates in Delaware was exacerbated by the unusually small size of the State and the familiarity of law enforcement officers with delinquent youth. Therefore, the recidivism figures below should be viewed with some caution.

Recidivism after 12 months

Of the 38 youths in the NCIA cohort, 23 youths were re-arrested. Thirty-three arrests occurred within a 12 month period following placement into the community; eight youths incurred more than one arrest. Fifteen of the 33 arrest charges were ultimately dropped, suggesting that the juvenile defence advocacy aspect of the programme was particularly effective in negotiating with arresting officers. After 12 months, four youths had been returned to the institution, and four had been transferred to adult jurisdiction.

The number of youths convicted of new charges after 12 months was 14. Of the 23 youths re-arrested, 13 remained in placement; they would otherwise have been removed from placement (this suggests that the defence advocacy component was effective, see above).

Overall, 12-month recidivism rates for the NCIA cohort were lower than those reported in comparative studies. It is noteworthy that, of the 14 youths convicted, each offence was less severe than any crime committed prior to selection for the experiment.

COMPARATIVE ANALYSES

Massachusetts, Utah, Pennsylvania, Florida and California

The NCIA cohort of 38 serious juvenile delinquents is a skewed sample of the Delaware juvenile justice system. The profile of the youth were such that they were more likely to be arrested and hence have a higher rate of recidivism

---

39   Snyder 1988: 10.

because they had scored highly on the risk assessment instrument. However, it is interesting to compare the NCIA cohort's 12 months post-placement recidivism to studies in other States, such as Massachusetts, Utah, Pennsylvania, Florida and California, for the same period.

The Massachusetts data is derived from the National Council on Crime and Delinquency (NCCD) study that included the records of all youths who exercised the Division of Youth Services (DYS) jurisdiction in 1985 and another group that derived from DYS secure facilities in 1984. Data on the proportion of youths re-incarcerated covers prisons as well as youths who were placed in DYS secure programmes after committing a new offence. The Pennsylvania data is based on a random sample of almost 600 youths placed, primarily in 1984, in 10 residential programmes.[40] The California Youth Authority data on arrests is taken from a sample of 2,200 youths who were released from youth authority institutions between 1981 and 1982.[41] The data on reconviction was taken from a 24 month follow-up of all juvenile court committed youths (2,522) released on parole in 1985.[42] The California Camps and Ranches data are from a special study conducted by the Program Research and Review Division of the California Youth Authority in 1988. This study examined a sample of 2,835 youths released in 1982 from juvenile correctional facilities operated by county probation departments. The measure of recidivism was the proportion of youths who had sustained delinquency petitions in juvenile courts or convictions in adult courts 12 months after their release.[43]

The Florida data is based on a sample of 1,664 youths released from a variety of public and private Florida juvenile correctional programmes in 1984. The recidivism measure was the proportion of youths who were convicted of a delinquent or adult criminal offence.[44] The Utah data was taken from an NCCD study of 248 youths who were committed to the Utah Division of Youth Corrections during 1983–84. Data is presented on the number of youths arrested within 12 months, as well as those with a sustained delinquency petition during that same period.[45]

Overall, the Delaware NCIA cohort had a statistically lower level of recidivism in the 12 month post-placement period than comparative data. The NCIA cohort recidivism compares favourably with other States. The reconviction rates after 12 months are the lowest at 36%, compared to Massachusetts (43%), Florida (44%), Utah (48%) and California (53%).

---

40 Goodstein and Sontheimer 1987.
41 Baird 1987.
42 Automated Services Branch 1988.
43 Wedge and Palmer 1986.
44 Tollett 1987.
45 Krisberg, Austin, Joe and Steele 1987.

However, the arrest rate for the Delaware group is the median at 61% of its comparison group (Massachusetts 55%, Pennsylvania 56%, California Youth Authority 70% and Utah 75%). This would suggest that the NCIA tracking and advocacy strategy was successful, as less youth were convicted despite a median arrest rate in comparison to other States.

Parallel developments in the UK

Referring to the historical period which covers the Delaware experiment, statistics released by the Home Office in 1994 indicated that the numbers of young people aged 17 or under who were convicted or cautioned in the UK decreased from 204,600 in 1983 to 129,500 in 1993. The overall fall in juvenile population correlated directly with the Department of Health and Social Security's Intermediate Treatment Initiative of 1983, which financed the establishment of 110 intensive schemes in 62 local authority areas to provide alternatives to custody (Rutherford 1992).[46]

An analogous experiment to the Delaware Juvenile Advocacy Project in the UK was the Children's Society Tracking Project in Kirklees.[47] Similarly, it targeted serious and persistent offenders who would have been sentenced to custody in the absence of intermediate treatment. The methodology of the tracking project[48] involved the offender meeting his or her tracker every day for four months, with meetings gradually decreasing in frequency, to address issues such as employment, education, personal relationships, and legal and probationary requirements. Projects such as this were successful in persuading magistrates in the UK that a serious hard alternative to custody existed which could benefit both the offender and the community, proving that 'serious and persistent offenders can be managed in the community'.[49]

LESSONS LEARNED

Case continuity versus fragmentation: a question of budgets?

The lack of rationalisation and continuity in the treatment of youths by the Delaware authorities was noteworthy. Moreover, the fragmentation and complications were compounded in the case of the NCIA cohort. In Delaware,

---

46 Intermediate treatment must be distinguished from CSP in that it focused less on the individual need of the juvenile and more on the nature of the offence.

47 Curtis 1989:96 *et seq.*

48 Following the granting by the court of a one year supervision order under the Children and Young Persons Act 1969, ss 7 and 12.

49 NACRO 1991:3.

for example, the DCYF was divided into four departments. The typical chronic juvenile offender or the youth's family was usually known to Child Protective Services and the Child Mental Health Division prior to being adjudicated delinquent and committed to DYRS. Most of the NCIA cohort had three caseworkers, one from each department, each with their own treatment plan for the youth based on the ethos and bias of their particular department.

In principal, where several departments were involved, case co-ordination meetings took place, facilitated by a trained arbiter, to develop a co-ordinated approach. In practice, once a youth had become criminalised, it was common practice for the other departments to attempt to close the cases and transfer them to the DYRS. The reason for this enthusiasm to 'pass the buck' could be that treatment for chronic juvenile offenders was expensive and each department had only limited budget resources. The criminalisation of the youth, therefore, provided an excuse to pass the case onto another department. Secondly, management of chronic offenders in the community is difficult and extremely time consuming. This was a survival practice in departments where morale and financial remuneration were often extremely low. The custom and practice of passing the buck to the DYRS by closing cases and, therefore, closing off access to specialised services, had become entrenched. Consequently, youths were essentially being deprived of potential post-discharge community services.

Following discharge into the community, supervising the NCIA cohort was time intensive work. The NCIA cohort, without exception, had violated probation orders in the past and the probation officers had developed an expectation of failure. The NCIA tracker worked alongside the probation officers, providing additional supervision and advocacy services in the event of a problem in placement or with the police, thereby reducing the propensity of probation officers to revoke probation and remove problematic youths from their caseload.

Tracking and monitoring strategies – best practice in juvenile justice

The NCIA cohort illustrated that, the greater the number of contact hours between the youth and the service deliverer, the more successful the placement. The NCIA case manager/tracker was an additional resource and advocate for the youth by virtue of having both developed the placement inside the institution and then taken responsibility for its facilitation outside the institution. A determination to keep the youth out of the institution was integral to the philosophy of the experiment.

Moreover, the tracking system provided a periodic review of the treatment and services being provided to the youth. It was a standard which allowed the youth to be heard, to be in touch with the outside world and to have access to an independent person to complain to. It was a standard which provided safeguards against one of the most serious forms of abuse of youths – abuse by the State (Art 25 of the UN Convention on the Rights of the Child 1989).[50]

Organisational dynamics – a closer look

Krisberg and Bloomberg 1983 argue that less than satisfactory results in juvenile justice establishments are often caused by a variety of 'organisational dynamics'. Indeed, Miller has indicated that such dynamics are often endemic and may even lead to organisational aims being obscured:

> Institutional politics are characterized by such Byzantine infighting that the average helping professional soon loses either direction or integrity.[51]

Analysts from the University of Syracuse Center for Human Policy had also noted this tendency over three decades ago:

> Many professionals think in terms of categories and segregated services. This is the way they have been taught to diagnose and prescribe. Thus, they may not have the philosophy or the skills needed to meet the requirements of conversion (de-institutionalization and community based placement). Retraining can provide only a partial remedy. There is a brick and mortar, formal organization of the professions, physical and organizational elements that stand as defenses against the onslaught of change.[52]

Returning to the Delaware experiment, NCIA encountered staff resistance at various levels of professional input. Noteworthy resistance to the project came from the contract management department responsible for authorising agreements with service providers. The staff of this department comprised mainly ex-senior case managers from within the Ferris Secure Institution who held their own personal opinions about the NCIA cohort members. Their new responsibilities were the management of contracts as opposed to the youths themselves. Undue difficulties were experienced at this stage of the experiment due to this dynamic.[53] Even after the experiment had run its

---

50   'A child who has been placed in by the competent authorities for the purpose of care, protection, or treatment of his or her physical or mental health, to periodic review of the treatment provided to the child and all other circumstances relevant to his or her placement' (Art 25).

51   Miller 1990:154.

52   (1969) *Boston Herald*, 20 September.

53   The three individual contract managers under the supervision of a co-ordinator found it difficult to distance themselves from their earlier job description: supervision of case managers at Ferris (charged with placing youth in the community). They attempted to supervise NCIA placement decisions. This resulted in delays and attempts to frustrate placement of the NCIA cohort. The underlying issue may have been that they resented outsiders coming in to place youth, an operation which they had previously supervised, and perhaps resented having to serve NCIA case managers in a contractual capacity.

course, the challenge remained for the State of Delaware to revive the spirit of innovation and the willingness to work with youths with difficult behavioural problems.

Serious offenders and placements in the community

The Delaware experiment appears to illustrate that the rationale behind decisions to exclude serious offenders from community based sanctions are flawed. Serious offenders appear to be as capable of complying with court restitution orders in community based placements as offenders with a shorter or less serious offending history and they appear able to draw on the rehabilitative benefits of it with no greater risk of offending (Umbriet 1989; Dunkel 1990; Weitekamp 1992; De Martelaere *et al* 1985; and Peeters 1985). Furthermore, it appears that the other experiments to date have tended to be overly cautious, focusing on low risk cases. This was not the case with the Delaware experiment.

Due process

Prior to NCIA involvement in Delaware, little attention was paid to whether the youth actually committed the offence for which he or she had received their current sanction.[54] All too often, the parents and youth accepted plea bargains in the absence of a lawyer or in the presence of a young inexperienced lawyer allocated at the eleventh hour with little time for preparation. In the event of an arrest of one of the cohort, the NCIA tracker ensured proper legal representation. The benefits of this practice were evident from the fact that 15 of the 33 arrest charges against the NCIA cohort were ultimately dropped. This suggests that the juvenile defence advocacy aspect of the experiment was particularly effective in negotiating with arresting officers to drop charges.

---

54 Every child alleged or accused of having infringed the penal law has at least the following guarantees:

(i) to be presumed innocent until proven guilty according to the law;

(iii) ... and to have the matter determined ... in the presence of legal or other appropriate assistance ...

The Beijing Rules expand on the right to legal assistance (r 15(1)). Throughout the legal proceedings, the juvenile shall have the right to be represented by a legal adviser or to apply for free legal aid, where there is provision for such aid in the country.

The existence of alternative sanctions and their effects on sentencing practice

A substantial number of youths would not have received services or have been placed under supervision by the court had these programmes not existed. The NCIA cohort, prior to the Krisberg and De Muro 1987 risk assessment, had all been determined appropriate for institutional placement because they had previously failed in community based placements available to DYRS. NCIA encountered initial problems with service providers as evaluations conducted independently by the NCIA cohort differed from State evaluations. A 1983 study of the classification of delinquents came to a similar conclusion: the less resources were available, the more a punishment orientated option was viewed as beneficial for the youth.[55] When the person making the diagnosis was aware of the spectrum of treatment alternatives, the diagnosis was less restrictive. Left with only the choice to institutionalise, institutionalisation would result. The experiment appears to illustrate that diagnosis virtually never determines treatment; rather, available treatment dictates diagnosis.

The development of more flexible sentencing options

The project appeared to encourage the creation of a new range of alternative sanctions for youths in the State of Delaware. New contracts were negotiated between the State and service providers, thus expanding the continuum of alternative placements for Ferris Secure Institution case managers. Moreover, new contracts were negotiated with service providers such as VisionQuest and Rebound in Colorado, projects which treat serious and chronic offenders.

On a community level, NCIA was also proactive in strengthening, where they existed, a wide range of flexible community based support measures for young persons, including after school programmes, development centres and recreational facilities to respond to the needs of the youths it placed in the community.[56]

Promotion and accountability

The dissemination of information about the project, the methodological approach adopted and the general promotion of an alternative sanctions approach were important aims of the experiment. This educational aspect of

---

55 Mulvey 1983.
56 The State of Delaware thereby addressed obligations under the Riyadh Guidelines, paras 33, 34 and 38.

the scheme was of primary importance for the caseworkers who would resume responsibility for the youth after the experiment. To this end, formal training sessions were held throughout currency of the project.[57] Building support in the Delaware community for the experiment was an underlying function of the project. The Delaware NCIA director addressed State officials, community groups and NGOs and regularly presented to local media on the CSP and alternative sanctions approach. This was particularly effective due to the small size of the State of Delaware. The importance of ongoing education and training, albeit formally or informally, of personnel, judges and other administration justice officials in international standards of juvenile justice cannot be understated.

No net widening occurred with the NCIA cohort

All disposal decisions deemed appropriate by the risk assessment instrument resulted in less restrictive placements being imposed. While the cohort for the Delaware experiment was well targeted, it was apparent from the review of all the Delaware cases that net widening had occurred in the past.

Lower cost of alternative sanctions

The growing fiscal crisis in public spending in the US dictates that the use of community based alternatives to institutionalisation will continue.[58] While the Delaware experiment was cost effective, budgets from the institution were not transferred to the alternative programmes in proportion to youth leaving the Ferris Secure Institution. In essence, the dollar amount of the cost of keeping a youth incarcerated in a secure facility was transferred to a community based community programme, thereby hindering the potential effectiveness of community based programmes.

Labelling

Prior to the De Muro and Krisberg 1987 report, the NCIA cohort had all been labelled as appropriate for incarceration, principally because they were

---

57 An attempt was made by the DYRS to set up a ghost NCIA team which used the CSP model. But it did not have the aftercare component and eventually the State reverted to its old system of case management. In order to succeed, the system must embrace the change: placement of youths must occur directly from the court in order that youths do not languish in the facility pending placement.

58 In the UK, the average custodial sanction was just 4.4 months. Nor are they cost effective: £311–£375 stg to hold a youth in custody (Home Office 1990c:110) compared with the costs of alternative sanctions such as intermediate treatment at £700 stg for each juvenile's complete placement (NACRO 1991:10).

difficult to manage and place in the community. Professional gain can arguably be achieved by defining young offenders as more delinquent than the facts warrant.[59] However, the State of Delaware, in hiring an independent agency such as NCIA, assisted this 'labelled' group of juveniles in re-establishing themselves in society, in the knowledge that the cumulative system prejudice would not follow them into the community to the same degree during this experiment.

Political will

This experiment did not take place in a de-politicised, managerial or technical realm, but was contingent upon broader political agendas and priorities such as the ACLU law suit. This experiment took place at a time in Delaware when progressive elements were present in the State. However, throughout the experiment, it was prey to knee-jerk and reactionary overhaul. The politics of the family court in Delaware was one such illustration.

According to the politics of the family court, political support is key to bringing about systemic change. There was an unusual tension between DYRS and the family court. The tension arose due to the frustration felt on the part of family court judges regarding their inability to control placements of youth. Following their adjudication by the family court, judges were only empowered to commit youth to the Ferris Secure Institution for a mandatory period of six months for certain felony offences. All other commitments were to DYRS for 'appropriate placement'. In practice, youths often languished at the Ferris Secure Institution for long periods prior to placement. In essence, the judges had the power to recommend a placement, but DYRS controlled the dispositions with an eye to their budget. The relationship reached a historic low point during the 1980–89 administration. The department was found in contempt of court for failure to place a youth at the alternative Glenn Mills Program. The charge was somewhat dubious but served to demonstrate the factions that exist within the juvenile justice system. The NCIA project was an initiative of DYRS, who also funded it, and was accordingly regarded with suspicion by the family court. Additionally, no family court judge had been appointed to sit on the working committee which had alienated them at the beginning of the process. Ten of the NCIA youth were committed on a mandatory basis. The family court therefore had jurisdiction and veto power over each NCIA client specific plan. Availability of alternatives determines diagnosis.

---

59 'If the patient improves, it can be attributed to the therapist's skill and treatment. If, on the other hand, the patient deteriorates, the therapist looks even more sophisticated, having predicted it all along. In this world, it is to no one's advantage to de-stigmatise labels, except those who are labelled. The process by which we label delinquents is more crucial than the label' (Miller 1990:194).

In the UK, central to the success of the Kirklees Tracking Project and other intermediate treatment initiatives was the involvement on the management committees of representatives of community agencies including the juvenile judges. The key to success was an effective local strategy involving an inter-agency approach subject to scrutiny and review.[60]

CONCLUSION

The Delaware Juvenile Advocacy Project stands as a small contribution to the alternative treatment and education programmes that are at the heart of the juvenile justice system in this era of 'getting tough' on youth crime. The need to combat the propensity of politicians to sacrifice innovation in juvenile justice to short term political popularity needs to remain central to any juvenile justice debate. In the UK, the introduction of the Crime and Disorder Act 1998 and the Youth Justice and Criminal Evidence Act 1999 has arguably continued the previous Conservative Government's commitment to a bifurcated approach to youth justice. This is leading to a focus upon punishment orientated sanctions for young offenders categorised as 'persistent' or as having committed a 'serious' offence. For such young people, the principle of welfare seems to have been lost.

With this in mind, programmes such as the Delaware experiment should be repeated, in the US and in Europe, particularly in the current climate, as they provide a humane alternative to incarceration for some young law breakers and may assist in helping them avoid falling deeper into a life of crime. Research in both the US and the UK clearly indicates that, for most young people, prison doesn't work. The reasons why projects like the Delaware experiment should be encouraged include:

- the recidivism rate for youth released from secure facilities is high;
- few programmes have been effective in reducing the recidivism of particular types of high risk youth;
- considerable evidence has suggested that projects such as the Delaware experiment are successful;
- the large majority of offenders in such experiments completed their orders successfully and with decreased levels of re-offending (and, when re-offending occurred, it was for less serious offences).[61]

The Delaware experiment will take its place in juvenile justice history as having adopted a youth orientated approach that recognises the young person

---

60 NACRO 1991:49.
61 Curtis 1989; NACRO 1991:52.

as a subject possessing fundamental rights and freedoms and stresses the need for all actions concerning youth to be guided by the best interests principal.[62] The importance of education and training, either formal or informal, of personnel, judges and other justice officials in international standards of juvenile justice cannot be understated.

Finally, the project enhanced humaneness and equity by reducing the use of secure confinement. We will continue to betray large numbers of young people unless custodial sentences are imposed only as a last resort, where no alternative way of protecting the public exists. The NCIA cohort of youths were all, without exception, the products of severely dysfunctional families known to social services for some time. For such young people, sensitive and supportive intervention is necessary because, as the UN Committee on the Rights of the Child has noted, 'unless the chain is broken, there is reduced hope for the individual child, let alone the rest of the family and future generations'.[63] It appears to be a wasted opportunity to treat the young person by placing him or her in a programme where the family has little or no input. We know full well that we shall never achieve an ideal society, but we must go on trying, otherwise, as Waldgrave 1995 has argued, the one we have may rapidly disintegrate.

---

62 This approach was recommended during a discussion on juvenile justice administration at the ninth session of the Committee on the Rights of the Child May–June 1995 (CRC/C43).

63 McKenzie 1982.

BIBLIOGRAPHY

ACPO (1998) *Reducing Anti-Social and Criminal Behaviour Amongst Young People*, London: Association of Chief Police Officers

Adamski, W and Grootings, P (eds) (1989) *Youth, Education and Work in Europe*, London: Routledge

Adler, R (1985) *Taking Juvenile Justice Seriously*, Edinburgh: Scottish Academic

Aichhorn, A (1925) (rep 1955) *Wayward Youth*, New York: Meridian

Ainley, P (1991) *Young People Leaving Home*, London: Cassell

Ainley, P (1994) *Degrees of Difference*, London: Lawrence & Wishart

Ainley, P (1999) *Learning Policy – Towards the Certificated Society*, Basingstoke: Macmillan

Ainley, P and Bailey, W (1997) *The Business of Learning*, London: Cassell

Ainley, P and Corney, M (1990) *Training for the Future*, London: Cassell

Ainley, P and Rainbird, H (eds) (1999) *Apprenticeship: Towards a New Paradigm of Learning*, London: Sage

Alford, F (1989) *Melanie Klein and Critical Social Theory*, New Haven: Yale UP

Allen, R (1996) *Children and Crime: Taking Responsibility*, London: Institute of Public Policy Research

Allen, R (1997) 'The age of innocence', 27 Criminal Justice Matters 17

Allen-Hagen, B (1988) *Children in Custody 1987*, Washington DC: Office of Juvenile Justice and Delinquency Prevention

Amnesty International (1998) 'Betraying the young: children in the US justice system', AMR 51/60/98

Amnesty International (October 1998) 'On the wrong side of history: children and the death penalty in the USA', AMR 51/58/98

Anderson, M (1983) *The Family*, Occasional Paper 31, London: OPCS

Andrews, D *et al* (1990) 'Does correctional treatment work? A clinically relevant and psychologically informed meta-analysis', 28(3) Criminology 369

Ariès, P (1973) *Centuries of Childhood*, Harmondsworth: Penguin

Aristotle (1962) *The Politics*, Sinclair, TA (trans), Harmondsworth: Penguin

Armstrong, G (1993) 'Like that Desmond Morris?', in Hobbs, D and May, T (eds), *Interpreting the Field: Accounts of Ethnography*, Oxford: OUP

Armstrong, G and Harris, R (1991) 'Football hooliganism: theory and evidence', Sociological Review, August

Aronowitz, A and DiFazio, W (1994) *The Jobless Future: Sci-tech and the Dogma of Work*, Minnesota: Minnesota UP

Ashworth, A (1994) 'Abolishing the presumption of incapacity: *C v DPP*', 6(4) Journal of Child Law 174

Ashworth, A and Hough, M (1996) 'Sentencing and the climate of opinion', Crim LR 776

Asquith, A, Buist, M, Loughran, N, Macauly, C and Montgomery, M (1998) *Children, Young People and Offending in Scotland: A Research Review*, Edinburgh: The Scottish Office Central Research Unit

Atkinson, J (1995) 'Review: Restorative justice: healing the effects of crime by Jim Consedine', 3(77) Aboriginal Law Bulletin 21

Audit Commission (1996) *Misspent Youth: Young People and Crime*, London: HMSO

Audit Commission (1998) *Better By Far: Preparing for Best Value*, London: HMSO

Automated Services Branch (1988) *Parole Performance Follow-up for the 1985 Releases to Parole*, Sacramento, CA: California Youth Authority

Awiah, J, Butt, S and Dorn, N (1992) 'Race, gender and drug services', ISDD Research Monograph No 6, London: ISDD

Back, L (1997) *New Ethnicities and Urban Youth Culture*, London: UCL

Back, L, Cohen, P and Keith, M (1999) *Finding the Way Home – First Takes*, 2 CNER/CUCR Working Paper

Bailey, V (1987) *Delinquency and Citizenship: Reclaiming the Young Offender 1914–1948*, Oxford: Clarendon

Baird, C (1987) *The Development of Risk Prediction Scales for the California Youthful Offender Parole Board*, San Francisco, CA: NCCD

Baker, JH (1990) *An Introduction to English Legal History*, 3rd edn, London: Butterworths

Bala, N (1994) 'Responding to criminal behaviour of children under 12: an analysis of Canadian law and practice', ONLINE: http://qsilver.queenssu.ca/law/bala/under12.htm

Ball, C, McCormack, K and Stone, N (1995) *Young Offenders: Law, Policy and Practice*, London: Sweet & Maxwell

Bandalli, S (1998) 'Abolition of the presumption of *doli incapax* and the criminalisation of children', 37(2) Howard Journal of Criminal Justice 114

Banks, M, Bates, I and Breakwell, G (1991) *Careers and Identities*, Milton Keynes: OUP

Barone, C, Weissberg, RP, Kasprow, J and Voyce, CK (1995) 'Involvement in multiple problem behaviours of young urban adolescents', 15 Journal of Primary Prevention 261

Barnes, M and Prior, D (1995) 'Spoilt for choice? How consumerism can disempower public service users', Public Money and Management, July–September, p 53

Barnes, HE and Teeters, NK (1951) *New Horizons in Criminology*, 2nd edn, New Jersey: Prentice Hall

Bates, I and Riseborough, G (1993) *Youth and Inequalities*, Milton Keynes: OUP

Baudrillard, J (1981) *For a Critique of the Political Economy of the Sign*, St Louis: Telos

Baudrillard, J (1983) *Simulations*, New York: Semiotext(e)

Baudrillard, J (1996) *The System of Objects*, London: Verso

Bauman, Z (1987) *Legislators and Interpreters*, Cambridge: Polity

Bauman, Z (1992) *Intimations of Post-modernity*, New York: Routledge

Bauman, Z (1997) *Post-modernity and its Discontents*, Cambridge. Polity

BBC Documentary (1998) *Children of Crime*, episode 1

Beck, U (1992) *Risk Society: Towards a New Modernity*, London: Sage

Beck, U, Giddens, A and Scott-Lash, J (1994) *Reflexive Modernisation*, Cambridge: Polity

Becker, H (1963) *The Outsiders: Studies in the Sociology of Deviance*, New York: Free Press

Belson, WA (1975) *Juvenile Theft: The Causal Factors*, London: Harper & Row

Benedict, R (1946) *The Chrysanthemum and the Sword: Patterns of Japanese Culture*, Boston: Houghton Mifflin

Bennett, T (1997) 'Out in the open – reflections on the history and practice of cultural studies', 10(1) Cultural Studies 1

Berridge, V (1999) *Opium and the People: Opiate Use and Drug Control Policy in Early 20th Century England*, 3rd edn, London: Free Association

Bingham LCJ (1997) 'Justice for the young', *Annual Lecture: The Prison Reform Trust*, London: Prison Reform Trust

Black, R (ed) (1987) *The Stair Memorial Encyclopedia of the Laws of Scotland*, Edinburgh: Bowker

Blackman, S (1995) *Youth, Positions and Oppositions*, Aldershot: Avebury

Blagg, H (1997) 'A just measure of shame? Aboriginal youth and conferencing in Australia', 37(4) Br J Crim 481

Blom-Cooper, L (1988) 'The penalty of imprisonment', from the Tanner Lectures, 30 November–2 December 1987

Bloomberg, TG (1983) 'Diversions, disparate results and unsolved questions: an integrative evaluation perspective', 20 Journal Research in Crime and Delinquency 24

Blumenburg, H (1983) *The Legitimacy of the Modern Age*, Wallace, RM (trans), Cambridge, Mass: MIT

Boateng, P (1998) 'Foreword', in Rutter, M, Giller, H and Hagell, A, *Anti-Social Behaviour by Young People*, Cambridge: CUP

Boateng, P (1999) paper delivered at Youth Court 2000: Implementing the Youth Justice and Criminal Evidence Act 1999, 6 July

Boethius, U (1995) 'Youth, the media and moral panics', in Forns, J and Bolin, G (eds), *Youth Culture in Late Modernity*, London: Sage

Bottoms, AE (1995) 'The philosophy and politics of sentencing', in Clarkson, CMV and Morgan, R (eds), *The Politics of Sentencing Reform*, Oxford: OUP

Bowlby, J (1946) *Forty-Four Juvenile Thieves*, London: Bailliére, Tindall & Cox

Braithwaite, J (1989) *Crime, Shame and Reintegration*, Cambridge: CUP

Braithwaite, J (1992) 'Reducing the crime problem: a not so dismal criminology', 25(1) Australian and New Zealand Journal of Criminology 1

Braithwaite, J (1993) 'Shame and modernity', 33(1) Br J Crim 1

Braithwaite, J (1996) 'Restorative justice and a better future', ONLINE, www.realjustice.org//braithwaite (30 March 1998), pp 1–13

Braithwaite, J and Mugford, J (1994) 'Conditions for successful reintegration ceremonies', 32 Br J Crim 139

Brake, M (1986) *Sociology of Youth*, London: Routledge

Brake, M (1990) 'Changing leisure and cultural patterns among British youth', in Chisholm, L, Büchner, P, Kruger, HH and Brown, P (eds), *Childhood, Youth and Social Change*, London: Falmer

Brodie, I (1996) 'School exclusion', 5 Fast Forward, winter, pp 6–7

Brownlie, I (1992) *Basic Documents on Human Rights*, 3rd edn, Oxford: Clarendon

Bruce, N (1985) 'Juvenile justice in Scotland: an historical perspective', unpublished paper presented to Franco-British Workshop, Edinburgh

Bruvold, WH (1993) 'A meta-analysis of adolescent smoking prevention programmes', 83 American Journal of Public Health 872

Bruvold, WH and Rundall, TG (1988) 'A meta-analysis and theoretical review of school based tobacco and alcohol intervention programmes', 2 Psychology and Health 53

Buckingham, D (ed) (1998) *Teaching Popular Culture*, London: Taylor & Francis

Burt, C (1925) *The Young Delinquent*, London: London UP

Bynner, J (ed) (1998) *Youth, Citizenship and Social Change*, Dartmouth: Ashgate

Campbell, A (1981) *Girl Delinquents*, London: Basil Blackwell

Campbell, C (1989) *The Romantic Ethic and the Spirit of Modern Consumerism*, London: Basil Blackwell

Cantwell, N (January 1998) 'Nothing more than justice', *Juvenile Justice Information Portfolio*, 3 Innocenti Digest

Carpenter, M (1953) *Juvenile Delinquents, Their Condition and Treatment*, London: Cash

Cavadino, P (1996) 'A case for change', in *Children Who Kill*, Winchester: Waterside

Cavadino, P (1997) 'Goodbye *doli*, must we leave you?', 9(2) CFLQ 165

Christie, N (1976) 'Conflicts as property', 17(1) Br J Crim 1

Clarke, J (1975) *The Three Rs – Repression, Rescue and Rehabilitation*, Birmingham: CCCS

Clarke, J and Newman, J (1997) *The Managerial State: Power, Politics and Ideology in the Re-making of Social Welfare*, London: Sage

Clelland, A (1995) *A Guide to the Children (Scotland) Act 1995*, Glasgow: Scottish Child Law Centre

Cloward, R and Ohlin, L (1961) *Delinquency and Opportunity: A Theory of Delinquent Gangs*, London: Routledge

Coates, RB, Miller, AD and Ohlin, LE (1978) *Diversity in a Youth Correctional System: Handling Delinquents in Massachusetts*, Cambridge, Mass: Bollinger

Cockburn, C (1987) *Two Track Training*, Basingstoke: Macmillan

Cohen, A (1955) *Delinquent Boys: The Culture of the Gang*, New York: Free Press

Cohen, J (1996) 'Drug education: politics, propaganda and censorship', 7 International Journal of Drug Policy 153

Cohen, P (1997a) *Rethinking the Youth Question*, Basingstoke: Macmillan

Cohen, P (1997b) 'Labouring under whiteness', in Frankenberg, R (ed), *Dislocating Whiteness*, Duke

Cohen, P (1999a) 'In visible cities', 3(1) Community Plural 284

Cohen, P (1999b) 'Apprenticeship *a la mode*', in Ainley, P and Rainbird, H (eds), *Apprenticeship: Towards a New Paradigm of Learning*, London: Sage

Cohen, S (ed) (1971) *Images of Deviance*, Harmondsworth: Penguin

Cohen, S (1972) *Folk Devils and Moral Panics: The Creation of the Mods and Rockers*, Oxford: Martin Robertson

Cohen, S (1973) *Folk Devils and Moral Panics*, St Albans: Paladin

Cohen, S (1985) *Visions of Social Control*, Cambridge: Polity

Committee Report on the Ninth Session, May–June 1995, CRC/C/43, Annex VIII, p 64

Committee on the Rights of the Child: UK and Northern Ireland, Annual Report, CRC/C/11/Add 17

Cooper, D (1995) 'Habit forming questions', 91(44) Nursing Times 36

Cornwell, A and Cornwall, V (1993) *Drugs, Alcohol and Mental Health*, 2nd edn, Cambridge: CUP

Cowperthwaite, DJ (1988) *The Emergence of the Scottish Children's Hearings System*, University of Southampton: Institute of Criminal Justice

Crofts, T (1998) 'Rebutting the principle of *doli incapax*', 62(2) JCL 185

Crown Prosecution Service (1997) *Annual Report*, HC 68, London: HMSO

Cumes, G (1997) 'Out of the court and into the conference', 35(1) Law Institute J 60

Curran, JH (1977) *The Children's Hearing System: A Review of Research*, Edinburgh: Scottish Office Central Research Unit

Curtis, S (1989) *Juvenile Offending: Prevention through Intermediate Treatment*, London: Batsford

Davidson, W *et al* (1990) *Alternative Treatments for Troubled Youth*, London: Plenum

Davis, J (1990) *Youth and the Condition of Britain*, London: Athlone

Davis, M and Bourhill, M (1991) '"Crisis": the demonisation of children and young people', in Stenson, K and Cowell, D (eds), *The Politics of Crime Control*, London: Sage

Deakin, B (1996) *The Youth Labour Market in Britain*, Cambridge: CUP

Dearing, R (Sir) (1993) *First Review of the National Curriculum and its Assessment*, London: NFER

Deleuze, G and Guattari, F (1977) *Anti-Oedipus: Capitalism and Schizophrenia*, London: Athlone

De Martelaere, A, Greenwood, P, Zimring, FE (1985) *One More Chance: The Pursuit of Promising Intervention Strategies for Chronic Juvenile Offenders*, Santa Monica, CA: Rand

De Muro, P and Krisberg, B (1987) *Adjudicated Youth in Delaware Who Need Secure Care*, San Francisco, CA: NCCD

DETR (1998) *Modern Local Government: In Touch with the People*, Cm 4013, London: HMSO

Donajgrodzki, A (ed) (1975) *Social Control in 19th Century Britain*, London: Croom Helm

Donaldson, R (1995) 'Mischief or malice?', Police Review, 24 March, p 16

Donzelot, J (1979) *The Policing of Families*, London: Hutchinson

Douglas, M (1970) *Purity and Danger*, Harmondsworth: Penguin

Douglas, M and Isherwood, B (1980) *The World of Goods*, Harmondsworth: Penguin

Dunbar, I and Langdon, A (1998) *Tough Justice: Sentencing and Penal Policies in the 1990s*, London: Blackstone

Dunkel, F (1991) 'Legal differences in juvenile criminology in Europe', in Booth, T (ed), *Juvenile Justice in the New Europe*, University of Sheffield: Joint Unit for Social Services Research

Dunkel, F (1990) 'Médiation déliquant-victime et reparation des dommages: nouvelle évolution du droit pénal et de la pratique judiciare dans une comparison internationale', in Dunkel, F and Zermatten, J (eds), *Nouvelles Tendances dans le Droit Pénal des Mineurs*

Duquette, D (1994) 'Scottish children's hearings and representation for the child', in Asquith, S and Hill, M (eds), *Justice For Children*, Dordrecht: Martinus Nijhoff

Dwyer, P and Wyn, J (1998) 'Post-compulsory education', 13(3) Journal of Educational Policy 256

Elias, N (1978) *The Civilizing Process: The History of Manners*, Vol 1, London: Basil Blackwell

Elias, N (1982) *The Civilizing Process: State Formation and Civilisation*, Vol 2, London: Basil Blackwell

Elliot, DS, Dunford, FW and Knowles, P (1978) *Diversion: A Study of Alternative Processing*, Boulder, CO: Behavioral Research Institute

Empey, LT (1982) *American Delinquency: Its Meaning and Construction*, Dorsey, IL: Wadsworth

Engels, F (1958) *The Condition of the Working Class in England*, Henderson, WO and Chaloner, WH (trans), New York: Macmillan

Evans, RI (1976) 'Smoking in children: developing a social psychological strategy of deterrence', 5 Preventive Medicine 122

Evans, R (1994) 'Making amends: victim-offender reconciliation', 68(6) Law Institute Journal 469

Evans, RI, Rozelle, RM, Mittelmark, MB, Hansen, WB, Bane, AL and Havis, J (1978) 'Determining the onset of smoking in children: knowledge of immediate physiological effects and coping with peer pressure, media pressure and parent modelling', 8 Journal of Applied Social Psychology 126

Ezell, M (1992) 'Juvenile diversion: the ongoing search for alternatives', in Schwartz, IM (ed), *Juvenile Justice and Public Policy*, London: Lexington, p 45

Farrington, D (1992) 'Juvenile delinquency', in Coleman, J (ed), *The School Years*, London: Routledge

Farrington, D (1997) *Understanding and Preventing Youth Crime*, York: Joseph Rowntree Foundation

Farrington, D (1997) 'Human development and criminal careers', in Maguire, M, Morgan, R and Reiner, R (eds), *The Oxford Handbook of Criminology*, 2nd edn, Oxford: OUP

Farrington, D and West, D (1990) 'The Cambridge study in delinquent development: a long term follow up of 411 London males', in Kerner, H and Kaiser, G (eds), *Criminality: Personality, Behaviour, Life History*, New York: Springer-Verlag

Featherstone, M (1991) *Consumer Culture and Post-modernism*, London: Sage

Feeley, MM and Simon, J (1992) '"The new penology": notes on the emerging strategy of corrections and its implications', 30 Criminology 449

Ferrell, J (1995) 'Urban graffiti: crime, control and resistance', 27 Youth and Society 73

Ferrell, J and Sanders, CR (1995) *Cultural Criminology*, Boston: Northeastern UP

Finlayson, A (1992) *Reporters to Children's Panels: Their Role, Function and Accountability*, Edinburgh: Scottish Office

Finn, D (1987) *Training Without Jobs*, Basingstoke: Macmillan

Fionda, J (1998) '*R v Secretary of State for the Home Department ex p Venables and Thompson*: the age of innocence? The concept of childhood in the punishment of young offenders', 10(1) CFLQ 77

Fionda, J (1999) 'New Labour, old hat: youth justice and the Crime and Disorder Act 1998', Crim LR 36

Fishman, M (1981) 'Crime waves as ideology', in Cohen, S (ed), *The Manufacture of the News*, 2nd edn, London: Constable

Fornas, J (1995) *Youth Culture in Late Modernity*, London: Sage

Fottrell, D (1999) 'Children's rights', in Hegarty, A and Leonard, S (eds), *Human Rights: An Agenda for the 21st Century*, London: Cavendish Publishing

Fottrell, D (2000) 'Assessing the impact of the children's convention', in *Revisiting Children's Rights: Ten Years of the Convention on the Rights of the Child*, Nijhoff: Dordrecht

Foucault, M (1977) *Discipline and Punish*, London: Allen Lane

Fox, L (1952) *The English Prison and Borstal Systems*, London: Routledge

Fox, S, 'Juvenile justice reform: an historical perspective', 22(6) Stanford Law Review 1

Frankenberg, R (ed) (1997) *Dislocating Whiteness*, Chicago: Chicago UP

Franklin, B and Petley, J (1996) 'Killing the age of innocence: newspaper reporting of the death of James Bulger', in Pilcher, J and Wagg, S (eds), *Thatcher's Children: Politics, Childhood and Society in the 1980s and 1990s*, London: Falmer

Freeman, M (1997) 'The James Bulger tragedy: childish innocence and the construction of guilt', in McGillivray, A (ed), *Governing Childhood*, Aldershot: Dartmouth

Frith, S (1983) *Sound Effects*, London: Constable

Frith, S (1996) *Performing Rites*, Oxford: OUP

Furby, L and Beyth-Marom, R (1992) 'Risk taking in adolescence: a decision making perspective', 12 Developmental Review 1

Furlong, A (1993) *Growing up in a Classless Society?*, Edinburgh: Edinburgh UP

Furlong, A and Cartmel, F (1997) *Young People and Social Change*, Buckingham: OU Press

Fuss, D (1989) *Essentially Speaking: Feminism, Nature and Difference*, London: Routledge

Gardner, JP (1997) *Human Rights as General Norms and a State's Right to Opt Out*, London: BIICL

Garland, D (1985) *Punishment and Welfare: A History of Penal Strategies*, Aldershot: Gower

Gelsthorpe, L and Morris, A (1994) 'Juvenile justice 1945–92', in Maguire, M, Morgan, R and Reiner, R (eds), *The Oxford Handbook of Criminology*, Oxford: Clarendon

George, M (1996) 'Practice focus: drugs – meeting the challenge', 8 Community Care 8

Gibson, B, Cavadino, P, Rutherford, A and Harding, J (1994) *The Youth Court: One Year Onwards*, Winchester: Waterside

Gilling, D (1994) 'Multi-agency crime prevention: some barriers to collaboration', 33 Howard Journal of Criminal Justice

Gillis, JR (1975) *Youth and History*, London: Academic

Gilroy, P (1987) *There Ain't No Black in the Union Jack*, London: Hutchinson

Gilvarry, E (1998) 'Young drug users: early intervention', 5 Drugs: Education, Prevention and Policy 281

Giroux, H (1996) *Fugitive Cultures*, London: Routledge

Giulianotti, R (1989) 'A participant-observation study of Aberdeen fans at home and away', *Working Paper No 2 on Football Violence*, Aberdeen: University of Aberdeen

Goddard, H (1927) *The Kallikak Family: A Study in the Heredity of Feeble-Mindedness*, London: Macmillan

Goldblath, P and Lewis, C (1998) 'Reducing offending – an assessment of research evidence on ways of dealing with offending behaviour', Home Office Research Study 187, London: HMSO

Goldson, B (1999) 'Punishing times for children in trouble: recent policy developments and the Crime and Disorder Act 1998', 11(4) Representing Children 274

Goodstein, L and Sontheimer, H (1987) *A Study of the Impact of 10 Pennsylvania Residential Placements on Juvenile Recidivism*, Shippensburg, PA: Center for Juvenile Justice Training and Research

Gottfredson, M and Hirshci, T (1990) *A General Theory of Crime*, Stanford, CA: Stanford UP

Graham, J and Bowling, B (1995) *Young People and Crime*, London: HMSO

Green, A (1996) 'Do police have a role in education?', 11(2) Druglink 19

Griffin, C (1985) *Typical Girls?*, London: Routledge

Grossberg, L (1997) *Bringing It All Back Home*, Chicago: Chicago UP

Hagan, J and Leon, J 'Rediscovering delinquency: social history, political ideology and the sociology of law', 42 American Sociological Review 1

Hagedorn, J (1988) *People and Folks: Gangs, Crime and the Underclass in a Rustbelt City*, Chicago: Lake View

Hagell, A and Newburn, T (1994) *Persistent Young Offenders*, London: Policy Studies Institute

Hall, GS (1905) *Adolescence, Its Psychology and Its Relations to Physiology, Anthropology, Sociology, Sex, Crime, Religion and Education*, New York: Appleton

Hall, S (1974) 'Deviance, politics and the media', in Rock, P and McIntosh, M (eds), *Deviance and Social Control*, London: Tavistock

Hall, S (1992) 'Cultural studies and its theoretical legacies', in Grossberg, L (1997) *Bringing It All Back Home*, Chicago: Chicago UP

Hall, S and Jefferson, T (eds) (1976) *Resistance Through Rituals: Youth Subcultures in Post-War Britain*, London: Hutchinson

Hall, S and Scraton, P (1981) 'Law, class and control', in Fitzgerald, M, McLennan, G and Pawson, J (eds), *Crime and Society*, London: Routledge

Hall, S, Critcher, C, Jefferson, T, Clarke, J and Roberts, B (1978) *Policing the Crisis: Mugging, the State and Law and Order*, London: Macmillan

Hall, S, Critcher, C, Jefferson, T, Clarke, J and Roberts, B (1981) 'The social production of news: mugging in the media', in Cohen, S (ed), *The Manufacture of the News*, 2nd edn, London: Constable

Hallett, C, Murray, C, Jamieson, J and Veitch, B (1998) *The Evaluation of Children's Hearings in Scotland: Deciding in Children's Best Interest*, Vol 1, Edinburgh: Scottish Office Central Research Unit

Harden, I (1992) *The Contracting State*, Milton Keynes: OU Press

Harris, S (1998) 'Bash victim's legacy of fear', *The Sunday Telegraph*, 14 June

Harris, R and Webb, D (1987) *Welfare, Power and Juvenile Justice: The Social Control of Delinquent Youth*, London: Tavistock

Harvey, D (1989) *The Condition of Post-modernity*, London: Basil Blackwell

Hay, D (1975) 'Property, authority and the criminal law', in Hay, D, Linebaugh, P, Rule, JG, Thompson, EP and Winslow, C, *Albion's Fatal Tree*, London: Allen Lane

Hazenkamp, J, Meeus, W and Poel, YT (ed) (1988) *European Contributions to Youth Research*, Amsterdam: Free UP

Hebdige, D (1981) *The Meaning of Subculture*, London: Methuen

Hebdige, D (1984) *Hiding in the Light*, London: Comedia

Hebdige, D (1988) *Hiding in the Light*, London: Routledge

Henry, S and Milovanovic, D (1996) *Constitutive Criminology: Beyond Post-modernism*, London: Sage

Hewitt, R (1981) *White Talk, Black Talk*, Cambridge: CUP

Higgins, L (1977) 'Personality variables in relation to panel members' (PhD thesis, University of Glasgow), in Curran, JH *The Children's Hearing System: A Review of Research*, Edinburgh: Scottish Office Central Research Unit

Hirschi, T (1969) *Causes of Delinquency*, Berkeley: California UP

Hobbes, T (1991) *Leviathan*, Tuck, R (ed), Cambridge: CUP

Hodgkin, R and Newell, P (1998) *Implementation Handbook for the Convention on the Rights of the Child*, New York: UNICEF

Hollands, R (1990) *The Long Transition*, London: Macmillan

Home Office (1990b) *Crime, Justice and Protecting the Public: Three Governments' Proposals for Legislation*, Cm 965, London: HMSO

Home Office (1990c) *Prison Statistics in England and Wales 1989*, Cm 12210, London: HMSO

Home Office (1990d) *The Sentence of the Court: A Handbook for Courts on the Treatment of Offenders*, London: HMSO

Home Office (1991a) *Guide to the Criminal Justice Act 1991*, London: HMSO

Home Office (1991b) *Safer Communities: Report of the Morgan Inquiry*, London: HMSO

Home Office (1993) *Aspects of Crime: Young Offenders*, London: HMSO

Home Office (1997a) *Criminal Careers of those Born Between 1953 and 1973*, London: Home Office

Home Office (1997b) *Tackling Delays in Youth Justice*, London: HMSO

Home Office (1997c) *Tackling Youth Crime: Reforming Youth Justice*, Consultation Paper, London: HMSO

Home Office (1997d) *No More Excuses – A New Approach to Tackling Youth Crime in England and Wales*, Cm 3809, London: HMSO

Home Office (1998) *Youth Justice – The Statutory Principal Aim of Preventing Offending by Children and Young People*, London: Home Office

Home Office (1999) *Probation Statistics of England and Wales 1997*, London: Home Office

Home Office and Lord Chancellor's Department Circular (1998) *New Powers for Youth Court: No 47/1998*, London: LCD

Home Office, Department of Health and Welsh Office (1998) *National Standards for the Supervision of Offenders in the Community 1995*, London: Home Office

Home Office Juvenile Offenders Unit (1998) *Crime and Disorder Act 1998 – Implementing the Act, Delivering the Aim*, London: Home Office Juvenile Offenders Unit

Home Office Juvenile Offenders Unit (1999) *Referral Orders – A Short Guide*, London: Home Office Juvenile Offenders Unit

Home Office Statistics (1998) *Criminal Statistics of England and Wales 1997*, London: Stationery Office

hooks, b (1992) *Black Looks: Race and Representation*, Boston, MA: South End

Hope, T and Shaw, M (eds) (1988) *Communities and Crime Reduction*, London: HMSO

Horder, J (1993) 'Pleading involuntary lack of capacity', 52(2) CLJ 298

Hough, M and Roberts, J (1998) 'Attitudes to punishment: findings from the British Crime Survey', Home Office Research Study 179, London: Home Office

Hough, M (1996) 'Drug misuse and the criminal justice system: a review of the literature', Drugs Prevention Initiative Paper No 15, London: Central Drugs Prevention Unit

Howard, C (1982) *Criminal Law*, 4th edn, Sydney: LBC

Howard, J and Zibert, E (1990) 'Curious, bored and wanting to feel good: the drug use of detained young offenders', 9 Drug and Alcohol Review 225

Howard League (1995) *Child Offenders: UK and International Practice*, London: Howard League for Penal Reform

Howard League (1998) *Sentenced to Fail*, London: Howard League for Penal Reform

Howard League for Penal Reform (1999) *Protecting the Rights of Children*, Briefing Paper 5, London: Howard League for Penal Reform

Hudson, BA (1996) *Understanding Justice: An Introduction to Ideas, Perspectives and Controversies in Modern Penal Theory*, Milton Keynes: OUP

Hudson, J, Morris, A, Maxwell, G and Galaway, B (1996) *Family Group Conferences*, Annandale: Australia Federation

Hudson, R (1998) '*Doli incapax*', 148 NLJ 60

Huizinga, D, Loeber, R and Thornberry, T (1994) *Urban Delinquency and Substance Abuse*, Washington DC: Office of Juvenile and Delinquency Prevention, US Department of Justice

Human Rights Watch (1997) *Juvenile Injustice: Police Abuse and Detention of Street Children in Kenya*, New York: Human Rights Watch

Human Rights Watch (1999) *Nobody's Children: Jamaican Children in Police Detention and Government Institutions*, New York: Human Rights Watch

Humphries, S (1981) *Hooligans or Rebels?*, London: Basil Blackwell

Hunter, M (1999) 'Team spirit', Community Care, 23 June

Hutton, W (1996) *The State We're In*, London: Cape

Ingleby Committee (1960) *Report of the Committee on Children and Young Persons*, Cmnd 1191, London: HMSO

Inglis, B (1975) *The Forbidden Game*, London: Coronet

Inglis, B (1977) *A Social History of Drugs*, London: Coronet

Irwin, I (1996) *Rights of Passage*, London: UCL

ISDD (1994) *Drug Misuse in Britain*, London: ISDD

ISDD (1996) 'News section', Druglink, p 4

ISDD (1999) *Report on Policy, Action and Trends*, London: ISDD

Izzo, R and Ross, R (1990) 'Meta-analysis of rehabilitation programmes for juvenile delinquents', 17 Criminal Justice and Behaviour 134

James, A and Jenks, C (1996) 'Public perceptions of childhood criminality', 47(2) British Journal of Sociology 315

James, A and Prout, A (eds) (1990) *Constructing and Reconstructing Childhood: Contemporary Issues in the Sociological Study of Childhood*, London: Falmer

Jameson, F (1991) *Post-modernism*, London: Verso

Jefferson, T and Hall, S (1978) *Resistance Through Rituals*, London: Hutcheson

Jenks, C (1996) *Childhood*, London: Routledge

Jessor, R and Jessor, SL (1977) *Problem Behaviour and Psychosocial Development: A Longitudinal Study of Youth*, New York: Academic

Jessor, R, Van Den Bos, J, Vanderryn, J and Costa, M (1995) 'Protective factors in adolescent problem behaviour: moderator effects and developmental change', 31 Developmental Psychology 923

Johnson, CA, Pentz, MA, Weber, MD, Dwyer, JH, Baer, N, MacKinnon, DP, Hansen, WB and Flay, BR (1993) 'Relative effectiveness of comprehensive community programming for drug abuse prevention with high risk and low risk adolescents', 58 Journal of Clinical and Consulting Psychology 447

Johnstone, G (1997) 'From experts in responsibility to advisers on punishment: the role of psychiatrists in penal matters', in Rush, P *et al*, *Criminal Legal Doctrine*, Aldershot: Dartmouth

Johnstone, H (1995) 'Interface of the Children's Hearing System and the criminal justice system', unpublished MSc thesis, University of Edinburgh

Jones, G and Wallace, C (1992) *Youth, Family and Citizenship*, Milton Keynes: OUP

Jones, M (1996) 'Full steam ahead to a workfare State', 24(2) Policy and Politics 83

Katz, J (1988) *Seductions of Crime: Moral and Sensual Attractions of Doing Evil*, New York: Basic

Kearney, B (1987) *Children's Hearings and the Sheriff Court*, London: Butterworths

Keating, H (1996) 'The Law Commission Report on Involuntary Manslaughter: (1) the restoration of a serious crime', Crim LR 540

Keene, J and Williams, M (1996) 'Who DARES wins? Drug prevention and the police in schools', 11(2) Druglink 16

Keith, M and Cross, M (eds) (1993) *Racism, the City and the State*, London: Routledge

Kelly, A (1996) *Introduction to the Scottish Children's Hearing Panel*, Winchester: Waterside

Kelly, E (1997) 'Not just saying no: media education and drugs awareness', 37 English and Media Magazine 8

Kilbrandon Committee (1964) *Report of the Committee on Children and Young Persons*, Cmnd 3065, London: HMSO

Kilkelly, U (1999) *The Child and the European Convention on Human Rights*, Aldershot: Dartmouth

Kilkelly, U (2000) 'The impact of the children's convention on the case law of the European Convention on Human Rights', in Fottrell, D (ed), *Revisiting Children's Rights: Ten Years of the Convention on the Rights of the Child*, Nijhoff: Dordrecht

King, M (1981) *The Framework of Criminal Justice*, London: Croom Helm

King, M (1997) 'The James Bulger trial: good or bad for guilty or innocent children?', in *A Better World for Children: Explorations in Morality and Authority*, London: Routledge

Knell, BEF (1965) 'Capital punishment: its administration in relation to juvenile offenders in the 19th century and its possible administration in the 18th', 5 Br J Crim 198

Krisberg, B, Austin, J and Steele, P (1989) *Unlocking Juvenile Corrections*, San Francisco, CA: NCCD

Krisberg, B, Austin, J, Joe, K and Steele, P (1987) *The Impact of Juvenile Court Sanctions*, San Francisco, CA: NCCD

Labour Party (1996) 'Tackling youth crime: reforming youth justice: a consultation paper on an agenda for change', in *Road to the Manifesto*, London: Labour Party

Lacey, N (1995) 'Contingency and criminalisation', in Loveland, I (ed), *Frontiers of Criminality*, London: Sweet & Maxwell

Lacey, N (1997) 'Criminology, criminal law and criminalisation', in Maguire, M, Morgan, R and Reiner, R (eds), *The Oxford Handbook of Criminology*, 2nd edn, Oxford: OUP

Lasley, JR (1995) 'New writing on the wall: exploring the middle class graffiti sub-culture', 16(2) Deviant Behavior 151

Lave, J and Wenger, E (1991) *Informal Situated Learning*, Berkeley, CA: California UP

Laybourn, A (1986) 'Traditional strict working class parenting – an undervalued system', 16 British Journal of Social Work 625

LeBlanc, L (1995) *The Convention on the Rights of the Child: United Nations Law Making on Human Rights*, Lincoln: University of Nebraska

Leigh, LH (1995) 'Liability for inadvertance: a lordly legacy', 58 MLR 457

Leiss, W, Kline, S and Jhally, S (1986) *Social Communication as Advertising: Persons, Products and Images of Well Being*, New York: Macmillan

Leng, R et al (1998) *Blackstone's Guide to the Crime and Disorder Act 1998*, London: Blackstone

Levi, G and Schmidt, J-C (1996) *Histoires des Jeunes en Occident*, Paris: Seuil

Levitt, MZ and Selman, RL (1996) 'The personal meaning of risk behaviour: a developmental perspective on friendship and fighting in early adolescence', in Noam, GG and Fisher, KW (eds), *Development and Vulnerability in Close Relationships*, New Jersey: Lawrence Erlbaum

Levy, A (1996) 'The sleep of legal reason', in Cavadino, P (ed), *Children Who Kill*, Winchester: Waterside

Lewis, J (1997) *The Road to Romance and Ruin*, London: Routledge

Lloyd, B, Lucas, K, Holland, J, McGrellis, S and Arnold, S (1998) *Smoking in Adolescence – Images and Identities*, London: Routledge

Lloyd, C (1998) 'Risk factors for problem drug use: identifying vulnerable groups', 5 Drugs: Education, Prevention and Policy 217

Lloyd Morris, S and Mahendra, B (1996) 'Doli incapax and mental age', 146 NLJ 1622

Lockyer, A (1992) Citizens Service and Children's Panel Membership, Edinburgh: Scottish Office

Lockyer, A and Stone, F (eds) (1998) Juvenile Justice in Scotland: Twenty-Five Years of the Welfare Approach, Edinburgh: T & T Clark

Longford (Lord) (1993) Young Offenders, London: Chapmans

Lord Chancellor's Department (1997) Time Intervals for Criminal Proceedings in Magistrates' Courts: No 297, London: LCD

Loveland, I (ed) (1995) Frontiers of Criminality, London: Sweet & Maxwell

Lury, C (1996) Consumer Culture, Cambridge: Polity

Lyon, D (1996) Post-modernity, Milton Keynes: OU Press

Lyotard, J-F (1984) The Post-modern Condition, Manchester: Manchester UP

Lyng, R (1990) 'Edgework: a social psychological analysis of voluntary risk taking', 95 American Journal of Sociology 851

MacDonald, R (ed) (1997) Youth, the 'Underclass' and Social Exclusion, London: Routledge

MacIntyre, A (1985) After Virtue, 2nd edn, London: Duckworth

MacKenzie, D and Uchida, C (1994) Drugs and Crime, London: Sage

Maguire, M, Morgan, R and Reiner, R (eds) (1997) The Oxford Handbook of Criminology, 2nd edn, Oxford: Clarendon

Manchester, AH (1986) 'Doli incapax: the criminal responsibility of the juvenile', 150 JP 6

Mapstone, E (1973) 'The selection of the children's panel for the county of Fife: a case study', 2(4) British Journal of Social Work 445

Marris, P and Rein, M (1974) Dilemmas of Social Reform: Poverty and Community Action in the United States, Harmondsworth: Penguin

Marsh, A and McKay, S (1994) Poor Smokers, London: Policy Studies Institute

Martin, F, Fox, S and Murray, K (1981) Children Out of Court, Edinburgh: Scottish Academic

Marx, K (1985) *Grundrisse*, London: Penguin

Maslanka, H (1994) *Adolescent Drug Use in Edinburgh: February 1994 Survey*, Edinburgh: Crew 2000

Matza, D (1964) *Delinquency and Drift*, New York: Wiley

Matza, D (1969) *Becoming Deviant*, New Jersey: Prentice Hall

Maxwell, GM and Morris, A (1993) *Family Victims and Culture: Youth Justice in New Zealand: No 4*, University of Wellington: Social Policy Agency, Institute of Criminology

May, M (1973) 'Innocence and experience: the evolution of a concept of juvenile delinquency in the mid-19th century', 17(1) Victorian Studies 7

McDiarmid, C (1996) 'A feminist perspective on children who kill', 11(1) Res Publica 3

McElrea, FWM (1993) 'A new model of justice', in Brown, BJ and McElrea, FWM (eds), *The Youth Court in New Zealand: A New Model of Justice*, Auckland: Legal Research Foundation

McElrea, FWM (1994) 'Restorative justice – the New Zealand youth court: a model for development in other courts?', 4(1) Journal of Judicial Administration 33

McGarrel, E (1988) *Juvenile Correctional Reform*, New York: New York UP

McKenzie, ER (1982) *The Kids Nobody Wants: Treating the Seriously Delinquent Youth*, Delta Institute

McLaughlin, E and Muncie, J (1996) *Controlling Crime*, London: Sage

McLeod, JL (1980) '*Doli incapax*: the forgotten presumption in juvenile court trials', 3 Canadian Journal of Family Law 25

McRobbie, A (1991) *Feminism and Youth Culture*, London: Macmillan

McRobbie, A (1994) *Post-modernism and Popular Culture*, London: Routledge

McRobbie, A (ed) (1997) *Back to Reality: Social Experience and Cultural Studies*, Manchester: Manchester UP

Measham, F, Newcombe, R and Parker, H (1994) 'The normalisation of recreational drug use amongst young people in the North West of England', 45(2) British Journal of Sociology 287

Melly, G (1989) *Revolt into Style*, Milton Keynes: OUP

Merrington, S (1998) *A Guide to Setting Up and Evaluating Programmes for Young Offenders*, London: ISTD

Merton, R (1938) 'Social structure and "anomie"', American Sociological Review 3

Meyer, P (1977) *L'Enfant et la Raison d'Etat*, Ennew, J and Lloyd, J (trans) (1983, *The Child and the State*), Cambridge: CUP

Miller, J (1990) *Last One Over the Wall*, Ohio: Ohio State University

Minow, M (1997) 'Governing children, imagining childhood', in McGillivray, A (ed), *Governing Childhood*, Aldershot: Dartmouth

Mitchell, G (1999) 'Children who kill', 12(1) Representing Children 20

Mitterauer, M (1992) *A History of Youth*, London: Basil Blackwell

Mizen, P (1997) 'Rights of passage', 56 Youth and Policy 61

Moh, J and Mirlees-Black, C (1995) *Self-Reported Drug Misuse in England and Wales: Findings from the 1992 British Crime Survey*, London: Home Office

Maloney Committee (1927) *Report of the Departmental Committee on the Treatment of Young Offenders*, Cmnd 283, London: HMSO

Moody, S (1976) *Survey of the Background of Current Panel Members*, Edinburgh: Scottish Office Central Research Unit

Moore, DB (1993) 'Shame, forgiveness and juvenile justice', 12(1) Criminal Justice Ethics 3

Moore, G and Whyte, B (1998) *Social Work and Criminal Law in Scotland*, Edinburgh: Mercat

Moore-Gilbert, B (1997) *Post-Colonial Theory*, London: Verso

Moore, TG (1995) 'In defence of *doli incapax*', 159 JP 347

Morris, A and Giller, H (1987) *Understanding Juvenile Justice*, London: Croom Helm

Morris, A and Maxwell, GM (1993) *Family Victims and Culture: Youth Justice in New Zealand: No 4*, University of Wellington: Social Policy Agency, Institute of Criminology

Morris, A and McIsaac, MW (1978) *Juvenile Justice? The Practice of Social Welfare*, London: Heinemann

Morris, A and McIsaac, MW (1985) *Scottish Juvenile Justice: A Case Study in the Operation of the Children's Hearings in Scotland*, unpublished thesis, University of Edinburgh

Morrison, W (1995) *Theoretical Criminology: From Modernity to Post-modernism*, London: Cavendish Publishing

Morrison, W (ed) (2000) *Blackstone's Commentaries*, London: Cavendish Publishing

Mounteney, J (1996) 'One year on DATs: how have they measured up?', 11(4) Druglink 8

Mulvey, EP (1983) *Amenability to Treatment*

Murphy, J (1992) *British Social Services: The Scottish Dimension*, Edinburgh: Scottish Academic

NACRO (1991) *Seizing the Initiative: NACRO's Final Report on the DHSS Initiative to Divert Juvenile Offenders from Care and Custody, 1983–89*, London: NACRO

NACRO (February 1997) *Nacro Youth Crime Section: Factsheet – Facts about Young Offenders in 1995*, London: NACRO

NACRO (September 1997) *Briefing Paper: Government Proposals for Change, the Crime and Disorder Bill*, London: NACRO

NACRO (1999) *Facts About Young Offenders in 1997*, London: NACRO

National Opinion Poll (1971) *Attitudes Towards Crime, Violence and Permissiveness in Society*, London: NOP

National Planning Group (1999) *Report on Care and Education Services for Young People with Behavioural Problems*, Edinburgh: Scottish Office

Newburn, T (1996) 'Back to the future? Youth crime, youth justice and the rediscovery of "authoritarian populism"', in Pilcher, J and Wagg, S (eds), *Thatcher's Children*, London: Falmer

Newburn, T (1997) 'Youth, crime and justice', in Maguire, M, Morgan, R and Reiner, R (eds), *The Oxford Handbook of Criminology*, 2nd edn, Oxford: OUP

Newburn, T (1998) 'Young offenders, drugs and prevention', 5 Drugs: Education, Prevention and Policy 233

Nichol, A (1995) 'The common law concept of *doli incapax*', in *Child Offenders: UK and International Practice*, London: Howard League for Penal Reform

Norrie, A (1993) *Crime, Reason and History: A Critical Introduction to Criminal Law*, London: Weidenfeld & Nicolson

Norrie, A (1997) 'Legal and moral judgment in the "general part"', in Rush, P, McVeigh, S and Young, A (eds), *Criminal Legal Doctrine*, Aldershot: Dartmouth

Norrie, K, McK (1995) *Children (Scotland) Act 1995: Green's Annotated Acts*, Edinburgh: W Green

Norrie, K, McK (1997) *Children's Hearings in Scotland*, Edinburgh: W Green

O'Malley, P and Mugford, S (1994) 'Crime, excitement and modernity', in Barak, G (ed), *Varieties of Criminology: Readings from a Dynamic Discipline*, Westport: Praeger

O'Shea, A (1998) 'A special relationship? Cultural studies, academia and pedagogy', Cultural Studies 513

Osgerby, B (1998) *Youth in Britain Since 1945*, London: Basil Blackwell

Parry, P (1992) 'Juveniles in criminal justice under stress', in Stockdale, E and Casale, S, *Criminal Justice Under Stress*, London: Blackstone

Parsloe, P (1975) 'The boundaries between legal and social work concerns in the hearing system', in Houston, D (ed), *Social Work in the Children's Hearing System*, Glasgow: Joint Committee for Further and Advanced Training

Pearce, N and Hillman, J (1998) *Wasted Youth: Raising Achievement and Tackling Social Exclusion*, London: IPPR

Pearson, G (1983) *Hooligan: A History of Respectable Fears*, London: Macmillan

Peeters, G and Peeters, J (1985) 'Een experiment van alternatieve sanctuies aan de jeugdrechtbank te mechelen', 1 Panopticon 34

Penal Affairs Consortium (1995) 'The doctrine of *doli incapax*', Paper for Children Who Kill Conference, British Juvenile and Family Courts Society

Pettit, P and Braithwaite, J (1993) 'Not just deserts, even in sentencing', 4(3) Current Issues in Criminal Justice 225

Phoenix, A and Rattansi, A (1998) 'Youth research in Britain', in Bynner, J, *Youth, Citizenship and Social Change*, Dartmouth: Ashgate

Pilcher, J and Wagg, S (eds) (1996) *Thatcher's Children?*, London: Falmer

Pinchbeck, I and Hewitt, M (1969) *Children in English Society*, London: Routledge

Piper, C (1999) 'The Crime and Disorder Act 1998: child and community "safety"', 62(3) MLR 397

Pitts, J (1996) 'The politics and practice of youth justice', in McLaughlin, E and Muncie, J (eds), *Controlling Crime*, London: Sage

Platt, A (1969) *The Child Savers*, Chicago: Chicago UP

Pollock, LA (1983) *Forgotten Children: Parent-Child Relations from 1500–1900*, Cambridge: CUP

Powis, B, Griffiths, P, Gossop, M, Lloyd, C and Strang, J (1998) 'Drug use and offending behaviour among young people excluded from school', 5 Drugs: Education, Prevention and Policy 245

Presdee, M (1994) 'Young people, culture and the construction of crime: doing wrong versus doing right', in Barak, G (ed), *Varieties of Criminology: Readings from a Dynamic Discipline*, Westport: Praeger

Radzinowicz, L (Sir) and Hood, R (1986) *A History of English Criminal Law and its Administration from 1750: The Emergence of Penal Policy*, Vol 5, London: Stevens

Raeburn, J (1994) 'Arguments for and against the use of volunteers as decision makers in the Children's Hearing System in Scotland', unpublished MSc thesis, University of Edinburgh

Ramsbotham, D (Sir) (1997) *Young Prisoners – A Thematic Review*, London: Stationery Office

Redhead, S (1993) *Rave Off*, Aldershot: Avebury

Redhead, S (1995) *Unpopular Cultures: The Birth of Law and Popular Culture*, Manchester: Manchester UP

Riddell, P (1989) *The Thatcher Effect*, London: Basil Blackwell

Roberts, K (1995) *Youth and Employment in Modern Britain*, Oxford: OUP

Robins, D (1984) *We Hate Humans*, Harmondsworth: Penguin

Robins, D and Cohen, P (1978) *Knuckle Sandwich*, Harmondsworth: Penguin

Rock, P and McIntosh, M (eds), *Deviance and Social Control*, London: Tavistock

Rose, A (1971) 'The history and sociology of the study of social problems', in Smigel, E (ed), *Handbook on the Study of Social Problems*, Chicago: Chicago UP, pp 3–18

Rose, J (1994) 'Procedures in children's hearings', 14 SLT 137

Roshier, B (1981) 'The selection of crime news by the press', in Cohen, S (ed), *The Manufacture of the News*, 2nd edn, London: Constable

Rothman, DJ (1984) *Conscience and Convenience: The Asylum and its Alternatives in Progressive America*

Royal College of Psychiatrists (1986) *Alcohol – Our Favourite Drug: A New Report of a Special Committee of the Royal College of Psychiatrists*, London: Tavistock

Rutherford, A (1992) *Growing Out of Crime: The New Era*, Winchester: Waterside

Rutherford, A (1998) 'A Bill to be tough on crime', 148 NLJ 13

Rutherford, J (ed) (1997) 'Young Britain', in *Six Soundings*, London: Lawrence & Wishart

Rutter, M, Maughan, B, Mortimore, P, Ouston, J and Smith, A (1979) *Fifteen-Thousand Hours: Secondary Schools and their Effects on Children*, Cambridge, MA: Harvard UP

Sagel-Grande, I (1991) 'Looking for one age', in Booth, T (ed), *Juvenile Justice in the New Europe*, University of Sheffield: Joint Unit for Social Services Research

Salecl, R (1993) 'Crime as a mode of subjectivisation: Lacan and the law', 4 Law and Critique 2

Sarre, R (1994) 'Juvenile justice in South Australia', 5(4) Criminology Australia 13

Sassen, S (1991) *The Global City*, Ewing, New Jersey: Princeton UP

Save the Children (1992) *Sixteen and Seventeen Year Olds at the Interface between the Children's Hearings System and the Criminal Justice System*, Glasgow: Save the Children

Schwartz, IM (1989) *Injustice for Juveniles*, London: Lexington

Scottish Children's Reporter Administration (1997) *Referral Timescales Flowchart – Statistical Year 1995*, Stirling: Scottish Children's Reporter Administration

Scottish Office (1993) *Scotland's Children: Proposals for Child Care Policy and Law*, Cm 2286, Edinburgh: HMSO

Scottish Office Statistical Bulletin (1991) *Children and Crime, Scotland 1989*, CRJ/1991/3, Glasgow: Government Statistical Service

Scottish Office Statistical Bulletin (1997) *Referrals to Reporters and Children's Hearings: Social Work Series*, Glasgow: Government Statistical Service

Scraton, P (1991) 'Whose "childhood"? What crisis?', in Stenson, K and Cowell, D (eds), *The Politics of Crime Control*, London: Sage

Scraton, P and Chadwick, K (1991) 'The theoretical and political priorities of critical criminology', in Stenson, K and Cowell, D (eds), *The Politics of Crime Control*, London: Sage

Scull, A (1977) *Decarceration*, Englewood Cliff, New Jersey: Prentice Hall

Sennett, R (1998) *The Corrosion of Character*, New York: Norton

Sereny, G (1998) *Cries Unheard: The Story of Mary Bell*, London: Macmillan

Sewell, T (1997) *Black Masculinities and Schooling*, Stoke on Trent: Trentham

Shelton, D (1987) 'Application of the death penalty on juveniles in the US', 8 HRLJ 355

Sherman, LW and Strange, H (1997) 'RISE', in *Working Papers: Nos 1–4*, Canberra: Australian National University

SHHD (1966) *Social Work and the Community: Proposals for Re-organising Local Authority Services in Scotland*, Cmnd 3065, Edinburgh: HMSO

Shireman, C et al (1986) *Rehabilitating Juvenile Justice*, Colombia: Colombia UP

Sibley, D (1995) *Geographies of Exclusion*, London: Routledge

Singer, S (1996) *Recriminalising Delinquency*, Cambridge: CUP

Skryme, T (Sir) (1994) *History of the Justices of the Peace*, Chichester: Rose

Slater, D (1997) *Consumer Culture and Modernity*, Cambridge: Polity

Snyder, HN (1988) *Court Careers of Juvenile Offenders*, Pittsburgh: National Center for Juvenile Justice

SOED (1964) *The Kilbrandon Report of the Committee on Children and Young Persons*, Scotland, Cmnd 2306, Edinburgh: HMSO

Soloman, K and Klein, M (1993) *Community Treatment for Juvenile Offenders*, London: Sage

Sparks, R (1997) 'Social theory and crime and punishment', in Maguire, M, Morgan, R and Reiner, R (eds), *The Oxford Handbook of Criminology*, 2nd edn, Oxford: OUP

Springhall, J (1986) *Coming of Age: Adolescence in Britain 1860–1960*, Dublin: Gill & Macmillan

Stafford, A (1982) 'Learning not to labour', 17 Capital and Class 55

Stanley, C (1996) *Urban Excess and the Law: Capital, Culture and Desire*, London: Cavendish Publishing

Stanley, C (1997) 'Politics and ethics in cultural criminology', 26 Crime, Law and Social Change 1

Statistical Bulletin Criminal Justice Series (1999) *Criminal Proceedings in Scottish Courts, 1997*, Edinburgh: Scottish Office

Stedman-Jones, G (1977) 'Class expression versus social control? A critique of recent trends in the social history of "leisure"', 4 History Workshop Journal 162

Stein, M (1997) *What Works in Leaving Care?*, Ilford: Barnardos

Steiner, HJ and Alston, P (1996) *International Human Rights in Context: Law, Politics and Morals*, Oxford: Clarendon

Strang Dahl, T (1995) *The Emergence of the Norwegian Child Welfare Law: Scandinavian Studies in Criminology*, University of Copenhagen: Scandinavian Research Council for Criminology, Vol 5

Straw, J (May 1997) speech to the Police Federation Annual Conference

Straw, J (1997) 'Preface', in Home Office, *No More Excuses – A New Approach to Tackling Youth Crime in England and Wales*, Cm 3809, London: HMSO

Sullivan, GR (1994) 'The presumption of incapacity, binding authority and retroactivity – a commentary on *C v DPP*', 49 Criminal Lawyer 1

Sutton, SR (1987) 'Social-psychological approaches to understanding addictive behaviours: attitude-behaviour and decision making models', 82 British Journal of Addiction 355

Swann, R and James, P (1998) 'The effect of the prison environment upon inmate drug-taking behaviour', 37(3) Howard Journal of Criminal Justice 252

SWSG (1991) *National Objectives and Standards for Social Work Services in the Criminal Justice System*, Edinburgh: Scottish Office

SWSG (1996) *National Objectives and Standards for Social Work Services in the Criminal Justice System: General Issues*, Edinburgh: Scottish Office

Taylor, I (1971) 'Soccer consciousness and soccer hooliganism', in Cohen, S (ed), *Images of Deviance*, Harmondsworth: Penguin

Taylor, I (1999) *Crime in Context*, Cambridge: Polity

Taylor, I, Walton, P and Young, J (1971) *The New Criminology*, London: Routledge

Thane, P (1981) 'Childhood in history', in King, M (ed), *Childhood, Welfare and Justice*, London: Batsford

Thompson, HS (1993) *Fear and Loathing in Las Vegas*, London: Flamingo

Thornton, S (1995) *Club Culture: Music, Media and Sub-cultural Capital*, Cambridge: Polity

Thrasher, FM (1927) *The Gang: A Study of 1,313 Gangs in Chicago*, Chicago: Chicago UP

Tollett, T (1987) *A Comparative Study of Florida Delinquency Commitment Programs*, Tallahassee, FL: Department of Health Rehabilitative Services

Toynbee, P (1999) *The Guardian*, 23 June

Tulkens, F (1993) 'Les transformations du droit pénal aux Etats-Unis: pour autre modéle de justice', in *Nouveaux Itinéraires en Droit, Hommage à Francoise Rgaux*, Bruxelles: Bruylant, Bibliothéque de la Faculté de droit de UCL

Turgot, A (1973) *Turgot on Progress, Sociology and Economics*, Meek, RL (ed), Cambridge: CUP

Turnball, P, Webster, R and Stillwell, G (1996) *Get It While You Can: An Evaluation of an Early Intervention Project for Arrestees with Alcohol and Drug Problems*, London: Home Office Drugs Prevention Initiative

Uggen, C, 'Reintegrating Braithwaite: shame and consensus in criminological theory', 18(4) Law and Social Inquiry 481

Umbriet, M (1989) 'Crime victims seeking fairness, not revenge: towards restorative justice', 3 Federal Probation 52

United Nations (1989) *UN Convention on the Rights of the Child 1989*, London: HMSO

Vague, T (1997) *Anarchy in the UK: The Angry Brigade*, Edinburgh: AK

Valentine, G (ed) (1996) *Cool Places*, London: Routledge

Van Bueren, G (1992) 'Child oriented justice – an international challenge for Europe', 3 International Journal of Law and the Family 381

Van Bueren, G (1993) *International Documents on Children*, Nijhoff: Dordrecht

Van Bueren, G (1995) *The International Law on the Rights of the Child*, Dordrecht: Martinus Nijhoff

Van Bueren, G (1996) 'Protecting children's rights in Europe', 2 EHRLR 169

Van Hoorebeeck, B (1997) 'Prospects of reconstructing aetiology', 1 Theoretical Criminology 510

Vennard, J and Hedderman, C (1998) 'Effective interventions with offenders', Home Office Research Study 187, London: HMSO

Verhellen, E, Eliaerts, C and Cappelaere, G (1987) *Alternatieve Sanctionering van Jongeren, Gent, Studieen Documentatie centrum voor Rechten van Kinderen*, RU Gent, Cahier 5

Vigil, JD (1988) *Barrio Gangs: Street Life and Identity in Southern California*, Austin, Texas: Texas UP

VisionQuest (December 1999) *Youth Justice Matters*, London: VisionQuest

Vold, GB, Bernard, TJ and Snipes, JB (1998) *Theoretical Criminology*, 4th edn, Oxford: OUP

Wagner, P (1994) *A Sociology of Modernity: Liberty and Discipline*, London: Routledge

Waldgrave, L (1995) 'Restorative justice for juveniles: just a technique or a fully fledged alternative?', 34(3) Howard Journal of Criminal Justice 228

Walker, DM (1980) *Oxford Companion to Law*, Oxford: Clarendon

Walker, N (1983) 'Childhood and madness: history and theory', in Morris, A and Giller, H (eds), *Providing Justice for Children*, London: Edward Arnold

Walkerdine, V (1998) *Daddy's Girls – Young Girls and Popular Culture*, Basingstoke: Macmillan

Wallace, C and Grootings, P (1996) *Youth, Education and Work in Europe*, London: Routledge

Walsh, C (1998) 'Irrational presumptions of rationality and comprehension' 3 Web JCLI, ONLINE: http://webjcli.ncl.ac.uk

Walvin, J (1982) *A Child's World: A Social History of English Childhood 1800–1914*, Middlesex: Penguin

Ward, C (1989) *Steaming In: Journal of a Football Fan*, New York: Simon & Schuster

Warner, M (1994) 'Little angels, little devils: keeping childhood innocent', in *Managing Monsters: Six Myths of Our Time – The 1994 Reith Lectures*, London: Vintage

Warner (Lord) (2000) Press Release, 29 March

Waterhouse, L, McGhee, J, Loucks, N, Whyte, B and Kay, H (1999) *The Evaluation of Children's Hearings in Scotland: Children in Focus*, Social Work Research Findings 31, Edinburgh: Scottish Office Central Research Unit

Watts, R (1996) 'John Braithwaite and *Crime, Shame and Reintegration*: some reflections on theory and criminology', 29(2) Australian and New Zealand Journal of Criminology 121

Wedge, R and Palmer, T (1986) *California's Juvenile Probation Camps: Comparison of Characteristics of Youth in Juvenile Justice Programs*, Sacramento, CA: California Youth Authority

Weinberger, B (1993) 'Policing juveniles: delinquency in late 19th and early 20th century Manchester', in *Criminal Justice History: No 14*, Westport, CT: Greenwood

Weiner, MS (1990) *Reconstructing the Criminal: Culture, Law and Policy in England, 1850–1914*, Cambridge: CUP

Weitekamp, E (1992) 'Can restitution serve as a reasonable alternative to imprisonment?', in Messmer, H and Otto, HU (eds), *Restorative Justice on Trial*, Dordrecht: Kluwer

White, R, Carr, P and Lowe, N (1995) *The Children Act in Practice*, London: Butterworths

White, R and Haines, F (1996) *Crime and Criminology*, Oxford: OUP

Wilkins, L (1964) *Social Deviance*, London: Tavistock

Williams, G (1954) 'The criminal responsibility of children', Crim LR 493

Williams, J (1986) 'White riots: the English football fan abroad', in Tomlinson, A and Whannel, G (eds), *Off the Ball*, London: Pluto

Williamson, H (1993) 'Youth policy in the United Kingdom and the marginalisation of young people', 40 Youth and Policy 33

Williamson, H (1997) 'Status zero youth and the underclass', in MacDonald, R (ed), *Youth, the 'Underclass' and Social Exclusion*, London: Routledge

Williamson, K (1997) *Drugs and the Party Line*, Edinburgh: Rebel

Williamson, S, Griffiths, P, Noble, A, Bacchus, L, Strang, J and Gossop, M (1996) 'Patterns of drug use amongst a sample of young offenders', *Report to Bexley and Greenwich Drug Action Team and Greenwich Safer Cities*, London: National Addiction Centre

Willis, P (1976) 'The cultural meaning of drug use', in Hall, S and Jefferson, T (eds), *Resistance through Rituals: Youth Sub-cultures in Post-War Britain*, London: Hutchinson, pp 106–18

Willis, P (1977) *Learning to Labour*, London: Saxon House

Willis, P (1990) *Common Culture*, Milton Keynes: OUP

Wilson, JQ (1991) *On Character*, Washington: AEI

Wilson, JQ (1993) *The Moral Sense*, New York: Free Press

Wilson, J and Herrnstein R (1985) *Crime and Human Nature*, New York: Simon & Schuster

Winterdyke, J (ed) (1997) *Juvenile Justice Systems: International Perspectives*, Toronto: Canadian Scholars

Wyn, J and White, R (1997) *Rethinking Youth*, London: Sage

Yablonsky, L (1962) *The Violent Gang*, New York: Macmillan

Yeatman, A (1994) *Postmodern Revisionings of the Political*, New York: Routledge

Young, A (1996) *Imagining Crime: Textual Outlaws and Criminal Conversations*, London: Sage

Young, J (1971) 'The role of the police as amplifiers of deviancy, negotiators of reality and translators of fantasy: some consequences of our present system of drug control as seen in Notting Hill', in Cohen, S (ed), *Images of Deviance*, Harmondsworth: Penguin, pp 27–61

Young, J (1972) *The Drugtakers*, London: Paladin

Young, J (1974) 'Mass media, drugs and deviance', in Rock, P and McIntosh, M (eds), *Deviance and Social Control*, London: Tavistock

Young, J (1997) 'Recent paradigms in criminology', in Maguire, M, Morgan, R and Reiner, R (eds), *The Oxford Handbook of Criminology*, 2nd edn, Oxford: Clarendon

Young, J (1999) *The Exclusive Society*, London: Sage

Young, P (1997) *Crime and Criminal Justice in Scotland*, Edinburgh: The Stationary Office

Youth Justice Board (1998) *Preliminary Advice from Youth Justice Board on Juvenile Secure Estate*, London: Youth Justice Board

Youth Justice Board (1999) *Planning and Performance Management – A Guide for YOTs*, London: Youth Justice Board

Zehr, H (1990) *Changing Lenses: A New Focus for Crime and Justice*, Scottdale, Penn: Herald

Zizek, S (1998) *Pleasure and Popular Culture*, London: Verso

Zuckerman, M (1979) 'Sensation seeking and risk taking', in Izard, CE (ed), *Emotions in Personality and Psychopathology*, New York: Plenum

Zuckerman, M (1988) 'Sensation seeking, risk taking and health', in Janisse, MP (ed), *Individual Differences, Stress and Health*, New York: Springer-Verlag

Zuckerman, M (1994) *Behavioural Expressions and Biosocial Bases of Sensation Seeking*, Cambridge: CUP

INDEX